# ENTERPRISE IN RADIO:
# WWL AND
# THE BUSINESS OF
# BROADCASTING
# IN AMERICA.

**C. Joseph Pusateri**
University of San Diego

## University Press
## of America™

Library of Congress Catalog Card Number: 79-9598

To four who may want to read it--

      Steve, Barb, Cathy, and Dave

And to one who I wish could--Dad

# TABLE OF CONTENTS

PREFACE

Business history has been defined as the written record of decision-making by individuals seeking a private profit from the production and distribution of goods and services.[1] Its glamour and social impact aside, broadcasting is essentially a business and, therefore, it too deserves the careful attention of any historian of American enterprise. Yet, that historian has thus far devoted relatively little attention to broadcasting despite the fact that it has emerged over the past half century as a crucial force in modern society.

As a result, broadcasting lacks some fundamental historical studies--a full scale account of any of its national or regional networks, a comprehensive treatment of the Federal Communications Commission and its predecessors, and solid biographies of the nation's key radio and television stations that emphasize their role as individual companies engaged in a rapidly evolving industry. For the business historian, this last type of study is essential; the biography of the firm is an indispensable building block upon which any general synthesis should be constructed.

A partial explanation for the failure of the historian to deal with these business organizations may lie in the fact that at the station level, they are essentially small establishments when compared to the corporate giants of petroleum, transportation or other well-documented industries. In addition, stations seem, at first glance, to have only a regional impact at most. But broadcasting is different than most other industries. Because of the physical characteristics of the radio spectrum, access to the public is closely regulated. Radio frequencies, unlike locations for plants or super markets, are a scarce commodity. Only a limited number of entrepreneurs can be granted the privilege of engaging in the business. Nevertheless, it is through the medium of these few stations, oligopolists in their own market areas, that the listening and viewing public who make up their audience and the potential advertisers seeking to reach that same audience are brought together. The story of the broadcasting station, therefore, is the story of the industry itself. An understanding of it is critical to an understanding of a central feature of life in twentieth century America.

This work is a history of a broadcasting station. The subject is WWL in New Orleans, licensed to Loyola University, a Catholic educational institution in the same city. Taking the air for the first time in March 1922, it was the first station in Louisiana and one of the earliest in the South and in the United States. Moreover, since the 1930's, it has been of substantial importance in the industry. Transmitting on a clear channel frequency with a strength of 50,000 watts, it counted itself among a small number of elite radio stations endowed by federal policy with the capability of reaching and influencing a public in large portions of the United States, an inter-regional audience. Concomitant with this status was another capability, that of significant commercial success. As a business enterprise, WWL more than fulfilled the profit expectations of its managers.

The ownership of WWL by a church-related university and, at the same time, its operation as a fully commercial enterprise was an exceptional situation in broadcasting. Educational stations were formed by the dozens in radio's infant years, but the overwhelming majority failed dismally. They rigidly adhered to non-commercial policies, seeing themselves as having only instructional and inspirational responsibilities, and thus they were unable to solve the complex economic problem of survival. A few did choose a path of limited commercialism, but they embraced it reluctantly, without enthusiasm, and consequently, without success. How the university authorities at Loyola came to grips with the same problem, the unique strategy formulated, and the decisions made--both bad and good--to implement the strategy will be a major feature of this history. Further, the special questions, theological as well as economic, posed by the engagement of a religious institution in commercial broadcasting form an important portion of the narrative as well. A recent journalistic critic of the media has caustically characterized broadcasting as "one part conscience and nine parts profit motive."[2] If that statement is even partially true, how did a university-owned station with denominational ties seek to rationalize the imbalance?

Another major aspect of WWL's history was its continuing relationship with governmental authority, a topic that cannot be ignored in a treatment of a regulated industry such as broadcasting. Inevitably, it forms a vital part of the life of any station, and WWL was no exception. The victories the New Orleanians won in Washington before and sometimes against the FCC and other federal agencies were in many ways a factor more telling in the fortunes of their enterprise than the broadcasting activities they engaged in at home.

Overall then, this will be the biography of a business for whatever its ownership, WWL's managers were moved primarily by the classic goal of profit maximization. The WWL experience, therefore, is a case study in the growth and development of commercial broadcasting in the South and in the United States. The focus of this history will be upon the radio era, the years from the first experiments in wireless telephony thru the moment when a prosperous AM service found itself forced to reach an accommodation with the new and threatening medium of television. More specifically, the study will follow WWL from its amateur antecedents to its initiation as a multi-service organization offering AM, FM, and TV.

Acknowledgements for whatever success this work may have should be extended to a large number of people, indeed too many to all be mentioned here, deserving as they certainly are. A special thanks, however, must go to the administration of Loyola University and to its President, Rev. James C. Carter, S.J., as well as to Mr. J. Michael Early, General Manager of WWL. They gave valuable support to the project by opening available records to me and by encouraging key staff members to cooperate. My thanks also to dozens of radio and television professionals at WWL, at other stations, and in the industry generally who allowed themselves to be interviewed and who answered my questions with candor, patience, and good humor. Some of these persons are mentioned in the text. Unfortunately, many others are not.

Certainly, librarians and archivists in New Orleans, Baton Rouge, and Shreveport, Louisiana, in Washington, D.C., and in New York City were an important aid in the research, with an individual recognition due Ms. Catherine Heinz, Director of the Broadcast Pioneers Library in Washington, for her generous assistance. I am also appreciative of the aid of Ms. Terry Smith who typed the final copy with diligence, speed, and accuracy, and of the willingness of Mr. Phil Johnson, News Director of WWL, to read the entire work and to comment helpfully on it. To Dr. Forrest McDonald of the University of Alabama goes my sincere gratitude for the active interest he took in this project and the encouragement he gave it. The revisions that resulted from his review

of the manuscript have made the work considerably
stronger than it would otherwise have been. Whatever
weaknesses remain, alas, are the sole responsibility
of the author. Finally, a specific salute to a former
colleague, Dr. Maurice P. Brungardt, who first suggested
the idea of the WWL story to a somewhat skeptical
departmental chairman. And, as always, to my wife,
Barbara.

C. Joseph Pusateri
San Diego, California
September 1979

# 1

## THE COMING OF RADIO TELEPHONY

New Orleanians scanning copies of the Times-Picayune over their breakfast tables on the morning of March 31, 1922, would have had little reason to expect the day would mark the beginning of a new era in mass communications in Louisiana. The morning newspaper carried no mention of the impending inauguration of the state's first broadcasting station. Radio would come to New Orleans and to Louisiana unobtrusively rather than with the fanfares and hoopla that would later surround the medium.

To be sure, the Times-Picayune would not wholly ignore radio that March day. A photograph of a Bridgeport, Connecticut barber was displayed on an inside page. The barber, a modern businessman, had installed a "receiving set" in his shop so that his customers could "listen to concerts, lectures, and other radio subjects" while their tonsorial needs were being attended. Barbers aside, however, primary attention that day focused upon a threatened nationwide coal strike rather than the new phenomenon of broadcasting.[1]

Nevertheless, the city's residents were generally aware of developments surrounding the emergence of radio, and some of them had directly participated in giving life to the infant. The incubation had indeed been a lengthy one. Prior to the nation's centennial in 1876, the telegraph was the only available means of rapid, long-distance communication. Then with the introduction of the telephone in 1876, a revolution in communications technology quickly unfolded.

The telephone made possible the transmission of a greater number of words per minute than the telegraph, but more important, the words could be transmitted in

plain speech rather than in some form of code.  The
next step was clear--could messages be transmitted and
received without the use of wires altogether?[2]  After
Heinrich Hertz, a young German physicist, demonstrated
the existence of radio waves in the 1880's, it was
Guglielmo Marconi, stimulated by Hertz's discovery,
who exploited their commercial potential, sending the
first "wireless" message across the Atlantic in 1901
and establishing a British company to provide a world-
wide maritime service.  Marconi, however, melded tele-
graphic code with his wireless system, and as a result,
it remained for a Canadian working in the United States,
Reginald A. Fessenden, to successfully superimpose
speech and music on a high frequency radio wave, thus
making what eventually would be termed "broadcasting"
possible.[3]

     In December 1900, Fessenden, utilizing a spark gap
transmitter at Cobb Island, Maryland, was able to send
intelligible speech by radio waves for a distance of
about one mile.  The result was less than satisfactory,
however, since the transmission was poor in quality and
accompanied by loud and unpleasant noises created by
the irregularity of the short spark bursts.  Fessenden
continued his experiments and in 1904 he requested the
General Electric Company to construct for him an
"alternator" capable of producing "continuous waves"
in the radio frequency range.  He was assigned Ernest
F. W. Alexanderson, a new employee of General Electric's
Schenectady plant and a talented, young, Swedish engineer, who was able to construct for Fessenden an
alternator with one kilowatt of power.  Completed in
September 1906, it was delivered to Fessenden at Brant
Rock, Massachusetts where his newly formed National
Electric Signalling Company maintained an installation.[4]

     Three days in advance of Christmas Eve 1906,
Fessenden notified both United States Navy and United
Fruit Company ships in the area of his intention to
present musical programs on December 24 and on New Year's
Eve, in effect the first radio broadcasts.  Fessenden
later described the content of the Christmas program:
"First a short speech by me saying what we were going to
do, then some phonograph music--the music on the phonograph being Handel's 'Largo.'  Then came a violin solo
by me...of which I sang one verse, in addition to
playing on the violin, though the singing, of course,
was not very good."[5]  During the following year
Fessenden continued his demonstrations of "radio telephony," extending the range of his transmissions to
Washington, D.C., five hundred miles away.[6]

Meanwhile, another early experimenter, Lee DeForest, part inventor and part radio missionary, had begun to attract attention. DeForest, whose 1899 Yale doctoral dissertation had dealt with "Hertzian" radio waves, succeeded in 1907 in interesting the Navy in his radio telephone system, and as a result won a contract for the equipping of America's "Great White Fleet" with his transmitting and receiving units. That Fleet's impending around-the-world cruise offered obvious possibilities for the boosting of radio telephony, a fact DeForest had not failed to notice. The DeForest Radio Telephone Company was formed earlier the same year. Spectacular promotions were his style--in 1908 he broadcast from the Eiffel Tower in Paris, in 1910 he aired two Metropolitan Opera Company productions from New York City, direct from the stage and featuring the voice of Enrico Caruso. The listening audience, in all cases, was limited to the small group of radio enthusiasts who had been forewarned of the broadcasts or who tuned in on their sets by accident, and to ship operators guarding the frequency.[7]

Indeed, such a sufficient amount of progress had been made by 1915 that David Sarnoff, young executive of the Marconi Wireless Telegraph Company of America, a subsidiary of the British corporation, was encouraged to address a memorandum to his General Manager. "I have in mind a plan of development which would make a radio a 'household utility' in the same sense as the piano or phonograph," he wrote. "The idea," Sarnoff proposed, "is to bring music into the house by wireless," and he labeled his system the "Radio Music Box." The memorandum brought no response from American Marconi, and Sarnoff put the idea aside only temporarily.[8]

As developments in radio unfolded in these years, the federal government had not been inactive. In June 1910 the United States Congress passed and President William Howard Taft signed the first American radio law. This initial legislation, dealing with wireless telegraphy, was prompted by concern for the only significant use for radio then envisioned--safety at sea. The Wireless Ship Act of 1910 applied to any vessel of the United States or to any foreign vessel leaving an American port. Under its provisions "an efficient apparatus for radio-communication, in good working order, in charge of a person skilled in the use of such apparatus, which apparatus shall be capable of transmitting and receiving messages over a distance of at least one hundred miles" was required in all ships carrying fifty or more persons. Significantly, the

administration of the law was placed in the hands of the
Secretary of Commerce and Labor, his Department having
jurisdiction over marine navigation. The Act thus
served as a precedent for the later continuance of radio
regulation in the Department of Commerce.[9]

In the following year a Radio Service Section was
established within the Department's Bureau of Navigation
to insure proper enforcement of the legislation. Moreover, in 1912 Congress returned to the subject of radio
yet again. First, in July, the provisions of the 1910
Act were extended to include cargo vessels; then in
August Congress passed the Nation's first comprehensive
radio regulation statute. A public, aroused by the
failure of radio communication to prevent the Titanic
disaster in April 1912, served as an effective incentive for governmental action.[10]

The Radio Act of 1912 required every station to
secure a license from the Department of Commerce and to
employ a licensed operator. The frequency bands, or
wave lengths as they were then classified, were also
defined for each category of service. Four such categories were indicated: ship, coastal, government, and
amateur (the latter being referred to as "private" in
the law). The amateur band was designated in the
shorter wave lengths, less than two hundred meters, thus
relegating the supposedly few such radio devotees in
the country to the higher and least desirable frequencies. In later years the limits of the authority
that the Secretary of Commerce could exercise under
the 1912 Act would become a major issue since in the
year of its origin, the Radio Act did not envision
broadcasting as a class of service to which it need
address itself. Attempts by Herbert Hoover, as Commerce
Secretary in the 1920's, to adopt the provisions of the
1912 legislation to the new situation created by the
emergence of the broadcast industry, were to meet
vigorous opposition from many fiercely individualistic
station owners of the next decade.[11]

The 1912 law served another purpose. It awoke amateurs to the realization that there was a significant
number of them scattered across the country. Under the
law "call letters," designated by the Commerce Secretary,
were assigned to each licensee, and a list of the radio
stations so licensed was published. The surprising
number of amateurs listed was a revelation, and a sense
of comradeship began to develop. Radio clubs sprang
into existence for the exchange of information since

there were few books that adequately dealt with the
subject of wireless communication. The contact tended
to reinforce the enthusiasm of the members and from
many such organizations came the early broadcasters
of the 1920's.[12]

Amateur enthusiasm received something of a temporary setback with American entrance into World War I
in 1917. The Radio Act of 1912 had provided that the
President "in time of war or public peril or disaster
may cause the closing of any station for radio communication and the removal therefrom of all radio apparatus."[13] Under this authority, the Radio Service in
April 1917 required the dismantling of amateur stations,
stipulating that "antennae and all aerial wires be
immediately lowered to the ground" and that equipment
be rendered generally inoperative. At the time, 8562
amateurs were licensed to transmit, and an estimated
125,000 Americans possessed receiving equipment. Both
sending and receiving, however, were banned by the wartime order.[14]

Even so, radio overall experienced a dramatic leap
forward with the impetus of America's overseas adventure.
The threat of a German severance of the transatlantic
cables brought an immediate governmental interest in
the utilization of alternative forms of communication.
In addition, the nation's armed services now sought
high quality transmitters and receiving sets for use in
the struggle against Germany and her allies and were
prepared to pay handsomely with generous congressional
appropriations. Patent disputes between corporate
giants such as American Marconi and the American
Telephone and Telegraph Company were set aside for
the duration and production forged ahead. And because
a key feature of the needed equipment was vacuum tubes,
two massive light bulb manufacturers, General Electric
and Westinghouse, were also drawn irrevocably into the
radio picture. General Electric, which had housed the
construction of the Alexanderson alternator for
Fessenden in 1906, also continued its development work
in that area. By 1918 it developed a 200,000 watt transmitter which President Wilson employed to beam a plea
directly to the German people for the overthrow of the
Kaiser. A prewar era, seemingly marked by the individual
inventor and radio promoter, was now about to give way
to a postwar dominance by large scale business organizations.[15]

The prohibition on the use of amateur receiving
sets was not lifted by the federal government until

1919; that on amateur transmissions remained in effect
until September 1920, though it seems safe to conclude
that a not insignificant number of operators had ignored both bans all along.  In any event, the removal
of the restrictions opened the door to the appearance
of the nation's initial broadcasting stations.[16]

Historians of broadcasting have never ceased dis-
puting which station among a half dozen contenders
rightly can claim the honor of being the first.  Among
those claimants is KQW in San Jose, California (now
KCBS in San Francisco) which, under the direction of
Charles D. Herrold, began something like primitive
broadcasts as early as 1909, before even call letters
were assigned.  Also vying for the title are Detroit's
WWJ, which began broadcasts of music programs under
the amateur call letters 8MK in 1920, and a University
of Wisconsin amateur station, 9XM (later Madison's WHA),
that was also transmitting music in the same year.  If,
however, the requirements be imposed that the station
must have been providing "a continuous program service"
and be licensed by the federal government as well, then
the claim of the station traditionally regarded as the
first, Pittsburgh's KDKA, seems most justified.[17]

During World War I the Westinghouse Electric and
Manufacturing Company became involved in the production
of radio equipment and in wireless telephony research,
both under the supervision of Dr. Frank Conrad, an
engineer and an amateur operator himself.  Conrad's
amateur activities, which had been licensed by the
Department of Commerce in 1916 as 8XK, were carried on
in the home workshop over his garage in a Pittsburgh
suburb.  Gradually they had begun to attract a considerable amount of attention.  A local music store
even began to provide phonograph records in return for
proper credit being given on the air, and a regular
schedule of "concerts" was introduced.  When a
Pittsburgh department store, noticing the interest in
Conrad's station, advertised in the Pittsburgh Sun
in September 1920 that it had receiving sets for sale
and that these sets could be used to tune in the Conrad
concerts, the commercial possibilities of broadcasting
dawned on a few Westinghouse executives.[18]

Moving quickly, they invited Conrad to build a
station at the Westinghouse plant itself which would
provide a regular and dependable service to present
owners and to future purchasers of radio sets manufactured by the company.  Thus at one and the same time

6

Westinghouse could produce the receivers and create a
market for them by the programming it broadcast over
its own station. The station would thus become a means
to an end, the sale of sets, rather than an end in itself. In October 1920 Westinghouse applied to the
Department of Commerce for a special license to operate
a broadcasting service. On October 27, the Department
replied, assigning the call letters KDKA, those of a
commercial coastal station rather than an amateur call
sign, and authorizing the use of a wave length of 360
meters (833.3 kc.), a channel relatively free from interference and a considerable distance from those frequencies used by amateurs. A shack was then constructed
on the roof of one of the plant buildings, a one hundred
watt transmitter assembled, and broadcasting begun on
the evening of November 2, 1920 with the results of
the presidential election held that day. The Harding-
Cox contest offered a golden opportunity to demonstrate
the public service potential of broadcasting and to
attract maximum attention to the station relaying the
election bulletins.[19]

An estimated 500-1000 listeners heard KDKA's
election night program, and when the station followed
up on succeeding evenings with regular programming, at
first only an hour in length but gradually expanding,
a national mania was born. Since there was little
interference from other stations as yet, KDKA's
signal, especially after it replaced its first transmitter with one of five hundred watts power, could be
heard at great distances from Pittsburgh. It quickly
became a mark of social sophistication in America to
casually remark in conversation with friends that one
had "picked up" KDKA or one of the other pioneer stations
the previous evening. Electrical shops were deluged
with requests for parts and department stores set up
special radio displays. Radio suddenly became a public
passion.[20]

Especially significant was the number of new stations spawned in the wake of the publicity attending
KDKA. During 1921, the year in which the Commerce
Department formally established "broadcasting" as a
separate service classification, twenty-eight new stations received licenses and took the air. But 1921
was a year in which the national economy experienced a
sharp and severe recession, and ten percent of the
labor force found itself unemployed by July. As a
result, the full effects of America's new-found in-
fatuation with radio were not felt until 1922, when

7

the economy regained its balance and began the upward climb that would characterize the decade as a whole. In the first three months of 1922, 109 fledgling broadcasters were licensed with the peak yet to be reached. The single month of May saw 97 licenses issued, and by December the total would be 570. Moreover, an estimated 400,000 receiving sets were now in use in the United States, a figure that would be almost tripled in 1923. Radio broadcasting had come to stay.[21]

The South and Louisiana, in particular, were not oblivious to these developments in radio telephony. The Commerce Department's 1913 list of "amateur radio stations" contained the names of only three Louisiana operators, all located in New Orleans, but by 1916, the state's number had increased to thirty-two, including amateurs in Shreveport, Covington, Baton Rouge, and Franklinton. Appearing on the 1916 list were some Louisianians who would play key roles in the emergence of broadcasting in the 1920's. William E. Antony of Shreveport, Dorr R. Simmons, and the Uhalt brothers, William and Joseph, of New Orleans were later to have important associations as broadcasters in the State. By June 1921, nearly the eve of the birth of the industry in Louisiana, the number of amateur stations totalled fifty, substantially exceeding the figures for other deep South states in the Commerce Department's Fifth District.[22]

Further, 1921 also marked Louisiana's first experimental broadcasting. Dorr Simmons, factory manager for the Interstate Electric Company, a large New Orleans electrical supply house, constructed "the first complete wireless instrument of its kind in the South" at his home in the uptown area of the city. Simmons and two neighbors began transmitting broadcasts of phonograph records in January 1921, and received responses from owners of receiving sets as far from their New Orleans location as Shreveport. Simmons claimed coverage of five hundred miles with his transmitter and predicted, somewhat modestly in view of KDKA's already achieved success, that he expected to see "wireless telephony developed to such a point that a band in one city can supply music for a dance in another many miles away."[23]

The first licenses issued to any private individuals or organizations in the South under the Radio Service's new "broadcasting" classification were granted in February 1922. They were secured by two utility companies, one in Alabama and the second in Arkansas. Montgomery Light & Water Power Company of Montgomery, Alabama received call letters WGH and the Pine Bluff Company, a subsidiary of Arkansas Light and Power, received WOK. As was the case with many early stations, however, the realities of broadcasting quickly overcame the glowing visions of the initial moments on the air with the result that both stations were soon deleted from the roster of those still operational.[24]

March 1922 saw nine more Southern stations joining the initial pair, including the first two in Louisiana. On March 21, Interstate Electric was authorized to broadcast, using the call letters WGV, and on March 31, the call letters WWL were assigned to Loyola University of New Orleans. Only WWL would actually take the air that March month, and thus, to it would fall the honor of beginning the history of broadcasting in Louisiana.[25]

2

THE STATE, THE SCHOOL, THE STATION


Louisiana in 1920 shared most of the characteristics of its sister states of the old Confederacy.
In a year when for the first time a majority of the
nation's population could be classified as urban
rather than rural, Louisiana's urban residents were
only 34.9% of its citizenry. Even so, that degree of
urbanization placed second only to Florida within the
South itself.[1]

Louisiana's high urban ranking was directly
attributable to the state's boasting the South's
largest city, New Orleans. In 1920 the Crescent
City's population numbered 387,219, nearly twice the
size of Atlanta, the nearest rival. Within Louisiana,
however, no urban area approached New Orleans in size.
The state capitol of Baton Rouge counted its population
at less than 22,000, while Shreveport, Louisiana's
second city in 1920, could muster some 44,000 only.[2]

The most striking demographic difference between
Louisiana and the remainder of the South has been the
former's distinctive French and Catholic heritage.
The first major settlements in the state were made by
the French in south Louisiana, and French influence
was increased even more by the advent of the Acadians,
exiles from French Canada who began arriving in 1760
and who settled the southern and southwestern parishes
of the state. Their "Cajun" culture became characteristic of that area. Northern Louisiana, on the other
hand, the parishes above the 31st parallel, saw a
population influx somewhat later and from a quite
different source. Not until after 1812 did immigration
begin there, and it was marked by the westward expansion of the Anglo-American, Protestant civilization of
the United States. Thus two different cultures divided

11

the state between themselves in an uneasy social and political détente.[3]

Both the French and the Anglo-American societies of Louisiana regarded agriculture as their economic mainstay. Three cash crops dominated farming in 1920-- sugar and rice in the south, and cotton in the north. In the antebellum years a substantial slave community was employed in their production, and by 1920 blacks still numbered 39% of the state's overall population. Unfortunately, the average Louisiana farm was valued at only $3,499, placing it far behind such Southern leaders as Texas ($8,486), Virginia ($5,501), and Florida ($5,212) as well as the national average of $10,284.[4]

In the 1920's industrial interests of some significance were making their presence felt in Louisiana. Sugar refining and lumber products were still the leaders, but petroleum refining had moved into third position and would displace the first pair by 1930. While oil and gas production were centered in North Louisiana, the largest refinery in the state was based at Baton Rouge and operated by the Standard Oil Company of Louisiana. Political power, which had long been a monopoly of the Bourbons, a planter-commercial aristocracy, was now being shared with industry. But the degree of industrial penetration should not be exaggerated. Louisiana at the end of the second decade of the century could still point to only 2,617 manufacturing establishments, placing it eighth among the eleven former Confederate states.[5]

With Louisiana's available supply of cheap labor not being sufficient to counterbalance its lack of a wide variety of raw materials and its relative distance from the mass markets of the East, the economic growth of the state was sluggish. While per capita personal income nationally averaged $223 in 1920, Louisiana's reached only $131. The effects were felt across a wide spectrum of the state's social and political life. As late as 1921, only some 70% of the 565,000 white and black children of school age were actually attending school. The depressed conditions of life in the Louisiana countryside would prove fertile soil for the rise of Longism in the 1920's.[6]

In New Orleans itself, a native French, Spanish, and black Creole population dating from colonial times, joined by a substantial number of Germans, Irish, and

Italian immigrants in the nineteenth century, formed
the community of 1920. Politically, power resided in
the Choctaw Club, the Regular Democratic Organization
of New Orleans or the "Old Regulars" as they were
generally known, organized in 1897 and still in control
at the close of World War I. The Old Regulars, finding
solid support in the conservative oligarchy of the city,
railroad and public utilities executives, commercial
factors, and the new industrialists, represented those
business interests effectively both locally and in Baton
Rouge. Despite occasional setbacks, the Choctaw Club
maintained a dominance over New Orleans politics and a
decisive influence in state affairs until the emergence
of Huey Long.[7]

Economically, the city's strength rested upon two
pillars--the port and its position as the financial
center of the Deep South and Southwest. In terms of
foreign trade, New Orleans was the nation's third
busiest port with Latin American imports forming the
bulk of the goods handled on the docks. Banking and
the cotton, rice and sugar exchanges were central to
the city's financial muscle.[8]

Perhaps the most startling fact regarding the New
Orleans economy was the degree to which it dominated
the state's. Its citizens earned half the personal income and its retail businesses transacted a full third
of the sales in Louisiana, despite New Orleans compri-
sing only 20% of the population. This economic hegemony
produced a substantial hostility in the rural sections
of the state, and especially in the Protestant North
where New Orleans' heavily Catholic orientation engen-
dered equal resentment.[9]

Despite this seeming wealth, the prosperity of the
city was narrowly based. New Orleans lacked any impressive industry. As late as 1939 it did not share in
the output of any of Louisiana's four major industries--
petroleum and sugar refining, lumbering, and chemicals.
What manufacturing there was tended to be light in
nature and the largest source of industrial employment
lay in the railroad repair shops. Yet because of the
overall size of the city and its available commercial
resources, it was not surprising that Louisiana's first
broadcasters should claim New Orleans as home.[10]

* * * * * * * * * *

The renowned Roman Catholic clerical order, the
Society of Jesus, first acquired property in New

13

Orleans in 1847 at the corners of Baronne and Common
Streets in the central business district.  Two years
later it established there the College of Immaculate
Conception, or as it was more generally known then,
the Jesuit College.  In 1889 land in the uptown area
of the city, across St. Charles Avenue from Upper City
Park (later Audubon Park) and in the vicinity of the
newly incorporated Tulane University, was acquired by
the New Orleans Province of the Society.  When enrollment at the downtown College passed 400 students in
1904 and the school was deemed overcrowded as a result,
Father Albert H. Biever, S.J., was assigned by Province
officials to found a new institution at the second
site.

Loyola College, as it was initially named, began
accepting its own students in September 1904.  Then
after some seven years of co-existence, the original
Jesuit College was transformed into a high school only,
and a 1912 Louisiana charter of incorporation was conferred upon the retitled Loyola University uptown.[11]

The 1922 broadcast grant eventually assigned the
young University marked, not the beginning of its radio
involvement, but a further step in a process by then
over a decade old.  Father Anton L. Kunkel, S.J., a
tall, stoop-shouldered Jesuit whose German accent be-
trayed his birthplace, had provided the impetus.  Kunkel
moved from Baronne and Common to the new Loyola College
in 1909.  As a physicist, he found himself drawn to
the work being done in wireless telegraphy, and he
quickly determined to participate in it.  Together
Kunkel and Biever bought $150 worth of radio parts from
the Electro Importing Company of New York, and Kunkel
undertook the task of constructing a receiving set and
later a transmitter.  He received assistance in the project from a young Immaculate Conception College graduate,
L.J.N. "Joe" du Treil.  Even though du Treil had a
regular employment with American Marconi as a wireless
operator, he devoted his spare time to collaborating
with the Jesuit physicist.[12]

Kunkel, in due course, assembled a spark gap transmitter, a beast of a machine that was described as "an
awe-inspiring piece of apparatus with its pyrotechnic
display rivaling the light and sound effects of the
good old fire cracker and cannon cracker days."
Another observer likened its horrendous noise to "a
daily repetition of the battle of Gettysburg."  Capitalizing on this growing body of experience, the
University determined in 1913 to organize a Wireless

14

Telegraphy School. Classes would be scheduled in the
evening and consist mainly of code practice and some
theory. The course of study was expected to be approximately six months in length. To serve as the School's
first Director, du Treil was recruited. Enrollment
averaged eight to ten students at a time, all expecting
to find eventual jobs as wireless operators on ships
or in coastal stations. When du Treil, who had retained
his position with American Marconi while simultaneously
directing the small University program, was transferred
by that company to Galveston in 1916, a succession of
one year appointments marked the School's administration
thereafter.[13]

With American entrance into World War I, the School's
facilities, as well as those on other campuses, were
taken over by the Armed Forces for their own training
purposes. A naval program was established at Loyola
with some two hundred sailors prepared for duty as wireless operators by the Armistice in 1918. Once the
wartime emergency had passed, University control was
resumed and classes for civilians, who proved to be
mainly veterans desiring a radio career, were opened
once again. Now styled the Radio School, its classes
were continued until June 1922 when the enterprise was
finally closed down, in large part because of substantial
competition from several similar operations in the New
Orleans area. It was, however, shortly before that
closing that the decision for broadcasting was made.[14]

* * * * * * * * * *

Early broadcasters did not establish their stations
with the classic economic aim of direct profit maximization. Rather they sought indirect benefits, if
they sought any at all. In 1922 radio stations were
begun in the United States for one of four basic reasons.
The largest number were the creations of business
organizations interested in the sale of radio sets.
Manufacturers, radio shops, and department stores all
saw broadcasting stations as devices for increasing
public demand for the receiving sets in their inven-
tories. They anticipated no revenues from the stations
themselves. A second group of broadcasters were businessmen who saw radio as a means of generating community
goodwill and of attracting favorable attention to themselves. Newspapers formed the major component in this
second group that looked upon investments or affiliations
with stations as part of normal promotional activities.
A Florida publisher commented in the summer of 1922 that
while there had been no direct benefits from his new

15

radio operation, "it was a good means of keeping the name of a morning paper impressed on the public mind during the hours when the paper was not for sale on the streets." Print journalism regarded the broadcast medium at this early date "as a toy, a rather complex and sophisticated publicity tool in which there was a growing public curiosity." A possible circulation increase for the primary activity, the newspaper operation, was the only payoff envisioned, and the contingency that radio might eventually become a dangerous competitor escaped consideration.[15]

Educational institutions and churches formed the third bloc of 1922 broadcasters. In January the Universities of Minnesota and Wisconsin were the first to receive licenses. They were followed by some sixty other college stations during the remainder of the year. Many were outgrowths of experiments conducted in the Physics Departments of the various schools; most were founded in bursts of enthusiasm but with very little money appropriated for expenses, thereby insuring a short life span. All anticipated a public appetite for educational programming that was never to materialize. Religious groups too found that early idealistic hopes of significant additions to their congregations through radio preaching were to be largely disappointed. Nonetheless, in the first euphoric days after the acquisition of a license, a college president or an energetic minister could entertain roseate visions of radio's sway not yet clouded by later realities. Finally, a smaller number of stations were established by broadcasters possessing no motives other than indulging their own love for technology. As one early observer noted: "They have gone into it merely to satisfy their desire for a hobby, or because they wanted to learn the tricks of the new game, or as a method of giving vent to their pent-up enthusiasm." This amorphous band of radio-struck zealots would likewise soon find broadcasting a harsh reality.[16]

Louisiana broadcasting in 1922, the year of its inception, followed all four of the patterns mentioned above. The first station licensed by the Commerce. Department, WGV on March 21, was a joint venture of the Interstate Electric Company and a daily newspaper, The New Orleans Item. Interstate Electric, one of the five local firms then listed as dealers in "radio supplies," was a large wholesale and retail electrical supply house located at Baronne and Perdido Streets in downtown New Orleans. Owned by Percival and Ferdinand Stern, it was, as mentioned previously, the

employer of Dorr Simmons, the originator of the first
radio telephone experiments in the state.  The Item,
an afternoon newspaper, claimed the second largest
circulation of the city's dailies, trailing the morning
Times-Picayune by a margin of 74,000 to 65,000 in 1920
figures, but well ahead of its afternoon competition,
the New Orleans States, which admitted an everyday count
of only 39,000 readers.17

    There is good reason to presume that it was Clarke
Salmon, the Item's associate managing editor, who first
proposed the joint venture.  Certainly, it was Salmon
who corresponded with the Radio Service Section's New
Orleans district office and its supervisor, Theodore G.
Deiler, on matters involving the station during the
spring of 1922 despite the license being formally granted
only to Interstate Electric.  Salmon undoubtedly knew
that newspapers in other sections of the country had already moved to cement relations with the new medium.
KDKA commenced broadcasts from the newsroom of the
Pittsburgh Post in September 1921, and in the same month
the Post began carrying the first program schedule published in a daily paper.  Some journalists were even
then moving to acquire licenses in their own name;
indeed, by the end of 1922, seventy publishers had
secured the necessary permission to go on the air.  It
was not a time for an aggressive and imaginative newspaper executive to hang back.18

    While WGV's license was granted on March 21, the
station did not immediately begin to broadcast.  The
delay, which the Item would later maintain was due to
a necessity for "the perfection of a few arrangements
for outside cooperation with points at a distance, and
the formulation of programs," would cost WGV whatever
distinction lay in being first on the air.  While Dorr
Simmons worked at the installation of a transmitter on
the seventh floor of Interstate Electric's Baronne
Street building, others were making preparations as
well.  On March 31, just ten days after WGV's, a
license was awarded Loyola University.  The Jesuits,
unlike the Item-Interstate planners, would not wait
even a single day before putting theirs to good use.19

    The specific inspiration leading to the establish-
ment of a Loyola station was developmental rather than
academic.  It was simply money and the need to raise
it.  In the spring of 1922 Father Edward Cummings, S.J.,
who had assumed the University Presidency in 1919,
announced a major campaign to raise $1,500,000 in funds
for the construction of six new campus buildings.  The

drive was accompanied by elaborate promotions: parades
on Canal Street, benefit contract bridge games, slogan
contests, a huge clock elevated over a downtown street
(its face featured fifteen hours, one for each
$150,000 collected), and whatever other eye-catching
public relations devices were available. A radio
station was another possible campaign tool. What
better way to convince prospective donors in a
technology-infatuated decade of the up-to-dateness of
an emerging college than by a little injection of the
KDKA magic into the New Orleans scene?

Responsibility for the project was given to
Edward T. Cassidy, then a Jesuit seminarian and
physicist who was serving as the current head of the
Radio School. Cassidy was able to secure the assistance of an old University friend, Joe du Treil, who
had returned to New Orleans in 1919 to become Assistant
Supervisor of American Marconi's Gulf Division, and who
in 1921 had joined the Radio Service Section's New
Orleans district office as a field inspector. Du Treil's
holding that key Commerce Department post would prove
both greatly beneficial to Loyola and a focus for some
controversy in years to come. Together Cassidy and
du Treil worked to secure the necessary equipment that
would bring broadcasting into being. Money was a first
problem, one which Cassidy solved by converting a $400
donation from a ship's captain for the purchase of
Radio School wireless equipment into the starting
capital of New Orleans' first radio station. Then he
and du Treil sought out their required hardware.[21]

On a ship docked in port they found a discarded
Morse code transmitter featuring huge coils, Leyden jar
condensers, vacuum tubes, all contained in a trunk.
After purchasing it and other parts with their available
funds, they modified the set to their needs, building
their own voice modulator. When completed, the composite equipment supported a microphone extending from
the trunk set on a long arched arm, much as in tele-
phones in use at the time. An antenna wire was then
strung from Marquette Hall, the only classroom building
on campus, to the steeple of the nearby Holy Name of
Jesus church. With installation accomplished, a
Department of Commerce authorization was requested.[22]

In 1922 such applications were filed with the
nearest district office of the Radio Service, which in
turn forwarded them to Washington for final approval.
The New Orleans Customs House headquarters of the
Fifth District served Alabama, Arkansas, Mississippi,

18

Oklahoma, New Mexico, Tennessee, and Texas, as well as
Louisiana. It was not until Friday morning, March 31,
that the telegraphed permission from Washington was
finally received. The federal approval stipulated that
broadcasting could be done on a wave length of 360 meters
(833.3 kilocycles, or kilohertz in today's terminology
for frequencies) with a transmitter of 100 watts power.
In addition the telegram assigned to the new station
the call letters which it would retain throughout its
long history--WWL.[23]

The letters had previously belonged to the Pacific
Mail Steamship Company's steamer San Jose but on
August 10, 1921, that vessel was unlucky enough to run
aground on the coast of Lower California. A salvage
party was dispatched from San Francisco to assist, but
all efforts to refloat the San Jose proved unsuccessful.
After ten days a decision was made to abandon her.
The call sign WWL, which had been assigned the doomed
ship's transmitter since 1920, now passed back into
the reservoir of designations available for reuse. The
letters, unlike many special combinations requested by
later stations, had no special significance in themselves
applicable to Loyola University. They were simply transferred to the New Orleans institution on a luck of the
draw basis.[24]

Without any advance publicity, Father Cummings
determined that WWL would take the air the same morning
that the telegram authorization was received. He recognized the publicity value inherent in being first and
that others in the city were nearing the flash point of
actual transmission. Thus on the morning of Friday,
March 31, 1922, he seated himself in front of the trunk
set's telephone-style microphone, and at 10:52 a.m.
began the history of Louisiana broadcasting. Appropri-
ately enough, perhaps, the state's premier station began
with a commercial.[25]

Cummings' opening speech was short, a three minute
fund-raising plea on behalf of the University's
building drive. In it he explained the role of
radio:

> We are organizing the radio operators
> in the state to spread the story of Loyola's
> needs. Will you lend your support to our
> campaign, both by radio and individual effort
> which will aid us in making Loyola University
> one of the greatest institutions of learning
> in the Southland?[26]

19

Cummings' appeal was then followed by a musical selection, Guiseppe Ferrate of Tulane's Newcomb College faculty playing an original piano composition. Edward Cassidy served as the program's announcer and exuded enthusiasm over the station's prospects. He bragged that the transmitter was "of the most modern type;" that while its present range was limited to some two hundred miles, that would soon be increased, and that daily broadcasts to farmers of "crops, weather, and agricultural reports" would be forthcoming. Such was the city's introduction to broadcasting.[27]

Immediately following the half hour broadcast, a hasty telephone call was placed to Immaculate Conception College downtown to determine if the program had in fact been heard. It had! Listeners there received it on a "catwhisker" crystal set. How many other New Orleanians, not warned in advance, heard the first broadcast is an open question. In early May, the Times-Picayune placed the number of listeners in the city at 3,000, but that estimate (really little more than a guess) followed a month of intensive publicity for the emergent stations. Given the unannounced nature of the first program, the fact that it was broadcast in a morning hour when most males interested in the novelty of radio were at work rather than home, and the prevailing custom of listening in evening hours when distant stations could be picked up on the primitive receivers available, it is doubtful that anyone other than an alerted few Jesuits and students at Baronne and Common actually formed the audience.[28]

Only after the belated publication of stories describing WWL's debut in the three daily newspapers two days later, were the city's residents aware of the birth of local broadcasting. Since none of those three papers had reporters present at the actual event, each was forced to rely upon prepared copy furnished by the University. Hence the first stories carried were identical. On succeeding days the Loyola station began evening programming, usually thirty minutes to one hour in length. On Sunday night, April 2, Cassidy, who had now assumed the role of WWL's first station manager, positioned a portable victrola before the transmitter and played into the microphone John McCormick's recording of "When Irish Eyes Are Smiling." Cassidy thereby became Louisiana's first disc jockey. The general nature of the programs broadcast in the first weeks of operation was a melange of fund-raising, live instrumental or vocal music, and recordings. On a typical evening, an initial building campaign talk was followed by a recording of a Thomas Edison speech, live cornet, piano, and tenor solos (the latter "I'll Take You Home Again, Kathleen), and concluded with a recording of the Edison Concert Band. At this very early date no serious thought was given to the copyright issues raised by the playing of recorded or live music on the air. All of the broadcasting originated in the third floor Physics lab of Marquette Hall, where the trunk set transmitter had been installed.[29]

The zest for radio of the Loyola administration in the spring of 1922 and the progress of its campaign for donations were in direct proportion. As a distinct lack of success became apparent in the funds drive, WWL came to appear as more and more of an unnecessary luxury. By early May, when only $90,000 of the needed $1,500,000 had been subscribed, one disappointed volunteer conjectured that too many prospective givers were "laboring under the erroneous impression that the Jesuits are wealthy." A final report given at a closing luncheon at the end of May revealed that pledges and cash of just $316,000 had been collected. The campaign chairman attributed the shortfall to "depressed business conditions." Cummings, however, was more caustic, referring to "the way our friends have failed us in the most critical hour of Loyola's history."[30]

In the face of these dismaying results and in the light of no long range commitment to broadcasting ever having been made by University officials, the station being viewed simply as a temporary donation-producing gimmick, WWL's future became highly uncertain. The strong probability existed that it might suffer the same mortality that soon would befall many others. By August 1924 the Department of Commerce had licensed 1,105 broadcasters but 572 of that number had already surrendered their licenses and retired from the field, a death rate of nearly 52%. The losers in the early radio game faced three impersonal challenges too difficult to overcome: high start-up costs, continuing and increasing operating expenses, and the absence of a tangible income from their broadcast activities.[31]

College-owned stations fared somewhat better than most in the first two problem areas but were, in the long run, defeated by the third. A 1924 industry survey revealed that the initial capital investment for college stations was invariably less than that required for non-collegiate facilities, usually under $3,000, since the equipment was ordinarily assembled in a

21

Physics Department, and since space was provided free of rent by the institution. Further, day-to-day operating expenses were kept in line by the fact that the college stations normally were on the air for short periods of time, often at irregular intervals, and that a non-paid staff (faculty members and students) and unpaid artists and performers were utilized. For such operations, annual operating costs of $1,000 or less, principally spent for equipment maintenance, were normal. Nevertheless, even those modest sums could quickly pose difficulties, especially as public pressure upon station owners to lengthen broadcast hours, to increase power, and to improve program quality began to build. With no income being provided by programming that was, of course, entirely non-commercial at this early date, many broadcasters inevitably asked themselves, "Does it really pay?" They understandably concluded that good will simply did not suffice; it did not pay the bills.[32]

The Loyola administration reached essentially that same conclusion by mid-June 1922 when it announced that WWL had been "closed down for the summer." A vague promise was given of a re-opening in the fall, but every indicator signalled a diminished Jesuit relish for radio. That interpretation was confirmed by an almost total lack of activity in the months that followed. The trunk set transmitter remained in its place in the third floor Physics lab and was used but "spasmodically and intermittently" between the summer of 1922 and the summer of 1923. Even with an only occasional use, costs were still regarded as excessive. In 1923 the large tubes of the transmitter that allowed it to perform at its authorized 100 watts were replaced by smaller and more economical tubes. Power was accordingly reduced to a meager ten watts at a time when other stations were urgently moving to increase theirs.

By the summer of 1923 WWL broadcasting was non-existent. The newspapers had not carried notices of past or future programming for months beforehand and the station existed in name only. The license, which under existing law required renewal every three months if it was to be retained, was re-applied for as necessary, thanks largely to the conscientiousness of Joe du Treil in the Radio Service office, but it was little more than a formality. No judgment could be reached other than to pronounce WWL in extremis, with death all but certain, probably sometime in 1924.[33]

# 3

## STATIC IN THE 360 JUNGLE

WWL was not the only broadcast station to take the
air in the spring of 1922. Rather, it quickly found itself joined by a rush of others, and almost overnight
an industry had begun to develop, though not to prosper,
in Louisiana. The outstanding feature of this early
stage in the state's radio history was an intense competition, indeed a race, between the three New Orleans
daily newspapers, each striving to launch stations under
their own banners. The Item initiated the dash by con-
triving the WGV venture with Interstate Electric, but
the Times-Picayune and the States were not far behind.
The WWL breakthrough on March 31 came as an unwelcome
shock to the three newspapers, but it was still possible
to salvage some considerable measure of value from a
radio affiliation, even if one could no longer claim to
be the first. It would be simple enough to largely
ignore the University station and instead to turn the
publicity guns loose on their own projects. Besides,
even if first was no longer possible, there still would
be great satisfaction in finishing ahead of the rest of
the journalistic pack.

The Times-Picayune was the next to move. Leonard K.
Nicholson, who had assumed the presidency of the Times-
Picayune in 1918, was mildly infected with radio fever.
Moving partially on his own and partially out of reaction to rumors of the Item plans, he sought out the
necessary technical expertise. He found it in the person
of Valdemar "Val" Jensen, an automobile salesman who
dabbled in amateur radio during his leisure hours. In
1922 Jensen was the used car manager of the Fairchild
Motor Company, but also a radio devotee. He operated a
licensed amateur transmitter from his home on New
Orleans' St. Patrick Street, and it was that equipment
and that home that Nicholson proposed to grandly desig-
nate as the broadcasting station of the Times-Picayune.

23

Without leaking word to his competitors or to the public, Nicholson received the required governmental authorization and his assigned call letters of WAAB in early April, and prepared for the station's surprise opening.[1]

Colonel Robert Ewing, the walrus-mustached publisher of the New Orleans States, was not lacking in aggressiveness even though his was the smallest in circulation of the city's three newspapers. He had managed to construct a Louisiana journalism empire, acquiring the States in 1900, and then adding to it the Shreveport Times and two Monroe papers, and he was a force in Democratic Party politics in the state. The broadcasting potential had not escaped him as well, and even before the Times-Picayune's station received its license, Ewing was already ordering up the same menu for the States. He chose for his technical talent Clyde R. Randall, manager of a storage battery company in the city, who combined an electronic knowledge with some previous show business experience. The station, to be installed in Randall's Calhoun Street home, would be licensed in both the name of the operator and of the States.[2]

Progress was, however, too slow to please Ewing. In an April 4 letter to a Louisiana Congressman, he admitted: "We are installing a Radio Broadcasting Station here on the States to send out news and a short entertainment daily and have already applied for a license from the Inspector for this district." But Deiler was proving an obstacle, refusing to recommend a license until the installation was complete. Ewing described his plight, hoping the Congressman could intervene: "This will delay even my publicity for several weeks more. As the parts arrive they are installed, but I must start my publicity now if I expect to beat some of the others."[3]

Help was not to be forthcoming. Two weeks later the situation had not materially changed. The station was still unfinished. John B. Draper, a States executive, reported to Ewing "that everything was in place but two 50-watt tubes," which had not yet been delivered. Draper promised: "The moment these 50-watt tubes are in place the Inspector will go out to the Plant and give us an inspection. As it stands it is impossible for him to do anything because his powers are limited to inspecting a station when it is in shape to operate and not before." The delay would put the States far behind in the radio race, and finally cause Ewing to

place less and less emphasis on his broadcasting
association as his less tardy competitors garnered
public attention.[4]

The Item was the first to openly publish its intentions.  On April 6, it splashed the WGV story
across its front page.  A page one editorial asked,
"What is WGV?" and answered its own question:

> Scarcely a dozen persons know today.
> Within two weeks there will be scarcely
> that many in and about New Orleans who do
> not know... This station will be opened
> formally within a short time under the
> joint auspices of the Interstate Electric
> Company and the New Orleans Item.  WGV
> will give a nightly program of concert
> music, Item news bulletins and theatrical
> arts for everyone within a radius of
> 300 miles or more.[5]

While the announcement indicated WGV's opening
was still some days off, that timetable was scrapped
when it became apparent that the Times-Picayune had
every intention of beating WGV to the air.  By late
afternoon on the same day, word reached the Item that
its newspaper rival was going on the air that very
evening.  The news jolted the Item strategists who had
not anticipated the Times-Picayune's preparations being
that near completion.  It is probable that Nicholson
had deliberately pushed ahead WAAB's inauguration in
order to lessen the impact of the WGV announcement.
In any event, the Item had only a few hours at most in
which to react.  Dorr Simmons was ordered to put WGV
on the air immediately and a hasty opening program was
formulated.[6]

Musicians were borrowed from the Strand Theater,
owned by Julian Saenger, a switch was thrown, "two
lamps set in the front of a polished black, instrument-
studded bakelite panel, suddenly glowed cherry red",
and WGV went on the air.  After an initial greeting, a
Strand orchestra violinist played "Mighty Lak a Rose,"
two vocalists dueted on "I'll Forget You," and a cellist
and a violinist combined on a pair of classical
selections.  New Orleans had its second station, and
the Item had won the intramural newspaper sweepstakes.
When the Times-Picayune's WAAB opened later that
evening, it found itself the state's third station.[7]

WAAB looked to Phillip Werlein's music store for
its program content.  It began with an Enrico Caruso
recording of "Memories of Naples," secured from
Werlein's.  Caruso was followed by another record, the
Dixieland Jazz Band's arrangement of "Lazy Daddy,"
which the newspaper claimed put "unmistakeable pep
into the air and the feet of those who were listening."
A little later two live cornet solos by the manager of
Werlein's "small goods department" were followed by the
same gentleman switching to a banjo.  WAAB's first night
programming ran two hours in length, the longest single
time segment broadcast to that time in the city.  Overall, the Times-Picayune's treatment of the story was
restrained and in keeping with the somewhat more aris-
tocratic and stuffy nature of the paper's journalistic
philosophy.  At no time did the newspaper state the
location of the station itself, thus giving the reader
the impression the transmitter had been installed in
the Times-Picayune's Lafayette Square headquarters
rather than in its actual site, the Jensen home.  The
newspaper also avoided any mention of WGV which had
begun broadcasts on the same day.[8]

The contrast with the Item's treatment of the same
story was stark.  A banner headline on April 7, "RADIO
CONCERTS START," topped breathless reporting of the
previous night's events.  The Item admitted it had not
intended to go on the air that Thursday evening but had
decided to do so as a result of the excitement created
by its announcement earlier that day.  It referred to
itself as "the first newspaper to take steps to bring
the new wonders of radio-telephony within the reach of
the people of New Orleans, Louisiana, and neighboring
states."  A formal opening on Friday evening was also
publicized with speeches by Mayor Andrew McShane,
President A.B. Dinwiddie of Tulane University, and
Archbishop John W. Shaw promised.[9]

The Item, moreover, used its tie with Interstate
Electric for a marketing promotion.  On this and
succeeding days, it vigorously advertised a "Junior
Item Receiving Set," being sold by Interstate Electric
for 75¢.  The set, which came in kit form and required
the buyer to assemble it himself, included "wire,
crystal, nut, bolt, tack, screw and switch already
cut to exact dimensions."  The only additional materials necessary, according to the advertising, were
"as much wood as there is in a cigar box lid and an
old round oatmeal package or mailing tube of cardboard."
When completed, the crystal set could, with the
attaching of earphones (available at Interstate Electric

26

for as little as $1.75 extra), tune in all the exciting programs being broadcast on WGV.  Even a contest was announced to be judged by Dorr Simmons, who was by now something of an instant civic celebrity.  For the best set built by anyone using the Item kit, a $25 order of radio parts from Interstate Electric was awarded. A few days later, the Item was offering a completely assembled receiving set together with earphones for any boy securing twenty new subscriptions to the newspaper.[10]

Both the Item and the Times-Picayune did agree on one matter, the effect of the radio activity on the city of New Orleans.  The morning newspaper referred to interest in the new medium as being "at fever heat" and reported that dealers in parts and supplies were "swamped with orders."  The Item termed the city "radio-mad" and claimed supply houses "were swept clean of material by a purchasing craze."  It added that the Sterns at Interstate Electric had been forced to add extra employees to package the popular crystal set kits.[11]

Broadcasting firsts of one type or another became an every day event that spring.  The first children's program was carried on WGV, "Uncle Wiggly Bedtime Stories," read by Suzanne France, a Strand Theater singer.  The same station presented the city's first radio drama--a production of a Shaw play, Dark Lady of Sonnets.  On May 6, WAAB held an amateur night talent contest with the winner promised three appearances on the vaudeville stage of the Palace Theater in New Orleans.  Mailed-in votes from the listening audience were to be the basis for the decision.  The eventual winners were two young sisters, Martha and Constance Boswell, whose later fame as pop singers would carry them far beyond Louisiana's borders.  And in early May, WAAB aired the first "remote control" broadcast. Jensen successfully placed microphones in the Jerusalem Temple and sent the sound of a musicale back to the transmitter in his home by means of an ordinary telephone line.  The Times-Picayune described it as having been done "with the same dependable volume, the same intensity and color, and with as little distortion as would be possible if the concert were being given in the sending room alongside the radio transmitter itself."[12]

Even more new stations were now coming on the air. On April 5, the Commerce Department licensed Tulane University's wireless telephone operation and designated

27

it WAAC, though the station did not actually begin broadcasting till a few weeks later. On April 22 the call letters WBAM were assigned a New Orleans realtor, I.B. Rennyson, who had become intrigued by radio's business possibilities. As Rennyson explained: "The idea struck me that real estate could be sold by use of the wireless telephone and I applied for government authority to broadcast." And on May 4, Colonel Ewing's States at last achieved its license, and as WCAG became the city's sixth station.[13]

It was not just New Orleans, though, that saw stations coming into being at this time in Louisiana. In Shreveport some broadcasting activity was taking place as well, and William E. Antony was at the center of it all. Antony, a telephone company employee, had long demonstrated his interest in radio, particularly by the operation of an amateur transmitter since 1916. In May 1922 he built and conducted from his home a short-lived station licensed to the Elliott Electric Company, and then in July he performed the same service for William G. Patterson's Glenwood Radio Corporation. Patterson, a Shreveport merchant, would eventually see his station, WGAQ, under new ownership and with the new call letters of KWKH, play a major and controversial role in the history of American broadcasting. As for Antony, except for one brief flirtation with station ownership in the late 1920's, he would confine his interests to the technical aspects of radio, and would become at KWKH one of the best known and most senior Chief Engineers in the South. Nowhere else but in New Orleans and in Shreveport did Louisiana broadcasting make an appearance in 1922.[14]

In New Orleans, where six stations were authorized to broadcast by mid-May, a major crisis had developed--a traffic jam on the one available wave length had to be unsnarled if radio was to perform any service for the community. The wave length confusion stemmed from a lack of foresight on the part of the Commerce Department. In granting licenses to the pioneer stations of 1921 and 1922, it had assigned them all to the same 360 meters. This created no great difficulty when only a single broadcaster existed in a community, though it did prevent out-of-town stations from being tuned in when the locals were on the air and for that reason "silent nights" were observed in many cities. But when additional stations jumped into the same market, chaos reigned supreme. Unless all those who wanted to broadcast would negotiate together some rational scheme for dividing the available time, the

28

tower of Babel would seem more intelligible. Unfortunately, such divisions were depressingly difficult to establish as the required meetings were thorny tangles of inflated egoes, grandiose ambitions, and pure rugged individualism. New Orleans was no exception, especially with three of the stations being the flagships of competing newspapers.[15]

Theodore Deiler, heading the Radio Service's District Office in New Orleans, found himself the man in the middle. Oral and written protests from disgruntled listeners and from unhappy broadcasters bombarded him at his Customs House desk. They demanded that the Radio Service or Secretary of Commerce Hoover or someone in authority establish order and put into effect by federal fiat a reasonable allocation plan. WWL was among those insisting upon action. Father Florence D. Sullivan, who in 1925 would become Loyola's fifth president, wrote an angry letter to Deiler on April 8, calling on the government official to arbitrarily assign WWL "at least one hour every night between 7:00 P.M. and 9:00 P.M." Sullivan warned that unless this time was set aside for the University's use, "our valuable installation which we developed before others came into the field will be rendered useless, and our U.S. permit to broadcast will be a fiction." Deiler, helpless to settle the controversy himself in the absence of any precedent or ruling from Washington, forwarded the correspondence on the problem to his immediate superior, the Commissioner of Navigation.[16]

He explained the stalemate that had been encountered, and noted that he had suggested that the stations arrive at their own plan, but self-regulation had been unsuccessful. In a classic understatement, Deiler added: "The fact that intense newspaper rivalry exists among the three newspapers of New Orleans considerably complicates matters." He openly asked for help, requesting that an "actual division of time" be dictated by Washington. The response was less than Deiler had requested but sufficient to accomplish his purpose. On May 3, A.J. Tyrer, the Acting Commissioner of Navigation, informed the New Orleans office that if local stations were unable or unwilling to come to an agreement among themselves, "the Secretary of Commerce has authority to specify in the licenses the hours these stations shall operate." In effect, Deiler was told to make one more try, but this time with a warning clearly stated to recalcitrant operators that if they could not agree upon a satisfactory solution, they would have to accept a Washington version of one.[17]

Armed with the threat, Deiler called another conference to meet in his office, and this time successfully hammered out a temporary modus vivendi. It was a
seven night a week rotating schedule, beginning each
evening at 6:30 P.M. and concluding at 10:00 P.M.[18]

Since no one expressed an interest in daytime broadcasting, when the tiny 10 to 100-watt transmitters then
in use lost most of their already meager coverage, those
hours were ignored. The newspaper stations of the Item
and the States fared the best in the division, with WGV
being the only one slated for programs seven nights
each week. The university stations collected only the
crumbs from the bargaining table with WWL being heard
just three hours weekly spread over three separate
evenings, and Tulane's WAAC allotted only time on
Friday nights. Since neither of the University stations
were especially active in programming by late May, with
Loyola's enthusiasm by this time experiencing the severe
chill already described, the academic institutions acquiesced in their less favorable assignments.

The most surprising drop-out, however, was the
Times-Picayune's WAAB, which did not appear on the
schedule at all. Unexpectedly, the city's largest newspaper had shrugged off broadcasting entirely. In im-
perial prose on May 14, it announced that it was no
longer interested in a radio association, and cited a
number of factors shaping its negative decision. Included among them was the uncertainty of the regulatory
situation, clearly a reference to the unsettled issue of
the limits of Department of Commerce authority, a matter
which would not be permanently resolved until 1927.[19]

Even more specifically, the newspaper pointed to an
increasingly worrisome patent problem: "A group of
associated enterprises, through control of certain
patent rights are in a position apparently to wield a
powerful influence on radio in the future." It also
admitted: "Many of the broadcast stations operating
today are doing so in technical violation of this
group's patent rights and could be closed down or at
least subjected to a costly court fight." The Times-
Picayune was rightly concerned with the implications
of a License Agreement reached on July 1, 1920 by the
American Telephone and Telegraph Company, its Western
Electric subsidiary, and the General Electric Company
and its newly organized subsidiary, the Radio Corporation of America. The Agreement, which Westinghouse
joined in 1921, seemingly gave AT&T, through an exchange
of patents, exclusive rights to the manufacture of

transmitters for broadcasting stations.  Nonetheless,
by 1923 only thirty-five stations were using Western
Electric equipment as opposed to that manufactured by
other companies or homemade by themselves.  Broadcasters could not help but wait uneasily for the first
sounds of the telephone giant's legal machinery being
set in motion.  While AT&T debated within its own board
room the best policy to pursue towards patent infringements, radio stations lived under a cloud of anxiety.20

     Perhaps, most important to the Times-Picayune was
the lack of a tangible return from broadcasting.  As the
newspaper phrased it:  "Nor have the brightest minds in
the newspaper world hit upon a scheme by which a broadcast station efficiently operated could be made even to
pay for itself."  Others shared the New Orleans' paper's
pessimism.  Radio Broadcast, in its inaugural issue of
May 1922, could offer no solution to the puzzle of station financing other than philanthropy.  The magazine
concluded that the "most attractive" alternative was
"the endowment of a station by a public spirited
citizen."  Comparing broadcasting to libraries, it
argued "there is no doubt that a properly conducted
radio broadcasting station can do at least as great an
educational work as does the average library."  Ironically, within a few months after the Times-Picayune's
public despair, the ultimate solution to bearing the
economic cost of station operation would be tested in
New York City.21

     On August 28, 1922, station WEAF, owned by AT&T,
initiated "toll broadcasting."  At 5:15 P.M. a spokesman for the Queensboro Corporation began the first of a
series of fifteen minute sales talks on behalf of
Hawthorne Court, an apartment development in Jackson
Heights.  The charge for the time furnished by the
station was $100, but broadcasts were said to have been
directly responsible for several thousand dollars worth
of apartment sales for the corporate sponsors.  In
September WEAF carried sales presentations for two more
business organizations, Tidewater Oil and American
Express.  Reluctance to conceive of radio as an advertising medium was difficult to overcome, though, despite
these early experiments.  After two months, WEAF was
successful in selling to sponsors only three hours of
air time, and gross income for the station was a paltry
$550.  In some quarters absolute hostility to the idea
had surfaced.  Printers' Ink referred to the possibility
as "positively offensive" to most Americans, and warned:
"The family circle is not a public place, and advertising has no business intruding there unless it is
invited."  Even the nation's respected Secretary of

Commerce, Herbert Hoover, spoke disapprovingly of the new development: "It is inconceivable that we should allow so great a possibility for service to be drowned in advertising chatter."[22]

Plainly, the emergence of advertising as the solution to the financial dilemma confronting broadcasting would be both slow and beset by a host of enemies. The Times-Picayune, therefore, while not demonstrating any appreciable imagination or gambling spirit, was certainly basing its decision to abandon radio on the hard realities of the moment. Costs, even if minimal in 1922 as compared to later years, were still uncompensated by any palpable gains. Once the immediate publicity values had been siphoned off, there appeared little reason to continue the enterprise. The other dailies, in part prompted by the Times-Picayune withdrawal, would soon beat the same retreat.

Thus the "Treaty of New Orleans," mediated by Theodore Deiler in May 1922, was marked by the conspicuous absence of WAAB. The eventual return of the station under Val Jensen's sole control was expected. For that reason open slots were provided in the schedule so that it might be slipped in at a later date. The weakness in the Treaty, a weakness apparent to all parties involved, was its failure to accommodate the future. It was predicated on the existence of only those stations already licensed. No mechanism was available for reconciling the demands of other stations that, without a doubt, would be spawned in the months ahead if the public's appetite for radio entertainment failed to diminish. No mechanism was even provided for an orderly assumption of the time thrown open by the default of an existing station. In both instances only a re-convening of the original negotiating sessions, with all their attendant difficulties, would suffice. The ultimate answer to the perplexities of wave length division lay in Washington and not in the local communities. Only when the Department of Commerce embarked on a policy of wave length differentiation among stations, was the 360 jumble eliminated.[23]

The groundwork for such action was already in place. In early February 1922 Hoover called for the convocation of a National Radio Conference. Referring to "the critical situation that has arisen through the astonishing development of the wireless telephone," he asked government and private representatives of various broadcasting interests to meet with him in

Washington. Fifteen official delegates were present
at the opening session on February 27 and heard Hoover
equate safeguarding the air waves from needless interference with conservation of the nation's natural
resources. While conflicting viewpoints prevented
the recommendations of the Conference from being more
than general, the delegates did strongly recommend ves-
ting "adequate legal authority for the effective control"
of both commercial and amateur radio in the Secretary of
Commerce.[24]

Acting under the encouragement given him by the
Conference's recommendation, and in the absence of any
congressional legislation, Hoover moved on his own to
alleviate the chaos. In August 1922 he made the first
attempt at classification of broadcasting stations by
establishing a new group termed "class B." They would
operate on a separate wave length entirely, 400 meters
or 750 kc. Class B stations were required to have
transmitters capable of 500 watts power and to use live
music only in their normal programming. Obviously,
Hoover was creating an elite group in this category.
He emphasized their special status by warning Class B
broadcasters that if they did not maintain acceptable
standards, they would be relegated by him back to the
no man's land of 360 meters. No New Orleans stations
qualified for the honor. None were broadcasting with
what was then regarded as "high power," 500-watts or
more.[25]

Hoover took even more sweeping action the following
year. Again, the recommendations of a National Radio
Conference, which like its predecessor had been summoned
by the energetic Commerce Secretary, featured as a primary aim an attempt to broaden even more the available
channels for broadcasting. The resulting resolution of
the delegates called for "making available all wave
lengths from 222 to 545 meters for public broadcasting,
the various possible bands to be assigned to different
stations, so as not only to reduce direct interference
but also to build up zonal regions of distribution."
Hoover quickly responded, setting up a new three-fold
channel classification. Class B stations, still the
elite, were to be assigned wave lengths between 300-
345 and 375-545 meters. Such stations were required to
use power of at least 500 watts and as much as 1,000
watts (1 kw.). A new intermediate group with "power
not exceeding 500 watts" was assigned positions
between 222 and 300 meters. This subdivision, it was
hoped, would include virtually all stations not quali-
fying for Class B, thus spreading the great mass of
licenses across the full range of the broadcast band.

Since serious doubt still remained as to the
legality of any coercive action undertaken by Hoover's
Department, a third category was shrewdly established.
Class C included any stations not desiring to move from
the 360 ghetto. Thus no broadcaster was required to
change wave lengths, and any such change was cloaked
in the guise of voluntary action. No new Class C
stations would be licensed. In 1923 classification
order was the effective beginning of radio spectrum
allocation. Shortly afterwards, again acting upon a
Conference suggestion, the Radio Service informed station operators that it was abandoning the wave length
terminology and substituting references to "frequencies."
Thereafter assignments were stated in terms of kilocycles rather than meters. By trial and error, a
federal regulatory policy was being shaped.[26]

WWL was one of the stations choosing to move on
to an uncrowded frequency in Class A. In July 1923 it
was assigned 1070 kc., a location on the radio dial which
it would hold for just one year until a 1924 change
shifted it slightly to 1090 kc. Yet with broadcasting
at a standstill at Loyola, WWL's frequency alterations
seemed of minor consequence.[27]

As if the struggling broadcasters of 1922 had not
enough burdens to bear, they found nature itself placing
another on their shoulders in the heated atmosphere of
summer evenings. Static became a disconcerting feature
of every program attempt. The States exclaimed:
"Static! The word which is on every radio fan's lips
these days! We have heard it, heard about it, thought
about it, dreamed about it, and finally, in much dis-
gust, cussed it."[28] Earlier the Item had been moved
to poetry of sorts by the maddening phenomenon:

> The melancholy days are come, the
> saddest of the year
> When static snaps across the skies
> e'en though the night be clear
> When all the headsets in the land
> will crackle, hiss and slam
> As though the stars were shifting
> gears and frying eggs and ham.[29]

As the summer months dragged on, static interference became more and more severe. It drove listeners
and broadcasters alike into never-ending discussions
on how to overcome it. Countless newspaper articles
offered advice but given the state of available

equipment and knowledge, the task was impossible to accomplish. The _States_ predicted, however, that "fame and fortune awaits the one who does it."[30]

Plagued by static, ensnarled in the tedious diplomacy of time division agreements, harassed by mounting costs and non-existent incomes, many broadcasters withdrew rapidly from their exposed positions in the new industry. In New Orleans the _Times-Picayune_ led off the parade to the rear, and once the city's leading daily made its decision, it was easier for the other two to follow. Program news gradually slipped from the front page to an inside page, from detailed stories to cryptic listings, and then finally to no mention at all. By mid-1923 WCAG's license had been officially transferred to Clyde Randall, and the _States_ had bowed out of any direct radio connection. A Sunday column, written by a local licensed amateur operator, Hubert de Ben, offering technical advice, was carried but no program or station news was included. The _Item_ likewise had ended its participation in the WGV venture, turning that station over to the undivided control of the Sterns and Interstate Electric. The Sterns maintained the operation until they too became discouraged with its future prospects, at last shutting the transmitter down permanently in 1924.[31]

I.B. Rennyson, the realtor with a taste for broadcasting, lost that taste rather quickly. WBAM was deleted from the Radio Service's list of active stations in October 1922. Tulane likewise lost interest in WAAC as it began to demand too expensive a lifestyle. Little programming was done after 1922 and the station was allowed to die a quiet death in 1925. By November 1923 the _States_ reported only three active New Orleans stations remained on the air--WGV (soon to expire), WCAG, and WTAF (a new station licensed in the summer of 1923)-- half the number broadcasting over a year before. Major problems, principally economic, had yet to be solved if the industry was to have a basis for growth. If there was in fact a pot of gold at the end of the radio rainbow, it was still a considerable distance off, and it would be someone other than the first New Orleans broadcasters of 1922 who would find it.[32]

# 4

## TROUBLED GROWTH, 1924-1925

In the life of any organization, decisive moments
will occur when it may take the path to growth or to
decay. For WWL such a moment presented itself in June
1924 with the assignment to the Loyola campus of a
short, slightly-built, thirty-five year old Jesuit with
a flair for electronics. The Reverend Orie L. Abell,
S.J., was the product of a mechanically inclined family;
his brothers were professional engineers and he himself
held a degree in physics. By nature a humble man, he
was at the same time exacting in his requirements, a per-
fectionist in his demands, and unafraid of stating his
own views in any argument in the most forceful terms.
He also possessed an extremely long memory, especially
for those battles which he had lost, and his memories
were not always kind. Capable of a single-minded dedication to projects or enterprises in which he believed,
Abell, more than any other individual, reversed the
downward slide of WWL and set the station on a course
towards eventual financial success.[1]

He arrived at the University as the new Chairman
of the Physics Department, replacing Edward Cassidy who
was leaving temporarily to pursue further theological
studies. Abell would head that Department for the next
eight years, though an increasing amount of his time
during that period would be devoted to the station
rather than to classroom duties. For the next thirteen
years, the fortunes of WWL and the Jesuit physicist
would be synonymous. When a separation did finally
come, it would not be without pain and some bitterness.[2]

Within weeks of his arrival, Abell had formed a
close association with L.J.N. du Treil. The federal
Radio Inspector continued to devote a significant portion of his evening leisure hours to experiments in the
Marquette Hall Physics Lab. Du Treil was soon successful in convincing the Jesuit that the now virtually

abandoned transmitter be rehabilitated and WWL resume
broadcasting. During the summer and early fall, Abell
rebuilt the old trunk set, increasing its power in the
process to 50 watts. On October 3, after months off
the air, WWL underwent an official rebirth, and Abell
announced the station would broadcast on Saturday
evenings for one hour from 8:00-9:00 P.M. The schedule
was devastatingly modest, but at least some activity
was again taking place.[3]

By now a complete believer in WWL's potential,
Abell was chronically discontent with the status quo.
Like most broadcasters of this period he sought increased station power almost as a goal in itself. Power
meant coverage and coverage translated into influence
to be used in whatever fashion management might dictate,
for economic gains or for fulfilling intangible educational or religious aims. But all rested upon power,
the number of watts with which a station was authorized
to transmit. Abell would never rest with the last amount
assigned. There was always a larger figure towards which
he could reach and for which he could strive. As a
result the Abell years were marked primarily by an in-
exorable climb in wattage, and the perquisites of this
increased power followed in direct proportion.

Less than two months after WWL resumed broadcasting
in the fall of 1924, Abell set about rebuilding the
transmitter yet again. He introduced "electrolytic" or
chemical rectifiers in order to eliminate a disagreeable
hum heard by listeners; he added a late model Western
Electric carbon microphone; and most important, he
boosted power to 100 watts. While Commerce Department
permission to use the increased power was not granted
until March 28, 1925, it seems possible that Abell was
utilizing it as early as January of that year. One
other change of significance for the station was made.
The transmitter itself was placed in a new home, a small,
square brick structure located at the south door of
Bobet Hall, the recently completed classroom building
constructed with the funds raised in 1922. The structure,
which had formerly housed the University's seismograph,
was just barely large enough for a single transmitter
operator and, as a result, required separate production facilities. A studio was arranged in a second
floor Marquette Hall auditorium--the station's first
separation of the two broadcast functions of production
and transmission.[4]

Finances remained a critical problem. The power
increase necessitated expenditures for which little

institutional support was forthcoming. Abell later recalled, somewhat caustically, that in these years he
had "received no encouragement, either financially or
otherwise from the University authorities towards the
upkeep of WWL." Rather the station had come to be regarded by them as "Father Abell's Hobby" and even
"Father Abell's Folly." He solved his problem by
turning part-time salesman. He negotiated an arrangement with the local distributor of an opaque projector
whereby Abell received a commission on each piece of
equipment sold to a prospect developed by the Jesuit.
The commissions were then devoted to the purchase of
transmitter parts and studio furnishings. Abell also
solicited a contribution from the Pastor of Holy Name
Church sufficient for the acquisition of the Western
Electric microphone ($125.00) in return for WWL's
broadcast of the 10:30 A.M. Solemn High Mass each
Sunday. That program was to become a permanent
feature of the station schedule. By utilizing his own
labor and the volunteered services of du Treil and some
willing students, the necessary manpower was coupled
with purchased parts to forge a newly active broadcasting
station.[5]

\* \* \* \* \* \* \* \* \* \*

While WWL was regaining the momentum lost in 1922,
radio in general and New Orleans' broadcasting in particular was experiencing an erratic and troubled growth.
One factor brightening the prospects for the industry
was the improvements being made in receiving sets. By
1925 the consumer could choose either an inexpensive
crystal set capable of receiving a signal from a distance of up to one hundred miles, or a far more superior
set employing vacuum tubes and requiring two separate
batteries, one for filament voltage and another for
plate current. Prices varied from $10-25 for crystal
sets requiring headphones to $100-500 for sets employing
as many as six vacuum tubes. Each manufacturer lauded
his particular model: Crosley, "The Height of
Efficiency"; Magnavox, "Magnavox Keeps the Stay-at-Homes
Happy"; RCA, "Get Long Range with RCA Radio"; Super-
Heterodyne, "The Rolls-Royce of Reception"; and
Paragon, "Aladdin's Lamp Outdone." The States estimated
in March 1924 that the average New Orleanian spent $100
for an assembled receiving set, though a substantial
percentage were still buying only parts and building the
set at home. Whereas the 1923 City Directory listed
just five shops dealing in "radio supplies," the 1925
edition listed seventeen under "radios and supplies"
including all major department stores.[6]

An improved device for listening was only half the equation, progress was also being made in transmission. The overall number of stations had not significantly increased; as late as 1926 it still remained below 600, but there had been a sizeable jump in the average power used per station. From .17 kilowatts in 1924, the figure had become .37 in 1925 and .66 in 1926. By 1929 average power for the first time surpassed one kilowatt or 1,000 watts.[7] The following table illustrates the shift in power distribution for stations in the decade:[8]

Station Power Distribution, 1923-1929

| Watts | 1923 | 1924 | 1925 | 1926 | 1927 | 1928 | 1929 |
|---|---|---|---|---|---|---|---|
| 0-100 | 409 | 389 | 355 | 269 | 331 | 297 | 246 |
| 100-500 | 159 | 136 | 184 | 175 | 258 | 263 | 209 |
| 500-1,000 | 11 | 16 | 23 | 58 | 66 | 79 | 95 |
| 1,000-5,000 | | | 18 | 29 | 45 | 61 | 58 |
| over 5,000 | | | | | 6 | 9 | 28 |

The ten years between 1923-1932 thus saw a major trend toward continuous and aggressive power increases for most licensees. During that period the total number of active stations rose by only 5.4%, but the power employed soared by more than 1400%. The philosophy Abell pursued at WWL was mirrored in the actions of other broadcasters of the period.[9]

The combination of increased transmitter power and more sophisticated receiving sets was also winning the technical battle against static. One New Orleans newspaper commented in late 1924 that "Old Man Static" certainly was "not cutting the capers he used to" in the light of these advances.[10] But if engineering problems were proving less intractable, others remained formidable and fresh concerns had arisen. One of these was an escalating dispute with the American Society of Composers, Authors, and Publishers--ASCAP.

As music quickly became the principal broadcast fare for the emergent stations of the early 1920's, ASCAP, the nation's dominant licensing or "performing rights" association, grew alarmed by what it perceived to be a decline in royalty payments stemming from the sale of sheet music and phonograph records. Radio was supposedly not only slaking the public demand for such items, it was also ignoring its own responsibility to respect copyright requirements. ASCAP, organized in 1914 by a group led by composer Victor Herbert, saw its

sole function to be a clearing house for the bulk
licensing of public performance rights held by its
members. It took the leadership in defense of those
rights. The matter was raised at the 1923 National
Radio Conference by J.C. Rosenthal, ASCAP general manager. Rosenthal warned the delegates that unless station
owners paid royalties to copyright holders, prosecutions
under the federal copyright law would follow.[11]

Broadcasters were outraged at the ASCAP demands.
They denied any deleterious effects upon the music industry. Indeed, they contended that radio exposure
helped popularize songs, multiplying sales of records
and sheet music. Moreover, radio was in no position to
pay royalty fees. Most stations earned no incomes in
this pre-advertising era, and, therefore, there were no
funds from which royalties could be paid. The editors of
Radio Broadcast, the newly established industry organ,
argued: "When a station can be shown to be on a paying
basis, then it seems proper for music writers to collect
as their share of the proceeds as much as seems reasonable, but to insist on large royalties while the game is
in the experimental stage seems very much like killing
the goose which might some day lay golden eggs for them."
The ASCAP executives, however, saw little validity in
those counter-arguments.[12]

Shrewdly, the association attacked on two fronts.
It demanded an annual license fee from each station
with amounts scaled upwards from $250. Simultaneously,
it pressed its case in the courts, winning a 1923 judgment against Newark's WOR, owned by the Bamberger department store, for the playing of "Mother Machree" without
payment of a royalty. Buttressed by the WOR decision,
and with broadcasters suddenly aware that under the
copyright law even "innocent infringement" could be
penalized by a $250 fine on each count, ASCAP was in a
commanding position. Stations were faced with two alternatives: they might avoid playing ASCAP material
entirely, and program only music in the public domain
or for which rights had been negotiated in some private
manner; or they must succumb to the ASCAP demand for an
annual license payment. Despite abortive efforts at
both boycotting ASCAP music and reversing the WOR precedent in the courts, stations gradually fell into line
by signing the ASCAP agreements.[13]

Even if the music license fee appeared moderate in
actual dollar terms, it represented another financial
drain on stations already hard-pressed to meet ordinary

day to day expenses.  Such burdens represented the principal reason why the fatality rate among early broadcasters reached a calamitous level by the summer of 1924,
almost 50% of those granted licenses since 1921.  And
ASCAP's was not the only license fee broadcasters found
themselves facing in these months, for AT&T was now
demanding a tribute as well.[14]

The telephone giant had been reluctant to move
against those broadcasters who had blatantly ignored its
patent rights since such an action, no matter how appropriate in purely legal terms, involved an enormous public
relations and political risk.  Further, it was clear
that many of the infringing stations had begun in innocent ignorance of the patents held by AT&T.  In view of
the probability that a substantial portion of the stations would not survive the financial rigors of daily
operation, the wisest course seemed to be one of restraint.  By 1923, however, the question became complicated by an increasing demand on the part of broadcasters
for telephone "pickup" lines to make remote control
programs possible.  If Bell System companies agreed to
the leasing of such lines to stations using outlaw
equipment, tacit approval of the patent infringements
could be implied.  A resolution of the issue was thus
inexorably forced upon the worried telephone officials.[15]

Two decisions were reached at a Bell System conference in February 1923.  Local Bell companies were
told to refuse remote lines to infringing broadcasters,
and at the same time plans were set in motion for the
offering of a license to such violators.  The license
agreement eventually submitted to the nation's radio
stations provided for a scale of fees ranging from $1
for churches and colleges to $3,000 for non-educational
commercial operations employing transmitters of 500
watts or more.  A minimum fee of $500 for smaller sta-
tions was set.  Criticism of the plan was met head on
by a vigorous defense of patent theory and principles.
H.B. Thayer, AT&T President, in a March 1924 statement,
argued:  "The laws of the United States provide for a
reward to those who make meritorious inventions in the
shape of control over the right to make, use and sell
such inventions."  Thayer pointed out:  "When the public became interested in entertainment by wireless
telephonic broadcasting, the Telephone Company arranged
so that these inventions could become available to the
public by purchase of apparatus at reasonable prices,"
and added that "the Courts have held that unless the
owners of patents protect them and prosecute infringements, the patents lapse."  The thesis was clear.

Unless AT&T moved to protect its valuable patents, they would be lost. It had no alternative. Yet at the same time, it would be magnanimous and forgiving. It would offer to license the violators at a reasonable cost so that the public would not be deprived of radio entertainment. Consoling statements were offered the public: "There is no need of any broadcasting station closing down. The freedom of the air is not in question."[16]

Radio Broadcast greeted the solution with some sympathy, commenting that "the fee is certainly no more than adequate to cover the various costly developments which the Telephone Company puts at the disposal of the licensee when he is operating one of their equipments." Others exhibited less understanding of the AT&T situation, and termed the fee excessive. For small stations without visible incomes, the license payment could be an insurmountable hurdle. Indeed, some New Orleans stations found it exactly so, the culminating financial burden that brought their own broadcasting activities to a halt.[17]

* * * * * * * * * *

Only one new New Orleans station actually emerged in 1923--WTAF, operated by Louis J. Gallo, a partner in a firm billing itself as "designers and builders of high-grade transmitting and receiving apparatus."[18] The following year, 1924, saw a good deal more action. The Coliseum Place Baptist Church became the first such institution in the city to acquire a broadcasting permit. Using the call letters WABZ, "The Station With a Message" was the product of the efforts of its minister, Reverend L. T. Hastings, a radio enthusiast who supposedly understood "the importance of radio in connection with a livewire church."[19] Following closely behind was the First Baptist Church, the city's second church to own a transmitter. Designated WBBS, it was destined to have a much shorter life span than the Baptist station which preceeded it.[20]

Two more stations joined the enlarging group in 1924. The first, WCBE, marked the official advent of a family name that would play a major role in New Orleans radio. A license, issued on February 15, 1924, was granted to the Uhalt Radio Company, a partnership of two brothers, William J. and Joseph H. Uhalt. In later years, the Uhalts would cite July 1923 as the actual starting date for their enterprise, but Commerce Department records indicate no earlier broadcasting class license than 1924. Natives of New Orleans,

they had both served as wireless operators aboard ship,
held amateur licenses, and opened a radio shop on Baronne
Street in the early 1920's  The younger man, Joe, was
born in 1899, attended school only to the third grade,
but was self-educated, becoming an avid reader and an
articulate speaker on a variety of subjects.  His career
in New Orleans broadcasting would span two decades.[21]

     The second station, WEBP, was a joint venture of
New Orleans Public Service Inc., the city's multi-
function private utility company and Crescent Amusement Company of Spanish Fort Park.  The Park, a popular
amusement area in the 1920's was also the location of
the station in May 1924.  President H. B. Flowers of
the utility company noted a connection between the name
of his own organization and the new venture:  "We
would be remiss in this ideal of public service had we
neglected to keep pace with some 15,000 radio owners
in New Orleans."[22]

     On a typical Sunday in April 1924, the stations in
operation in the city divided the time thus:[23]

11:00 A.M.-12:30 P.M. WBBS "Morning Service and Sermon"
 1:00 P.M.- 2:00 P.M. WCBE "Dinner Concert by Strecklin's
                           Melody Boys"
 8:00 P.M.- 9:00 P.M. WABZ "Evening Service and Sermon"
10:00 P.M.-12:00 P.M. WTAF Various musical performances

     On Mondays Clyde Randall's WCAG could be heard, and
on Fridays Tulane's WAAC did occasional broadcasting.
When WEBP was added, the schedule was rearranged again,
giving the new station four evenings with Saturday
becoming a "silent night."  Even with the stations now
operating on different frequencies, early broadcasters
were still loath to program against each other, preferring instead to rotate their on-the-air hours, thus
requiring the listener to shift the dial as one station
signed off and another signed on.[24]

     Each owner attempted to meet the financial strain
of broadcasting in his own way.  Clyde Randall labelled
his station "the invisible theatre" and began selling
"tickets" to his listening audience.  "Pit" seats were
offered for fifty cents each, while "box" seats were
priced at five dollars.  Randall promised the revenue
so raised would be used to secure "the highest class
professional talent."  WCBE, WTAF, and WEBP, owned by
business firms, received their support directly from
company treasuries.  Nevertheless, the announcement of

the special AT&T license fees posed even those stations serious problems.[25]

Quickly denouncing the imposition as excessive and worse, some non-institutional stations found themselves required to ask for public aid. Only WEBP, relying on the resources of New Orleans Public Service, forwarded to AT&T the necessary $500 and applied for a license. The States rallied to the support of the remaining broadcasters, noting that since they gave "their time, money and equipment to entertain us night after night," it would be "a calamity sure enough for them to be forced to close down." It asked readers to contribute one dollar each to a fund for meeting the necessary cost.[26]

By late July, despite the States' efforts, only WCAG had successfully raised sufficient funds and had joined WEBP as AT&T licensees. The Uhalts at WCBE and Gallo at WTAF had fallen short and, rather than risk a confrontation with the Bell System, temporarily took themselves off the air. The three institutional stations, WWL and the two Baptist churches, faced with only a token one dollar fee, experienced no interruption in their programs. The States, the only newspaper publishing significant information on radio developments in New Orleans in 1924, chided a public which it felt had been too slow to respond to the plight of the stations. It warned "those who listen to radio shouldn't hesitate to feed the kitty."[27]

Ironically, WCBE and WTAF were soon joined off the air by the station that had been the first to secure an AT&T license, WEBP. In mid-September New Orleans Public Service announced its intention to suspend operations of WEBP because of "apparent lack of interest on the part of the public." Like other broadcasters before it, the utility company had found no tangible returns in broadcasting and the cash box value of good will questionable indeed.[28]

But if New Orleans lost stations in the fall of 1924, their absence was more than balanced by the buoyant news that the Crescent City might soon have its first Class B 500 watt, "high power" station. In early October the States had commented "there is a lot of talk about it, but nothing is being done." The difficulty, according to the newspaper, lay not in the $25,000 plus required for initial installation, but the more than $20,000 per year necessary "to maintain it properly." Only an operation backed by major business

organizations ready to accept substantial outlays without the prospect of any corresponding income could
make the enterprise a reality.[29]

The wish was granted later in the fall. On
November 9, the States was able to proclaim:

> A great, big 500-watt radio station for
> New Orleans! A real, honest-to-goodness
> Western Electric broadcasting station, with
> all the trimmings of the big stations that
> local listeners tune in on every night in
> other cities--and then some! Remote
> control! Big studios! Day time programs--
> and everything![30]

Two major New Orleans corporations were combining
in a joint venture to bring the city's first Class B
station into being. The original idea may well have
stemmed from the aggressive and controversial General
Manager of the Saenger Amusement Company, E.V. Richards.
A rough-hewn, self-made man who many regarded as
ruthless, Richards had become associated with Julian
Henri Saenger in the operation of motion picture houses
in eleven Southern cities and in Central America. From
a vaudeville-nickelodeon begun in Shreveport in 1911,
the Saenger Amusement Company had snowballed into an
organization owning more than 150 theatres. In 1917,
it opened the Strand Theatre in New Orleans, the "first
deluxe motion picture theatre in the South." It was
from the Strand that musicians were rushed to WGV to begin that station's programming in 1922.[31]

Joining Richards and Saenger in the venture was the
Maison Blanche Company, Louisiana's largest department
store. Representing the store were S.J. Schwartz, Jr.,
its Vice President, and Treasurer Edgar Newman. Both
were quick to disavow any intention of commercializing
the project. Schwartz claimed, perhaps a bit too
hastily to be believed: "We are not putting it in for
the purpose of boosting our radio department, but
rather with the idea of Maison Blanche service to the
community." The division of responsibility between the
two corporate parties to the undertaking quickly became
clear. The department store would furnish the studio
space, on the thirteenth floor of the Maison Blanche
building, while Saenger would supply the talent, provided largely by the artists regularly or occasionally
playing on and for the theatre company's vaudeville
stages. Lastly, to manage the entire affair, the
hiring of Clyde Randall was announced in early February

1925. The veteran radio man was induced to give up his own station, WCAG, and to join the new enterprise. By mid-summer, WCAG, one of New Orleans' earliest assigned call letter sets, was deleted from the Commerce Department's list of active stations.[32]

The project was federally licensed on April 16 with the call letters WSMB (the last three letters representing Saenger-Maison Blanche) assigned. The frequency of 940 kc. was designated as its dial location, and authorized power was stipulated at 500 watts, making it by far the city's strongest station. Broadcasting did not actually begin until April 21 and then only after considerable fanfare. The Item-Tribune, the Sunday version of the New Orleans Item which in 1924 had begun publishing a Morning Tribune to compete directly with the Times-Picayune, distributed a "special souvenir edition" dedicated to WSMB. It featured a sprawling picture lay-out of the facilities and lengthy and breathless descriptions of plans and personnel. The publicity noted, for example, that in the main studio: "Restful lounges, wrought iron chairs, Castillian settees, and a deep webbed carpet, concentrate the voice waves into the microphone and insure perfect modulation. A concert grand piano, and soft-tinted candelabras add a cozy and colorful touch." Not surprisingly, the whole was termed the "South's finest radio station" by the States, while its afternoon competition promised, somewhat vaguely, that WSMB meant "prosperity for the people of New Orleans."[33]

The Item had a rather special stake in the proceedings. After two years of relative coolness towards radio, a distinct contrast to the exuberance it manifested in the spring 1922, the journalistic pendulum had swung back to enthusiasm again. In early 1925 the Sunday Item-Tribune suddenly blossomed forth with a full page and sometimes more of "Radio News," and a neglected subject was once again being covered. The Item's fresh interest was understandable. It had negotiated a working agreement with WSMB whereby the station broadcast Item news bulletins at various times daily. They originated from a remote studio set up on the third floor of the newspaper's own building, a ten foot square cubicle in which a young Item reporter, Ted R. Liuzza, read the available copy. It was to be a second radio honeymoon for the newspaper, and like the first, it too would not last.[34]

Remote lines were also maintained to the Saenger Amusement Company theatres in the city, the Strand and

the Liberty (and later the Saenger when it was constructed in 1927), from whose stages live performances
were transmitted. There was, of course, a certain
business risk for Saenger and Richards in their association with WSMB. In the first years of the twentieth
century, some two thousand theatres featured vaudeville
acts. With the advent of silent movies, an accommodation
of sorts had been arrived at since those motion pictures
could still be combined with vaudeville performances,
as the Saenger houses were successfully doing in 1925.
But radio posed a potentially more dangerous threat.
It had the effect of sapping vaudeville acts of their
novelty as songs and stories which had previously taken
a year or more to cross the country could now do so in
a matter of weeks only. The popularity of radio thus
might translate into declining theatre admissions, and
for Saenger Amusement to voluntarily embrace the in-
truder represented an act of faith of sorts. Saenger
executives were gambling that the exposure vaudeville
artists received on WSMB would encourage theatre
attendance to see the same performers in person rather
than the reverse. It was a gamble destined to be ultimately lost as a combination of network broadcasting,
the advent of talking pictures, and the hard times of
the depression doomed vaudeville to a virtually complete extinction by 1933.[35]

During its first year WSMB quickly took the lead
among New Orleans stations. Broadcasting six days a
week with Sundays silent, its programs fell into three
distinct blocks. From 12:30-1:30 P.M. it transmitted
a "Noonday Hour Musical Program" complete with Item
news bulletins. This block represented a breakthrough,
the first systematic effort at daytime operation of any
of the city's stations. A second block of time was
utilized from 6:30-7:30 P.M. for "dinner concerts,"
followed later in the evening by the principal segment,
usually 8:30-10:30 P.M. It was altogether the most
extensive programming per week ever taken on to that
time by a local radio organization, and it established
standards that competitors were required to emulate.
No commercial announcements were carried other than
the publicizing of Maison Blanche merchandise and the
current play bills of Saenger theatres. Within six
weeks of its inauguration, the station had already
received 40,000 letters, postcards, and telegrams from
listeners in every state in the nation as well as Canada,
Mexico, and Cuba. A newspaper exclamation that "New
Orleans is at last on the air!" seemed to be well borne
out by the developing facts.[36]

* * * * * * * * * *

The Department of Commerce's Radio Service Bulletin listed nine New Orleans stations with licenses in force as of May 31, 1925:[37]

| Call Letters | Licensee |
| --- | --- |
| WAAB | Valdemar Jensen |
| WAAC | Tulane University |
| WABZ | Coliseum Place Baptist Church |
| WBBS | First Baptist Church |
| WCAG | Clyde R. Randall |
| WCBE | Uhalt Brothers Radio Company |
| WOWL | Owl Battery Company |
| WSMB | Saenger-Maison Blanche |
| WWL | Loyola University |

Of the nine, two, WAAC and WCAG, would surrender their licenses before the end of the year. WAAB, inactive at the end of May when the list was drawn, would return to the air in January 1926 under a new designation--WJBO (Jensen Broadcasting Organization)-- but with the license still held by Val Jensen. WOWL were the new call letters of Louis Gallo's former WTAF, now operated by the Owl Battery Company, local manufacturers of storage batteries. The station under its new owners would have a short life span, however, suspending operations by the summer of 1926. As for the Uhalts' WCBE, which had temporarily left the air when AT&T had imposed its fee schedule in the spring of 1924, the necessary financial arrangements had finally been concluded, allowing the station to resume broadcasting some six months later.[38]

Overall, Louisiana boasted fourteen licensed stations by mid-1925. Besides the nine in New Orleans, Shreveport claimed two, and Alexandria, Baton Rouge, and Jennings one each. The state's figures compared most favorably with the remainder of the South, as did the city's as well. Elsewhere in the region, Tennessee showed ten active stations, Florida seven, and Georgia and Arkansas but six each. Only Texas' twenty-five surpassed Louisiana in the Old Confederacy. Further, New Orleans' nine broadcasters placed it well ahead of all other urban areas of the South, as befitting the region's largest city. Yet the active stations in New Orleans in 1925 were, with the exception of WSMB, small-scale operations with uncertain futures. Thus despite three years of eager effort and considerable ambition,

49

broadcasting's foothold in the Mississippi Delta remained tenuous indeed.[39]

# 5

## NEW LAW, NEW POWER, NEW QUARTERS

For the young radio industry, 1926 was a year of turmoil. The jerry-built regulatory system erected by Secretary of Commerce Herbert Hoover collapsed under the shock of twin legal blows, one delivered by a federal district court, the second by the Department of Justice. Both stemmed from the same case, the United States vs. Zenith Radio Corporation. Eugene L. McDonald, Zenith president, challenged Hoover's authority to assign a station to a specific frequency or to restrict its broadcasting hours. Usurping a frequency supposedly allocated only to Canadian broadcasters, Zenith's Chicago station, WJAZ, forced a federal prosecution.[1]

To the dismay of the Washington officials the decision of the United States Court for the Northern District of Illinois, rendered on April 16, 1926, upheld the Zenith contention. It found that there was indeed "no express grant of power in the act (Radio Act of 1912) to the Secretary of Commerce to establish regulations." Before appealing the decision to higher court, Hoover referred the matter to the Attorney General for an opinion, and thereby received yet another rebuff. On July 8 that office announced itself in agreement with the Zenith findings. The Secretary of Commerce, it informed Hoover, was required to issue broadcasting licenses when requested, and could not specify wave lengths or frequencies, assign hours of operation, or limit power to be used. The opinion effectively removed whatever authority was heretofore exercised by the Commerce Department, and made the issuance of licenses purely a perfunctory matter.[2]

Following upon the Justice Department opinion, Commerce found itself admitting to inquiring licensees that "each station is at liberty to use any wave lengths they may desire." The result was a stupefying confusion.

51

Hoover himself pronounced broadcasting in "imminent danger of chaos," and the events that followed seemed to bear out his prediction. Despite a plea from him for broadcasters to impose a voluntary self-regulation on themselves and to avoid interfering with each other as well as those channels reserved for Canadian use only, wholesale disruptions followed.[3]

With no supervisory authority controlling their actions, stations "pirated" frequencies in use by other operators and "jumped" their power to whatever level they desired. Proper separation between stations in the same community was often ignored. Instead of the normal fifty kilocycles, separations were reduced to less than ten at times, with the result that stations began "blanketing" each other, and providing listeners with gibberish instead of intelligible programs. In self-defense stations resorted to legal action, requesting injunctions and similar court orders against interfering pirates. Further, some 220 new broadcasting applicants, who had previously been denied licenses by Hoover on the grounds that the existing channels were too crowded, now demanded and received permissions to go on the air, further complicating the deteriorating situation. The chaos did serve to convince most broadcasters as well as governmental officials of the imperative need for new regulatory legislation. Congress was not long in responding.[4]

Pressure upon that body had been intensifying as the crisis deepened. In December 1926 Calvin Coolidge added his voice to the clamor, calling for action in his Annual Message to the Congress. He warned that "the whole service of this most important public function has drifted into such chaos as seems likely, if not remedied, to destroy its great value." The basis for the congressional action which followed was a Senate bill drafted by Clarence C. Dill, a Democrat from the state of Washington. Dill had been drawn into the radio issue almost by accident, having earlier proposed as a favor to friends, an amendment dealing with the broadcasting-ASCAP controversy. Suddenly finding himself regarded as the Senate's only radio "expert," he later described his role as that of a "one-eyed man among the blind." After some modification by a joint Senate-House conference committee, Dill's handiwork passed the House on January 29, the Senate on February 13, and received the presidential signature on February 23, 1927.[5]

The Radio Act of 1927 created a bipartisan Federal
Radio Commission consisting of five members, appointed
by the President with the advice and consent of the
Senate.  Each member was to be selected from one of
five zones into which the law divided the country.
The third zone contained most of the South including
Louisiana.  Power was vested in the Commission to
classify radio stations, assign frequencies, decide
upon power and hours of operation for any station,
regulate the equipment used, and make rules with respect to chain or network broadcasting.  The Act also
stipulated that the Commission should move toward equal
service for all parts of the country.  It required "such
a distribution of licenses, bands of frequency of wave
lengths, periods of time for operation, and of power
among the different states and communities as to give
fair, efficient, and equitable radio service to each of
the same."  The last requirement would prove the focus
for considerable debate during the Commission's first
year in existence.  The Commerce Department retained
some responsibility under the Act.  The Secretary was
to receive all applications for station licenses, pre-
scribe the qualifications for and issue licenses to
individual radio operators, inspect transmitters, and
report violations to the Commission.  The Radio Service
of the Department was now separated from the Bureau of
Navigation and reorganized as the Radio Division, headed
by a Chief under the direct supervision of the Secretary
of Commerce.  As the FRC had no field service of its
own, it depended upon the Radio Division for its investigations.  Not until 1932 were the personnel of the
Division transferred to the FRC itself, becoming the
Commission's Division of Field Operations.[6]

Admiral William H.G. Bullard was selected as the
first FRC Chairman.  Born in Pennsylvania in 1866, a
graduate of the Naval Academy, and the Director of
Naval Communications before his retirement from active
duty in 1922, Bullard was to serve only a few months as
Chairman before his death in late November 1927.  He
would be succeeded by Judge Ira E. Robinson, a West
Virginia jurist.  More significantly for Southern
stations, the Commissioner representing zone three was
Judge Eugene O. Sykes of Mississippi.  Sykes, a
Democrat, had been a Justice of the Mississippi State
Supreme Court before his appointment by Coolidge to
the FRC.  In 1932 he would assume the Chairmanship of
the Commission, and when that body was superseded by
the Federal Communications Commission in 1934, he would
become one of the original members of the new regulatory agency.  It was Bullard, Robinson, and Sykes

whose actions would touch the fortunes of WWL and other
Louisiana stations most directly.[7]

The immediate problem facing the FRC at its first
meeting on March 15, 1927, was the turmoil created by
the aftermath of the Zenith decision, a condition in
which, according to one Commissioner, "anarchy reigned
in the ether." On April 17 the FRC took its first step
to clear up the accumulated confusion, ordering a change
in the frequencies of 129 stations that had been operating at dial locations other than those originally
authorized by the Department of Commerce. General
reallocations that altered the frequencies used by
virtually every station on the air soon followed. WWL
thus found itself in changed circumstances as a result
of the FRC action in 1927.[8]

* * * * * * * * * *

WWL had not taken advantage of the 1926 disarray
to seize a new frequency or inflate station power. As
Abell later proudly stated: "WWL bided its time and
observed the spirit of the Radio Law of 1912, refusing
to profit at somebody else's expense." There had, in
fact, been no great incentive to do so as Abell admitted
the station broadcast a total of only 75 hours during
the whole of that year. With the formation of the FRC,
however, Abell no longer held back. In July 1927, he
wrote Theodore Deiler, still the local Radio Supervisor,
requesting an increase in WWL power to 5,000 watts (5
kilowatts) and a more favorable frequency than the
1090 kc. presently being occupied. Copies of the letter
were sent to Commissioner Sykes and to the two United
States Senators from Louisiana as well as the state's
Governor in hope of winning their endorsement of the
project.[9]

The scheme was nothing if not audacious. A 100
watt station broadcasting little more than one hour per
week was requesting an enormous increase in its power
to a level that would place it among the nation's most
important radio operations. Moreover, the increase was
being requested despite the fact that the financial support offered WWL by the University had been scanty indeed
in the past, and a five kilowatt installation would
require a probable expenditure of $10,000. In the last
respect Abell now found himself in a somewhat better bargaining position than earlier. The death of an incumbent University President in early 1925 brought the
Reverend Florence D. Sullivan, S.J., to the post.
Sullivan, who had participated in many of the early

54

WWL broadcasts in 1922, was distinctly more sympathetic
to the enterprise of radio than earlier Jesuit Presidents,
and more willing to give Abell's visions freer rein.
Yet it was undoubtedly too much to expect that the FRC
would approve, at least in one step, such a stride upward in radiated power. On November 16, the Commission
replied to the Abell application with a partial grant.
WWL power was boosted but only to 500 watts, a sizeable
increase in itself. Meanwhile, as a part of a general
reallocation of the broadcast band, the station's
assigned frequency was shifted to 1220 kc., a higher
and somewhat less desirable position on the dial. The
Commission, in its order to WWL, seemed to have delicately
balanced advantage and disadvantage in its blending of
power and frequency. In any event the FRC decision
transformed WWL into the second most powerful New Orleans
station in terms of wattage, trailing only WSMB whose
output the Commissioners swelled to 750 watts.[10]

Abell filed a "vigorous protest" with the FRC,
claiming its reduction of the WWL power increase application was unfair both to Loyola and to Louisiana.
Nevertheless, since the 500 watt transmitter would, in
Abell's words, "form the driver for the 5,000 watt
amplifier," construction went forward. At the same time
he continued to press the WWL case for five kilowatts.
Preparatory to the design and assembly of the 500 watt
transmitter, Abell and the ever-present du Treil
traveled to Texas, visiting stations in Galveston,
Houston, Dallas, and Fort Worth and inspecting the equipment employed by each. Particularly helpful was W. E.
Branch, Chief Engineer of Fort Worth's WBAP. Branch
had done a good deal of radio research and experimentation, especially in adapting a mercury arc rectifier to
transmitters. He placed his findings at the disposal of
the WWL representatives. Upon returning to New Orleans,
du Treil undertook the task of designing both the 500
and the hoped-for 5,000 watt transmitter, while Abell
with the assistance of two Jesuit brothers, handled the
assembling and installation. The entire apparatus was
completed in the workshop of the University, often
using already available materials.[11]

Meanwhile, steps were being taken to raise the funds
which would eventually be needed for the construction of
the five kilowatt transmitter. Abell was forecasting
a favorable FRC decision in the not-too-distant future
and preparing accordingly. He and Sullivan called upon
the assistance of a University affiliated social-
religious organization, the Catholic Alumni Sodality of
Loyola. Under the scheme finally agreed upon, the

Sodality would guarantee a $10,000 bank loan secured
from Canal Bank & Trust. Abell estimated that amount
would be necessary for equipment and for new studios
suitable to a 5 kilowatt station. Simultaneously, a
public funds drive was launched, seeking donations from
the community at large which would, hopefully, make
the guarantee signed by Sodality members superfluous.
Beginning in March 1928 and continuing for the remainder of the year the campaign brought in contributions
ranging from one dollar to the $1,000 provided by the
Fourth Degree Knights of Columbus and the $500 tendered
by Archbishop John W. Shaw. A different form of contribution was received from the city administration.
Abell and Sullivan negotiated a contract with municipal
officials whereby the New Orleans Police Department was
allowed "the privilege of making use of the station
any hour of the day or night in connection with its
police work." In addition, WWL agreed to broadcast
descriptions of stolen automobiles. In return for this
access, the city was obligated to pay the station
$2,500 yearly. It might thus be argued that the very
first WWL sponsor was the Police Department.[12]

On March 7 the initial $2,500 payment from the city
was received, and on April 19 the second--to cover the
calendar year 1929--was accepted. Thus $5,000 of the
necessary $10,000 had that quickly been raised. By
April 1929 the total of all contributions reached
$9,101, short of the original goal but sufficient for
the purpose. Testing of the transmitter began in May
with the formal inauguration date set for July 3, 1928.[13]

Not only a new transmitter but new studio facilities
as well were readied for the July inaugural. Space on
the ground floor of the recently constructed Bobet Hall
was made available as a permanent home for the station.
Included was a 20 x 25 foot studio "well draped and
apparently well appointed" containing a Baldwin Piano,
a turntable, and thick sound-proof padding on the walls.
Also completed was an adjacent 20 x 20 foot waiting
room separated from the studio itself by a glass par-
tition. Later this would serve as an auxiliary studio
and a Western Union teletype machine would be installed.
The transmitter was housed in the "power room," a
smaller cubicle located closest to the main entrance
to the building. It featured a bank of 2 1/2 feet tall
mercury arc rectifier tubes immersed in oil for cooling.
Abell was to find that the "arc" would prove most tem-
peramental. The tubes would have to be physically
rocked back and forth in order to be "fired" when the
power was turned on. Further, they had the annoying

habit of quitting entirely during broadcasts, until
they were rocked once again. After considerable
exasperation and experimentation, Abell devised an
"automatic shaker" consisting of a solenoid actuated
by the direct high voltage current of the mercury arc
itself. Not until a Corpus Christi, Texas, station
engineer suggested a modification in the apparatus
was the problem fully corrected. Atop the building
two fifty foot steel towers were implanted with an
antenna consisting of a half dozen wires strung between
them. In this fashion WWL entered its adolescent years
in 1928.[14]

The formal initiation of the new facilities on
July 3 was carried out with the by-now customary
ceremonies. Present were the usual dignitaries
including the Mayor and Theodore Deiler representing
the Radio Division and the FRC. The inaugural program's announcer was Jean Pasquet, a local pianist
employed by D. H. Holmes Department Store, who had
volunteered his services. The musicians and singers
who performed were likewise volunteers. Broadcasting
plans promising "a better music period each Tuesday
and Saturday evenings at 8 P.M." were publicized, but
within weeks that schedule had been increased. By
December the station had operated a total of 300 hours
during 1928, a 400% increase over its 1926 figure. The
schedule consisted of programming on Monday, Wednesday,
Friday, and Saturday evenings along with Sunday mornings
and afternoons. Tuesdays and Thursdays were silent.
Programming fell into two basic categories--classical or
semi-classical music and lectures, usually by Loyola
faculty members. Its decorum was obvious, its popular
appeal was not.[15]

Abell's plans called for even more increases in
broadcasting time. He predicted that during the first
quarter of 1929 alone, WWL would be on the air for a
minimum of 150 hours. He envisioned five nights per
week and daytime programs on Saturdays and Sundays. To
handle the load, the only available announcers were
Pasquet and a Loyola senior, Jefferson Davis Bloom,
who also assisted Abell with the engineering duties.
Pasquet and Bloom, as well as the artists who appeared
on the station at this time, were unpaid volunteers.
Bloom occasionally even tripled as talent himself,
entertaining on a guitar and the musical saw. Abell
too faced multiple duties, serving as WWL manager,
chief engineer and designer of the five kilowatt transmitter, while maintaining his teaching responsibilities

as Chairman of the University's Physics Department. But as the extent of WWL activity continued to grow, it became clear that the stage of voluntarism was passing and that of professionalism was about to begin.[16]

The operation of a 500 watt transmitter in the up-town residential area of New Orleans was not greeted with universal approval. Complaints quickly began to arise from University neighbors, one even referring to the station as "a public nuisance." Deiler, heading the Radio Division's New Orleans office, found himself the repository for the unhappiness expressed. Deiler was not unsympathetic to the complainants. In September he informed Washington that while WWL's equipment was "very neatly installed," the station was located "in the heart of a very fine residential section and their operation severely interferes with other transmissions." He also warned that the granting of the application for 5,000 watts would result "in the station blanketing over three quarters of the listening population of New Orleans." He argued that the FRC should require the location of any future five kilowatt transmitter "at least five miles from the city limits." Loyola had declined to do so voluntarily.[17]

Deiler found on his desk criticism of another sort-- criticism that involved the conduct of his own staff in relation to WWL. Unnamed "radio interests" in the city had leveled the charge of conflict of interest against du Treil and his close association with the University station. Deiler reported fully on the situation to Washington. He explained that du Treil had indeed designed the current transmitter at WWL and was "planning the engineering details" for the next. But Deiler pointedly noted that the work had been done in the Radio Inspector's spare time with no neglect of his regular duties, and that du Treil was receiving no compensation for his efforts. Nevertheless, Deiler asked for guidance from Washington on how to handle the matter. An answer was quickly forthcoming. The Radio Division's Solicitor ruled that employees "should have no connection with the construction or operation of any station which they, undoubtedly, will be later called upon to inspect." Plainly, du Treil must sever his WWL connection.[18]

When the ruling was communicated to du Treil and Abell, the latter characteristically refused to accept it as final. Blaming the jealousy of WWL competitors for its arising at all, Abell countered by writing directly to W. D. Terrell, Radio Division Chief. Using

reasoning at times difficult to follow, Abell maintained
du Treil was "absolutely freer and less hampered in
fulfilling the duties of his office than he would be
otherwise, for the very reason that Loyola is deeply
obligated to him." Then the Jesuit suggested a simple
solution; someone else should make the inspections of
WWL in the future. He added that depriving the station
of du Treil's services would "work a great hardship
upon us." Terrell was prepared to compromise. He informed Abell that du Treil could continue but "in an
advisory capacity only." The actual work of design and
construction must be carried on by WWL's own staff.
Deiler, on the other hand, remained unsatisfied. Opposed
to the operation of a high power transmitter in the
residential section of the city, he regarded du Treil's
participation in it in any way as a contradiction of his
own policies and "a situation that will be very much
against the interests of the general listening public."
Nevertheless, the matter seemed settled. None of the
parties could perceive at this point that the issue
would be raised again in less than two years, and that
the question would be the focus for an acrimonious
legal debate.[19]

* * * * * * * * * *

While Abell was successfully heightening the impact
of WWL, two more stations entered the New Orleans scene.
WJBW, "The Friendly Broadcasting Station," had been
licensed in 1926 to Charles C. Carlson, a self-employed
electrician, who utilized his home for a studio. Carlson
introduced the city's first female announcer, his wife,
Louise Elsie Carlson, who also served as program
director. The station remained a small, independent
operation as it tenaciously continued broadcasting
activities until its eventual demise in 1949.[20]

More directly a problem for WWL in the years ahead
was the transformation of the Uhalts' WCBE. By 1927
the eldest Uhalt brother, William, had dropped out of
the partnership, relocated to Houston, and established
a station there. The younger of the brothers, Joseph,
carried on the operation in New Orleans with significant
changes. In June 1927 the studio was moved to the top
floor of the De Soto Hotel in the central business district. At the same time a working relationship, akin
to WSMB's with the Item, was established with the New
Orleans States. A remote studio was similarly established at the States for the broadcasting of news and
sports items. Then on May 10, 1928, the station's
call letters were officially changed to WDSU. In

soliciting the change, Uhalt explained to Deiler: "The requested call letters stand for W being the government letter, D for De Soto Hotel, S for New Orleans States, and U for Uhalt Radio Broadcasting Company."[21]

The States began its second honeymoon with radio with the customary self-inspired excitement. With a grand opening of WDSU scheduled for the summer of 1928, the newspaper headlined: "Greatest Radio Station in New Orleans" and "De Soto Hotel, States, and Uhalt in Combine." An investment of $35,000 was claimed, and, significantly, network broadcasts were promised: "According to present plans, (WDSU) will be linked in on the New York 'chain' seven days a week, thus bringing New York's famed Broadway to Canal Street." Six weeks later, with opening night slated for July 6, the States was deploring the fact that no previous New Orleans station had been carrying chain programs, for which it claimed the city's radio listeners had been clamoring. It again promised "WDSU is going to do its utmost to provide them."[22]

There seems little doubt that interest in receiving programs of the recently established chains or networks on a local rather than a distant station was building in Louisiana. Deiler explained in his correspondence with Washington that atmospheric conditions in the summer months made it virtually impossible to receive out-of-town network stations, and that programs produced by local broadcasters were "very ordinary." The attraction of top-name New York talent being featured on network radio shows was, therefore, great indeed.[23]

In 1941 the Federal Communications Commission defined a network as "the simultaneous broadcasting of an identical program by two or more connected stations." Using that definition, the first network broadcast could be said to have taken place on January 4, 1923, when a program on WEAF, AT&T's New York station, was also aired on WNAC in Boston. More commonly, networking is dated from 1924 when stations connected to WEAF began broadcasts of the Eveready Hour, sponsored by the National Carbon Company. By the end of 1925, AT&T had a network or chain of twenty-six stations extending as far west as Kansas City. But the most decisive step toward the creation of chain broadcasting on a fully national scale took place in 1926 when the Radio Corporation of America purchased WEAF from AT&T, and utilized a subsidiary of its own, the National Broadcasting Company, to assume the network operations it had acquired. By the summer of 1927, just six months after its establishment, NBC had two different chains carrying programs: a "Red" network of fifteen stations including WEAF, and a "Blue" network of ten stations. There was an additional group of eight stations affiliated with both chains. Then in September 1927, NBC found itself with competition when the Columbia Broadcasting System was launched with an initial sixteen affiliates. Network broadcasting had come to stay.[24]

Networks made possible the distribution of higher quality programming to all parts of the nation, but from an economic standpoint their primary effect was to open the door to the enormous profit potential of the industry. For the first time sponsors had a means of conducting efficient and effective nationwide advertising campaigns through radio. Attractive programs could be created as vehicles for commercials that would be broadcast at specified times in virtually all the key cities of the nation.

From the standpoint of a local station, a number of economic advantages existed in network affiliation. An affiliate would have access to the larger listening audience attracted by chain programs, thus allowing the station's own rates for local and national "spot" advertising to be set at a higher and more lucrative level. Equally significant for a struggling station, as an affiliate it would receive a revenue from the carrying of network commercial fare.

These arrangements for compensating affiliates differed between chains. From 1927 to 1930, NBC paid most of its stations $50 per evening hour and $30 per daytime hour for commercial programs carried, while charging them $45 per evening hour and $25 for an equivalent daytime hour for the sustaining programs it provided. The only exceptions were a few affiliates located in major markets so necessary to NBC that the local outlets could insist upon both increased rates for commercial and decreased rates for sustaining programming. In 1930 regular sustaining charges were reduced, and in 1932 they were to be replaced entirely by a flat $1,500 monthly fee.

The CBS arrangement for station compensation took a somewhat different form. Beginning in 1929 the network agreed to pay each station a specified hourly rate. This rate varied with such factors as the size and importance of the market served and the demand for coverage of that area by national sponsors. A distinction was made between an evening and a daytime hour with compensation for the latter one-half the former. Then in return for the stations waiving payment for five hours of evening commercial time per week, CBS agreed to supply all sustaining programming free. This last feature of a CBS contract held a considerable attraction for smaller affiliates struggling to find and support quality local shows of their own. It was much simpler to just relinquish that time to the network and rely on the CBS creative resources and talent budget, at least until the home community could be more effectively scoured for willing sponsors.

While the majority of both NBC and CBS stations were compensated at a rate in the neighborhood of $50 per evening hour of chain commercial programming, the charges to advertisers by the networks were of a quite different magnitude. These charges were indicated on a network rate card. The CBS card, for instance, listed the stations available, the groupings in which they must be purchased, and the individual station rates, which ranged from $125 to $1,250 per "converted" hour during the 1930's. The rate applicable to each affiliate was determined by the network after a consideration of the outlet's market, relative popularity, power, physical coverage, and the price at which time was sold to national advertisers for spot business. A formula was used to translate the less valuable daytime and after midnight periods into the equivalent of evening prime time units, hence the term "converted" hours. NBC employed much the same system for billing its advertisers.

Also a feature of the standard affiliation contract by the 1930's was a network option time clause. A CBS contract, beginning in 1929, gave the network an option on all the broadcasting time of the station for the chain's commercial programming. This arrangement was modified slightly in 1937 when CBS agreed an affiliate need not air network commercial programs for more than fifty converted hours per week. But since CBS had, in fact, never yet exercised its options for as many as fifty converted hours, the change was only theoretical. A similar system for network option time was not inaugurated at NBC until 1933.[25]

Not surprisingly, the multiple attractions of a chain contract became almost irresistible for broadcasters once networks established their permanence. Uhalt, therefore, was quick to act on his own promise

of chain programs for New Orleans.  Shortly after the
July opening of WDSU, he traveled to New York to meet
with officials of NBC.  While the conference resulted
in WDSU's carrying at least one NBC program, a speech
by the Democratic nominee for the Presidency, Al
Smith, on August 22, the network proved to be more
interested in Uhalt's rival, WSMB, which joined that
chain in March, 1929.  Faced with defeat in his attempt
to secure an NBC affiliation, Uhalt and P. K. Ewing,
the States' Radio Editor who had moved over to WDSU to
handle special events announcing, sales, and act as the
owner's principal lieutenant, turned to CBS.  There
they found a more receptive situation and by February
1929, WDSU was already carrying Columbia network programs.[26]

Uhalt did not credit the entire success of his
station to simply a network affiliation.  Rather, he
boasted of WDSU's sports activity as the decisive
factor.  In 1927 he noted that his station was the first
to broadcast "the play by play details of every baseball game played on the road by our home club in the
Southern League."  Indeed, the station was the first
not only to broadcast baseball but football and boxing
as well.  The events that took place away from New
Orleans were "recreated" from cryptic wire reports.
The announcers, P. K. Ewing or Uhalt himself or others,
added their own embellishments to the story--the noise
from a pencil being rapped on a table became a bat
meeting a ball, etc.  The technique was accepted by a
still unsophisticated listening public without noticeable objection.[27]

The broadcasting schedule of the new WDSU generally
matched that of WSMB, its principal competitor, with
one innovation, an early morning hour from 7:00-8:00
A.M. six days per week.  Power, however, remained at an
unsatisfactory 250 watts on a less than desirable frequency, 1320 kc., until another general FRC reallocation
in the fall of 1928.  The nationwide shuffle of stations,
made necessary by Congress' passage of the so-called
Davis Amendment (of which more later), worked dramatic
changes in the fortunes of New Orleans broadcasters.
The arrangement scheduled to take effect at 3:00 A.M.,
eastern standard time, on November 11, 1928, reflected
the following alterations in power and frequency for
New Orleans:[28]

| Station | Former Power | Former Frequency | New Power | New Frequency |
|---------|--------------|------------------|-----------|---------------|
| WABZ | 50 watts | 1260 kc. | 50 watts | 1200 kc. |
| WDSU | 250 watts | 1320 kc. | 1,000 watts | 1270 kc. |
| WJBO | 100 watts | 1140 kc. | 100 watts | 1370 kc. |
| WJBW | 30 watts | 1260 kc. | 30 watts | 1200 kc. |
| WKBT* | 50 watts | 1190 kc. | 50 watts | 1420 kc. |
| WSMB | 750 watts | 1010 kc. | 750 watts | 1320 kc. |
| WWL | 500 watts | 1220 kc. | 500 watts | 850 kc. |

*formerly WBBS

Clear gains and losses were apparent. WSMB had
not secured a power increase and had slipped to a
somewhat less desirable frequency. WDSU, on the other
hand, had taken a stride forward by moving to the one
kilowatt level. Its attractiveness as an affiliate to
CBS was plainly enhanced. As for Abell and WWL, the
FRC reallocation was an enormous triumph. Not only was
the station shifted to a highly desirable cleared
channel frequency, 850 kc., but a construction permit
at last authorizing the installation of the five kilowatt transmitter was issued by the FRC. For the time
being power remained at 500 watts, but only until the
new equipment was properly in place. With the new
power would come an altered program policy as well,
bringing major revisions in the nature of the WWL operation. Only one small cloud hovered over the good news;
WWL was not to occupy its channel alone. The FRC had
thrown the New Orleans Jesuits into a forced sharing of
the frequency with Shreveport's KWKH, a station owned
by one of the most notorious and controversial of the
nation's broadcasters, W. K. Henderson, "the Bolshevik
of radio." If Abell and his associates expected a
normal, professional relationship between the two
stations, they would be quickly disillusioned. The
Commission had handed them a five year war that would
finally end only when one of the belligerents was
forced out of the industry altogether.[29]

# 6

## THE CLEAR CHANNEL WAR--ROUND ONE

During radio's formative years the President of the
University of Wisconsin optimistically concluded that
the new medium was "the deadly enemy of the demagogue--a
ruthless revealer of 'hokum.'"  His judgment was not
borne out by events.  In the 1920's the infamous "goat-
gland surgeon," Doctor John R. Brinkley, used the vehicle
of his Milford, Kansas, station, KFKB, to bilk millions
from naive, trusting, and desperate patients.  And for
almost a decade in the 1920's and 1930's an unvarying
formula--"Hello, world, doggone ya! This is KWKH in
Shreveport, Lou-ee-zee-ana, and it's W.K. Henderson
talkin' to ya..."--introduced the South's most potent
pitch man and radio rabble rouser.[1]

Henderson's daily radio audience stretched across
the bulk of the United States.  In 1932 a congressional
ally boasted from the floor of the House of Representatives that Henderson's voice was heard not only in
every Southern state but in "every state in the
Mississippi Valley from Canada to the Gulf, and, in
short, every state with the possible exception of two
or three states on the Pacific and some of the Northeastern states."[2]

Henderson's controversial broadcasting style delighted the majority of his listeners while simultaneously offending and infuriating the others, including
a substantial number of public officials in Washington.
His influence, for good or harm, was felt in politics,
in economics, and in the shaping of governmental policy
towards the emerging broadcast industry.  In an era of
radio history that has been rightly termed "a sal-
magundi of blunders and power grabs," Henderson stands
out as one of the more flamboyant and important personalities.[3]

Henderson was a successful businessman in a wholly unrelated field when radio first burst upon the scene in the early 1920's. Born in Bastrop, Louisiana, in 1880, he moved to Texas while still a small boy. After completing his education at St. Edward's College in Austin, he found employment with his father and for a period operated a garage business of his own. In 1918 when his father died, Henderson inherited the family enterprise, assuming the presidency of Henderson Iron Works and Supply Company located in Shreveport. Manufacturers of machinery, mill, and oil field supplies, the firm was already one of the most successful businesses and largest employers in the city when the younger Henderson took control.[4]

Meanwhile, station WGAQ had been licensed to William G. Patterson in June 1922, but by 1923 had encountered financial difficulties and was seeking fresh capital. At that point Patterson first approached Henderson, by then not only a prominent businessman but also vice-president of the local Chamber of Commerce. In order to interest his unimpressed prospect, Patterson proposed reading one of Henderson's own letters over the air. As Henderson described the experience, Patterson "placed some kind of a little cabinet with dials on it on my desk and he intended to take a letter and go to some distant part of town and read this letter to me." A short time later, as Henderson recalled: "I was at work at my desk and the first thing I knew I heard a frying, whirring, buzzing noise and then a faint sound or two--a human voice." Altogether the experiment was hardly a success. Patterson persisted, however, and by 1924 finally prevailed.[5]

In 1924 Henderson was instrumental in the calling of a conference that temporarily established the station as a partnership of Patterson, the city's largest newspaper, its principal hotel, and himself. The partnership was shortlived. Before the end of the same year Henderson bought out all but Patterson and was the owner of a three-quarters interest in WGAQ. From that point on, he dominated the operation, a Class A station then broadcasting on a wave length of 252 meters (1190 kc.) with 150 watts of power. Patterson offered explicit testimony of the new Henderson role early in 1925 by requesting the Commerce Department change the call letters of the station to KWKH "in honor of W.K. Henderson who so unselfishly has given of his time and money to the development of his community."[6]

But within a year Henderson was to become a notorious name to public officials in Washington charged with regulating broadcasting. Henderson, like many individualistic and aggressive station licensees, was dissatisfied with both his dial location and his authorized power. He determined to take matters into his own hands. Though he increased power to one kilowatt despite a new Commerce Department grant of only 500 watts, Henderson denied committing any illegal act. Proudly he boasted to Theodore Deiler: "We have a Federal Court house here and, if I have violated any laws, the right officials to find me will not have any trouble."[7]

A few weeks later Henderson was again brought to the attention of Deiler's New Orleans office. The Shreveport businessman had arbitrarily moved his station's signal to 950 kc. rather than the authorized 1150 kilocycles. Louis L. McCabe, one of Deiler's radio inspectors, could only report: "Arguments with Mr. Henderson seemed to be of no avail, and he even told me to inform our office to save our postage as he did not care to correspond on the subject." Henderson insisted that he was violating no law by occupying whatever wave length he desired and by broadcasting with whatever power suited his fancy. By April 1926 his antics had begun to attract considerable attention with even the New York Herald-Tribune commenting upon the impasse.[8]

It was at that moment that Henderson's stand was indirectly upheld by the federal court decision in the Zenith case. He had won a victory, and it served only to enhance the substantial esteem in which he already held his own opinions in disputes with public officials.

Within the KWKH organization, William G. Patterson, Henderson's forgotten partner, was finding his position untenable. Not surprisingly, the two partners soon parted company with Patterson quickly starting up his own Shreveport station operation, utilizing the call letters KSBA. In addition to abandoning Patterson, Henderson also forsook the city of Shreveport itself. He moved the studios and transmitter to his own estate at Kennonwood, Louisiana, eighteen miles north of the city. There a single building adjacent to the main residence housed the transmitter, the record library, and the main studio. Supplementary studios were located in the residence including a small upstairs room adjoining Henderson's own bedroom from which Henderson

could broadcast at odd hours or whenever the whim
seized him. On the second floor of the residence were
also located "dormitories" for the unmarried male and
female staff of the station. Other buildings on the
estate housed the married personnel. Finally, another
auxiliary studio was set up in the owner's office at
the Iron Works in Shreveport. Eventually, during the
hard times of the depression, the operation took on the
aspects of a commune with staff members eating food
grown on the estate as well as using Kennonwood as a
home.[9]

The newly established Federal Radio Commission found
its relations with the volatile Henderson no more placid
than the Commerce Department's had been. The initial
mass reassignment of stations ordered by the FRC in
April 1927 placed KWKH on a frequency of 960 kc. with
power of one kilowatt. But Henderson again paid little
attention to prescribed limits on his transmitter power,
using as much as three kilowatts instead. As a result,
in August 1927 the Commission recommended to the Justice
Department the criminal prosecution of Henderson for
"illegal operation" of a broadcast station, specifically
the use of "excessive power" on more than forty occasions
in June and July of 1927 alone. The recommendation was
the first such ever made by the FRC, and if convicted,
Henderson could have been liable for fines totaling
$20,000. However, the case was never pressed by the
Justice Department--possibly because Henderson temporarily subsided in the use of unauthorized power, and
possibly because KWKH was already regarded as one of
the most popular Southern stations.[10]

Indeed, Henderson had enlisted a considerable
amount of public support in his campaign for more power.
A barrage of letters exploded on the desks of FRC
members and other governmental bureaucrats. Some even
reached the President. In September 1927 a Paducah,
Kentucky, listener to KWKH angrily demanded action from
President Calvin Coolidge: "Do not we citizens have
any say so in our Radio Question; why cannot we have
super power at KWKH in Shreveport?... Don't we tax-
payers and voters have any say so for our own southland?"[11]

Henderson neatly joined his own private campaign
for more power with a regional issue, that of equal
treatment for the South as a whole. Since broadcasting
had, in fact, been slower to develop in that section of
the country, he was capitalizing on a valid complaint.

In fact, he went far towards assuming the leadership of
the cause. With the vehicle of one of the more powerful Southern stations at his disposal and with his
willingness to challenge Washington officials, he was
a most effective spokesman for the regional chauvinism
being expressed on the question.

The Radio Act of 1927 had called for "fair, efficient, and equitable radio service" to each of the
regions of the nation, but by 1928 many Southerners
denied that clause was being effectively implemented.
They pointed out that zone 3, including the bulk of
the Southern states, actually contained the largest
population of any of the five zones but the smallest
number of stations and only 7.8% of total national
station power. While some Dixie partisans were
willing to admit that the situation had not been the
result of intentional discrimination and were simply
seeking justice for the future, Henderson was much less
ready to concede the good intentions of governmental
regulators. He charged them with "denying the South
free speech by denying the Southern stations power when
they want it." He chose as his particular target
Commissioner Sykes who he accused of betraying the
region he was obligated to protect.[12]

Most infuriating to the FRC was the style of
Henderson's on-the-air fulminations. He openly referred to the FRC as "parasites" and "sapheads" and
sprinkled his broadcasting conversation with "hell"
and "damn." By January 1928 Judge Sykes was requesting
the Radio Division conduct an investigation of Henderson
whose "very strong language about numbers of officials"
was proving especially offensive. Dutifully, the
Division's field inspectors began making verbatim transcripts of KWKH broadcasts and forwarding them to
Washington as possible future ammunition. There was
much to transcribe. As Henderson's relations with
both the Commerce Department and the FRC began to
deteriorate, his own role in his station's programming
increased. Devoting more time to KWKH and less to the
Iron Works, the station's program content began to
degenerate into extended monologues by the station
manager, punctuated by some recorded music and a small
number of live singing or musical groups, the latter
invariably unpaid, amateur talent.[13]

The FRC defended itself against the Henderson
attacks as best it could. Admiral Bullard, the
Commission Chairman, admitted the South was "not particularly well represented in the broadcasting field"

69

but denied the FRC was responsible. Rather, the disparity was simply due to the region's own lack of energy. He noted, somewhat coldly: "If the people of the South do not want broadcasting stations and do not make applications for them, the Commission can not take any action whatsoever." Sykes voiced a similar defense, denying the validity of the discrimination charge and claiming instead that the FRC had been "quite sympathetic" to Southern needs. Congressional support was also forthcoming with sympathy expressed for the vilified Sykes and references on the floor of the House of Representatives to "an unscrupulous broadcaster in Louisiana."[14]

In response to the popular feeling incited by Henderson and others, Representative Ewin L. Davis of Tennessee drafted an amendment to the existing radio law stipulating that each section of the nation was "entitled to equality of radio-broadcasting service, both of transmission and reception." The Davis Amendment, which became law on March 28, 1928, placed upon the FRC the heavy burden of carrying the required equality into effect. During the summer of 1928 the Commission sought to work out an allocation of broadcasting stations with respect to frequency, power, and hours of operation that would conform as closely as possible to the dictates of the Davis Amendment. The first step toward that end was the issuance of General Order No. 40 on August 30. Under its terms forty frequencies were set aside for stations on cleared channels with the aim of delivering a better service for rural listeners remote from the usual city-based transmitters. In a victory for the South, the forty cleared channels were to be allocated equally, eight to each zone. Henderson regarded the FRC decision as one for which he was in large part responsible. General Order No. 40 was soon followed by the announcement of specific new assignments for stations, including the fateful placing of KWKH and WWL on the same 850 kc. frequency, effective November 11.[15]

Sharing the same frequency necessarily required the negotiating of a time division agreement between the two stations. For that purpose Henderson travelled to New Orleans and confronted Father Abell. The apparition was more than a little unsettling for the Jesuit. Henderson sported "sparkling diamonds" on his tie and finger, and, in honor of the candidate he supported in the 1928 presidential race, wore an Al Smith brown derby as well as "loud socks with the embroidered name of Al Smith prominently displayed on

them." Abell, whose background had been a somewhat
sheltered one--born in a small town of South Mound,
Kansas, educated in religious schools in Albuquerque
and Denver, and entering the Society of Jesus at the
age of eighteen--may have been a bit out of his element
in dealing with the stormy petrel from Shreveport.
Nevertheless, an agreement was soon reached.[16]

Since neither Henderson nor WWL had any particular
interest in the daylight hours, the first division concerned itself only with evenings. On Mondays, Wednesdays,
Fridays, and Saturdays, WWL was to broadcast between
the hours of 6:00-9:00 P.M., while KWKH would go on the
air at 9:00 and sign off at midnight. On Tuesdays and
Thursdays the hours would be reversed. On Sundays the
only WWL programming would be the Solemn High Mass in
the morning at 10:00 and a brief evening lecture on a
religious topic during the dinner hour. In the fall of
1928 a series of lectures on Catholic Church history
was being delivered by Wallace A. Burk, S.J., Chairman
of the University's History Department, at that hour.
Other than the Sunday morning Mass, no daytime programs
were scheduled.[17]

The newly created clear channels were highly
desirable commodities since possession of one enabled
a broadcaster to reach large sections of the country
with his signal. Each clear channel station would
operate with a five kilowatt or more transmitter and
would, under the nature of the system, be guaranteed
freedom from interference. The FRC defined its purpose
in creating the forty privileged channels as bringing
"a fair diversity of programs to every home in the
United States, including the remote 50,000,000 of our
population on farms and ranches, in the mountains,
along the coasts, and in towns, villages and cross-
roads, more than 100 miles from any broadcasting
station." Henderson's possession of a clear channel
and his controversial record and questionable conduct
on the air inevitably left him an obvious target for
rival broadcasters seeking a better situation for themselves. As for WWL, its forced marriage with KWKH
destined it to a share in any challenge to the latter's
assignment.[18]

In the first months of 1929 such a threat
materialized. A Tulsa, Oklahoma, station, KVOO, owned
by the Southwestern Sales Corporation of which
William G. Skelly, president of the Skelly Oil Company,
was the principal, had found the fall 1928 FRC reassignment not to its liking. Formerly occupying a frequency

71

of 860 kc., it was now being ordered to shift to a less
desirable dial location, 1140 kc., and to divide time
with an Alabama station. While 1140 was one of the
eight clear channels allocated to the South, coverage
would be considerably less than the lower frequency
KVOO had been required to abandon. Hence Skelly opened
a campaign to acquire the channel assigned to KWKH and
WWL, thus precipitating the first major confrontation
between rival broadcasters before the new FRC.[19]

Placing the best possible face on his move,
Skelly argued that KVOO was simply seeking justice for
the state of Oklahoma, "a fair deal in the location of
wave lengths," and that he was attempting to spare the
state "obscenity, slang and vulgarity over the air."
The Shreveport station, according to the Oklahoman,
was being "used largely for personal attacks" and was
not being "conducted in a dignified manner." Skelly
admitted his action was directed at KWKH primarily,
but since it involved an attempt to gain undivided
control of the Louisiana channel, it would also
necessarily result in the ousting of WWL from its
assignment as well.[20]

The Louisiana counter-attack took a variety of
forms. Both WWL and Henderson relied upon endorse-
ments solicited from private citizens and from public
officials, but the Shreveport station operator carried
his response far beyond the expected. He launched an
invective-filled assault on Skelly and on the Skelly
Oil Company that came to have little logical relation
to the merits of the pending case.

The Federal Radio Commission scheduled a hearing
on the KVOO application for February 20, 1929. In
these early days of the FRC's existence, hearings were
generally held before the entire Commission. Later a
system of examiners was begun with each of those
officials, after presiding over a hearing in which
written evidence and oral testimony was submitted, forwarding to the Commission a report containing specific
recommendations. The KVOO hearing, however, would use
no examiner; the battle was joined before the Commissioners themselves.[21]

Abell solicited support for WWL wherever he could
find it. Within the University it came especially from
a fellow Jesuit, Wallace A. Burk. As a close personal
friend of Abell's, Burk had found himself being drawn
closer and closer to the WWL operation. He was, as

already noted, delivering lectures on religious history as a chief feature of the station's Sunday programming. Now Burk became involved in the station's
business affairs for the first time. Within two years
he would assume the title of Faculty Director, re-
lieving Abell of that responsibility. In late January
1929 Burk sharply criticized the KVOO action, terming
it an "injustice to Loyola." He called for citizens
of the state to sign specially prepared affidavits
addressed to the FRC and testifying to the worthwhile
service being provided by WWL. He boasted that several
hundred such documents had already been forwarded to the
Commission.[22]

From outside of Louisiana aid came through a prominent Catholic laymen's organization, the National
Council of Catholic Men. Headed by an enterprising
Paulist priest, John J. Burke, C.S.P., the NCCM had
earlier lobbied for WWL in the New Orleans station's
successful effort to gain increased transmitter power.
The organization was following a general policy of
supporting any Catholic broadcasters embroiled with
federal regulatory authorities. Now it provided the
legal services of its executive secretary, Charles F.
Dolle. In a late January letter to the University,
Dolle disdained receiving any compensation for himself
and suggested instead that "any honorarium you might
wish to send me would be gratefully received and the
money turned over to our organization." In the hearing
that was to follow Dolle served as the principal
attorney representing WWL.[23]

Assistance was also soon forthcoming from
Louisiana's elected officials. Congressmen and United
States Senators announced their support for the KWKH-
WWL cause as a war of words began to resemble a mini-
civil war between two sovereign states. Most prominent
in offering assistance was the newly elected Governor
of Louisiana, Huey P. Long, Jr. The fiery young
Governor denounced the KVOO application as an "attack
on the state's medium of advertising and her commercial
interest" and promised a vigorous protest to the FRC
from his office. Long went even farther. He appointed
a "special attorney" to represent himself at the hearing
in order to "safeguard the radio interests of the state."
In reality, the attorney, J.J. Grimmett of Shreveport,
served as counsel for KWKH as well as the state of
Louisiana at the hearing.[24]

Long's support was not unexpected. Henderson had
been one of the Kingfish's earliest backers and had

raised $10,000 during the politician's first and unsuc-
cessful gubernatorial campaign in 1924. The two men had
met during World War I when Long acted as Attorney for
a plaintiff bringing a suit against Henderson. Striking
up a friendship thereafter, Long soon began handling
legal matters for the Shreveport businessman. In
addition to monetary campaign contributions, Henderson
rendered substantial assistance to candidate Long by
allowing him use of the powerful KWKH facilities on an
almost unlimited basis. Long was thus given ample
opportunity to perfect a potent radio style well before
his emergence on the national stage. Moreover, the
KWKH facilities proved invaluable in April 1929 when, as
Governor, he successfully but barely withstood a determined legislative effort to impeach and remove him
from office. Long was not even required to speak from
the KWKH studios. Instead remote broadcasts were often
arranged from the Governor's various public meetings
or even from his bedroom. Invariably he spoke without
notes or manuscripts, quoting the Bible, telling rural
jokes, and flying into towering rages against his
enemies. The style bore a remarkable similarity to
that of Henderson himself and it seems fair to conclude
that each undoubtedly played a key role in shaping the
other's radio personality.[25]

The political weight thrown into the struggle
against KVOO by the Governor was thus a friendly quid
pro quo, but Henderson was not content to rely on that
alone. Unwilling by nature to remain on the defensive,
he tore into the leader of the opposition, William G.
Skelly. In one on-the-air attack after another,
Henderson branded Skelly a liar, hi-jacker, drunk with
power, contemptible, and an armed robber. He called
upon his listeners to boycott Skelly Oil products, and
in a final flight-of-far fetched-fancy referred to
Skelly's son-in-law, a Shreveport resident, as "a
German spy." Not unreasonably, Skelly protested to
the Commission that he had been "attacked, maligned,
and misrepresented" by the KWKH broadcasts. He could
only term the Henderson tactics "unethical," a restrained piece of understatement.[26]

On another flank Henderson was also engaging in
affidavit collection maneuvers. In January newspapers
both in Louisiana and outside of the state suddenly
began carrying paid advertisements labelled: "Help
Radio Station KWKH Keep Its Wave Length." The ads
featured a tear-out blank which the reader was asked
to carry to a notary public. Before the notary the
blank was to be signed attesting that KWKH was the

individual's "favorite" station and that the FRC was implored to allow KWKH to "retain its present status." The affidavits were then to be dispatched to Henderson for use in the up-coming hearing. By early February Henderson called the response "overwhelming" and claimed to be employing twenty persons just for "receiving, sorting, and packing affidavits."[27]

On behalf of WWL, Abell and Burk travelled to Washington by train to join Dolle at the scheduled hearing. From Shreveport on February 19, Henderson too set out but in a grander style. He rented a private railroad car to transport himself, his family, and friends, taking care to have broadcasted in advance his itinerary. The result was crowds at each stop bearing additional affidavits and calling upon Henderson to deliver back-platform addresses. No further proof was necessary of the impact of the broadcasting medium in the hands of a shrewd and dynamic manipulator.[28]

In addition, Henderson focused public attention on the massive outpouring of public support supposedly represented by the testimonials. An airplane was chartered to carry a portion of the documents to Washington with the gesture being, of course, well publicized. Even more publicity was received, though this unexpected, when the plane crashed in Alabama, shortly after taking off from a stop in Birmingham. There were no serious injuries. Since Henderson was carrying the bulk of the affidavits with him, their desired effect was not significantly diluted by the accident.[29]

By now the case had attracted considerable national attention. Because of the throng of spectators seeking admittance to the hearing, the Commission quickly chose to move the site to a large auditorium in the Department of Interior building. There on February 20, the proceedings got underway. On the first day testimony from the KVOO applicants were heard. Not until February 21 did the Louisiana stations present arguments in defense of their assignment. Burk testified that the topography of the New Orleans area was not conducive to good signal coverage on a higher frequency. He also pointed out that atmospheric conditions in the Gulf South made it impossible to pick up stations at great distances, thus making it more essential that the area have its own powerful broadcast operations. Moreover, since Mississippi had not been assigned a clear channel station of its own, the WWL-KWKH combination actually served the needs of both states. Abell's testimony which followed also pursued a technical defense for retention of the channel.[30]

Henderson's appearance on the stand the same day took the hearing in quite another direction. Beginning with his now famous "Hello, World, doggone ya!", he quickly asked permission of the Commission to present his affidavits. When assent was given, two black station employees dressed in uniform with the letters KWKH on their caps wheeled in three immense red, white, and blue packing cases, placing them on the auditorium stage to the delight of the audience and the dismay of the Commissioners. Henderson had made his point. The wooden cases contained 163,000 affidavits theoretically testifying to public satisfaction with the current operations of KWKH. The Times-Picayune estimated the total weight of the "evidence" at two tons, four thousand pounds.[31]

After order had been restored, another uproar was to shortly break out again. Harsh words between Henderson and Skelly's "German spy" son-in-law erupted into a fist fight between Henderson and Skelly himself. The police were called upon to intervene. The hearing was by now degenerating rapidly. Its tone was not uplifted either by an unprecedented and bitter verbal onslaught upon Henderson by a member of the very Commission seemingly sitting in judgment on the case. Commissioner Orestes H. Caldwell shocked the room by launching into a public excoriation of the KWKH owner. Henderson was accused of character assasination by his slanders of public officials, and Caldwell held him especially responsible for the recent death of the FRC's first chairman, Admiral Bullard, who had supposedly succumbed to the vicious attacks made upon him by the Louisianan. Caldwell pleaded with his fellow Commissioners to revoke altogether the broadcasting privileges extended to KWKH. On that rather unjudicial note, the substantive portion of the hearing concluded.[32]

WWL emerged from the proceeding generally unscathed as the real cannonballs flew only between Shreveport and Tulsa. Some criticism of the New Orleans station had surfaced, primarily dealing with the narrow appeal of its regular programming. An impression had been left that WWL had not "measured up to the opportunity presented by a clear channel." Nevertheless, since the Commission in its original 1927 mandate had been denied any authority to censor programs unless they offended public decency, it was apparent an FRC decision would not be made on those grounds. As for Henderson, despite a harrowing cross-examination from KVOO attorneys

charging him with everything from libel to failure to
identify phonograph records played on the air as recordings and not live performances (in accord with an
FRC order), and despite the Caldwell attack, he had
resolutely weathered the experience and appeared un-
chastened.[33]

Now the waiting for the verdict began.  Not until
June was the Commission's decision made public.  When
it was, it proved to be a complete victory for WWL and
KWKH.  The application of KVOO for the 850 kc. frequency was denied and the status quo remained in effect.
Surprisingly, the decision held that the charges against
Henderson had not been "substantiated to the satisfaction
of the Commission."  Caldwell's pleas for punitive
action failed to win over a majority of his colleagues.
In the case of WWL, since the FRC could find no violation
in its operations, it reasoned correctly that there was
no justification for withdrawing its right to operate
half-time on its clear channel.  It followed logically
also that in view of the satisfactory WWL performance,
the most that KVOO could hope for would be a shift from
time-sharing on one frequency to time-sharing on another,
an insufficient gain to warrant the move being made.
KVOO quickly filed an appeal of the decision with the
Court of Appeals in the District of Columbia but then
withdrew the motion within a month without explanation.
The Oklahoma station in the future would take no further
action in the matter.[34]

The episode would have three short-run effects.
For Henderson it marked yet another victory in
Washington, increasing thereby his complete confidence
in himself.  Within weeks of the decision he was well
launched on an entirely new crusade, one destined to
be his most famous, a full scale war on the nation's
retail chain stores.  The chain store war would bring
him back to the bar of the FRC but this time with much
less satisfying results.  For WWL also a measure of
over-confidence was bred by the KVOO decision.  Abell
especially became convinced that Henderson had survived only because of his association on the channel
with WWL.  Abell later wrote regarding Henderson that
"it would have gone hard with him, and in all probability
he would have lost the decision" had it not been for
WWL's good record.  As a result Abell and the Loyola
administration felt themselves freer to take a hard line
in future negotiations with Henderson, and they fully
expected that in any disagreement between the two
Louisiana broadcasting enterprises, the FRC would
without a doubt find in New Orleans' favor.  The months

ahead would painfully disabuse them of that belief.[35]

Finally, the KVOO case would quickly cause the FRC to alter its own hearing procedures. In its 1929 Annual Report, the Commission warned that stations soliciting affidavits and petitions to support their cases before the FRC were engaging in "a regrettable practice." The effect was to only create "an encumbrance of the record without particular significance." The Commission conjectured that the supposed support was "usually more indicative of the diligence of the broadcaster than of the popularity of the station." Henceforth the Commissioners would not accept or consider such "evidence." In May 1929, while testifying before a congressional committee, the General Counsel for the FRC admitted the new rule stemmed directly from the Henderson fiasco. When asked by a Senator on the committee whether he or the Commission had actually read any of the KWKH affidavits, the attorney replied wryly: "I must stand on my constitutional rights."[36]

The case, spectacular as it was, had reflected no great credit on any of its parties including the judging authority. What was even worse, for three of the parties--WWL, KWKH, and the Commission itself--the 1929 experience would be only the first round in a continuing series of battles. The Louisiana clear channel over the next five years would prove a prize for which a good deal of political and economic blood would be shed.

COMMERCIAL EXPECTATIONS AND REALITIES, 1929-1931

Orie Abell had not campaigned for increased power
and a more favorable dial location for WWL simply to
continue the narrow interest programming that had characterized the station's efforts during those early years
of existence.  Abell's vision of WWL took quite another
form.  The added expense of maintaining the new five
kilowatt transmitter, put into service on Easter Sunday,
March 31, 1929--seven years to the day after the station
had first taken the air--was obvious.  More important
to Abell, however, was the potential he saw in WWL for
providing a continuing income for the University.  Given
a fresh policy direction, Abell was convinced, the station could not only meet its higher operating costs out
of revenues of its own, but also act as a continuing
endowment for Loyola.  There need only be a decision by
the University administration to allow the station to
"sell time," to adopt a frankly commercial format.[1]

Loyola's President, Father Florence Sullivan, was
sympathetic to the goal, even though the operation of
the station as a commercial venture would entail changes,
possibly of a troublesome nature.  The present almost
wholly educational, religious, and fine arts programming
would to a considerable extent be replaced by fare of a
more popular, perhaps too popular, type.  How would such
programs and the advertisements that accompanied them
comport with the image and dignity of a church-related
educational institution?  Might the revenues generated
be more than offset by a loss of community good will?
How much censorship would the Jesuits have to exercise
or even be able to exercise over live shows performed
by artists who might not reflect the same values as the
station licensees.  Further, a frankly commercial policy
would undoubtedly mean an expansion of the WWL staff,
now consisting of virtually Abell alone serving as
manager, chief engineer, announcer, and program director.

Hired employees, accounts to be sold and maintained, management strategies to be planned and implemented-- all these and more implied an expertise in broadcasting and in the business world in general not necessarily possessed by clerics and teachers. Would day-to-day control of WWL activities have to be relinquished to laymen not associated with the University, and if so, under what terms? All these issues and more were debated by Sullivan and Abell as they struggled to formulate a policy in early 1929.[2]

There were at hand local precedents for the operation of a commercial station, though not by a university. By the spring of 1929 nine stations remained on the air in Louisiana, five in New Orleans and four in Shreveport. Of that number six were classified as commercial in varying degrees. In New Orleans WDSU (now a CBS affiliate), WSMB (now an NBC affiliate), and WJBO were already offering time to advertisers. Their example and that of radio nationally provided Abell with the encouragement needed to contemplate commercialism.[3]

By 1929 the number of radio sets in use in the United States had passed the ten million mark, an increase of over 100% from just five years before. Moreover, surveys soon revealed that the average American could be found listening to his set four to six hours daily. As for Louisiana, the 1930 census placed "radio families" at 11.2% of the state's total number of families, a figure which compared closely to the South's overall 11.9%, but was dramatically smaller than the 76.4% counted in the Northern states. While the potential radio audience of the South was relatively weak, so were its available broadcast facilities, thus lessening competition. But Abell was not confining his attention solely to his own region; the assignment of WWL to be a cleared channel with a five kilowatt transmitter allowed it to deliver to any national sponsor, in the evening hours where the bulk of its schedule lay, an inter-regional audience. A wall map of the United States, Canada, and Mexico in the main WWL studio featured multi-colored pins indicating points from which listeners had responded to broadcasts with letters or telegrams. Within two weeks after the new transmitter was put in service, the pins marked Vancouver, Saskatchewan, Ottawa, Quebec, Nova Scotia, British Honduras, Mexico City, and Vera Cruz as well as numerous points in the West, Midwest, and South.[4]

* * * * * * * * * *

80

Meanwhile, major national developments on the business side of the broadcasting industry were unfolding, heightening the income possibilities for an emerging commercial station such as WWL. Advertisers were discovering that radio could be an effective means of moving products, even without the costly purchase of network programming. Better than satisfactory results could be attained by sponsoring time, weather or news reports over selected stations scattered across the country or by the insertion of advertising messages into locally produced programs. Such insertions could be purchased at a nominal cost and roughly correspond to the traditional classified advertisements of a newspaper. Thus the "spot announcement" offered a new avenue for the effective use of radio as a marketing tool for both the local and the national advertiser, and an important source of income for the individual station, especially one without network affiliation.[5]

In response to the demand for radio time, a new middleman structure took shape. The advertising agency had for years served as the standard representative of the firm with a product to sell, and had acted as the instrument through which advertising was prepared and placed, principally with print media. But agencies knew little of radio in general and even less about particular stations in distant parts of the United States far removed from an agency's own headquarters ordinarily located in New York City or Chicago. Conversely, the station operator usually lacked the means and the practical knowledge needed for initiating the contact himself with either the sponsoring firm or its representative, the agency. To bridge this gap another type of intermediary appeared--in the late 1920's, the "time broker," and by the mid-1930's, the "station representative." This new intermediary fulfilled two basic needs. It was he who secured for the agency necessary station information regarding rates, listenership, and available hours and programs; it was also he who actively sought new business from agencies and sponsors for his client stations, and who heralded the efficacy of broadcasting as an advertising medium.[6]

Aiding considerably in the rise of spot advertising was the introduction of electrical transcriptions which made their debut in 1929. These wax disks enabled an advertiser to produce a program, give it a permanent form on a record, and then have it broadcast over any station he chose at a time of his own pleasure. While some of the largest business organizations utilized

the "E.T.," as witnessed by the popular Chevrolet
Chronicles series of 1931, it was the medium size
manufacturers or distributors selling to a national
market who found them most useful.  Those companies
possessed resources too limited or aimed at market
areas too restricted for network broadcasting.  With
the production of higher quality transcriptions, they
actually came to be preferred programming fare on
smaller stations where their only competition was in-
ferior local talent.  Even a suspicious Federal Radio
Commission, concerned that the use of the E.T. would
deceive a gullible audience into believing it was
hearing a live program, could not diminish the employment of the new program vehicle.  While the Commission's
General Order No. 78, issued on December 5, 1929,
required an explanatory announcement:  "This program is
an electrical transcription made exclusively for broadcast purposes," the caution had no appreciable effect
on their popularity with stations and sponsors alike.[7]

   As commercial programs became prevelant on the
nation's radio stations, so also did published rate
cards quoting charges for the use of each broadcaster's
facilities.  Rates were usually offered for units of
one hour, a half hour, and a quarter hour as well as
lesser periods down to one minute of time.  Gradually
even the one minute rate was subdivided into prices
for 50, 75, or 100 words.  Distinctions were drawn
between day and evening programs with the dividing line
set at 6:00 P.M., and separate rates were frequently
quoted for local and national advertisers with the
latter averaging at least 50% more than the former.
This disparity was most often justified by the argument that the national account was able to utilize all
of a station's signal coverage and potential audience
while the local merchant sold his goods in only a segment of the station's market area.  At least some
industry spokesmen, those dealing with national accounts,
regarded the rate difference as blatant discrimination,
a classic example of charging "whatever the traffic
would bear."  Nevertheless, the higher national rates
persisted and became institutionalized within the industry.  Also quickly acquiring the status of common
practice was the allowance of a commission of 15% for
advertising agencies and another for time brokers and
station representatives.  The necessity of paying double
commissions to these middlemen for national accounts
placed with the station was a major factor too in the
inflation of rates charged non-local business.[8]

The sales tool for which the sponsor was paying had taken on greater sophistication by 1929. Early practice had been based on the theory that indirect selling alone would be tolerated by the listening audience. As a result commercial announcements contained little more that a mere mention of the sponsor's name, usually in the title of the program itself. Typical of this approach was the Happiness Boys, featuring Billy Jones and Ernest Hare and sponsored by the Happiness Candy Stores of New York City, who went on the air for the first time in December 1923. Aside from the often repeated catch phrase, "Happiness Is Just Around the Corner," no direct selling was done. During 1928 and 1929, however, a more aggressive approach began to be developed. The latter year saw the first dramatized announcements produced for Fels Naptha Soap. In one a cautious uncle required his niece to prove her housekeeping ability before bequeathing her the family estate. Needless to say, she successfully demonstrated her prowess by means of the sponsor's product.[9]

Soon some commercial announcements had acquired the smoothness of Graham McNamee's opening for the Coca-Cola Program in November 1931:

> Good evening, ladies and gentlemen of the radio audience. This is Graham McNamee, happy to be offering you the refreshment of another sparkling Coca-Cola program. Familiar melodies you love, beautifully played by Gustave Hoenschen and the all-string orchestra, Lewis James as soloist.... So just lean back at your ease and enjoy it with us tonight. And then tomorrow remember that whatever you're doing, you can always pause and refresh yourself around the corner from anywhere. Take a minute from your busy day. Relax at a cool cheerful soda fountain with ice-cold Coca-Cola. It will leave you refreshed--off to a fresh start.[10]

* * * * * * * * * *

Thus as WWL contemplated the adoption of a strategy of full commercialism in 1929, the necessary institutional structure in the industry to make that strategy successful was nearing completion, and advertising techniques were already coming into use that would remain generally permanent features of broadcasting's business practices. A station, even without network affiliation, could expect to mine important sources of revenue through spot advertising, which by 1931 totalled an estimated $32 million or 46% of all broadcast advertising expenditures for the year. Abell, sensing the drift toward a near total victory for commercialism, sought to place WWL in line with the industry's obvious future and to reap for Loyola thereby the accompanying rewards.[11]

But before any action could be taken, an immediate problem of an unusual nature required solution. Sullivan recognized a major difficulty was the Code of Canon Law of the Catholic Church. Under Canon 142: "Clerics are forbidden to engage personally or through another in business or to carry on commerce whether for their own benefit or for that of others." Furthermore, the Epitome of the Institute of the Society of Jesus, a compilation of canon law and Jesuit rules that provided an up-to-date summary for the Order after the 1918 revision of the Code, added to the restriction. Paragraph 533 of the Epitome quoted Canon 142 for "diligent observance" by Jesuits, and then went even farther. It prohibited "even the appearance of profit-seeking." Examples were cited, but the question of the sale of advertising time on a radio station was, obviously, new. It did not fit the categories delineated. Canon 142 itself merely repeated a rule passed by the Church Council of Elvira held in the year 324, and enunciated again in an encyclical of Pope Benedict XIV in 1741.[12]

When WWL embarked upon the policy of commercialism in 1929, it soon found itself facing the issue of Canon 142. The Superior General of the Society of Jesus called Father John W. Hynes, rector of Loyola's Jesuit community, to Rome to investigate whether the operation of a commercial station violated both the canon law and the Society's own rules. In response, Hynes sought out the Spanish Jesuit canon law scholar, Antonio M. Arregui, who had authored a commentary on the Epitome. Arregui prepared an opinion presented to the Superior General to the effect that the operation of a broadcasting station and the selling of its time was no more of a business venture than that of publishing a religious newspaper or magazine. According to Arregui, some columns in those were used to convey substantive information, while other blank pages or space were sold for advertising to pay for the costs of publication, with the overall purpose being the support of a worthy cause. So also on a radio station, a certain amount of time would be used for religious

and educational messages, while other time, like the
extra pages in a magazine or newspaper, could be sold
for a revenue. The analogy may not have been altogether
appropriate, for Arregui probably did not realize the
volume of commercial programming that WWL was carrying
on in relation to the educational and religious portion
of its schedule. The paramount purpose for which WWL
existed after 1929 was to furnish a flourishing source
of endowment funds for the University which held its
license. By largely abandoning the objective of
directly propagating the faith, both religious and
academic, it survived and it insured the ultimate
economic viability of the institution that established
it. Thereby, it was at least indirectly supportive of
that same first objective. Arregui's argument carried
the day, no matter what its accuracy, and the commercial
era of WWL was not brought to a premature end.[13]

Abell and Sullivan also sought out the lay business
support which they believed necessary to put their
enterprise on a sound foundation. They found it in the
offices of the Standard Fruit Company, one of the
pioneers in the development of the banana industry in
Latin America. Headquartered in New Orleans, it was
controlled by the Vaccaro-D'Antoni interests. Salvador
D'Antoni arrived in the United States at New Orleans
in 1886. He quickly went into business operating a
boat and selling fruit on the lower Mississippi
River. One of his principal suppliers was Joseph
Vaccaro, a Crescent City produce wholesaler. Eventually,
a partnership resulted with D'Antoni serving as the
general manager of the firm's new ventures in Honduras
where banana and coconut plantations were being established. In 1923 the Standard Fruit and Steamship
Company was incorporated, but it still remained
basically a family alliance with control in the hands
of Joseph Vaccaro and his two brothers, and Salvador
D'Antoni (who had married Joseph Vaccaro's daughter
in 1899) and his sons Blaise and Joseph. Their investments broadened even more in 1923 when the Vaccaro
brothers purchased the downtown Grunewald Hotel. The
old structure was quickly demolished and a new building
constructed in its place. Finished in 1925, the hotel
was renamed the Roosevelt, and as such, it would
eventually play a major role in WWL's history.[14]

Standard Fruit was not a surprising choice for
Sullivan to make. The corporation's principals had
maintained close ties with the University and with
the Jesuits. Both D'Antoni sons had been educated in
Jesuit schools including the downtown College of

Immaculate Conception and Loyola itself. A series of meetings between Standard Fruit officials and the Jesuit planners hammered out an approach acceptable to both sides. A new corporation, the WWL Development Company, Inc., was chartered by the state of Louisiana and an agreement formalized between it and the University on October 29, 1929. Under the terms of this first agreement, Loyola granted to WWL Development "the exclusive right to contract for the broadcasting over said station of all matter and programs for which compensation in money is paid." In return Loyola was to be credited with "an amount equivalent to the gross revenues" of WWL Development each year after expenses had been paid. In effect, the new corporation was being given the management of the station, but it would exercise that authority on a non-profit basis, for all revenues over and above expenses would be funneled into the University's treasury. One other restriction was placed upon the managing company--"the character of all matter to be thus broadcasted" remained subject to University approval. In this way a concern on the part of some Jesuits regarding the possibility of embarrassing or offensive programming being aired was alleviated.[15]

Two thousand shares of capital stock were initially authorized of which fifty were subscribed at $100 each, all purchased by Standard Fruit. Three office employees of that organization served as the first Board of Directors of WWL Development even though they played no part in contributing the original capital. In 1931 they would resign, to be succeeded by a new Board made up of local businessmen without connection to Standard Fruit; but until that time, the Vaccaro-D'Antoni firm would maintain a general but loose supervision over the business affairs of the station. The account books were maintained in the Standard Fruit office, all bills were paid from that location, and a WWL manager seeking the most minor supplies--stamps, for instance--was required to secure them from the banana importers.[16]

Abell, admitted that the arrangement was "a little more involved than was really necessary." The rationale for the holding company device was variously explained. One early station employee suggested that its purpose was to create an entity which could assume legal responsibility for the station's activities and could be the target of law suits, if necessary, without the University also being held liable. In view of the program control retained by the University under the 1929 agreement, it is extremely doubtful that this was the original intention. Ten years later a Loyola

86

President described WWL Development as "a corporation
of convenience which saves us Priest-Educators from
dealing in the commercial world." At the same time
another Loyola Jesuit close to the station recalled
that WWL Development came into being when "it was seen
that it would be improper to have Priest-Educators in
the business world to be worried about contracts, about
the sale of time, whether or not a party should be contacted, and such matters as those." In 1930 Wallace
Burk explained the company consisted "of a number of
businessmen who are supposed to develop our station
commercially." He added: "As a university, a religious
institution, we do not like immediately to embark upon
any directly commercial enterprise."[17]

It seems most likely the formation of WWL Development met the desires of both Loyola and Standard Fruit.
For the University administration it offered a means of
escaping direct violation of the constitution of the
Society of Jesus and the canon law prohibition against
engaging in business ventures. It also provided a
method of marshalling outside contributions in the form
of both capital and services. The latter would be
especially critical during WWL's early months as a
commercial station, a period prior to the standardization
of internal routines and practices that would only
evolve with time and experience. In effect, the
Standard Fruit intervention allowed the station to make
the transition to its new policy with a minimum of trial
and error. For Standard Fruit, on the other hand, WWL
Development offered a means of overseeing its $5,000
gift to the University, and making more certain its
efficacious use. When it appeared, as it would in 1931,
that the difficult transition period had been safely
passed, then control was passed to others and more
authority vested in the station's own staff.

The management company plan as formulated for WWL
was unique. It can be noted that less than two months
after the signing of the WWL Development agreement,
another university station took an ostensibly similar
step. WGST, an Atlanta station licensed to Georgia
Tech, had fallen on hard times. It elected to lease
its entire operation to Southern Broadcasting Stations,
Inc., a private corporation which maintained control
until 1943. The WGST case, however, differed markedly
from that of WWL in that Southern Broadcasting retained
a healthy share of the profits of the enterprise and
made no pretense to being anything other than it was,
a privately owned firm interested in an increasing
return on its own investment. In another variation,

Cornell University in 1932 sold the bulk of time available on its station to the Elmira Star-Gazette for commercial resale, while retaining a small portion for its own educational programming. Again the newspaper assuming de facto control was a profit-making organization, and in that respect departed from the WWL Development case. The design arrived at in New Orleans in 1929 was a unique accommodation to the problem at hand.[18]

The transition to commercialism began even before the October signing of the WWL Development agreement. In anticipation of that step, the station's first salaried employee was added to the staff in early September. Jean Pasquet, a musician who had participated regularly as unpaid talent in previous WWL broadcasts, now resigned his position with a local department store to take on the combined duties of Program Director, Announcer, and Sales Manager. His salary was placed at $150 per month with no provisions for commissions on new accounts attracted to the station. Abell remained as Station Manager, as well as Chief Engineer and Transmitter Operator, in addition to his teaching duties in the Physics Department.[19]

Again, in anticipation of the WWL agreement, an official announcement of the new commercial policy was made in advance. The October 1929 issue of Radio Advertising, compiled by Standard Rate and Data Service and the industry's official handbook of station charges, published for the first time national rates for WWL time sales. In previous years the station had simply been listed with the notation: "Does not sell time." Rates for "General Advertising" were now shown as follows on that first national rate card:[20]

(6:00 P.M. to 12:00 Midnight)

|          | 1 time   | 13 weeks | 26 weeks | 39 weeks | 52 weeks |
|----------|----------|----------|----------|----------|----------|
| 1 hour   | $150.00  | $142.50  | $135.00  | $127.00  | $120.00  |
| 1/2 hour | 90.00    | 85.50    | 81.00    | 76.00    | 72.00    |
| 1/4 hour | 50.00    | 47.50    | 45.00    | 42.50    | 40.00    |

(7:00 A.M. to 6:00 P.M.)

|          | 1 time  | 13 weeks | 26 weeks | 39 weeks | 52 weeks |
|----------|---------|----------|----------|----------|----------|
| 1 hour   | 75.00   | 71.25    | 67.50    | 63.75    | 60.00    |
| 1/2 hour | 45.00   | 42.75    | 40.50    | 38.25    | 36.00    |
| 1/4 hour | 25.00   | 23.75    | 22.50    | 21.25    | 20.00    |

88

The data was generally comparable to other stations
in WWL's category--an independent clear channel station
with 5,000 watts of broadcast power. The usual agency
commission of 15% was provided for, and the rates were
specified as applying only to air time with the costs
of talent extra. The station announced it would "gladly
assist the advertiser in securing talent and arranging
programs." The right "to omit or alter programs not
acceptable to the station management" was also stipulated. The station further pointed out that it was
"equipped to handle programs by electrical transcription,
using double turn-table." In general the first WWL
commercial information differed little from that being
published by competitors within and outside the state of
Louisiana.[21]

Despite the October rate announcement, WWL did not
abandon its non-commercial status until December 3 when
a fifteen minute sales talk was carried for the General
Research Laboratories of Des Moines, Iowa. The contract,
secured by Pasquet, called for the program to be continued for thirteen weeks with the product "some kind of
a radio appliance." No other details remain available
on this initial commercial account. Others were soon
added, however, with the first month's time sales
totalling $360. Abell and Pasquet regarded the amount
as "encouraging."[22]

New program features were also being added, including a dance music remote broadcast from the
Restaurant de La Louisiane four evenings per week, and
in an innovation, two weekday afternoons from noon
until 2:00 P.M. The string trio received no talent
fees. The restaurant and the musicians exchanged the
entertainment for the publicity opportunity. The
galloping popularity of NBC's Amos 'n' Andy, already a
national phenomenon that had inspired a comic strip
and phonograph records as well as sending hordes of
customers into radio shops, fostered its own local
copies. In New Orleans the show was Smoky Joe and Tee
Tain, aired nightly by WWL beginning in 1929. Struc-
tured as a comic serial and running for years on the
station, the Negro impersonators put their characters
into one far-fetched situation after another. In January
1930 the two had supposedly wandered by mistake into a
zeppelin hanger and switched on the airship's engine
instead of the lights. As the program information described their plight: "Now they are up in the air in
a runaway zeppelin and don't know what to do. Their
fate may be known by tuning in on WWL next Monday
night."[23]

More remote broadcasts were introduced in 1930, offering greater scheduling variety. Among them were organ concerts from the recently constructed Loew's State theatre. The orchestral organ installed in movie houses had become standard broadcast fare. WSMB especially had been featuring such remote pick-ups from Saenger-owned theatres since that station's establishment in 1925. Later in 1930 a Canal Street store was the scene of yet more WWL organ programming as the Kress variety store housed an instrument claimed to be valued at $50,000. But each of these remotes entailed a line cost of some $35 for the necessary telephone circuit because of the considerable distance from the central business district and the French Quarter to the WWL studios located far uptown.[24]

To save a portion of this expense, Abell determined to terminate remote lines at a centrally located downtown studio. Such a studio would also provide a convenience for visiting or local talent who would not have to be asked to travel across the city to the University and, therefore, might be more amenable to an invitation to appear before the WWL microphones. As a result Abell and Pasquet opened negotiations with the Monteleone Hotel, located in the French Quarter near Canal Street, for the station's first permanent remote studio. The space, secured in August, consisted simply of a single room but it came to serve as both a solo studio and a "cubby-hole" sales office. Abell built a "remote speech input amplifier" and a switching panel for it, and estimated that new facility and its equipment saved the station $25 per month on each remote location.[25]

In May 1930, WWL employed electrical transcriptions for the first time. A series of programs titled High, Wide and Handsome and distributed by Stanley Recordings was used as the content for shows sponsored by Gliddens Paint Company. The talent cost for the transcriptions as well as the time charges were borne by the sponsor. Other accounts, mainly sold by Pasquet, included at this early date an insurance company, an automobile dealer, a ladies' dress shop, and two department stores.

During the first quarter of 1930 Abell placed gross revenue from time sales at $820, but as the year progressed the figures improved even more. The month of August alone, the same month in which space in the Monteleone was rented, saw total billings of $2,080.75, the best thirty day period to that time. Principally responsible for the excellent summer income was a

90

heated campaign for the United States Senate between
Huey Long and the incumbent, Joseph E. Ransdell. Both
sides bought large quantities of air time, and WWL
shared in the political largesse. With the election
being held in early September, it was inevitable that
the income for that month would show a decline. It
did, to the more realistic figure of $950. Nevertheless,
the last five months of 1930 saw billings of over
$5,000.

Profit estimations at this early date are few and
unreliable. Abell himself placed the August net profit
at $1,600 but it seems certain that figure was highly
inflated. With much of the office work of the station
being done by Standard Fruit, and with Abell admitting
the electrical power expense of the station was being
absorbed by the University in its "advertising" budget,
realistic cost figures for the broadcasting operation
were simply not being computed. It would be some months
more before accounting methods began to give a reliable
picture of the station's financial health.[26]

An expansion of hours on the air accompanied the
growth in commercial accounts. By the fall of 1930
the station was broadcasting from 8:00 A.M.-1:00 P.M.
daily except Sunday. On Sundays daytime programming
covered the periods from 10:00-11:15 A.M. (Mass from
Holy Name Church) and noon - 4:00 P.M. Evening time
was still shared with KWKH. On Monday, Wednesday,
Friday, and Saturday, WWL was heard from 6:00-9:00 P.M.
On Tuesday and Thursday it was heard from 9:00 P.M. -
1:00 A.M., and on Sunday nights it had a short segment
from 6:00 - 7:45 P.M. Naturally, Henderson was
scheduled for the evening periods in which WWL was not.
A total of 57 hours per week were now being programmed
by Abell and Pasquet, a massive increase over just two
years before, for instance, when only 300 hours were
scheduled during the whole of 1928.[27]

Widening the broadcast day was a step not confined
to WWL. The principal stations of the city were following the same course, with the lead being taken by
WSMB. The Saenger-Maison Blanche station had fashioned
a breakthrough; it began in September 1930 continuous
programming from 7:00 A.M. until midnight, seven days
per week. This unprecedented length of time on the
air was made possible only by the availability of network shows. The quantity of locally-produced programming remained essentially the same while more and
more NBC entertainment, both sponsored and sustaining,
was heard on WSMB.

91

Uhalt and his WDSU were quickly forced to defend themselves against their chief competitor's tactic by duplicating the maneuver. As the CBS affiliate in New Orleans, WDSU too had network shows available to it which it quickly threw into the gap to fill the newly opened blocks in its schedule. Other than WWL, however, the city's independent stations, without great resources of their own or outside assistance in the form of network ties, were unable to follow suit. The effect inevitably was to relegate the surviving independents--WJBO, WABZ, and WJBW--to even more of a minor league status, and to make the entrance of new broadcasters into the field increasingly difficult.

With the slump in the nation's economy more painfully apparent each passing week, the threshold of entry into the business of broadcasting in a competitive community quickly came to be set at a level virtually unreachable for any but the wealthiest of individuals or organizations. Only in small to medium sized markets without existing or adequate service already available, were good opportunities still to be grasped. In Louisiana, a Monroe businessman such as laundry-owner J. C. Liner, could in July 1930 still successfully establish a KMLB in his own community which lacked any other local station. New Orleans, on the other hand, already served by six competing stations, would see no new facilities activated until after World War II.[28]

The expansion of WWL broadcasting hours was accompanied by a similar expansion of its staff. With the station on the air nearly sixty hours per week, it was physically impossible for Abell to be on duty during the whole period. For that reason, Raymond N. Toups was taken on at the beginning of September 1930 as WWL's second full time employee. Ray Toups' interest in radio had existed for some time. In 1924 he had won a "Freed-Eisemann five tube Neutrodyne" in a New Orleans States-sponsored contest for writing the best 300 word essay on the subject, "Radio in the Home Today--and Tomorrow." Later he worked for a local radio sets and parts dealer. In joining WWL as its first paid "operator," he shared duties with Abell.[29]

One month later another new staff member was hired by Abell, a staff member whose background differed markedly from others involved in New Orleans radio. Arthur C. Pritchard had been born in London in 1887. With the outbreak of World War I, he joined the British Army, quickly rising to the rank of Captain. Wounded in combat and invalided home, he volunteered for a

92

Liberty Bond selling campaign in the United States in
1918. When the Armistice was signed while he was still
touring America, he determined to remain in this country.
He had taken a fancy to New Orleans, one of his tour
stops, and after his discharge in 1919, entered the real
estate business in the city. Possessing a flair for
dramatics as well as a charming English accent, he
soon became involved in local stage productions. It
was in that activity that he first caught Abell's
eye and was induced to join the WWL staff. With the
onset of the depression slowing real estate sales to a
crawl, Pritchard felt he had nothing to lose by testing
the broadcasting waters. "Captain" Pritchard, as he
was universally known, thus became the station's third
full-time employee.[30]

Taken on as a staff announcer, Pritchard rapidly
found himself filling an even more responsible position
as the station's first major internal policy disagreement brought with it a personnel shuffle. Abell later
wrote bitterly of periodic individuals who portrayed
themselves as Moses predestined to lead WWL into a
promised land of radio riches, and who sometimes
successfully were able to convince the University
administration to allow them the chance despite protests
from the station managers. In September 1930 two such
"prophets" appeared in the persons of a former Tulane
football star and a colleague associated with a local
advertising agency.[31]

They proposed to the University administration a
plan whereby at least seven hours per week of sponsored
programming would be guaranteed in return for an even
division of the net income. On November 12, 1930, a
contract between the "time brokers," who in effect
now possessed a lease on the station's available time,
and WWL Development was signed. Pasquet and Abell
vociferously opposed the contract, claiming that the
station was being handed over to men with absolutely
no experience in broadcasting, and pointing out that
"gratifying and encouraging" progress without the use
of time brokers was already being made. When their
protests were ignored, Pasquet resigned in January 1931,
feeling that the contract was an unfavorable reflection
on his own record in the year he had spent as sales
manager of WWL.[32]

Ironically, the brokers followed soon after
Pasquet. By April it had become obvious that they were
unable to deliver on their promises. Only two hours
and seven minutes per week of time had been sold and

the station's billings had plunged to $300 monthly.
As a result the contract was cancelled by mutual consent, but not before serious damage to the station's
income had been done. Never again would WWL avail
itself of the services of time brokers. Indeed time
brokers as a class were being subjected to wide criticism in the industry for the variety of questionable
practices in which many of their type engaged. By the
end of 1931 their role in broadcasting was fast being
reduced, and they themselves were disappearing from the
scene to be replaced by reputable station representative firms.[33]

Following fast upon the conclusion of the broker
episode, a new staff lineup was established at the
station. Father Wallace Burk was formally appointed as
Faculty Director, thus giving that historian the responsibility of serving as the liaison between WWL
Development and the University administration on the
one hand and the station on the other. As Burk later
described the post, he was "in full and absolute control
of the entire operation." Nevertheless, it seems certain
that Burk, long a close friend of Abell's, probably
deferred to the latter on crucial matters involving
the station, especially in the technical or engineering
field. Also gaining new stature in the organization
was Captain Pritchard who now assumed the post of
General Manager, theoretically placing him second only
in authority to Burk. As for Abell, he was limited in
his formal duties to the posts of Technical Director
and Chief Engineer, but in actuality his influence still
touched, if not dominated, all phases of the operation
through his close personal relations with the other
management personnel.[34]

One of Pritchard's first actions as General Manager
was the June appointment of Albert S. Foster as Sales
Manager. Al Foster was to prove a controversial figure
in WWL history, but none would ever doubt he was a born
salesman. Though only twenty-eight, he was already a
radio veteran. At the age of nineteen he had loaded up
an old auto with radio parts in New York City and set
out across the country selling his wares as he went.
A year later he was working as a set salesman for a
large manufacturer, eventually landing in Atlanta where
he found new opportunities with WGST. A successful
record there resulted in his being brought to New
Orleans in 1930 to take over the active management of
WSMB. That station, directed by the hard-driving
E. V. Richards, was ready for a change. Concerned that
it was losing ground to Uhalt's WDSU, the other network

94

affiliate in the city, Richards fired Clyde Randall, who had brought WSMB into being in 1925, and replaced him with Foster. Within a relatively few weeks Foster wrought a substantial number of changes, instilling new life into the Saenger-Maison Blanche enterprise. He purchased a new transmitter, remodeled the studios, and most important, put WSMB on a continuous broadcasting schedule of seventeen hours per day. In commenting upon this show of energy, one newspaper admitted that "the new gang over at WSMB uncorked some big-time ideas about operating a radio station."[35]

Nevertheless, Foster also found himself a victim of Richards' ready axe less than two months after his appointment. The official explanation given was that Foster had only been hired "for construction purposes and was therefore replaced upon the completion of the job." More likely the two men had found themselves incompatible, with the stern Richards being unable to accept Al Foster's free-spending and free-wheeling style. Foster was immediately succeeded by Harold M. Wheelahan, a figure-oriented accountant who had been employed by the Saenger organization even before the founding of WSMB. A private man and a strict, tough executive, Wheelahan would never win a popularity contest with his staff, as Foster well might have; but Wheelahan pleased Richards, instituted tight fiscal procedures at the station, and remained as its manager until well after the Second World War. Foster, meanwhile, was out of a job.[36]

Foster was, therefore, available and interested when Pritchard approached him in the spring of 1931 about handling sales for WWL. Burk, however, was more than a little wary. The Jesuit had heard Foster described as "difficult" and was reluctant to hire a potential problem. It was only after considerable persuasion on Pritchard's part that Burk finally relented. Abell, who would always prove a Foster partisan, certainly lent his potent weight to the Englishman's arguments too. The new Sales Manager was given no regular salary but placed instead on a 25% commission on all business he secured. It was his task now to repair the damage done by the disastrous time broker experiment.[37]

Thus by the middle of 1931 the WWL organization had finally begun to resemble that of larger and more successful stations, and a definite division of labor and responsibility was at last emerging. Further refinements would follow but the essentials were now in place.

A management team had been forged and it was this team of Burk, Abell, Pritchard and Foster that would be required to face W. K. Henderson and to fight the remaining rounds of the clear channel war.

# 8

## DAYLIGHT BURGLARS AND CLEAR CHANNELS

The "Hello World" man was on a rampage. W. K. Henderson, fresh from his victory over the state of Oklahoma, had chosen a new enemy--the nation's retail chain stores--and was storming the barricades of his opposition each evening. His battlefield was 850 kc., and his weapon was KWKH, a broadsword that he wielded with a single-minded determination.

Henderson was the first to employ the medium of radio for a concerted attack on the mushrooming economic phenomenon of chain stores, but he was not the first to raise the issue itself. The Hudson's Bay Company, chartered by the British Crown in 1670, can be regarded as the oldest chain organization in the Western Hemisphere, although most historians trace the beginnings of chain store merchandising in a modern sense to the establishment of the Great Atlantic and Pacific Tea Company's first store in the New York City of 1858. By 1913 A & P was operating over 500 stores, and by 1930 the number had reached a peak of 15,700. The A & P example was copied by firms in nearly every major retail goods category: F. W. Woolworth and S. S. Kresge in limited-price variety stores, Kroger and National Tea in A & P's own grocery line, United Cigar Stores in tobacco products, Walgreen's in the drug field, and others.[1]

In 1929 the Bureau of the Census defined a chain as a grouping of "four or more stores in the same general kind of business, owned and operated jointly, with central buying, usually supplied from one or more central warehouses." The 1929 figures compiled by the Bureau revealed that 10.8% of all retail units in the nation could be classified as chain stores under its definition, but that they accounted for 22.5% of total retail sales. In some fields they completely dominated the trade. About 90% of variety store volume was controlled by chains, almost 50% among shoe stores, and nearly 40% in groceries. In Henderson's own Louisiana, chain store sales in 1929 were just 13.2% of the state's retail total, actually a small percentage when compared with Pennsylvania (24.2%) or New York (23.9%) as well as with the national average. The same pattern of below average market shares held for the other Southern states too. Yet anti-chain store activity gathered its momentum in the rural distrust of these same Southern states, and with the propagandizing of a fiery champion such as Henderson, it "fanned out into the nation as a whole."[2]

As early as 1922, the National Association of Retail Grocers had formally suggested a legal limitation on the number of chain stores in a single community, and Missouri grocers followed-up by securing the introduction of an anti-chain store bill in the next session of their legislature. The bill called for a graduated tax on chain store units, the tax increasing as the number of units multiplied. While the bill did not pass, it did signal the nature of the fight to come during the next decade.[3]

The smaller merchant and his allies leveled a variety of charges against the chains. Among those indictments were the following:

1) Chains impoverished local communities by sending the profits they earned to larger cities, especially New York, and by refusing to patronize local suppliers.

2) They deprived local young men of opportunities for advancement by relying on imported management and by their absentee ownership.

3) They tended toward the creation of monopolies by forcing out competition through unfair trade practices and low wages.

4) They refused to bear their share of the local tax burden.

5) They destroyed the "flavor" of the community by their policies of standardization of goods and marketing practices.[4]

The truth of the various charges was irrelevant; they had the appearance of truth to many Americans and that was sufficient.  Additional anti-chain store measures were debated by state legislatures in the 1920's, reaching a peak in 1927 when no less than thirteen were under consideration, most in Southern states.  Maryland, North Carolina, and Georgia actually saw bills become law.  The Maryland law flatly prohibited the operation of more than five chain stores in a single county and imposed a $500 license fee on the stores as well.  North Carolina also levied a license tax, this one of a more modest $50, on each store operated by a firm with six or more.  Georgia followed the same pattern as North Carolina but set the tax at $250.  Each of the three laws was quickly declared unconstitutional by the appropriate state supreme courts, but the legal reversals did nothing to lessen the general anti-chain store climate.  By 1930 the National Chain Store Association sadly noted that "trade-at-home" campaigns were being carried on in more than 400 communities in the United States, supported principally by the smaller merchants and businessmen of those towns.  It was into this volatile situation that "Old Man" Henderson boldly marched in the fall of 1929, quickly establishing himself as the nation's "most important anti-chain store campaigner."[5]

He later claimed that his actions were prompted by a provocative speech delivered in the fall of 1929 by a local Shreveport banker:  "I was sitting in my office, reading the home paper, when my eye fell upon a speech which had been delivered before one of the city clubs by my fellow townsman," Phillip Lieber.  The speech was titled "The Menace of the Chain Store" and so impressed Henderson that Lieber was invited to give it again, this time using the facilities of KWKH.  According to Henderson:  "This he did.  While he was talking I was so stirred by his words that I could hardly wait for him to come to the end of his address."  When Lieber's remarks were finished, Henderson stepped to the microphone and added "a few of my own in language that would be pretty damn plain."  Henderson's career as an anti-chain store campaigner was thus launched.[6]

Over the months ahead, he devoted little time to anything else.  The affairs of the Iron Works were ignored, ordinary station programming and advertising pushed aside, and the bulk of the available time devoted to "talks on the chain store menace," which he was delighted to find "brought a wonderful response from the masses."  Undoubtedly, he quickly grasped the empathy of a basically rural audience for his populist attacks on large-scale economic enterprises controlled by distant and sinister Eastern interests.[7]

His tirades attracted swift attention, especially because he minced no words in assailing the chains. He castigated them on the air as "dirty low down daylight burglars" and as "damnable low down thieves from Wall Street." He bellowed that he wanted "every damn penitentiary in America to open up and give me all the thieves and burglars they have," and he would "exchange them for the damn chain stores, those college guys that come down from Wall Street to gyp you." Warning listeners that trading with chain stores would cause them to become "slaves of the money crowd," he denounced "the short weight trickery of these contemptible daylight burglars" and called them not price "leaders, but bleeders."[8]

Inevitably, Henderson's abusive language raised questions of propriety on the air, but he only scorned the criticism he received for his salty harangues. Characteristically, he defended himself: "Hell! I have to cuss. My vocabulary is limited and I can't express myself unless I do." He also used the criticism as a point from which to counterattack: "It's a hell of a come off when a man cannot talk about the chain stores.... The newspapers cannot print anything about the truth regarding chain stores. Of course, they take advertising and cannot print anything because they are too damn yellow to print it."[9]

Nevertheless, he could not for long avoid a confrontation with governmental authority. In January 1930, Senator Clarence Dill, by now widely regarded as the watchdog of radio in the Congress, rose in the upper house to express his concern with Henderson's antics. Describing the language used on KWKH as "a disgrace to this country," Dill called upon the FRC to take action. The Senator related that he had been "traveling on a train on Friday night west of Minneapolis, and the radio on the train brought in (Henderson's) swearing and abuse as clearly as though the station had been 20 miles away." According to Dill, "women with children in the car" requested that another station be tuned in. As a result, the legislator felt a duty to the public "to call attention to this abuse of the use of the radio."[10]

Yet despite the existence of a section in the Radio Act of 1927 forbidding the use of "any obscene, indecent, or profane language" on the air, the FRC was

slow to take formal action against Henderson. The
regulatory body exhibited this marked restraint in
part because the 1927 law creating it had specifically
enjoined it from exercising "the power of censorship"
and from interfering "with the right of free speech
by means of radio communications." Further, no adequate standard as yet existed whereby it could have
readily determined whether Henderson had overstepped
the bounds. When told by an irate Dill in a hearing
before the Senate Interstate Commerce Committee that the
language used on KWKH was "billingsgate," the current
FRC Chairman Ira Robinson thoughtfully replied that
billingsgate was probably not a violation of the law.
Questioned more specifically regarding the use of the
words "hell" and "damn" on the air, the core of the
criticism, Robinson admitted that he simply was not
sure they were in fact outlawed by the 1927 act. He
added: "The question is how far can we go in the
matter of censorship and still preserve the liberty of
the people in their right to freedom of speech."[11]

In the practical realm, the FRC could not fail to
recognize KWKH's obvious popularity. A 1930 Radio
Digest poll based on ballots mailed in from listeners
to the nation's various stations had revealed KWKH to
be the "South's Most Popular Radio Station." The
metallic cup shaped like a microphone awarded by Radio
Digest and the attention Henderson was receiving, even
in such establishment periodicals as Nation's Business,
symbolized the political problem faced by the FRC.
Any move to revoke his license or to call upon the
Department of Justice to prosecute the Shreveport broadcaster could result in voter-listeners taking out their
displeasure with a Republican-dominated Commission on
the party itself in an election year. Even Dill was
forced to ruefully admit his criticism of Henderson had
quickly produced "a flood of letters and telegrams to
me from all over the country on both sides of the
question." The cautious Senator felt compelled to
state that his remarks regarding KWKH should not be
interpreted in any way as a defense of chain stores.
The lesson was obvious. Henderson was a "no-win"
political issue, and one best avoided by the prudent
public official.[12]

The Federal Radio Commission, caught in the middle,
chose the mildest of reprimands, the issuance to KWKH
of a thirty day probationary license renewal instead
of the usual ninety days. The move was sufficient,
however, to extract from Henderson a promise of better
behavior and less "cussin" in the future. He telegraphed

Congressman John Sandlin of Louisiana, pledging that he
would refrain from using "hell" and "damn" in his radio
talks though he still did not regard the words as profane in themselves. Dill, attempting to repair some
political damage done to himself by the episode claimed
to "really have done a service to those who want to
permit Mr. Henderson to fight the chain store movement...
because if he had not stopped using language violating
the law he would undoubtedly be taken off the air." The
FRC soon followed with the issuance of a regular license
to replace the probationary grant. It appears probable
that the Henderson experience played a key role in
shaping the standard developed by the FRC and the courts
in the very next year, 1931, a standard that determined
what constituted profanity on the air.[13]

Meanwhile, Henderson had thrown himself completely
into the anti-chain store crusade. He later remembered
that during the winter of 1929-1930 "I remained inside
one building (at Kennonwood) for 38 days, without going
out to the sidewalk, and devoted about 18 hours a day
on the fight against the chain stores." He was soon
considering the purchase of time on "relay stations"
so that listeners in the Northeast and the Northwest,
the only areas not satisfactorily reached by KWKH's
signal, "can be certain of clear reception." He also
transferred the station's ownership from himself individually to a new entity, the Hello World Broadcasting
Corporation, though actual control remained, naturally,
in his hands alone. The transfer was made, in part, to
separate the affairs of KWKH from those of the Iron
Works which had fallen upon hard times. By 1930, as a
result of the early depression and of Henderson's own
negligence, the Iron Works had passed into receivership
with a substantial outstanding debt. He blamed the
financial setback on disloyal and untrustworthy employees
and on the machinations of the chain stores and their
allies: "I was cut off from all financial aid from
banking institutions, for they have crippled me in
every way they could." With the Iron Works in serious
trouble but with the station attracting more attention
than ever, Henderson as President of Hello World Broadcasting had the opportunity to manipulate the affairs
and the revenues of the healthy enterprise to suit the
needs of the distressed firm. The opportunity was not
wasted.[14]

While Henderson never claimed to have initiated the
anti-chain agitation, he did boast that he "hotted it
up." In line with that role and with an eye to his
clouded business affairs, he moved in early 1930 to

establish a nationwide organization to ostensibly assist
him in the chain store struggle. Originally naming it
the "Merchant Minute Men" and later the "Modern Minute
Men," the membership numbered over 32,000 by September 1,
1930. A dues contribution of $12 was required with
about 60% of the total collected by mail in response
to Henderson's constant radio appeals. The remainder
represented the work of bonded agents hired by him to
travel the countryside soliciting candidates for the
organization. The agents worked on commission, keeping
$3 out of each $12 secured from new members. Auxiliary
groups were even formed with women's and youth clubs
created. At the height of the operation, KWKH was employing dozens of girls to handle a flood of mail with
the money contained in the letters placed in barrels ·
in the office until such time as they were full enough
to be hauled to the bank. Some $350,000 had been
collected by the end of the first nine months of 1930.[15]

In October 1930 the first and only national convention of the Merchant Minute Men was held in Shreveport. Henderson sent invitations to each of the 35,000
members of the organization as well as to other selected
individuals, especially prominent politicians who might
be sympathetic. The invitation was signed simply, "Old
Man Henderson." When the first session of the convention was called to order in Shreveport's municipal auditorium, some one thousand delegates from twenty-four
states were said to be present.

The public officials in attendance included the
Governor of Louisiana, Huey P. Long, who proclaimed
that the meeting marked "the beginning of a fight to
end a slavery more far-reaching than human slavery that
existed before the Civil War." Long denounced chain
store operators as "bloated plutocrats" who "grapple
at the throats of the people of America." In their
final session on October 22, the delegates elected
Henderson as president of a renamed "Modern Minute
Men," thus effectively broadening the membership beyond
small merchants, and called upon the FRC to give KWKH,
termed the "mouthpiece of individual thought," power
equal to any station in the country as well as undivided
time on its clear channel. For Henderson it was a
successful meeting though most of the larger newspapers
of the state virtually ignored the proceedings.[16]

The MMM effort was not Henderson's only fund-raising
venture in 1930. He also established something he
titled the "Save Our Roads Club." Again a combination
of radio appeals for dues and traveling membership

drummers was utilized. This time dues was set at a more
modest one dollar figure, of which fifty cents was retained as a commission by any agent inducing a live
prospect to join the body. The villians of the Save
Our Roads effort were truck and bus lines, which
Henderson somehow connected to his other campaign.
Truck and bus operators were vaguely "like the chain
stores waiting for the tax payers, after they had the
bonds voted and sold, that they are in debt for...and
then they come in and destroy our roads and highways,
and at the same time they are destroying our railroads."
Ironically, despite Henderson's populist rhetoric and
his anti-bigness fulminations, the principal backers of
the Save Our Roads project seem to have been the railroads. He later admitted that the Missouri-Pacific, the
Texas and Pacific, and others had made contributions to
the campaign. The total amount collected by the "Club"
in this period averaged $3,000 monthly, not an insig-
nificant figure but considerably less than from the MMM
operation. In neither venture was an accounting of
the money or its use ever made to the membership, and
in all cases the funds were deposited in the name of
the Hello World Broadcasting Corporation with Henderson
free to use it however and for whatever he wished.[17]

A substantial amount of direct selling for products
in which Henderson had a vested financial interest also
began to punctuate his nightly monologues on political
and economic philosophy. One of the most popular items
was Hello World Doggone Coffee, which he lavishly advertised and exorbitantly priced at one dollar per pound
when coffee on grocery store shelves cost only a
fraction of that figure. The coffee can featured a
brown label with red lettering, a picture of Henderson,
a facsimile of his signature, and the legend: "Shreveport on the Air--Shreveport Everywhere." The label
also bragged that the coffee had been "blended from the
highest grades, selected especially for fine drinking
qualities, strength and aroma" and was "guaranteed
100% pure by Radio Station KWKH." Henderson would inform the FRC some months later that he paid 46¢ per
pound for the coffee which was prepared for him by a
Shreveport grocer, and that between February and
September of 1930, he sold 48,953 pounds. When questioned from time to time about the high price of the
product, the broadcaster had a standard reply: "Any
idiot knows a pound of coffee isn't worth a dollar--
you're paying for the picture."[18]

Also marketed on KWKH was a biography of the station's favorite philosopher--The Life of W.K. Henderson--

104

sold at one dollar per copy. The first nine months of
1930 saw almost 5,000 copies purchased by eager fans.
From time to time other items were added to the list of
products: Hello World Syrup, pecan trees, life insurance, real estate, "lucky" elephants carved from ivory
(on which the station received 40% of the cash price of
each sale), and even oil wells in Texas.[19] In 1931
Henderson informed his listeners:

> Some of my good friends, good oil men,
> who has (sic) reliable information about
> this field, have asked old man Henderson if
> we will get together and form an oil company,
> and call it the Hello World Oil Syndicate and
> Development Company. If you want to gamble
> or take a little chance, I believe we can all
> make a little money. This station through
> its announcer and honest old man Henderson
> will see to it that you can't buy over $100
> worth, and we are going to do the best we
> can with your money.[20]

Very little local or national advertising of a
conventional nature was aired by KWKH. Its "Night
School of the Air," as Henderson styled it, was not
especially interested in or conducive to ordinary broadcast marketing. He dreamed larger dreams, and his
answer to those critics who charged that his aims were
not idealistic, but only directed towards helping
W. K. Henderson get rich was a crisp, "Suppose I do?"[21]

* * * * * * * * * *

As a matter of course, Henderson's burgeoning
national reputation was bound to collide with the
limitations of KWKH's time-sharing agreement with WWL.
The Loyola administration was not altogether surprised
therefore when Henderson laid before it a request that
WWL relinquish to him almost all its evening hours in
order that he might more effectively press his anti-
chain store crusade. Henderson's request was swiftly
refused. Burk, Abell, and Sullivan had determined
that Henderson's "language and methods were...beneath
the dignity of a university and of a religious institution." Perhaps equally important, the proposal, when
discussed with New Orleans business and social leaders
close to the school, met with cold hostility. Henderson's antics had won him no friends among the conservative New Orleans establishment. Abell opposed the
overture for an additional reason. The Jesuit felt
any time so given up would be lost to WWL forever, and

105

therefore such a step would be tantamount to a station suicide. As a result he vigorously supported the WWL decision in early 1930 to refuse "in no uncertain terms."[22]

Henderson was not so easily put off. He invited the WWL officials to come to Shreveport and see for themselves the scope of the KWKH operation. Wallace Burk dutifully made the journey in April 1930, but "more in the hope of showing Henderson the unreasonableness of his request...than for any other reason." Burk returned to confirm that the activity at KWKH was indeed hectic with thousands of letters received each day, hundreds of guests visiting the studios in person, and a force of sixty girls employed as office staff. But the WWL decision remain unchanged. In the face of this refusal, Henderson turned to threats. He was through asking for what he regarded as "a reasonable favor," and as he warned in an interview with the University president: "Since Loyola won't give me the time, I'll take it away from you." Sullivan at that point returned ultimatum for ultimatum, promising Henderson that if KWKH filed with the FRC for full-time on the channel and lost its fight, Loyola would immediately itself apply for full-time to drive the Shreveport station off the frequency and, the Jesuit predicted, WWL would win that fight. The second round of the Clear Channel War was about to begin.[23]

True to his word, Henderson promptly asked the Federal Radio Commission for permission to operate full-time on 850 kc., and to install a new 30 kw. transmitter, thus tripling his power. Shrewdly, Henderson determined to base part of his case on supposed technical deficiencies existing in the WWL operation. On June 10, in response to a request from the FRC for an "immediate investigation" of the WWL equipment, Theodore Deiler had filed an evaluation with the Radio Division in Washington. Deiler reported that while the station's programs were "very mediocre," the apparatus was "a very neatly constructed and installed composite installation." He still disapproved of the transmitter being located in a residential section of the city, but readily admitted that overall WWL was being "run in a very high class manner."[24]

The Deiler report fell far short of Henderson's expectations. The Shreveport firebrand was certain that serious deficiencies existed in WWL's technical performance, and an objective investigation would bring them out. He immediately renewed his request for such

a check but this time he pressed "that some other supervisor make a careful inspection of the equipment of the
Loyola station, together with the power they are now
using." The implication was more than clear. Henderson
was charging that the relations between Deiler's New
Orleans field office of the Radio Division and the
University were much too close for complete objectivity
to be maintained. Abell consistently denied any
favoritism existed and, ironically, claimed the reverse:
"As a matter of fact, we have never considered Mr.
Deiler as particularly well disposed towards our station." In the face of the Henderson insinuations, W. D.
Terrell, Radio Division Chief, felt no alternative but
to call for a new inspection of WWL and to ask the
Atlanta office, rather than Deiler's New Orleans office,
to carry it out. It was to prove a contentious step.[25]

Henderson's decision to focus upon WWL technical
problems was astute. Even Abell admitted they did
exist. He had recently installed an improved modulation
system, but the required adjustments were delicate and
"a considerable amount of experimenting had to be done."
As a result, Abell acknowledged, "WWL frequently broadcast on a power considerably below five kilowatts." To
Abell's consternation, however, the Atlanta inspectors
did not wait until after he had corrected the situation
to make their visit. Instead they arrived unannounced
on the evening of July 13, and the station was scarcely
prepared for their coming.[26]

The visitors were Atlanta Supervisor of Radio,
Walter F. Van Nostrand, Jr., and his assistant. When
they entered the WWL transmitter room, they found a
young temporary employee, L. D. Freret, in his first
week at the station, on duty at the controls. Abell
was in the adjoining studio as the on-the-air talent
at that moment. Freret's vague answers to the difficult
questions directed at him by the Radio Division officials,
a quick examination of the equipment, and a determination
that the station was broadcasting that evening with
power of slightly over one kilowatt, far below its
authorized strength, had done the damage before Abell
was able to break away from the program in progress and
intervene. Abell's hurried explanations of the low
power and general condition of the transmitter failed
to impress Van Nostrand. The inspection was over in
less than an hour, and the written report that followed
reflected the disastrous experience.[27]

On July 17 the team from Atlanta filed their
evaluation of the WWL situation. It was a scathing

document. They concluded the transmitter was "very
crude in construction," and even more dramatically,
termed it "a death trap." They noted with alarm that
"none of the equipment is screened or shielded, wire
carrying high voltage all over the room without any
protection, and some of the panel meters are 'hot,'
rendering the equipment exceedingly dangerous to anyone
who enters the room." Van Nostrand recognized, of
course, the disparity between his own report and that
filed a month earlier by Deiler, and he had an explanation for the variance--gross favoritism. In a separate
"additional report" written the following day, he
criticized severely the "very close connection" between
Loyola and Deiler's office, a situation supposedly
compounded by the fact that both Deiler and du Treil
held Master's degrees in science from the University.
Van Nostrand charged further that "Deiler's action in
knowingly permitting Mr. du Treil to maintain such
close contact with this institution and build equipment
for its radio station constitutes gross misfeasance of
office." Even the physical state of Deiler's own
offices were called to account by Van Nostrand who,
after a visit to them, denounced the premises as "in a
filthy and uninviting condition" and as a "disgrace to
the service."[28]

Despite the damning nature of the report, a copy
did not reach the hands of the WWL management until
early September, almost two months after it had been
submitted by Van Nostrand. Only when Charles F. Dolle,
the station's Washington counsel, secured a copy and
forwarded it to Father Sullivan in New Orleans did the
extent of the indictments finally become clear.

Sullivan reacted bitterly, as was to be expected.
He denounced the Van Nostrand report as containing
numerous "inaccuracies" and "unjust and absurd comments,"
and he accused the Atlanta Radio Supervisor of having
"been actuated by an ulterior motive." The Jesuit did
not elaborate on what the unspecified motive might have
been. Moreover, Sullivan called on Deiler to refute the
unfounded charges against WWL. This Deiler was fully
prepared to do for his own competence was in question.
In a September 13 letter to Washington, Deiler admitted
the Loyola station had been operating on low power at
the time of the Van Nostrand visit, but he claimed the
cause was "a defective radio frequency choke, which was
replaced a few days after the inspection." He further
defended the WWL facilities arguing that the composite
transmitter would compare "favorably with some factory
built equipments," and he denied vigorously there was

any real shock danger. According to Deiler, in order
to contact any high voltage, one would have to stand on
a chair and reach behind the panels, an unlikely procedure for the casual observer. Deiler made no reference,
however, to Van Nostrand's "additional report" dealing
with the conduct of the Radio Division's New Orleans
office. It is likely that Deiler had not even been made
aware of its existence yet.[29]

Matters stood thus when an FRC Hearing Examiner,
Elmer W. Pratt, called the parties together on September
22 in Washington for a presentation of evidence and
testimony on the KWKH full-time application. The hearings lacked the "spectacular display," as one newspaper
phrased it, of the KVOO proceedings the previous year,
but the stakes for WWL were just as high. Representing
the station again was Charles Dolle, as he had in 1929,
and traveling to Washington to testify once more were
Burk and Abell. Henderson, as usual, was the center of
the show, and all of the first day's session was taken
up with the direct testimony and the cross-examination
of the Shreveport broadcaster.

He concentrated upon two lines of argument. First,
he contended that WWL was "inadequately equipped and
managed to be permitted to continue use of one of the
forty cleared channels of the nation." To support this
conclusion, he relied heavily upon the Van Nostrand
report. Rather than a clear channel serving a national
audience, WWL was instead, according to Henderson, a
"local" station only with a signal limited to short
distances. He offered to let it share time with a
small Shreveport station he had just acquired a few
months before, KWEA. That station had been the property
of William E. Antony (hence the call letters KWEA),
one of the earliest Louisiana broadcasters and in 1930
KWKH's chief engineer. The license was transferred to
Hello World Broadcasting Corporation in March when the
station was operating on a frequency of 1210 kc. with
the tiny power of 100 watts. Henderson seems to have
picked up the station in part as a favor to Antony and
partly with a view to eventually moving its location
to Baton Rouge, at that time a city without any broadcasting of its own. Secondly, Henderson claimed the
clear channel should be his alone because "the people
want me to have it." He argued that the added power
and time were necessary to carry on his essential
educational campaigns against the various evils
threatening the nation.[30]

The Times-Picayune, no friend to Henderson, decided that he had not made a favorable impression as a witness. The newspaper pointed specifically to numerous "evasions and his flippant answers" while testifying. Abell himself referred to Dolle's cross-examination as "masterly," and certainly it must have been an uncomfortable afternoon for the witness. Dolle was able to bring out the fact that some $151,800 of the funds collected by the various KWKH campaigns had apparently been used to pay off the overdue debt of the Iron Works, rather than for the purpose for which they had been contributed originally. He was also able to show that Henderson had only the haziest ideas as to his station's expenses, overhead, and profits.[31]

On the following day both Burk and Abell testified. The former praised WWL for its use of local talent and for its general avoidance of recordings in its musical programs, neither policy being hallmarks of KWKH's schedule. Burk also noted that "only an insignificant portion of the total time" of WWL was devoted to Catholic subjects, a peripheral matter not really raised in any substantial way as yet by Henderson, and then in a surprising concession, stated that the University stood ready to drop all Catholic-oriented shows from its programming "if the Radio Commission believes the time can be used otherwise to greater advantage, or if there is objection to it from any substantial portion of the public." Earlier, Burk, in an obvious reference to Henderson, denounced "the use of a broadcasting station to array one group of the population against another and to broadcast propaganda material almost exclusively."[32]

Abell's role in the WWL case was to refute as much as possible the evidence contained in the Van Nostrand report. He exhibited blueprints and photographs, cited an approval of the WWL transmitter room by the New Orleans city electrician, and called Van Nostrand's judgment "a gratuitous assumption made after an inadequate inspection." The Atlanta inspector himself, Abell described as "not very well qualified or very familiar with the regulations that he is supposed to enforce." The Times-Picayune, at least, was impressed by Abell's performance, concluding that he had "picked to pieces" the adverse report.[33]

The two days of hearings left unresolved a key issue--the quality of WWL's technical performance. Conflicting evidence had been presented, and some resolution of the question was required before Examiner

Pratt could issue his recommendation to the Commission. Understandably, therefore, a third opinion was sought and another inspection ordered. This time the task was placed in the hands of two other Radio Division staff members, Arthur Batcheller and William J. McDonell. They visited the WWL facilities in early November and submitted their report to Washington the same month. Essentially, in a victory for Abell, they upheld Deiler's original evaluation.

Batcheller and McDonell, unconnected to either the New Orleans or the Atlanta Radio Division offices, found that while "the transmitter proper and wiring are not as neatly installed" as might be desired, the situation did not prevent the apparatus from functioning properly. Regarding the electrical shock threat raised by Van Nostrand, they determined "this equipment is dangerous only in the sense that all high voltage equipment is dangerous to those who enter the room." The new report added: "Persons not having business to transact in the transmitting room are excluded from it," and commented approvingly on "a sign posted on top of the filter bank bearing the inscription 'THINK, 10,000 VOLTS!'" In a separate report Batcheller and McDonell exonerated Deiler of any wrong-doing, declaring that he was "administering the duties of his office in accordance with the general policies of the Radio Division."[34]

The new findings were a body blow to the KWKH case. The only argument of substance which Henderson had put forward in support of his application for full-time was the alleged technical deficiencies existing at WWL. With that position now largely eroded, the weight of the decision shifted to Henderson's own conduct as a broadcaster, hardly the ground upon which he wished the matter settled. Therefore, the recommendation of the Examiner, issued on January 20, 1931, should not have been unexpected. What might have shocked him, however, was the harsh tone of Pratt's opinion. Pratt detailed Henderson's method of operation, agreed that the broadcaster was "an interesting radio personality," and then sliced him to ribbons. Henderson, according to the Examiner, was guilty of using "derisive and abusive language," and of contravening, at least in spirit, the sections of the Radio Act of 1927 dealing with proper on-the-air behavior. Most damning of all, Pratt stated that there was indeed "strong indication that Station KWKH is being used by an ingenious man for the purpose of soliciting funds for his personal aggrandizement and the settlement of his personal obligations." Pratt recommended to the Commission a denial of KWKH's

111

applications for both full-time and the increase in power as not in the public interest.[35]

Henderson's reaction to the Examiner's findings was predictable. In order to sway the Commission to reverse Pratt's verdict, he employed a mixture of public appeals and threats of unilateral action as well as the conventional legal steps, filing exceptions to the Examiner's report and requesting an opportunity to present an oral argument before the FRC members. On the very day the report was made public, Henderson signed a four page blast at the federal government's regulation of broadcasting. Addressed to several members of the United States Senate and inserted into the Congressional Record by Senator Tom Connally of Texas, the letter was an open challenge to Washington.[36]

It began with a denunciation of the "electrical and radio monopoly" and a charge that this combination was being "specially favored by the Radio Commission." Proceeding to describe KWKH as "the only medium of publicity, with reach and spread, that can be relied on and used to combat the present destructive system of monopoly," it pictured a vast conspiracy being organized against the Shreveport station "to limit to the minimum the scope of publicity" available to it. Henderson then quickly shifted to the well-trampled ground of states' rights and portrayed himself as the defender of the true construction of the Constitution. He saw himself in heroic terms: "If the Constitutional right of the National Government to foster and protect monopolistic tyranny can only be resisted and met by offering myself as a burning sacrifice on the altar of liberty and an untrammeled medium of communication, then I say to all enemies of Constitutional Government and the Shylock of the jingling guineas--Come and get me." He proclaimed that the question must be tested, and that he knew no better way to do so "than to disregard the allocation of time and power granted the State of Louisiana."[37]

Henderson's reference to the State of Louisiana was significant. He was depending upon support from the now increasingly famous Senator-elect and Governor of the Pelican State, Huey Long. In a broadcast of January 26, Henderson described Long as being "of the uncompromising conviction that the State of Louisiana cannot...be deprived of the control of the air within the borders of Louisiana." To Theodore Deiler, that support appeared to mean more than simple legal assistance. Deiler warned the Radio Division in Washington that Henderson was boasting the State Militia would be

used to protect KWKH against federal action. Whether
Long ever, in fact, offered the use of the militia for
such a purpose is highly doubtful. No evidence other than
Henderson's post-Pratt fulminations exists for the
offer. Indeed, as will be shown shortly, Long may
actually have been in the process of abandoning the
alliance with the fiery broadcaster and instead drawing
much closer to WWL, the other antagonist in the clear
channel struggle. A break between Long and Henderson
was not far in the future.[38]

Despite his bluster, as the days passed Henderson
made no actual move to violate KWKH's time or power
limitations. As Deiler informed Washington, with no
indication of license violations having taken place, it
was becoming apparent that Henderson had "no intention
of carrying out this plan at the present time." This
conclusion was confirmed by information from one of
Deiler's assistants, Louis McCabe. In mid-February,
McCabe spoke to both Henderson and his lawyer, and the
station owner had not only promised to abide by the
rules but had also been "courteous and cooperative."
It seems clear, therefore, that Henderson's first out-
bursts after the publication of the Pratt report had
been largely for public effect, probably to divert
attention away from the damaging personal evidence contained in the document. In addition, he now faced a
serious threat to his very continuance on the channel.
In keeping with Father Sullivan's original threat and
taking its cue from Pratt's searing indictment of
Henderson's conduct, Loyola had filed an application
of its own, requesting unlimited time on the frequency
as well as an increase in power to 10,000 watts.
Henderson would, for a time, become the courteous
Southern gentleman.[39]

The original application of Hello World Broadcasting
was now referred back to the hearing docket and consolidated with the new WWL application. A hearing date of
June 11 was set, and again Elmer W. Pratt would serve
as the examiner. Once more Abell and Burk traveled to
Washington, this time accompanied by Father Hynes, who
succeeded Sullivan to the University Presidency in
March. Dolle represented Loyola as counsel, as he had
in the 1929 and 1930 proceedings. Since the September
hearings had explored the merits of KWKH's case ex-
tensively enough, those findings were simply made a part
of the new record and the concentration in June 1931
was upon presentation of evidence dealing with WWL.[40]

The WWL officials came armed with resolutions from various New Orleans civic groups endorsing the station's application for full time and enhanced power. The Chamber of Commerce, Board of Trade, and the City Council, among others, supported the request. Financial information was also submitted to prove the station could bear the expense of the higher-powered transmitter. As to programming, Burk testified that preliminary talks had already been held with NBC looking towards WWL becoming a second New Orleans affiliate of that organization. With NBC operating both a Red and Blue network since 1927, the plan was distinctly feasible. However, as Burk admitted ruefully: "They did not think they could hook up with us as a half-time station." The line of argument was clear, unlimited time for WWL would mean more national programs for the city and for the larger area of nighttime coverage.[41]

The discussion of a network link also left an opening for Henderson, and in a pre-hearing affadavit, he pounced upon it. He accurately pointed out that KWKH was the only independent station of ten kilowatts or more on a clear channel in the nation. He then gravely warned that if WWL was granted undivided use of the 850 kc. channel, and that station went ahead with plans for an NBC connection, the result would be "completing the chain broadcasting monopoly to one hundred percent and reducing independent thought and opportunity of education of the people to zero except as a few local stations might broadcast." Henderson raised another significant issue--the nature of Loyola's relation to its broadcasting station. He charged that the University could not have it both ways. It could not portray itself as an educational institution operating a station as a part of its instructional mission while at the same time conducting the affairs of WWL in the same manner as that of any other fully commercial broadcast licensee in the country. He offered statistics attempting to prove that the amount of religious and educational programming carried on KWKH far exceeded that on the University-owned station. Indeed, Henderson placed the "educational" figures for his operation at 42.1% of the total program time while that for WWL at only 10%. Needless to say, there was a question of defining what could legitimately be termed educational. Henderson's figures were delightfully soft in that respect. Nevertheless, he had raised an issue that would haunt WWL again and again over the next quarter century in controversies ranging from the granting of federal income tax exemptions to the awarding of television franchises.[42]

Despite the Henderson arguments, the June 1931 hearings lacked the fireworks of either the KVOO contest of two years before or of the first KWKH-WWL encounter of 1930. Elmer Pratt's second report, made public September 12, represented no substantial victory for either side. The denials of KWKH's twin applications, originally published in January, were continued, as expected. Loyola fared somewhat better. Pratt concluded that the power increase would "promote the economical and efficient use of radio facilities by improving and increasing service on that channel," and Loyola was "financially able properly to construct, maintain, and operate the proposed new transmitter." Taking cognizance of the earlier heat generated over the technical issue, he acknowledged that the present WWL transmitter was "faulty in construction," but he agreed that the proposed new equipment would conform "to modern engineering standards." Not so pleasant news was Pratt's other judgment. He determined that New Orleans already had "an abundance of radio service from a number of stations, and there is not a sufficient showing of a need for more time for WWL to warrant a finding that public interest, convenience or necessity would be served by the granting of the increase in hours of operating requested." He added that there had been an insufficient showing by WWL "of proposed programs or availability of talent" to warrant full-time. The New Orleans station had gotten but half a loaf.[43]

If the WWL management was disappointed in the Examiner's report, their spirits were buoyed by its immediate aftermath. Al Foster, the station's newly hired and aggressive Sales Manager, took the lead. Calling Henderson directly, he invited the Shreveport man to a conference in New Orleans; the subject matter was a new time division. Meeting with Henderson at the Monteleone Hotel were Foster and Captain Pritchard. Their aim was to convince KWKH's owner to turn over to WWL virtually all of the daylight broadcast hours in return for a slight increase in evening time. Foster and Pritchard reasoned correctly that Henderson's ego was massaged sufficiently only by his nighttime national audiences, and that the reduced coverage available during the day bored him. They well remembered his remarks in the 1930 hearings: "I don't fool with it in the daytime. I probably get up in the morning early when they are on the air and say to the housewives, 'Please don't go to the chain stores. This is old man Henderson talking.' And I am through with it then until late in the evening." On the other hand, Foster sensed the enormous commercial potential in those same

daylight hours for a station willing to launch an energetic selling campaign. The exchange, therefore, seemed
desirable. When the conference broke up in the late
afternoon of September 14, Foster had a Henderson signature on a new time-sharing agreement. Delighted with
his accomplishment, he rushed uptown to the University
to secure Hynes' acceptance as well. When the Jesuit
hesitated and asked, "Are you sure this is a good
deal?", Foster replied, "Absolutely!" Abell agreed. He
termed the agreement the foundation of WWL's later
commercial success.[44]

Under the old division, the Loyola station had
broadcast 57 hours weekly, of which some 22 were classified as evening. The new plan allotted WWL almost 85
hours weekly, a nearly 50% programming increase, while
only slightly reducing the nighttime hours from 22 to 17.
The agreement called for KWKH to be on the air from
6:00 A.M. until 8:00 A.M. each morning except Sundays,
and each evening from 8:30 P.M. until midnight (7:45 P.M.
until midnight on Sundays). Meanwhile, WWL would have
unbroken control of the entire period from 8:00 A.M.
until 8:30 P.M. six days per week, and from 10:00 A.M.
until 7:45 P.M. on Sundays. The solid blocks of time
offered enormous opportunities for a shrewd and dynamic
Sales Manager, and Al Foster was well qualified to
recognize and to take advantage of the possibilities.
The time-sharing contract was to be in force for a
minimum of one year, and could be renewed.[45]

While the agreement still did not make a network
affiliation possible, it did pave the way for a more
profitable operation as an independent. Moreover, it
lessened considerably the disappointment with the
FRC's long-awaited decision in the clear channel case.
That ruling was handed down on December 4, 1931. It
contained few surprises, as the Commission upheld
Examiner Pratt on each point at issue. Repeating
nearly verbatim every critical comment on the KWKH
operation made by Pratt, it forcefully rejected that
station's now hopeless applications. Yet at the same
time, while approving a power increase, it did not
grant WWL's petition for unlimited time, arguing, as
did the Examiner, that the New Orleans broadcasters had
"failed to show that sufficient program material is
available to insure the successful full time operation."
Hidden between the lines of the decision was the implication that if WWL bolstered its proposal in the programming area, the FRC might well look with favor on
another application. It was plain that Henderson had
little to hope for from another journey to Washington,

116

and that he had been fortunate to retain his license at all.[46]

One might indeed question why, in view of the evidence, the Commission had not already taken such a step.  Part of the explanation, perhaps, lay in the fact that the evidence itself may not have seemed entirely conclusive.  Henderson, in effect, was being given the benefit of the doubt.  Not to be overlooked also were the obvious political considerations involved in revoking the license of as popular a broadcaster as the Shreveport radio maverick.  The regulation of broadcasting has always been, in the words of a recent study of the subject, an "intensely political process," and the FRC particularly, according to one observer, "operated on a level only slightly above that of the old-fashioned ward heelers."[47]

Just as important, however, was the vulnerable legal and constitutional position of the Commission in these years.  The Radio Act of 1927 had been "a far more daring legal experiment than generally has been recognized."  Passed in an era when governmental regulation of economic enterprise was hardly in high favor, the FRC's authority was constantly being challenged in the courts.  During the seven years of its existence, federal judges decided some sixty controversies involving the FRC, two-thirds of them touching upon the agency's basic power to regulate broadcasting at all. An especially debatable issue was the right of the Commission to revoke existing licenses because of the past performances of licensees.  Not until appeals by the owners of stations in Kansas and California were denied by the Court of Appeals for the District of Columbia in 1931 and 1932, was it a settled point of law that an FRC refusal to renew a license did not deny an owner his First Amendment rights of free speech. Thus at the time the KWKH-WWL struggle was taking shape, the FRC had yet to firmly prove itself in the courts. The Commissioners were still slow to use the ultimate power of withdrawing broadcast permits.[48]

As for the two Louisiana stations, the September 1931 time-sharing agreement marked a cessation of hostilities.  But the period that followed was to be only a truce, not a final peace; more rounds in the Clear Channel War were yet to be fought.  In the meantime WWL's management would be concentrating upon preparations for ten kilowatt operations, preparations that once again would involve a shift to new quarters.

117

## THE ACHE AND PILL STATION OF THE NATION

The decision to expand WWL operations in 1932 contained equal measures of vision, courage, and fool-
hardiness.  The nation was then mired in a deepening
depression and economic statistics were dismal.  The
New York Times' "Weekly Index of Business Activity,"
which had stood at 114.8 in June 1929, plummeted to a
low of 63.7 by early 1933, and the number of unemployed
in the land ranged upwards of fifteen million.  One
writer said of the depression:  "It was like a raw wind;
the very houses we lived in seemed to be shrinking,
hopeless of real comfort."[1]

The times offered no brighter prospects in Louisiana.
Like most states of the Deep South, Louisiana had not
shared significantly in the business prosperity of the
1920's, and the depression only aggravated an already
distressed condition.  Per capita income was slashed
from a poor 1929 figure of $415 to a disastrous $239 in
1932.  Louisiana farmers who had received just $170
million for their crops in 1929, were forced to settle
for only $59 million in 1932.  And the New Orleans
experience was little better.[2]

At first the city fathers assumed an optimistic
stance, bravely claiming that the business depression
had less impact on the South than on any other section.
But my mid-1930, the signs of trouble were unmistakeable.
Letters to the editor began to frequently appear in the
daily newspapers commenting upon the unemployment problem, sometimes offering crank solutions.  In December
1930 Mayor T. Semmes Walmsley put forward his own
solution--an orange selling campaign.  For just $2.70
a box, "carefully selected needy persons" would be
allowed to purchase oranges which they in turn were
permitted to peddle on busy corners for whatever profit
they could earn.  Within the month over 250 vendors were
in business on New Orleans' streets.[3]

Stronger action was obviously necessary. Retail
sales in the city by 1933 had eroded to 62% of their 1928
level and spendable income in 1932 declined by almost
60% from four years before. Unemployment was above
the national rate and the average wages of factory
workers who still retained their jobs were calculated
at less than an "emergency budget" for a family of four.
In early 1931 the Mayor formed the New Orleans Welfare
Committee, a body whose purpose was the provision of
relief and the finding of work for the unemployed. By
the summer of 1932 the Committee was providing part-
time employment for some two thousand jobless men. The
work consisted principally of grading streets, mowing
lawns, and collecting rubbish. The make-work projects ·
were invariably inadequate in the fact of the massive
problem, as the depression in New Orleans was "sharper
and more severe" than in other major Southern cities and
in the nation as a whole.[4]

Broadcasting, however, suffered less dislocation
than other American industries as the audience for its
product continued to swell. The number of radio sets
in use in the United States in the depression year of
1932 reached eighteen million, twice the figure of
just four years before. The hard times did stabilize
the number of stations in the nation with only 604 active
licensees in 1932, a slight decrease from each of the
two preceding years but a sharp drop from the 1927 high
of 681. The major impediment to the investment of new
capital, in short supply already in view of the prostrate
condition of the overall economy, was the high threshold
of entry into an industry characterized by its technological nature.[5]

For a five kilowatt station in 1931, invested
capital averaged nearly $170,000 and equipment alone
$80,000. Annual maintenance costs, including salaries
and replacement parts, represented an additional burden
of some $20,000. An increase in power to ten kilowatts,
such as WWL was about to undertake in 1932, meant even
higher dollar amounts. Further, there was no guarantee
of profits if the necessary investment was made. A
1932 Federal Radio Commission survey revealed that over
one-third of the country's stations reported losses
rather than profits in their operations. Significantly,
the loss rate was nearly 40% for stations using five
kilowatts or more of transmitter power. For the industry as a whole, gross receipts declined during the
first four years of the decade, reflecting the general
state of the economy, but by 1934 a turnaround was at
last experienced.[6]

With the public's continued purchasing of receiving
sets, with broadcasting usurping a mounting share of
the advertising revenues formerly enjoyed by the print
media, and with the Federal Communications Commission,
established as the FRC's successor in 1934, forcing new
license applicants to prove that a particular market
could indeed support an additional station without
rendering economic damage to existing licensees (thus
effectively discouraging many new entrants), the later
depression years brought smiles to the faces of industry
accountants. The broadcasters' rate of return on investment rose from 11% in 1934 to 23% by 1939. Thus if a
station owner could survive the setbacks of the early
1930's, better days would soon be on the way. The result
was a substantial reward for owners with grit and vision.
The decision-makers at WWL fell into both categories.[7]

The Loyola station's own figures for 1931 showed
a slight profit of $463 for the year, and billings
reached $24,200. Much of the overall sales gain was the
result of the persistent efforts of the new sales manager,
Al Foster, who tramped Canal Street from end to end,
calling upon every possible business prospect. One of
his earliest successes was a $1,500 contract with the
Krauss department store, not only WWL's largest to that
date but also an effective wedge in convincing other
concerns to sign as well.[8]

Without a chain connection, however, WWL remained
a struggling independent, inevitably destined to an
also-ran position behind the local network affiliates.
In early 1932 Price, Waterhouse & Co. carried out a
CBS-ordered nation-wide "audit" to determine relative
station popularity in every major market. The firm of
public accountants mailed questionnaires to names chosen
at random from the phonebooks of seventy-two cities.
Each questionnaire asked the respondent for the call
letters of the stations to which he regularly listened.
Price, Waterhouse termed the results "the only adequate
measure of station preference." For New Orleans, the
single Louisiana city surveyed, the data was not surprising. WSMB led the field as 86.1% of the replies
listed that NBC affiliate as regularly heard. Close
behind was the CBS station, Uhalt's WDSU, with a mark
of 82.5%, but the gap between the two leaders and their
remaining competitors was staggering. WWL held third
place, but its 23% was unimpressive in the light of the
WSMB and WDSU figures. Even weaker were the showings
of WJBO (18.2%), WABZ (4.8%), and WJBW (1.9%). The
Price, Waterhouse audit did not measure, of course,
WWL's non-local coverage. Its five kilowatt signal

and clear channel guaranteed it a rural, evening audience that other weaker-powered New Orleans stations, including the network affiliates, could not reach. Yet for local sponsors, the New Orleans market alone was significant, and therefore the independents faced a difficult path to survival, much less any substantial success.[9]

The WWL planners had no taste for the hazardous road of the independent. Discussions with NBC, as described earlier, had already begun, and only the shared-time status with KWKH seemingly prevented a satisfactory conclusion of the arrangements. Recognizing that clear fact, the New Orleans management was continuing to press the struggle with Henderson for complete control of the Louisiana clear channel. As Abell candidly admitted: "Full-time meant a good chain contract, and a chain contract meant a quick road to better programs, a better class of business and large financial returns." Both Abell and Burk regarded such a contract as inevitable, especially in view of the station's newly authorized ten kilowatt strength, and they soberly predicted that the operation could eventually produce an annual net income to the University of $100,000 or more. They were especially vehement in their opposition to the periodic suggestion, made both by outsiders and by members of the Loyola community itself, that the station be sold for whatever immediate price it might bring. Abell particularly deplored the fact that too many voices in the University "woefully undervalued the possibilities of WWL as a money-maker." He did not.[10]

In the meantime, as an independent, WWL would garner all the business, both local and national, that it could in order to earn acceptable profits. In this regard, the rates it charged national advertisers had increased substantially since the first published figures in 1929. In fact, they had basically doubled and become more complex. National advertising rates for WWL time, as of October 1, 1931, stood at the following:[11]

(6:00 p.m. to 8:30 p.m.)

|  | 1 time | 13 times | 26 times | 39 times | 52 times |
|---|---|---|---|---|---|
| 1 hour | $300.00 | $285.00 | $270.00 | $255.00 | $240.00 |
| 1/2 hour | 180.00 | 171.00 | 162.00 | 153.00 | 144.00 |
| 1/4 hour | 108.00 | 102.60 | 97.20 | 91.80 | 86.40 |

(5:00 p.m. to 6:00 p.m.)

|  | 1 time | 13 times | 26 times | 39 times | 52 times |
|---|---|---|---|---|---|
| 1 hour | 210.00 | 199.50 | 189.00 | 178.50 | 168.00 |

| | | | | | |
|---|---|---|---|---|---|
| 1/2 hour | 126.00 | 119.70 | 113.40 | 107.10 | 100.80 |
| 1/4 hour | 75.60 | 71.82 | 68.04 | 64.26 | 60.48 |

(8:00 a.m. to 5:00 p.m.)

| | | | | | |
|---|---|---|---|---|---|
| 1 hour | 180.00 | 171.50 | 162.00 | 153.00 | 144.00 |
| 1/2 hour | 108.00 | 102.60 | 97.20 | 91.80 | 86.40 |
| 1/4 hour | 64.80 | 61.56 | 58.32 | 55.08 | 51.84 |

A new category of "Announcements" was also added
and described as one hundred words to the minute with a
minimum of one minute and a maximum of five. For these
a separate set of rates were published:[12]

### Night Rates

| | 1 time | 13 times | 26 times | 39 times | 52 times |
|---|---|---|---|---|---|
| 5 minutes | $35.00 | $33.25 | $31.50 | $29.75 | $28.00 |
| 3 minutes | 25.00 | 23.75 | 22.50 | 21.25 | 20.00 |
| 1 minute | 15.00 | 14.25 | 13.50 | 12.75 | 12.00 |

### Day Rates

| | | | | | |
|---|---|---|---|---|---|
| 5 minutes | 21.00 | 19.95 | 18.90 | 17.85 | 16.80 |
| 3 minutes | 15.00 | 14.25 | 13.50 | 12.75 | 12.00 |
| 1 minute | 9.00 | 8.55 | 8.10 | 7.65 | 7.20 |

These rates were somewhat higher than those charged
national advertisers by WWL's major New Orleans competition. The disparity reflected the Loyola station's
greater coverage, especially in the evening hours. WDSU
was still operating with one kilowatt of power while
WSMB yet retained its original 500 watts, and neither
were broadcasting on a cleared channel. But in the hands
of the aggressive Al Foster, rate cards meant little.
Foster was more than willing to "go off the card" and
make whatever bargain he could with a prospective
sponsor.[13]

In doing so, Foster was following practices that
had become endemic in the industry. Small independents,
faced with dimming financial prospects in the depths
of the depression, were especially willing to accept
accounts at virtually whatever figures sponsors might
dictate. The economic strain also prompted station
managers to agree to carry advertising of doubtful
quality and honesty. Patent medicines were thus given
a new lease on life in the early 1930's. Reputable
newspapers and magazines throughout the nation had
ceased to carry such dubious copy, but hard-pressed
broadcasters preferred to choose survival over high

standards.  In 1929 the National Association of Broadcasters issued its first important statement on radio
advertising.  The pronouncement included a promise to
refuse "fraudulent, deceptive, or obscene" copy and a
pledge to exercise "great caution in accepting any
advertising matter regarding products or services
which may be injurious to health."  Nevertheless, in
an era when few broadcasters belonged to the Association,
the NAB's power to influence industry actions was
slight.  Not until after the establishment of the
Federal Communications Commission in 1934 and a crack-
down by that agency, were the stations pressed to
tighten their sales policies.  It may also be noted
that the belated clean-up campaign was simultaneous
with a generally brightening profit picture in the
industry, thereby allowing a fresh devotion to the
public interest to work no damage to the income potential of radio properties.[14]

Another form of questionable practice introduced
in these years was payment by accounts "per inquiry"
or "P.I.," as it was termed.  Under this system the
station was compensated on the basis of the number of
inquiries it received as a result of broadcasting the
advertiser's appeal, rather than at its usual time card
rates.  In a typical situation, a station might be paid
fifteen cents for each request for a product sample
resulting from the airing of an announcement or a
sponsored program.  In this way the broadcaster's
ordinary charges for time were completely nullified, and
he found himself selling access to his facilities not
on the basis of the real worth of that access, but
instead on the basis of a fluctuating measure of value
over which he could exercise only partial control at
best.  Further, the type of product usually offered in
this mode served only to bring it to added disrepute.[15]

The fruits of Al Foster's diligence as WWL sales
manager were the acquisition of a substantial number of
these patent medicine and P.I. accounts, many of them
associated with country music performers, who were
dubbed in the idiom of the time, "hillbillies."  The
volume of such accounts rose sharply after the inauguration of the ten kilowatt transmitter in 1932, with
the result that WWL was soon scornfully labeled by its
competitors "the ache and pill station of the nation."

Standard practice, in the words of one WWL
employee of the period, was to "promote the hell out
of the P.I. items," particularly if the mail response,
by which the station's fee would be determined, was

slow in coming. The product would be pushed throughout
the day, and especially on the evening hillbilly music
programs that were most effective in reaching the large
and distant rural audience. The Loyola authorities were
more than a little discomforted by the direction programming and advertising on the station had taken, and
from time to time Father Hynes, the University's President, expressed himself on the subject to Pritchard.
The latter recalled that Hynes often complained of "too
much of this patent medicine business" and of the country
music format. Pritchard's continuing rejoiner was to
point to the rising income figures of the broadcasting
operation and to explain that "people who buy patent
medicines only want to listen to hillbillies." Hynes
would leave less than satisfied but reluctantly
acquiescent.[16]

The nature of the patent medicine, P.I. commercials
carried can be seen in the following two samples from
WWL advertising copy of the early 1930's:

> If you are one of the many folks bothered
> with disagreeable colds all the time, the
> kind that go from one right to another, and
> cheat you out of a lot of fun, make a resolution
> that you are goin' to do somethin' that may
> make your life happier, more enjoyable--
> that you're goin' to give Peruna a chance
> just to see if it won't help you, as so many
> others say it has helped them to spend entire
> winters free from bad colds. You see, Peruna
> is a tonic that helps build up cold-fightin',
> cold-chasin' resistance so you may dodge
> bad colds. If you have a cold now, take
> Peruna to help build up your cold-chasin'
> resistance so it may not only knock out the
> torture of your present cold, but also try to
> keep free from bad ones in the future. Your
> druggist can supply you with a large sized
> bottle. Your money back if you're not
> satisfied with the results. If you'd like,
> a generous sample bottle of Peruna will be
> sent to you absolutely free. Just send your
> name and address to Peruna, care of WWL. Give
> the Peruna way a chance to knock out the
> torture of colds and to help you stay free
> from bad colds the rest of the winter. Think
> of it. You can get all this simply by sending
> in a penny postcard to Peruna. So be sure and
> send for yours today.[17]

Friends, if you are suffering from
stomach trouble, due to excess acid, I want
you to have Willard's Message of Relief.
This vital message explains the marvelous
Willard Treatment, for heartburn, poor
digestion, poor appetite, acid dyspepsia,
gassiness and stomach ulcers that are due to
or persist because of excess acid. If such
stomach trouble results in headaches or loss
of sleep; if you are unable to eat the foods
you need, because you're afraid of the pain
and misery they may cause; if these conditions
interfere with your work, and perhaps with
your earning power, then you owe it to your-
self and to your family, to get this helpful
message and find out about the remarkable
Willard Treatment. This unique formula has
brought definite relief to stomach sufferers
all over the United States. Well, no matter
how long you have suffered or what you may
have tried in the past, remember this...you
must get relief, you must get satisfactory
relief, or the Willard Treatment won't cost
you one penny. Be sure to read the money-
back agreement. Friends, you have everything
to gain, and nothing to lose, so if you
suffer from stomach trouble, due to excess
acid, I urge you to get Willard's Message at
once, and read it over in the quiet of your
own home. I will be glad to send it to you,
without cost, without obligation. Simply
drop me a postal card or letter asking for
Willard's Message, and this valuable booklet
will be sent to you, free, through the mail.
Remember the address--Willard's Messenger,
in care of WWL, New Orleans.18

Whether the product was Peruna, the Willard Treatment, or Grove's Tasteless Chill Tonic, as well as many
others, the image of the station underwent a considerable
change. Programming dominated by amateur performers
and salon music had, in the space of less than two years,
given way to a rural and regional orientation in both
advertising and entertainment. By 1934 WWL's logs
were populated by Lou Childre and Wiley Walker, country
singers who billed themselves as the Crazy Water
Crystal Boys; Jerry Behrens, the Yodeling Guitarist;
Tex Cole and his Drifting Cowboys; the Four Crazy
Hickory Nuts; J. E. Mauney and his Caroline Ramblers;
the Country Break-Downs; the Fiddling Bees; Smiling
Henry Berman's Village Barn; and perhaps most popular

126

of all--the Pickard Family. The latter were a long-time
fixture in the WWL schedule and attracted an enormous
audience response. During one Christmas season, a
picture of this family of country music singers was
offered to their listeners in exchange for a Peruna
boxtop. It produced a flood of mail, including 7,000
letters in a single day, the largest number received
by any performers on the station prior to World War II.[19]

What strides WWL's management was making in developing the revenue potential of the broadcasting operation,
were made without the support of the city's newspapers.
In this respect the New Orleans experience duplicated
that of other communities. The decade of the 1920's
had been the "friendly" period in newspaper-radio
relations, an era in which publishers laid stress on
the different appeals of the two media and on the
possibility of actually using radio to promote circulation. One newspaper executive conjectured that it
would be of benefit by "creating more and more of a
demand for the complete facts which are briefly touched
upon in radio broadcasts." Moreover, cooperation
probably was mutually beneficial since there seems
little doubt that the rapid growth of broadcasting
during the Twenties was due in no small part to the
newspaper publicity given the new medium.[20]

Even within the friendly period, some voices were
raised in warning. In February 1922 the Associated
Press advised its members against allowing wire service
news to be broadcast by radio. The admonition was without effect; too many newspaper members of the A.P. also
owned or had working relationships with emerging stations. Three years later the American Newspaper Publishers' Association moved more directly to the heart
of the problem. Taking cognizance of a trend toward
the commercialization of broadcasting, it self-servingly
declared at its 1925 annual meeting that "direct advertising by radio is likely to destroy the entertainment
and educational value of broadcasting and result in the
loss of the good-will of the public." It called upon
ANPA members to refuse to publish "free publicity" on
sponsored programs. Within months newspapers in New
York City acted, organizing a boycott of radio news and
requiring program schedules to be placed only in paid
advertisements. Nevertheless, favorable income
statistics overcame all misgivings during the decade.
The newspaper share of the advertising revenues amassed
by all media had in fact risen from 70% in 1919 to 80%
in 1928, and in the latter year, radio's share was a
skimpy 1.4%. No serious challenge had been posed as
yet.[21]

With the advent of the depression, however, attitudes abruptly changed. In the face of the economic slump, many advertisers reduced expenditures for newspapers while those for radio continued to climb. Publishers inevitably concluded that radio's growth had been a major contributor to their own losses. One later analyst has agreed and suggested the more intensive audience research done by broadcasters, a recognition by advertisers that the editorial position of newspapers and public opinion were increasingly at variance, the belief that radio was "depression-proof" since it was a cost-free form of entertainment for its audience, and the rigidity of print journalism's space rates in the 1930's, were largely responsible for the alteration in media competition. The radio share of gross advertising spending rose from 1.4% in 1928 to 6.6% in 1931 and to 12.3% in 1935. By 1939 the figure had reached 19.8% and, for the first time, surpassed magazines.[22]

A special problem arose over the subject of radio news. Radio had begun beating the press at the latter's own game--the rapid reporting of fast-breaking news stories. The old-fashioned special edition was all but completely eliminated by the bulletins broadcasted by station announcers. Eventually, newspaper owners would learn that when major events were reported on the air, the brief bulletins actually whetted the public's appetite for the additional details which only a printed story could provide. But for the moment, war rather than co-existence seemed the order of the day.[23]

This concern over radio's intrusion into the reporting of news was the predominant issue at the 1931 meeting of the ANPA. Again the Association urged its members "to make broadcasting stations pay for the publication of their programs," but it also added a call for "a conference with the great news-gathering agencies to devise a means of restricting the broadcasting of news to the newspapers and the agencies." On December 11-12, 1933, an even broader conference than that envisioned by the publishers was finally held at the Biltmore Hotel in New York City. Representatives of the ANPA, the various wire services, and the two broadcasting networks participated and formulated the so-called "Biltmore Program." Slated to go into effect on March 1, 1934, the plan established a Press-Radio Bureau from which stations were to receive sufficient news to fill a single five minute broadcast in the morning and a second in the evening. Each broadcast

was to be unsponsored. Only bulletins of "transcen-
dental importance" would be furnished for airing at
other times of the day.[24]

While the Biltmore agreement bound the network-
owned stations, it could not control independents or
even all the local chain affiliates, and upon that rock
it foundered. Rebel services such as Transradio Press
were quickly established to supply news to those stations that refused to conform. Further, the agreement
quickly came under the hostile scrutiny of Washington.
The ever-present Senator Clarence Dill denounced it as
"a failure" that "satisfies nobody because it flies
in the face of progress." He pointed out that local
broadcasters were "trying all sorts of schemes to furnish news by radio in violation of the spirit of the
agreement." Ultimately, the Press-Radio Bureau concept
collapsed in the face of its opposition. By 1935 the
United Press and the International News Service had
withdrawn and chosen instead to sell material directly
to stations for sponsored broadcasts, thus precluding
any possibility of the Bureau's success. While the
episode was a fiasco of sorts, it demonstrated the
panic experienced by the traditional print media in its
competition with the upstart radio industry.[25]

Much the same trepidation was exhibited by
Southern journalists in the early depression years.
In 1931 the Advertising Committee of the Southern
Newspaper Publishers Association recommended that "radio
programs be classified as paid advertising, and so
marked." Twelve months later the SNPA was clamoring for
the wire services to discontinue furnishing news to
broadcasters. The New Orleans experience evolved
similarly. Throughout the 1920's close relations had
existed between the two media, with the newspapers
having been responsible, as described earlier, for
bringing into being some of the city's first stations.
Again in 1927, the States had played a role in the
establishment of WDSU, the first CBS affiliate in New
Orleans. By March 1931, however, the States had broken
with Uhalt and WDSU and was seeking new radio ties. It
found them temporarily in Loyola's WWL. An arrangement
was reached whereby Thomas Ewing Dabney, a popular
States newspaperman, would also become WWL's "official
News Commentator." Utilizing copy from the States,
Dabney handled two fifteen minute news programs daily,
each carried directly from a small remote studio constructed by Orie Abell himself in the newspaper's own
downtown building. The innovation proved relatively
popular as Dabney, who possessed an effective radio

personality, gradually won an increasing following.
But then the city's dailies, following the lead of press
associations and publishers nationally, reversed their
policies and imposed a publicity blackout.[26]

On June 10, 1932, the journalistic axe fell on
radio in New Orleans. On that day, and without any
advance warning to their readers, the newspapers of the
community ceased carrying any information about radio--
no news articles, no radio columns, no station schedules--
in short, broadcasting as an activity no longer existed.
Though none of the three managements publicly acknowledged the fact, it was patently clear that the States,
the Item, and the Times-Picayune had agreed beforehand
on a common policy. There is some indication that not
only had an understanding been reached among them, but
that it was also enforced by a sizeable penalty (rumored
as $10,000), to be forfeited by the newspaper that
first broke the pact and carried any non-paid radio
information.[27]

Remonstrances were to no avail; the publishers
appeared unyielding. Pritchard approached the Times-
Picayune executives on behalf of WWL, arguing the
station's connection to the University placed it in a
different category than the usual broadcasting enterprises, but with no success whatsoever. The blackout
continued. The newspapers seemed determined to place
their economic woes on radio's shoulders. All had
suffered from the deepening depression--advertising space
sold in the Times-Picayune, for example, had decreased
from 20 million agate lines in 1926 to barely over 11
million in 1933. Circulation for all the daily papers
had declined as well. The States, already buffeted by
the death of its long-time publisher, Colonel Robert
Ewing, in April 1931, would shortly find itself in
such difficult straits that it would sell its entire
operation to the Times-Picayune in July 1933. Thereafter,
the latter newspaper corporation continued the publication of the States, but with a business policy
common to that followed by the parent organization.[28]

The only cracks in the blackout were paid advertisements inserted by the stations themselves or their
supporters. Maison Blanche, the major department store
holding a substantial interest in WSMB, quickly utilized
its regular retail advertising to publicize the station.
A cryptic log was carried, listing programs and times
amid the displays of the usual merchandise of the store.
In later months, the retailer used separate small boxed
ads, labeled "By Courtesy of Maison Blanche," to convey

the program information. The same technique was
employed by WDSU, utilizing the advertising of another
of the area's department stores, Feibleman's, an operation associated with the Sears-Roebuck chain. Again
only the most cryptic data was included, but the very
appearance of the listings served the purpose of at
least confirming the continued existence of the station.

WWL was unable to employ any business concerns to
act for it in this fashion. Occasionally, a notice
would be placed in a newspaper promoting a single program, with the item paid for by the sponsor. Again
occasionally, the full schedule for a particular day
would be displayed in a small, boxed ad accompanied by
the brief statement: "Paid For by Friends of WWL."
Aside from these irregular items, no significant journalistic notice was taken of the Loyola station for more
than two years.[29]

Not until May 24, 1934, was unpaid radio information again carried, and then only for the two network
affiliates, WSMB and WDSU. Just as suddenly as it had
been dropped in 1932, the program data, without prior
warning, appeared again. Only the barest essentials were
printed, the time and the name of the show, usually
without elaboration or enthusiasm. The listings were
often incomplete--the Times-Picayune titled its version,
"Highlights of Radio," and the Item, "Best Spots on the
Air." Because the schedules were incomplete, for some
months after the re-appearance of the free radio data,
Maison-Blanche and Feibleman ads continued to be employed as publicity vehicles for their respective
stations. This partial lifting of the blackout seemed
directly connected to the creation of the ill-fated
Press-Radio Bureau. That body's operations began in
the spring of 1934 after the Biltmore conference had
repaired relations between publishers, wire services,
and networks. In recognition of the modus vivendi,
the affiliates of the networks in New Orleans were
once again publicly acknowledged. No other local
stations, however, were given such recognition in 1934;
WWL would have to wait until well into 1935 for such a
lofty concession and the smaller independents years
longer.

For WWL the blackout came at a particularly troublesome time. Just as its managers had come to believe
that the station had finally passed through adolescence
and was entering young adulthood with the inauguration
of the 10,000 watt transmitter in 1932, it was unable
to secure any significant publicity for the event.

131

Even though New Orleans broadcasters were supporting a
small weekly periodical called Radio Time in order to
counter the effects of the newspaper actions, the effort
was inadequate. Radio Time carried complete schedules
for all of the city's stations, but its distribution
inevitably fell far short of the circulation of the
major metropolitan papers. Thus the substantial publicity that stations received in the 1920's was absent
completely in the fall of 1932 when WWL began its ten
kilowatt service. Outside of a single congratulatory
advertisement inserted in the States by a WWL account,
the Krauss department store, the event passed unnoticed
in the regular press.[30]

Preparations for the event had begun considerably
earlier, immediately after FRC approval of the power
increase in December 1931. A necessary first step was
the purchase of a ten kilowatt transmitter, since
Loyola had promised the Commission that the equipment
utilized this time would be modern and factory manufactured, not a jerry-built composite as in the past.
Burk and Abell opened negotiations with both RCA and
Western Electric, and shrewdly placed the two giant
organizations in the position of bidding against each
other for the WWL contract. RCA was especially anxious
to win the battle since it had previously sold no transmitters in the Gulf states region. Western Electric,
on the other hand, had equipped WDSU and WSMB, though
each of those installations was smaller than the WWL
specifications. The victor in the contest proved to be
RCA with whom a contract was signed in January 1932.
The price for the transmitter along with associated
studio and remote equipment was $59,000. The pur-
chaser was WWL Development, then undergoing a reorgani-
zation of its own.[31]

The three Standard Fruit employees who claimed
nominal membership on the WWL Development board since
1929 were now replaced, and a new board of directors
created representing a broader spectrum of the city's
business community. Assuming the posts of directors
were Andrew Fitzpatrick, John Legier, Larz A. Jones,
Edward E. Lafaye, and Charles I. Denechaud. Each held
a token single share of WWL Development stock, while
the University held forty-five shares in its own name.
Fitzpatrick, a prominent New Orleans banker, accepted
the presidency of the new board. John Legier, who
became the board's treasurer, was a banker and a lawyer
as well. A particularly strong voice in the body was
supplied by Edward E. Lafaye, a former Commissioner of

132

Finance for the city of New York and a successful wholesale coffee dealer. Larz Jones headed two regional railroads, the Alabama and Vicksburg and the Vicksburg,
Shreveport and Pacific. Charles I. Denechaud's connection
with Loyola was destined to be a lengthy one. Born in
New Orleans, he had attended the downtown Jesuit College
and then received a Tulane law degree in 1901. He served
as a legal counsel for the University from its 1912
chartering until his death in 1956. His would be a major
role in shaping overall WWL policy, and in protecting
the station's interests in a succession of legal battles.
In 1932 he was elected secretary of the revamped board
of directors.[32]

Representing a wider segment of the New Orleans
business establishment, the board was in a position
to serve as an effective advisor to the station's management when called upon, and also to evaluate the quality
of managerial success. Day to day decision-making,
naturally, continued in the hands of the Faculty
Director and the Station Manager. Indeed, Arthur
Pritchard later commented that he himself met with the
board on only a handful of occasions during his whole
tenure as Station Manager. Moreover, both the original
1929 agreement between WWL Development and the University
and a "supplemental agreement" signed in January 1933
left no doubt that "the conduct of the station and the
character of all matter to be broadcast is and shall
always be under the absolute control and subject to the
unconditional approval of the University." In addition,
the gradual expansion of WWL operations dictated that
it take control of its own internal business routines,
and so the office services formerly provided by Standard
Fruit in those first, halting months of commercial
operation were no longer required. The station thus
disengaged itself from that financial backer, as it
sought an infusion of new advice and capital elsewhere.[33]

Fresh capital was required, not only for the purchase of the RCA transmitter and studio equipment, but
also for the establishment and furnishing of new locations
for each. The answer to the problem of securing the
needed investment funds was found in an adjunct organization of the University, the Marquette Association for
Higher Education. It had been chartered in 1907, when
its first task was the construction of the main administrative and classroom building on the campus, Marquette
Hall. Once the structure was completed, attention was
directed to the acquisition of real estate, especially
property contiguous to the University. To further that

purpose it received in 1926 a legacy of nearly $250,000 from the estate of a wealthy donor friendly to Loyola. It was a portion of those funds that WWL would now call upon to finance the next step in its growth.[34]

The arrangement was not simple. The Marquette Association purchased 1,250 unissued shares of WWL Development stock for $125,000, thereby becoming by far the largest stockholder in that corporation. Since Loyola's Jesuit community was, in turn, the only stockholder in the Marquette Association, WWL Development thus remained firmly in the University's hands. In effect, holding companies were pyramided. With this infusion of capital, the necessary equipment would be purchased for the station by the Development Company, and a revised financial arrangement with the University concluded. Under its terms, agreed to in January 1933, WWL Development expended a total of $80,000 for the ten kilowatt transmitter, studio equipment, and furnishings. It now sold those items to the University for the same amount with payment represented by a demand note bearing 5% interest.

WWL Development retained the right to contract "for all broadcasting time over said station, for which compensation in money is paid" and promised each October to credit the school with the gross revenues earned by the station, after deducting operating expenses, a 5% interest on any funds advanced by the company if revenues were insufficient to meet those expenses, the 5% interest on the promissory note, and beginning in 1936, an annual payment of $10,000 on the principal. In this fashion the 1932 expansion was financed. The entire investment represented a conviction on the part of the WWL management, the businessmen-advisors of WWL Development, and the Loyola administration that radio offered a profit potential far beyond the sizeable funds being currently expended. In 1932, that was a conviction built more on hope than hard evidence. As yet, there had been little to demonstrate that sizeable profits could be earned, especially by a station operating independent of any network affiliation and in the depths of a national depression.[35]

Bearing out those impressions were the results of WWL's initial period of 10,000 watt service. For the first eleven months of 1933, broadcast time sales totaled $48,395, but expenses were even higher, $67,376. Those expenses included almost $20,000 in talent costs, $11,000 in commissions, and nearly $15,000 of staff salaries. Legal fees incurred in the clear channel fight with KWKH added to the burden. Prospects, despite Abell's optimism, did not seem inviting.[36]

Burk and Abell were, nevertheless, not deterred by any voices of caution as they planned for their station's expansion. They realized that a part of their plans must necessarily be new sites for both WWL's transmitter and its studios. Deiler's Radio Division field office had long been opposed to the transmitter's location on the campus, and the increase in power would make any continuance there impossible. In addition, Abell termed the need for new studios "imperative." While he admitted the Bobet Hall premises were adequate in their physical layout, they were too far removed from the downtown area for the convenience of artists who might be attracted to appear on any scheduled programs. A separation of transmitter and studio was inevitable now, with the former moving to some rural site and the latter to the busy central business district.[37]

The first location to be secured was that for the transmitter. The place was the old Troudeau Plantation near Kenner, Louisiana, some twelve miles by 1932 automobile road from Loyola, and within "the shadow of the Mississippi's east bank levee." Since the ground chosen was already under cultivation as a truck garden, there was no necessity to clear it of trees. While the surface was dry, the water level was no more than eighteen inches below, thereby convincing Abell that "a good ground system" was certain. In the weeks that followed the March 1932 acquisition of the land, a one story brick building to house the transmitter was constructed. The antenna system consisted of twin 200 feet high towers, and was designed by a Bessemer, Alabama, firm to withstand hurricane winds of 125 miles per hour. Delivered, it was priced at $6,000. The actual erection was handled by the Nashville Bridge Company and required a five week effort. While the transmitter itself was of RCA manufacture, Abell personally handled the installation, with help from any available willing hands at the University. By mid-August the work was complete and tuning began, with testing carried on between midnight and 6:00 A.M., as prescribed by FRC rules. Abell deemed the results "gratifying" since letters were received in response to the signal from as far away as New Zealand.[38]

While Abell supervised the transmitter activity near Kenner, Burk took charge of the search for new studios. He had already announced that the new ten kilowatt operation would "place New Orleans upon the radio map of the world," and he was determined to find

135

space for the station's broadcasting operations in keeping with WWL's new stature. The remote studio at the Monteleone Hotel was still being utilized, but the management of that hostelry proved less than willing to provide more radio space and the current amount available there was wholly inadequate. Burk now looked elsewhere, and once again the principals of Standard Fruit offered a solution.[39]

They suggested the newly constructed Roosevelt Hotel on University Place near Canal. The site had earlier been the location of the Grunewald Hotel, opened in 1893, but the Grunewald was sold in 1923 to a syndicate headed by the Vaccaro family, founders of Standard Fruit. The old 1893 structure was demolished, a new building erected in its place, and christened the Roosevelt. Managing the enterprise for the syndicate in 1932 was an individual whose rise in wealth and in political influence was little short of meteoric-- Seymour Weiss. Born in Abbeville, Louisiana, the son of a Jewish merchant, his formal education had not gone beyond the third grade. After working in a New Orleans shoe store, he was hired to manage the barbershop of the Roosevelt in 1926. In quick succession he was then named the Hotel's Assistant Manager, Associate Manager, and in 1931, its Vice President and Managing Director. Three years later, as head of the New Orleans Roosevelt Corporation, he would buy out the Vaccaros and become the Hotel's principal owner.[40]

Weiss also acquired a powerful friend in the person of Huey Long. The two men first met in 1928 when Long established his gubernatorial campaign headquarters in the Roosevelt, and soon Weiss "learned to love and admire" the Kingfish. Long, in turn, respected Weiss' elegant manners and expensive tastes as well as the hotel man's ability as an executive. Weiss became one of the politician's closest confidants and the keeper of Long's personal treasury. The Roosevelt also became recognized as "the bailiwick of Long forces." For WWL to move its studio operations to the Roosevelt meant, therefore, a closer relationship with the political organization that was increasingly dominating Louisiana life.[41]

Weiss, according to Abell, was at first skeptical about the value of a WWL connection, preferring instead to house a station with a network affiliation and undivided time on its own channel. Nevertheless, with the Vaccaro blessing, an agreement was rapidly concluded. The Roosevelt agreed to supply space for WWL facilities, rent free, and in return the Hotel would be given recognition in every station break, along with a thirty minute broadcast of the Hotel's orchestra during the daytime and another such program in the evening. The quarter hour station break announcements would specify: "This is Station WWL, from its studios in the Roosevelt Hotel." In the years to come, broadcasts of the dance music from the soon famous Blue Room of the Roosevelt would become a regular feature of much of the nation's nighttime radio listening. The station, the Hotel, and the big bands that performed in the Blue Room all benefited from the publicity generated. Abell and Burk believed that WWL alone transformed the Roosevelt into a profit-making vehicle for the first time. Certainly, the skepticism that "Colonel" Weiss, as Burk referred to him, had first felt turned to a genuine delight with the broadcasters.[42]

The Roosevelt was not anxious in 1932 to sacrifice revenue producing guest rooms to the radio needs, so the WWL executives settled for a large "somewhat irregularly shaped hall" that formerly had been a short-lived indoor miniature golf course. Now unused, the second-floor hall offered the possibilities of being converted into satisfactory facilities. Burk himself drew plans for that conversion, plans calling for three studios, the largest of which measured 18 x 36 feet, a control room and office space. By early October, the station had successfully moved from the old location in Bobet Hall to its new home in the Roosevelt.[43]

On October 2, 1932, a Sunday, 10,000 watt operation began with the broadcast of a High Mass from Holy Name Church on the campus and a special inaugural program from the new studios. The higher level of power placed WWL in a select group of stations. At the beginning of 1932 only four other stations in the FRC's Southern zone matched or surpassed WWL's increased strength of signal--two in Texas, one in Arkansas, and, of course, Henderson's KWKH. Operations in 1932 and 1933 were still being conducted at a loss, but gradually the pre-conditions to an eventually profitable broadcasting business were being laid.

# 10

## THE CLEAR CHANNEL WAR--THE FINAL ROUND

Simultaneous with the inauguration of ten kilowatt operations, the WWL managers readied themselves for the final round of the clear channel struggle. One of the maneuvers in the WWL strategy had already begun to unfold--the winning away of W. K. Henderson's principal political support, Senator Huey P. Long. As described earlier, the friendship between Long and Henderson had pre-dated the former's rise to power, and during Long's electoral campaigns, Henderson had supplied heaping quantities of both financial support and KWKH broadcasting time. Even Long associates, including the rabble-rousing Reverend Gerald L. K. Smith, were given the use of the station's facilities for programs of their own, while Longite opponents were conversely denied radio time. In view of this close relationship, a Loyola announcement in December 1930 that it was awarding the Governor and Senator-Elect an honorary Doctor of Laws degree undoubtedly came as a shock to Henderson, following so closely as it did the bitter September KWKH-WWL hearings.[1]

The University quickly admitted the award was out of the ordinary. It was "departing from its custom of conferring such honors at regular graduation exercises" in the spring only in view of the Governor's "exalted office and manifold duties." Instead the ceremony would take place in February with New Orleans' Municipal Auditorium rented for the occasion. One newspaper predicted "a throng that will probably set a record for its kind in the history of the city and the state." Not only were seating arrangements prepared to accommodate 12,000 spectators within the auditorium, but loud speakers were placed to carry the speeches to an expected overflow outside.[2]

The citation read at the ceremony laid great weight upon Long's various political accomplishments and referred to him as "a man of action, with ideas born of outstanding vision, who cares to fight for the realization of his ideals, watchfully waiting, working continually." Later, Long's biographer, T. Harry Williams, would judge the politician pleased but not overwhelmed by the honor. Nevertheless, it can be noted that Long devoted a chapter in his autobiography to the episode and quoted the citation in full. Williams also concluded that the University's primary motive, "the real reason for the award," was Long's responsibilty for the passage of a state law making free textbooks available for the first time to Louisiana children, including those enrolled in Catholic schools. It seems just as likely, however, that the University administration had the clear channel war well in mind when the decision was made to singularly recognize the Kingfish.[3]

Geographically, Long and Loyola had moved closer as well. Two years before WWL's shift to the Roosevelt, where Long maintained a permanent suite and where a chief New Orleans lieutenant presided, he transferred his law offices to the recently constructed Pere Marquette Building in the downtown central business district. The new office building, erected on the site of the previous Jesuit College, was owned by the Society of Jesus.[4]

The facilities of WWL were, with the shift to the Roosevelt, now easily available to Long, and he purchased sizeable blocks of time for political broadcasts. Pritchard recalled Al Foster returning to the station one evening in high good humor. The sales manager happily related how he had just visited Long, sold the Senator $1,000 worth of air time, convinced him to pay cash in advance for it, and then prevailed upon one of the Kingfish's bodyguards to provide an escort back to WWL. Long, there is reason to believe, had even offered the University a gift of $10,000 to assist in the conversion to 10 kw. in 1932. The offer was declined.[5]

Certainly, an understanding between Long and WWL's owners had been reached. He had promised assistance to the New Orleans station and John Hynes, Loyola's President, was not hesitant to ask for it. Hynes took notice of a growing estrangement between Long and Henderson and its happy consequences for WWL. As the Jesuit guardedly wrote the Senator in February 1932, Long could now act "with even greater freedom because you have been liberated from your obligations to a certain party."[6]

That "certain party" reached his own conclusion and
voiced them on the air in his usual blunt terms. By
the fall of 1932, Henderson was denouncing what he
believed plainly to be a Loyola-Long alliance. The
University "had put a cap" on Long and granted him an
honorary degree, expecting "that with this almighty
and godly power" WWL would have no difficulty in wresting
the channel from KWKH. He accused the New Orleanians
of inflated egoes, developed "by transfusion from that
dictator, Hooey P. Long." The Jesuits, Henderson
ranted, were "licking boots with the dirty low down
politicians, moving into a hotel used by the dictator
of politics who has this state in charge at this time."[7]

Despite Henderson's public forebodings, what
support Long might have given to the WWL cause in the
final round of the clear channel war was not readily
apparent. The round had, in fact, begun with Henderson
striking the first blow. In June 1932 he served notice
upon WWL that he would not renew the time-sharing agreement due to expire in September. His purpose may simply
have been to secure better terms by re-opening negotiations. If so, he was shocked by the WWL response, for
two days later that station officially informed Henderson
it would once again press for full time on the frequency
in a new application to the FRC. Responding to the
application and to the failure of the two Louisiana
stations to arrive at a mutually agreeable time-sharing
formula, the Commission designated the matter for hearings in February 1933, the fourth set of hearings in
which those same broadcasters had participated since
1929.[8]

Again the parties traveled to Washington to testify,
and again Burk, Hynes and Abell along with Pritchard
and Denechaud made the journey from New Orleans.
New faces were also present in 1933. In addition to
Denechaud and Dolle, WWL was to be represented by a
Washington-based firm of attorneys, Webster, Segal and
Smith. The lead in the case would be taken by the
fresh counsel, Paul M. Segal and B.M. Webster, Jr.,
with the latter handling the crucial cross-examination
of Henderson himself. But attorneys were not the only
new entrants into the litigation. Applying for KWKH's
half of the channel was the just organized International
Broadcasting Corporation, headquartered in Shreveport.
The company's principal was a wealthy oil man and prominent Shreveport citizen, Sam D. Hunter, who the
hearing examiner, noticeably impressed, would refer to
as "a public spirited citizen of high moral standing

and a man of refinement and culture." It seems likely
that the Hunter venture represented the belated response
of the conservative Shreveport business establishment
to the increasingly unacceptable Henderson antics.[9]

The weeks and months immediately prior to the
February 1933 hearings were disastrous for Henderson
as both his financial and his radio empire began to
steadily crumble. Moreover, as it became clear that he
would have to face attacks from both WWL and from Hunter
with little ammunition to use in his own defense, the
tone of his broadcasts became more strident than ever.
Deserted by his long-time political ally, Huey Long,
in deep financial difficulties, and faced with the
imminent prospect of meeting a hostile FRC once again,
Henderson desperately sought to rally his one resource,
his listeners, by appealing to their possible religious
prejudices. The struggle for the channel became a
Protestant-Catholic issue in his appeals for support:
"I say to you Methodists, Baptists, Episcopalians, are
you going to sit still and let a Catholic institution
claim the entire wave length of 850 kilocycles?"[10]

As the date for the opening of the FRC hearings
drew closer, Henderson's anti-Catholic attacks grew
more frantic. He accused them of "putting on a
whispering campaign" against him in order to "hold the
wave length from the rest of the religious sects," and
he somewhat awkwardly asked his audience: "Why should
the Catholics under the caption of Loyola University,
supported by the political influence of the Kingfish
of Louisiana, rob away from the rest of people and
religious denominations and take a whole wave channel."
Finally, in January 1933, he turned his attention to
the Catholic menace to the nation as a whole. He cited
"statistics" that supposedly revealed over sixty percent
of all federal government officials were Catholic, that
Catholics made up three-quarters of the teachers in the
public schools of the country's principal cities and
ninety percent of the police forces of those same
communities. He claimed West Point and Annapolis were
"dominated by Catholics," that "the men who shot
Roosevelt, Garfield, and Lincoln were Roman Catholics
or dominated by Catholics," and that "bridge dynamiters"
and "bomb throwers" were invariably also Catholic.
Later, under Webster's intense cross-examination in the
hearings, Henderson grudgingly admitted that he did not
believe "all of it was true," but he refused to retrench
on his general position.

Under Webster's questioning, Henderson also acknowledged appealing for funds in his broadcasts "to
carry on this expensive fight before the Federal Radio
Commission." Ruefully, he disclosed that, unlike previous years and appeals, "very little" was forthcoming
from his unseen audience. In the depths of the
depression, Henderson's largely rural following had no
cash to spare for anything but their own necessities
of life. The Shreveport broadcaster's own business
empire lay in ruins as well. The Iron Works had long
since passed to his creditors with Henderson claiming
a loss of $1,000,000 in its collapse. In 1932 another
venture, the Henderson Timber, Land and Investment Company, failed, and finally, in November of the same
year, he was forced to file a personal bankruptcy
petition listing unpaid obligations of $1,381,596.
Nevertheless, he claimed that those disasters in no
way affected the fortunes of the Hello World Broadcasting Corporation since he now was only a minor stockholder in that company. In late 1931, seeing the probable future course of events, Henderson transferred
Hello World's stock to his sister and aunt, retaining
just ten shares for himself as opposed to almost ten
thousand held by his relatives. The charade created
no illusions in the mind of the FRC Examiner, however;
he quickly determined Henderson still exercised the
practical control of KWKH and the "last say" in its
affairs, and that "none of the stockholders have anything to do with the management of the station which
remains in his hands."[12]

A financial statement for Hello World Broadcasting,
dated December 30, 1932, and filed with the FRC
Examiner, revealed the station's precarious situation.
The only assets of real value were the equipment and
furnishings, listed at some $44,000 after depreciation.
Also carried on the statement as assets, but totally
valueless in actual worth, were over $140,000 in
accounts and notes receivable due from Henderson himself
or his other bankrupt enterprises, plus $200,000 common
stock investment in the now defunct Iron Works and the
Timber venture. Cash on hand totaled just $288, and
some $2,000 in back salaries was still owed to station
employees. Henderson referred to those loyal staffers
as "Chinese labor" since "they work for nothing."
Liabilities were not large, consisting principally
of nearly $28,000 owing on two bank loans, but with
virtually no income coming in to the station, with
operating costs continuing unabated, and with constant
legal fees, only the liquidation of the fixed assets
and thus of the station itself, could meet the existing

obligations. For the last four months of 1932, KWKH
showed a net loss of $6,404. Henderson's other broad-
casting outlet, KWEA, had already gone off the air
entirely. Ellis A. Yost, the FRC Examiner in the
hearing, concluded in an almost tongue-in-cheek understatement Hello World Broadcasting was "not a strong
financial corporation."[13]

If Henderson's experience before Examiner Yost was
defensive in nature, the case for WWL had a much more
positive tone. Burk, Abell, Pritchard, Hynes, and
Denechaud, supported by local and federal officeholders
from Louisiana, argued the case for WWL's sole control
of the channel. Particular emphasis was placed upon
the fact that WWL was the only New Orleans station
capable of providing reliable radio service to rural
residents in much of Louisiana, Mississippi, and Alabama,
an area encompassing a population of almost two million.
Attention was also drawn to the nature of WWL programming,
which included the only educational features being aired
in the city. Pritchard testified only 20% to 30% of all
programs were sponsored while the rest were carried on
a sustaining basis. Left largely unspoken, of course,
was the management's fervent desire to eliminate many
of the sustaining shows, and to substitute network programming for the bulk of the local features carried.
In general, the argument was constantly used that full
time on the channel would particularly result in both
more public service programming and profitable operations
for the first time.[14]

Sam Hunter's International Broadcasting Corporation
proposed the installation of a ten kilowatt transmitter
on the shore of a lake ten miles from the center of
Shreveport. An initial investment in equipment of
$60,000 was anticipated, the entire sum to be furnished
by Hunter. A shrewd promise, formulated with Henderson's
record in mind, was offered that KWKH, under new operators, would be conducted "on a high plane," but no
specific details as to program plans were submitted
other than a desire to secure a network affiliation.
The case for International Broadcasting was primarily
based on the controversial past performance of KWKH's
present management.[15]

The hearings were concluded on February 20 but it
was not until April 8 that Ellis Yost submitted his
recommendations to the FRC. Yost dwelled at length on
Henderson's financial condition, the questionable
advertising KWKH carried on in the past, the lack of

144

commercial relations with Shreveport's business community, chain store attacks (citing, for example, the
reference to Montgomery Ward as "the most damnable
contemptible thieves...Monkey Ward"), and myriad personal assaults on individuals, groups, and institutions
with which the Shreveport station owner had come into
conflict at one time or another. Yost noted that under
FRC regulations an applicant requesting the facilities
already assigned to another licensee "must establish
by competent evidence that the proposed transfer and
use of such facilities would serve the public interest,
convenience, and/or necessity." WWL, in his opinion,
had satisfactorily met that requirement. There was
"a greater public need" in New Orleans for the time
utilized by KWKH than in Shreveport, and the transfer
would result "in a more equitable distribution" of
service within the state. As to International Broadcasting, it had failed, in Yost's view, to prove that
either the "available talent" or the "public need for
the service" were sufficient for it to be granted a
share of the channel. Henderson was given short shrift
in the Examiner's conclusions: "The financial qualifications, the public service heretofore rendered and
the public service proposed to be hereafter rendered...
do not warrant a finding that the continued operation
of Station KWKH would serve the public interest, convenience or necessity." Thus, in April 1933 the WWL
management confidently believed they had finally
achieved their goal; after a four year campaign, the
New Orleans station appeared on the verge of full control and unlimited time on its assigned frequency.16

Henderson, meanwhile, faced a disheartening situation. If the FRC upheld the Examiner's recommendation,
as it seemed likely to do, his career in broadcasting
would not only have reached an apparent finale, but he
would have succumbed to a foe for whom he felt only
animosity, the New Orleans broadcasters of WWL. Their
feud had continued on the air as well as off. Pritchard,
especially, had taken great pleasure in taunting the
Shreveport man and ridiculing his crusade against "the
nasty little chain stores." Henderson, in turn, spoke
acidly of "that mealy-mouthed Englishman" in New Orleans.
To surrender the field to WWL was more than Henderson
was prepared to accept; therefore, he chose the only
viable alternative yet open to him, selling his station
to Hunter's International Broadcasting Corporation.
The sale, recommended by his attorneys and concluded
in early June, carried a purchase price of $50,000 and
a necessary stipulation that it was contingent upon
FRC approval of the re-assignment of the KWKH license.
Better Hunter than Loyola.17

The sale would be meaningless, however, if the FRC
could not be persuaded to reverse the recommendation
of its own Examiner and to maintain a share of the 850
kc. frequency in Shreveport. To bring about this reversal, Henderson and International Broadcasting joined
forces. The former continued to blast on the air the
alleged WWL-Long alliance, and the latter turned to
political figures for support. The Louisiana clear
channel war was brought to the attention of two Democratic party Senate stalwarts, Majority Leader Joseph T.
Robinson of Arkansas and the respected Senator Pat
Harrison of Mississippi. Knowing of Robinson's bitter
antipathy towards Huey Long, the International Broadcasting officials warned of the presumable consequences
of WWL gaining full time on a clear channel. Robinson,
who was serving as one of the special targets of Long's
ridicule in the Senate, was quick to react. Recruiting
the assistance of Harrison, another anti-Long conservative, they turned to the White House, newly occupied in
1933 by Franklin Roosevelt.[18]

By July 1933, Roosevelt and Long had found themselves at odds over a number of pieces of early New Deal
legislation, notably those dealing with banking, industrial recovery, and veterans' benefits. FDR had come
to see Long as a man dangerous not only to New Deal
policy but also to the President's own political future.
He had determined, therefore, to strip the Senator of
much of his influence, especially control over federal
patronage posts in Louisiana. Diminishing, or at least
not expanding, the prominence of a supposed Long-
inclined radio station fit well with the decision to
"write Long off."[19]

Robinson and Harrison, accepting the argument that
WWL was Long-controlled, approached Louis Howe on the
White House staff with the details of the situation as
they understood it. Howe was the new President's oldest
and closest advisor and in many ways Roosevelt's "alter
ego." Having particular jurisdiction over patronage
distribution, he was also FDR's "personal political
agent, gauging every move with a cautious glance toward
1934 and 1936." Since Howe was customarily assigned
"the most nasty and delicate jobs," the curbing of Huey
Long was his special task. Moving rapidly, he contacted
in turn Commissioner Thad H. Brown, who was acting as
FRC Chairman while Judge Sykes attended a Mexican conference; the only Roosevelt appointee on the FRC,
Democratic lawyer James H. Hanley; and Herbert L. Pettey,
the Secretary of the Commission. The message was the
same in each case; the White House was concerned that

"no injustice" be done to the good citizens of Shreveport.[20]

That message was received loud and clear by the
Democrats on the Commission, now in the majority for
the first time. Apparently, even though Commissioners
had already tentatively agreed to affirm the Examiner's
report of April, a new vote was called and the three
Democrats (Sykes, Brown, and Hanley) reversed their
positions and Yost's recommendations as well. The
likely replacement of the FRC with a Roosevelt-favored
"communications commission," whose members had not as
yet been selected but which might include some of the
present Commissioners, certainly did not serve to
strengthen the regulatory body's independence from
political influence. The problem of executive or
legislative branch interference was not, by any means,
unknown to the FRC even before the Louisiana case.
Rumors of wardheeler politics permeating the operations
of the Commission were already current.[21]

After 1930 appointments to the FRC had primarily
been lawyers rather than the "technical experts" who
served in earlier years. The shift meant the selection
of men whose ties to politics and political power
were even closer than their predecessors. Roosevelt,
as well as other Presidents, was not unwilling to
communicate his opinions and advice on pending cases
to the Commissioners whose positions derived from his
own largesse. For WWL, the result was an FRC decision
of September 15, 1933, that Orie Abell angrily described
as the "Big Steal."[22]

To the bewilderment of the New Orleanians, the FRC
unexpectedly reversed the recommendations of the
hearing Examiner, Ellis Yost. In its decision, the
Commission noted that WWL still had available for
commercial sale a considerable portion of its current
time on the air. That fact contradicted the station's
contention that additional time was necessary for a
profitable operation. On the other hand, the Commission
took pains to point out that KWKH was "the only broadcast station in a position to deliver a really service-
able signal over a great area centering in Shreveport."
Yet, even though Yost had argued much the same fact
with regard to WWL, no mention was made of the New
Orleans station's similar role. Only the vaguest of
explanations was given for the FRC ruling. There was
said to be simply no need for "additional broadcast
facilities in the New Orleans area" such as to warrant

"the deletion of the Shreveport station." The KWKH
license was ordered transferred to International Broadcasting and time-sharing between the two Louisiana
stations was continued for the indefinite future.[23]

It was not the FRC's finest hour. The decision
offered a weak and generalized rationale for the
reversal of a detailed and strongly argued Examiner's
Report. The intrusion of politics seemed plain, and the
WWL team reacted accordingly. Paul Segal, WWL's
Washington-based legal counsel, promised an appeal of
the FRC order to the Circuit Court in the District of
Columbia and termed the ruling "unconscionable." Abell
was even stronger in his denunciation, calling the
verdict "one of the most unjust decisions ever handed
down by this politically-bossed FRC." In later months,
Senator L. J. Dickinson, an Iowa Republican, charged
on the floor of Congress that FRC Commissioner Harold A.
Lafount would not be appointed to the newly organized
Federal Communications Commission because Lafount had
"failed to vote according to instructions from the White
House" in the Louisiana case. Not unexpectedly, Huey
Long too charged "pressure exerted from the White House"
had determined the FRC ruling. Long called for the
appointment of a special congressional committee to
investigate the matter, a suggestion that was never
acted upon by the Senate. The NAB journal, Broadcasting,
also reported the common understanding that the
Commission had been "ordered" by the Roosevelt administration to decide the issue in favor of the Shreveport
interests.[24]

But the FRC was not through reversing itself; one
more twist was yet to come. Determined not to accept
the verdict or to rely solely upon the courts to bring
them justice, WWL mounted a political counter-offensive.
Father Hynes boarded a train for Washington to confront
Senators Robinson and Harrison in person and to convince
them that no real ties existed between the University
station and Huey Long. Meanwhile, Father Burk also
journeyed to Washington to assault the Roosevelt administration directly, meeting with both Louis Howe and
with Postmaster General James A. Farley, since the
latter was serving as an unofficial New Deal liaison
to the Roman Catholic community in the United States.[25]

To buttress their protestations of independence
from the Long machine in Louisiana, WWL's management
shrewdly initiated a "no politics" policy in its programming. The station would no longer carry political
speeches or advertising of any kind. The ostensible

explanation offered was based on the station's clear channel occupancy. It was argued that WWL's huge rural audience outside of both New Orleans and the Louisiana area would be disinterested in presentations tied to local or state political issues and elections. In actual fact, the strategy was designed to prevent the station's use by Huey Long, thus verifying to FDR that Henderson's charges of an alliance were unfounded. Long himself never publicly reacted to the change in WWL policy; he merely shifted his New Orleans radio usage to the facilities of Uhalt's WDSU. Further, he denied any association with the clear channel case, claiming only "grapevine" knowledge of the matter at issue. Ironically, the "no politics" formula, originated in late 1933, would far outlast the situation for which it had been established. Two years later in September 1935, Huey Long would face an assassin's fatal bullets, yet two decades later WWL radio was still refusing to air any local political broadcasts.[26]

The assurances tendered to the White House by WWL were apparently sufficient. Abell was informed by the returning Burk and Hynes that Howe had promised them "some way would be found to give WWL full time." The Chicago-Tribune, no admirer of the incumbent President, also reported that FDR was trying to extricate himself from a potentially disadvantageous position with Catholic voters "by some concession to the New Orleans station." Particularly worrisome to the administration in Washington was the possibility that, in view of Henderson's earlier anti-Catholic statements, the FRC decision might be interpreted as an indirect reflection of New Deal religious preferences. To avoid any additional escalation of a local case that was already becoming too important nationally, pressure was again applied to the ever-pliable FRC.[27]

With only a few weeks remaining in its own life before it was to be succeeded by the new FCC, and without a formal hearing, the FRC announced on June 8, 1934, the settlement of what Broadcasting termed "one of the most agitated cases in radio history." WWL and KWKH were each granted full time status but on two different frequencies. Under a "special experimental authorization," WWL was to operate on an unlimited time basis on 850 kc. while KWKH was moved to 1100 kc. The new KWKH frequency was also in use by WPG in Atlantic City and by WLWL in New York City, but with the installation of a directional antenna for the Shreveport station, interference could be avoided. The expenses incurred by KWKH in changing frequencies were to be underwritten by WWL, and Loyola

149

agreed to withdraw its appeal of the September 1933
FRC ruling still pending in the Circuit Court. Essen-
tially, a delicate political problem had been solved
with a favorite political device, the compromise.
Though the Shreveport Times headlined its report of the
FRC solution, "KWKH Winner of Fight for Full Service,"
Abell and his colleagues regarded it as a victory for
New Orleans.[28]

While WWL's sole occupation of the disputed 850 kc.
frequency was designated as temporary and experimental,
it would in fact prove permanent. On the other hand,
KWKH could hardly regard itself as securing better than
a draw at most in the struggle. It gained a new frequency assignment, but one at a higher and therefore
less desirable dial location, and one restricted somewhat by the operations of two Eastern stations. If a
clear loser emerged from the affair, it was most likely
the FRC itself. The inglorious conduct of that regulatory agency produced no remorse when it passed from
existence in July 1934, replaced by the FCC.

A clear winner was Franklin Roosevelt. The White
House had been victorious in three ways. It had been
able to render a political favor for the anti-Long
forces in Louisiana and in the United States Senate,
and at the same time it also deprived Long of a powerful radio voice which had previously been available
to him. The Louisiana stations upon which the Kingfish
was now forced to rely delivered much less coverage to
him than WWL. Finally, by eventually securing the clear
channel for Loyola, the Roosevelt administration was
able to placate Catholic supporters of the New Orleans
station's cause and extract the President from a
possible religious backlash. Certainly, the Louisiana
clear channel war bears out the conviction of governmental skeptics that genuine political independence for
regulatory officials is "unsustainable against presidents or governors who wished to interfere with
scientific deliberation, or thwart it through the
appointment of cronies and hacks." The KWKH-WWL experience offers the historian of broadcasting additional
evidence that the regulation of that communications
medium has indeed been an "intensely political process."[29]

The new owners of KWKH began immediate negotiations
with the Columbia Broadcasting System, one of the chains
that Henderson took such delight in reviling, and soon
the station became the 100th affiliate of that network.
In 1935 its ownership changed once again, this time
passing to the Times Publishing Co. Ltd., publishers of

the Shreveport Times. Since that newspaper was controlled by the Ewing family, the former principals
in the New Orleans States, the same interests that
helped promote the establishment of broadcasting in the
Crescent City, returned to the industry once more.
During the 1940 gubernatorial campaign in Louisiana,
candidate Earl Long, Huey's brother, secured time on
KWKH for political speeches. Each time the earthy
Earl lapsed into the use of "hell" or "damn" on the
air, he was cut off by the station's engineers. Clearly,
KWKH was no longer a Henderson station.[30]

The forgotten man in the settlement of the clear
channel war was W. K. Henderson. With the sale to
Hunter affirmed, he lost his radio voice. From time to
time he made "guest appearances" on KWKH during the year
following the FRC decision, but thereafter he faded
rapidly from sight. Only occasional glimpses of him
were seen. For a brief period he traveled the country
in a trailer caravan under an official appointment made
by Governor Richard W. Leche. Henderson was billed as
"Louisiana's ambassador to America." On June 28, 1935,
he placed an advertisement in the Shreveport Times,
headlining it: "I'm Still W. K. Henderson." The text
read: "I have everything I used to have except money.
I'm not in any business and I don't know what business
I'd get in if I had money. But you can bet I'm still
Old Man Henderson to my friends throughout the land."
Pointedly he suggested: "Maybe you have some ideas to
our mutual interest. Two plus two still makes four
with me." His address was included to facilitate communication.[31]

A few years after the publication of that ad,
Henderson was stricken with a paralysis resulting
from complications that followed a wasp sting on his
face. He spent the last six years of his life,
until his death on May 28, 1945, in a helpless condition. Interviewed during that final illness, he
seemed characteristically unrepentant: "I was right
you know. I was right about the chain stores. I was
right about the government control of radio. I guess
I was fighting for free speech and free enterprise."[32]

What conclusions can be drawn from Henderson's
stormy career? Certainly his radio battles did help
shape both public and governmental responses to real
problems. He influenced the course of broadcast regulation and, sincere or not, he was the nation's most
important anti-chain store campaigner. That campaign
eventuated in the passage of laws temporarily inhibiting

151

or penalizing the growth of retail chains in 27 states by 1939, and the most stringent of those laws was passed in Louisiana. Historian Richard Hofstadter once analyzed "the paranoid style in American politics." The characteristics of that style, he found, included conduct and speech that is "overheated, oversuspicious, overaggressive, grandiose, and apocalyptic in expression." The individual engaging in the behavior "constantly lives at a turning point, it is now or never in organizing resistance to conspiracy. Time is forever just running out." While the description fits the Shreveport broadcaster's career, the explanation presumes a real though fanatical devotion to principle. It may not correlate with Henderson's eye for the main chance and for simple survival.[33]

Opportunism rather than deep personal commitment seems more his dominant motivation. Like other depression demagogues, he played upon the "prejudices and passions of the population by tricks of rhetoric and sensational charges, by specious arguments, catchwords and cajolery." But no matter what his personal sincerity or personality compulsions, Henderson did represent a significant phase in the life of the broadcasting industry in America. In an era of emerging network supremacy, he epitomized, in his own bizarre and complex way, a fast receding figure, the fiercely independent, outlandishly unpredictable radio maverick. Few of his type would be seen again.[34]

# 11

## A PROFIT-MAKING ENTERPRISE--AT LAST

There was no exaggerating the importance of radio
to Depression-mired America.  Their loyalty to the
medium seemed almost irrational.  Social workers testified that poverty-stricken families would choose to
surrender an icebox or furniture or even a bed before
they would part with their radio sets.  Radios somehow
symbolized lifelines to the outside world that must be
preserved at virtually any cost.[1]

Given that degree of popular addiction, the broadcasting industry experienced a boom which grew in intensity as the nation struggled back to economic
equilibrium in the middle and late years of the 1930's.
By 1937 the Gross National Product of the United States
finally regained the level it had last reached in 1929,
while unemployment fell below 15% for the first time
since the early moments of the Depression.  Broadcasting's
recovery, if indeed it ever experienced a real slump
at all, was even more rapid.  The Federal Communications
Commission estimated that some 8,000,000 receiving sets
were sold to the public in 1936 alone, and that altogether some 45,000,000 sets were in use across the
nation, a total investment of $1,350,000,000.  During
the worst economic crisis in the country's history, the
number of radios in use had more than doubled, from
18,000,000 in 1932 to 45,000,000 just four years later.[2]

Moreover, the rest of the industry's statistics
were equally buoyant.  Over a thousand factories were
engaged in the manufacture of sets, tubes, transmitters,
and other equipment, and more than four thousand re-
tailers were exclusively involved in selling this output
to the public.  There were, at the time of the FCC
report in 1937, seven hundred active stations divided
into four general classes--clear channel, high power
regional, regional, and local.  The clear channel

stations, operating on forty uncluttered frequencies, utilized power of up to 50,000 watts, though one, WLW in Cincinnati, had begun using in 1934, on an experimental basis, "super power"--500,000 watts--making it the most powerful station in the world.[3]

In addition, three national chain organizations operated four coast-to-coast networks, and twenty-five regional network groups also existed. The largest and oldest of the chains, NBC, established in 1926 and a subsidiary of RCA, managed two systems--the Red and the Blue networks--and counted 161 affiliates by 1938. Second in size and established a year later than NBC, was CBS, controlled by William S. Paley and his associates, with 113 affiliated stations. The smallest network, the Mutual Broadcasting System, had been founded in 1934 and was largely under the control of the Chicago-Tribune and R. H. Macy & Company in 1938. It claimed 107 affiliates but they tended to be smaller stations on less desirable frequencies. Together, the three national organizations transacted almost half the total commercial business done by America's broadcasters. Their network time sales grossed over $46,000,000 in 1938, as compared to $101,000,000 for the entire industry.[4]

Particular types of sponsors were also becoming especially prominent in the radio advertising of the 1930's. The networks sold nearly 20% of their available time to companies vending toiletries and almost 19% to food accounts. On the non-network level, commercials for food products were the most prevalent, with drugs, apparel, and autos following closely after. But equally as influential were the major advertising agencies. By the early years of the decade, virtually all sponsored network programs were packaged by the "radio departments" of those agencies. The department heads, as Erik Barnouw has noted, "became an elite, besieged by time salesmen, producers, directors, and performing artists." Network approval of the programs developed by the agency executives became perfunctory.[5]

Many programs being supplied for broadcasting were little more than vaudeville moved to radio. Comedy and musical shows dominated, though as the decade closed drama was becoming increasingly popular. More talk and less music seemed the overall trend. An NBC survey revealed only 10.8% of that network's time devoted to drama in 1932, but 20.1% by 1939. Nevertheless, comedians and singers were kings of the hill, as Eddie Cantor, Amos 'n' Andy, Ed Wynn, Rudy Vallee, Fred Allen,

Jack Benny, and others attracted enormous audiences. On
any weekday evening in 1936, over 50% of the nation's
sets were tuned in to a family's special favorites.[6]

While most of radio's output was assimilative
rather than original, having been borrowed from the
vaudeville stage, the concert hall, or the legitimate
theater, it did make at least one unique contribution--
the adult daytime serial or "soap opera," as it was
derisively named. One observer deemed it "the great
invention of radio, its single notable contribution to
the art of fiction." Ma Perkins, one of the earliest
and longest lived, had first been heard as a local show
on Cincinnati's WLW, only to be quickly picked up by the
NBC Blue network in 1933. The indomitable Helen Trent
began on CBS the same year. The fall season of 1933
marked a major turning point in scheduling when CBS
introduced "block programming," the placing of several
serials in back to back fifteen minute time slots.
Until then they had been scattered throughout the day,
and they were not mutually supportive. Now one served
as a lead-in to another, and the housewife was encouraged never to turn a dial to a different station.
Within a few years more than half the commercial network time on weekdays was devoted to serial dramas, and,
by 1941, one could be found in every quarter hour
between 10:00 A.M. and 6:00 P.M., with two available in
most periods.[7]

Children's serials supplemented the soap operas.
Blending adventure and fantasy, they dominated the hours
after-school and prior to the beginning of the major
evening shows. In 1931 The Shadow and Little Orphan
Annie made their appearance, to be joined by The Lone
Ranger and by Jack Armstrong in 1933. As the years
passed, the serial plots were tailored to the issues
of the moment. During World War II, Tom Mix battled
for weeks a mysterious giant terrifying the Western
countryside. The cowboy hero finally won out,
unmasking the giant as only a huge balloon manipulated
by sinister Japanese agents for reasons totally inex-
plicable. In like manner, heroines of soap operas
in the war years suddenly found themselves kidnapped by
Nazi saboteurs rather than the garden variety of villians
of the 1930's.[8]

In the late Thirties, network programs comprised
50-70% of the average affiliate's daily schedule with
the remainder either local live talent or electrical
transcriptions. The use of transcriptions ranged from
10% on an affiliated station to as much as 85% on an

independent. The improved quality of the E.T., greater
sales aggressiveness on the part of firms marketing
them, a larger available variety, as well as a reduction
in their price, encouraged their wider usage. Sponsored
programs likewise were more common than ever before,
but the NAB Code stipulation that commercials should be
limited to no more than 15% of any daytime hour and 10%
of an evening hour was honored more in theory than in
practice.[9]

In 1936 the Bureau of the Census published what it
believed to be "the first complete measure of the extent
and character of the radio broadcasting business." The
study, based on 1935 statistics, revealed that net
revenue for the nation's stations had totaled $56,000,000
for the year, and 71% or $40,000,000 stemmed from the
direct sale of radio time by licensees. An additional
$12,500,000 was derived from network payments to affili-
ates for carrying commercial programs offered by the
chain organizations, and some $2,500,000 was earned
through selling the services of station talent. The
direct time sales of broadcasters were two-thirds local
and one-third to national advertisers. Naturally, the
more powerful stations drew the majority of their incomes
from national sources, both major advertisers and networks, while their weaker competitors relied primarily
on local businessmen as their financial mainstay.[10]

Broadcasting on the individual station level was
not a lucrative profession during the 1930's, especially
while the Depression was at its worst. The average
weekly wages of radio artists and announcers varied
from a low of $21 on the small 100 watters to a high of
$63 on 50 kw. operations. Technicians earned similar
salaries; office and clerical personnel did even worse.
At many stations, salesmen worked only on a commission
basis with no salary guarantee, while some on-the-air
staff members accepted positions without pay of any
kind, simply in hope that wages would eventually be
offered. One later WWL announcer, Don Lewis, recalled
accepting a six month probationary job at WDSU in 1933,
his first in radio, with only the promise from Joe
Uhalt of "car fare and lunch money." In 1935, Louisiana
stations, specifically, averaged just nine full time
employees and weekly wages of just $21-22 for announcers
and artists, placing the state far down the scale in
the national tabulations of both categories.[11]

Still, Louisiana had made some significant broadcasting gains during the decade. Between 1930 and 1934
the state had acquired over 98,000 new radio homes, an

increase of nearly 200% over the figure for the earlier year, the largest percentage gain in the United States. Total radio homes in Louisiana in 1934 stood at 152,000 or 31.4% of all homes in the state. While Louisiana still lagged badly behind the national figure (60%), it did out-pace all other Southern states except Florida (40%), Virginia (39.2%), and Tennessee (33.7%). By 1937, with an improving economy, Louisiana radio homes would number 260,000, and of those 90,800 could be found in Orleans Parish alone.[12]

New stations also made their appearance in Louisiana in the 1930's. Baton Rouge, after some false starts in the 1920's, took the air on a permanent basis in 1934. In 1932 the license for WJBO, a station dating back to Val Jensen's association with the Times-Picayune in those first frenetic days in the spring of 1922, was transferred to the Baton Rouge Broadcasting Company, owned primarily by Charles P. Manship, Sr., publisher of the capital city's only two newspapers. Jensen's New Orleans station was thus moved to Baton Rouge with a new management placed in charge. In 1937, WJBO joined the NBC Blue network.

The year 1935 saw three Louisiana cities, all previously without broadcasting facilities, acquire them for the first time. In Lake Charles, radio executives formerly associated with Shreveport's KRMD, secured an FCC license, and as the Calcasieu Broadcasting Company, established KPLC, operating with a daytime power of 250 watts. In Lafayette, the same partnership organized the Evangeline Broadcasting Company and put KVOL on the air in July 1935. In Alexandria, the third new broadcasting venture of 1935, KALB, went on the air, licensed to the Alexandria Broadcasting Company and transmitting with just 100 watts power in the daytime only.[13]

Meanwhile, elsewhere in the state no other major changes had taken place in the general station lineup. Shreveport boasted only three stations (KWKH, KTBS, and KRMD) since the demise of KWEA, Henderson's ill-fated second operation. KMLB continued on the air in Monroe, and New Orleans, now minus the re-assigned WJBO, counted just five stations. One of those New Orleans enterprises was, however, experiencing alterations in both its call letters and its ownership during the 1930's. Originally designated WABZ and licensed to the Coliseum Place Baptist Church, the control had been for a time transferred to Samuel D. Reeks and the call letters changed to WBBX. But when Reeks ran into difficulties, the station once more became the property of the Church, and in 1934, it was re-identified, this time as WBNO, in keeping with a new location in the Hotel New Orleans. It would continue under that style and ownership until 1939 when the facilities would finally be sold to James A. Noe, who secured permission from the FCC to use the call letters, WNOE. Noe, who was born in Kentucky, moved to Louisiana after World War I and soon became a wealthy businessman with substantial oil interests. He also became active politically, developing a close association with Huey Long. In 1932 he won election to the state Senate, and in 1935 to the position of lieutenant governor. When O. K. Allen, Long's hand-picked successor as governor, died unexpectedly, Noe served as Louisiana's chief executive for four months until a special election was held. While his tenure in the mansion lasted less than half a year, he was "Governor" Noe for the rest of his life. WWL was to hear a good deal from Noe when television made its appearance on the scene after World War II.[14]

With those thirteen stations, five of them in New Orleans, broadcasting in Louisiana entered the decade of the 1940's. But for WWL, the previous half dozen years, from the attainment of full time status on its clear channel in 1934 to the end of the 1930's, would be decisive. In those six years, WWL would wrest the broadcasting leadership of the state and of much of the South from its competitors, and convert the red ink of its early income statements to solid and consistent profits.

WWL initiated full time service on October 2, 1934, broadcasting from 7:00 A.M. until midnight, seventeen continuous hours. The date also marked the second anniversary of the station's residence in the Roosevelt Hotel studios. The day featured a special evening program in which Loyola's President, Father Hynes, offered an address of thanks to all friends of the University who had given their support in what he called "the long and bitter campaign" for sole control of the channel.[15]

There was no immediate change in the program content of the WWL schedule. Country music, featuring a variety of hillbilly groups, still dominated. In that orientation, WWL was hardly alone, however. Southern radio stations, beginning with WSB in Atlanta in 1922, featured country music from the first, and they were followed by such large Midwestern stations as Sears-Roebuck's influential WLS in Chicago. The latter aired a country entertainment program in 1924 which eventually evolved into a popular and long-running National Barn Dance. Likewise, WSM in Nashville began a barn dance show in 1925, and when Program Director George Hay noted on the air in 1926 that it was following a classical music presentation, he commented: "For the past hour we have been listening to music largely from Grand Opera, but from now on we will present 'The Grand Ole Opry!'" The name, of course, stuck and survives to the present. For the independent station such as WWL, in a time when talent budgets were small, hillbilly singers and musicians were attractive. They were available, cheap, and popular.[16]

WWL scheduling also assumed some of the regional character of southern Louisiana. While the New Orleans broadcasters did not follow in the footsteps of KPLC in Lake Charles and offer French language programs in the 1930's, the flavor of the Cajun culture was represented. In this vein, Walter Coquille portrayed a comedy character named Telesfore Boudreaux, Monsieur le Maire of Bayou Pom Pom. In 1934 the Mayor of Bayou Pom Pom and his adventures with his neighbors--Robleau, the long suffering utility man, as well as Fifi Le Blanc, the Mayor's "best friend," and Pete Patalano, the "ica man"--could be heard on Monday, Wednesday, and Friday evenings on WWL at 7:00 P.M. One critic judged the show "one of those God-sent patches of sunshine in a sky now nearly solid cloud."[17]

The Loyola station was also boasting the city's only "official News Commentator" in the person of Irving Victor, who used the spelling Ervin Viktor for publicity purposes. He joined WWL when the Roosevelt studios were opened after work on the New York stage and as a newspaperman. By early 1934, he was handling two news programs daily, one scheduled at 12:45 P.M. and the other at 6:45 P.M., with the first sponsored by "Cooling, Refreshing, Invigorating--Eagle Beer." Viktor's voguish and pretentious opening line on each broadcast--"Mr. and Mrs. New Orleans, Louisiana, and points East, West, North, and South--Greetings and Salutations--and, Heigh-ho!"--became quickly familiar to his listeners. Since no local station could afford to employ a full-time news commentator, Viktor was required to double as an announcer. He performed that chore all too well; his ability as a "selling announcer," especially on P.I. accounts, soon resulted in his receiving offers from larger stations. He left WWL in 1936 for a position on a Chicago station at a substantially increased salary.[18]

With the inauguration of 10,000 watt operations and the larger studio facilities, and in anticipation of the expanded scheduling that followed undivided time on the 850 kc. frequency, other new personnel were soon joining the staff. Some of these were to have long and important careers with WWL. James V. "Jimmie" Willson became Program Director in 1934. Billed as "the best announcer in New Orleans," he was better known for his singing voice which was featured in a succession of sponsored and sustaining shows during the decade. Another early mainstay was Karl Lellky. Born in Sweden in 1905, he traveled to the United States in 1928 and joined WWL four years later. He served as the staff pianist, the leader of the WWL String Trio, and the arranger and conductor for the impressively named WWL Little Symphony Orchestra. His wife, Maureen, a violinist, also played in the String Trio which performed on Sunday afternoon programs that featured dramatic readings.[19]

Especially important to the future of the station were two other staff members who were hired in these transition months--Henry Dupre and Irvine "Pinky" Vidacovich. Dupre was a native New Orleanian, born in 1906 and graduated from the old Jesuit College in 1925. For two years after his graduation, he performed in juvenile and character parts for the St. Charles Stock Company, a New Orleans theatre group, before leaving for New York and a hoped-for stage career there. When a family illness called him back to Louisiana in 1932, he decided to linger. Applying to WWL for a job, he emphasized his Jesuit educational background, and was able to secure a position as a part-time announcer.

In 1933 he was given a show of his own. Called Souvenirs, it featured poetry readings, and was carried by the station on a sustaining basis for the first few weeks until Al Foster successfully sold it to the Ouliber Coffee Company. Dupre's "talent fee" for the program was originally two dollars a broadcast, which he supplemented eventually by collecting his poems into a book and selling the volume for fifty cents a copy. His strength, however, lay in his abilities as a master of ceremonies. A marvelous "straight man," he served as a foil for a parade of studio comedians, and he delighted in participating in radio stunts. It might be broadcasting from atop a one hundred pound cake of ice on Canal Street while wearing only a bathing suit (the result of losing a Sugar Bowl bet), or from the bottom of the Mississippi River in a diver's outfit.

He seemed equal to any emergency or situation. When
the Mayor of Bayou Pom Pom staggered into the studio
one Christmas Eve "boiling drunk," Dupre ad-libbed a
show with him that supposedly featured the Mayor
tipsy. When the program finally limped to its conclusion, Coquille turned to Dupre and exclaimed: "Henry,
that was wonderful; we are going to do that again."
Dupre shot back: "Like hell we are." He felt he had
aged ten years in thirty minutes.

Souvenirs was followed in a few years by Street
Broadcast, a public participation show done at first
in front of the Loew's State Theatre on Canal Street
and later at other locations. Passers-by would be
interviewed and each would receive a coupon for a
"Carioca Cooler," the drink sponsor's product. The
program lent itself especially to free plugs for the
ventures and wares of influential New Orleanians. From
such efforts eventually evolved the single most popular
program in the city's radio history, the Dawnbusters.
Dupre would succeed Jimmie Willson as Program Director
after several years and, in the space of more than two
decades with WWL, hold virtually every possible staff
position at the station outside of engineering and
sales.[20]

Closely associated with Dupre, as the years passed,
was Pinky Vidacovich. A native of Buras, Louisiana,
he was a well-regarded musician and orchestra leader
when he made a first appearance before WWL microphones
in 1932. On Sunday afternoons at 1:30 in 1933, his
orchestra was billed as the Hillcrest Little Symphony
on a program paid for by Hillcrest Dairies. Later
his band became the regular WWL studio orchestra, and
was featured in all manner of musical broadcasts under
a variety of names. Gradually, with the inauguration
of the Dawnbusters in 1937, Pinky's comic genius began
to blossom. Having come to New Orleans at the age of
three, speaking only French, he had a strong grasp of
the flavor of Cajun culture, and he employed it effectively in what seemed countless skits, usually performed
by himself and Henry Dupre. Through the years that
followed, Pinky wrote perhaps 15,000 scripts, each
approximately 3-3¼ minutes in length. As one WWL
veteran later recalled: "With Pinky's superb writing
of sketches and songs, Henry's talent doing voices and
ad libs, and a band that just wouldn't shut up,...the
Dawnbusters became an institution." The institution
was to endure for over two decades, and Vidacovich came
to be regarded as "a modern-day minstrel using 20th
century methods to immortalize in song and playlet

161

the customs of a rapidly vanishing race."[21]

It has been said that broadcasting, like a newspaper or a billboard, is essentially an advertising vehicle, "a conduit through which a vendor crying his wares may be heard by propsective purchasers." Certainly, a growing number of such vendors were, by 1934 and 1935, availing themselves of the conduit of WWL. The number of unsponsored or sustaining programs had declined significantly with the 1932 increase in power and the 1934 attainment of full time on a clear channel.[22]

Daily schedules reflected a heavy musical orientation until the acquisition of network affiliation. The musical bias was understandable, production costs were less, relying primarily upon the salaried staff musicians of the station who were already available and who could be employed in a multitude of programs under a countless number of different names and titles. When an outside orchestra was used, it usually performed for publicity only until a sponsor was found. The schedules also lacked any significant Loyola University character. One casualty of the shift of the studios from the campus to the Roosevelt was educational programming. Other than High Mass on Sundays and infrequent presentations by various University departments, in the 1930's averaging fifteen minutes per week, the station might as well have been owned by any private enterprise firm. In 1939 a brief "Thought for the Day" program was added to the schedule at 6:45 A.M. It featured a succession of Jesuit Fathers over the years, and was carried as a remote broadcast from the Loyola campus.[23]

The product of the enhanced commercial activity could be read in WWL's income statements. Whereas time sales for 1933 totaled something over $50,000 and operations were conducted at a loss, the 1934 figures showed a gross income of $115,760, and even after "rent" to Loyola of nearly $20,000, as well as federal and state income taxes, a final profit of $3,617 was shown, the first earned on any significant volume of business. The year 1935 proved even better. Gross income reached $187,783 and stemmed from three sources:[24]

| | |
|---|---|
| $ 15,625 | network programs (Nov. & Dec. only) |
| 133,514 | national advertisers |
| 38,644 | local advertisers |
| $187,783 | total |

Even after a substantially increased rent to
Loyola of $49,984, the WWL Development figures reflected
a net profit after taxes ($869) of $4,905. The station
was finally a profit-making venture, and it would remain
that way. Moreover, the income to the University was
rapidly beginning to approach the amounts Abell had all
along felt WWL was capable of generating. What he did
not anticipate was how much beyond his original vision
the station would eventually travel.[25]

Operating expenses were the lion's share of WWL
costs in 1935. Included in this category, naturally,
were salaries and commissions. The former were not
impressive. The staff orchestra earned $125 weekly--
as a group, not individually. Even Pritchard, the
station manager, received but $200 monthly. He did,
however, have the opportunity to supplement that amount
by commissions earned on time sales for which he was
responsible. Indeed, sales department commissions made
up the largest single cost items on the 1935 statement.
Pritchard's commissions totaled $5,236 for the year, but
Al Foster did considerably better than that. The most
highly paid staff member on the station, Foster's
commissions reached almost $14,000 during the year. The
size of those commissions would prove in the future to
be a matter of some bitter disagreement between the WWL
management and the University's administration.

Renewed negotiations with the two principal broadcasting networks were the inevitable result of the clear
channel war victory. WWL had never made any secret of
its desire to acquire a chain affiliation, and talks
with both NBC and CBS had been held intermittently
over the past few years. But the discussions always
foundered on the rock of divided time on the channel.
Now with that obstacle removed, CBS acted quickly to
add WWL to its lineup. Of course, CBS already listed
a New Orleans affiliate, WDSU, but that station lacked
the two advantages that WWL could bring to any agree-
ment--10,000 watts and a clear channel. A 1933 CBS
Listening Areas survey placed the extent of WDSU's
primary coverage with its 1 kw. transmitter at 17
parishes or counties containing a total population of
858,000 in Louisiana and Mississippi. The number of
radio homes in that coverage area was set at 75,000
plus. A secondary listening area for WDSU was calculated
as including 56 additional parishes or counties, a population of 1,375,000 and 41,600 radio homes. The method
of determination of these zones should be explained.
During a week in October 1933 a sixty second message
was read by a local announcer, offering to listeners a

163

free "souvenir radio booklet." The announcement was
made for seven days, in the morning, the afternoon, and
the evening. All mail received in response by a station
was then forwarded to the CBS headquarters in New York
where it was audited by counties for each affiliate.
Counties with twenty-five or more requests per thousand
population were classified as primary coverage; those
with ten to twenty-five requests as secondary.[27]

Four years later, after WWL had become a CBS
affiliate, a similar survey was completed. The figures,
now broken down into daytime and evening listening areas,
revealed the advantages that the Loyola station brought
to the network. The primary daytime listening area now
comprised 74 parishes or counties with a total population
of 2,160,000 and 270,000 radio homes. It included not
only Louisiana and Mississippi, but portions of Alabama
and Florida as well. The after-dark listening area was
also impressive, and the survey revealed that 95% of all
radio families in Orleans Parish claimed listening to
WWL "sometime in the evening."[28]

Also adding to the attractiveness of WWL for the
Columbia network was the fact that Abell, ever hungry
for more power, filed an application with the FCC on
November 17, 1934, requesting authority to broadcast
with 50,000 watts. If granted, the boost would place
the station among the industry's elite, for only WLW
in Cincinnati with its temporary and experimental 500,000
watts service, could boast of more power. Thus with
the future as well as the present in mind, the contract
with WWL was signed by CBS on November 24, 1934. Uhalt
at WDSU was notified that the network was taking its
business elsewhere after the expiration in 1935 of the
agreement already in effect. Joe Uhalt's reaction to
the loss of his CBS affiliation was a bitter one, and
his relations with the Loyola station would thereafter
remain strained as long as he controlled WDSU. He was
able, however, to quickly secure a new chain tie, this
one with the Mutual network, the new chain that had
come into existence only the previous year. The Mutual
association was to last only two years as WDSU switched
to the NBC Blue network in 1937 and maintained that
affiliation until 1943 when NBC Blue evolved, under
federal government pressure, into the American Broadcasting Company--ABC. Meanwhile, WSMB continued to
carry the more popular programs of NBC Red, remaining
the only other network station in the city until
WNOE joined MBS in the 1940's.[29]

164

In early 1935 the station charge for WDSU on the CBS rate card was $225 per evening hour. When WWL became the affiliate in the last two months of the same year, that figure was raised to $250. There was no significant change again in the quoted rate until 1938 and WWL's step up to 50,000 watts. At that point CBS placed the new rate at $375; the following year it was raised once more, this time to $400 where it remained for the next decade. As already noted, WWL's share of the rate for two months of affiliation in 1935 totaled over $15,000.[30]

Not considered until later was the serious question of how a CBS affiliate could exercise effective control over the programming it broadcast when its entire time was optioned to the network. As the FCC eventually pointed out, it was the station and not the network which was licensed to serve the public interest, and which had a responsibility to serve the needs of its local community. Not until 1937 did CBS introduce a clause into its affiliate contracts allowing the possibility of rejection of network commercial programs: "In case the station has reasonable objection to any sponsored program or the product advertised thereon as not being in the public interest, the station may, on three weeks' prior notice thereof to Columbia, refuse to broadcast such program, unless during such notice period such reasonable objection of the station shall be satisfied." But even then, given the scanty advance information that affiliates received on up-coming network shows, the provision was of little value. The FCC recognized the reality:

> It is obvious that from such skeletal information the station cannot determine in advance whether the program is in the public interest, nor can it ascertain whether or not parts of the program are in one way or another offensive. In practice, if not in theory, stations affiliated with networks have delegated to the networks a large part of their programming functions.[31]

The entire situation was further complicated by the fact that the networks had virtually conceded the production of commercial programs, the ones that would actually be most listened to by the public, to the major advertising agencies. Thus for a local affiliate such as WWL, the determination of what its listeners would hear was made, to a significant extent, in the offices of New York advertising executives. For WWL this

165

situation posed a special paradox. The Loyola University agreement with WWL Development in 1933 had been careful to stress "the character of all matter to be broadcast is and shall always be under the absolute control and subject to the unconditional approval of the University." In part this strong statement simply reaffirmed that the licensee retained control over operations, as required by the law, but there was also contained in its meaning the cautious attitude of generally conservative religious educators towards placing too much unfettered authority in the hands of laymen. Now, however, faced with the compelling attraction of network affiliation and the bright economic future it promised, the same caution was conspicuously absent. In the pragmatic choice between WWL becoming a continuing endowment for the University or its substantially reflecting the educational and religious character of its owners, the first alternative was chosen as the greater good for the institution. That course, once chosen, would never see a significant deviation.[32]

On Saturday, October 2, 1935, WWL officially became a member of the Columbia Broadcasting System. That evening a special CBS show was carried over the network. Titled "A City of Constrasts," it originated in the WWL studios and for sixty minutes dramatized the history of New Orleans. The program was produced by Jimmie Willson and its score arranged by Karl Lellky. It gave nationwide attention to the city and to the new CBS outlet.[33]

The immediate change in the WWL schedule resulting from affiliation was wrought primarily in the evening hours. In December 1935, for instance, the hours between 6:30 P.M. and 9:30 P.M. were completely occupied by the network. Names such as Eddie Cantor, Phil Baker, Wayne King, Guy Lombardo, Myrt and Marge, the New York Philharmonic and others now appeared. It was no coincidence that the New Orleans newspapers, which for some months had recognized only the existence of the two network stations, WSMB and WDSU, now suddenly blossomed forth in 1935 with the WWL log as well. The remaining independents, on the other hand, continued to be ignored. A few vestiges of the old programming remained, however. The Pickard Family and some other hillbilly groups were still squeezed into whatever available time slots existed. Abell and Burk and Pritchard and Foster had not altogether forgotten the formula that put their station solidly into the black for the first time.[34]

# 12

## THE TWILIGHT OF THE ABELL YEARS

When the Federal Radio Commission shifted KWKH to 1100 kc. in 1934, clearing the 850 kc. channel for WWL, it also created an unexpected new quarrel for the New Orleanians. In an especially delicate situation, the Loyola Jesuits now found themselves pitted against another influential Roman Catholic religious order, the Missionary Society of St. Paul the Apostle--the Paulist Fathers.

In 1925, the Paulists, utilizing some $100,000 derived from donations to the Society, established a radio station in their rectory on West 50th Street in New York City. They cited as their goal the presentation of "talks on religious, social and literary subjects and discussions of interest of the present day." A featured part of the programming would also be the broadcasting of a Sunday evening service from the Paulist Church, "the magnificent singing of the internationally famous Paulist Choristers," and sermons by "distinguished preachers." The plans for the station received the friendly support of Patrick Cardinal Hayes, Archbishop of New York, and other Church authorities. The Department of Commerce authorized the new station to operate on a frequency of 1040 kc., with power of 5,000 watts, and with the call letters WLWL. But a year later, the Department assigned another New York station to the same frequency, requiring the Paulists to share time with the newcomers. The federal intrusion was roundly denounced by the Paulists as an "overt, deliberate, and outrageous discrimination against a high-grade non-commercial radio station with an unrivaled program of cultural entertainment and of instructive talks on religious, ethical, educational, economic and social questions, in favor of a mere dispenser of jazz and cheap amusement."[1]

Then, in a dizzying succession of changes over the next six years, WLWL was bounced from one new frequency to another--780 kc., 1020 kc., 810 kc., and finally 1100 kc., where it was required to share the channel with WPG of Atlantic City and later, KWKH. Even more infuriating to the WLWL owners, they were limited to a specific maximum number of weekly broadcast hours, 15½, a condition they described as being "brought to death's door" by the FRC's curtailment of their air time to a "starvation allowance." The FRC, on the other hand, contended that during the brief period in which the Paulist station had operated with unlimited time at its disposal, it made use of only three to four hours daily. Moreover, the Commission pointed out the more than twenty other stations active in the New York metropolitan area, raising the fundamental question of the indispensability of the WLWL endeavor. The FRC added that the others already carried educational and religious programs "to a considerable extent."[2]

The Paulists, led by their Father Superior, John B. Harney, C.S.P., had no intention of surrendering. They first attempted to convince the FRC to modify the time division between WLWL and WPG, asking for half time on the frequency. When the Commission, in February 1934, refused to agree, Harney decided to attack on a wider front. He admitted: "Neither the justice of our claims, nor repentance for its own unfair discrimination against us had budged the Federal Radio Commission one inch." Therefore, Harney merged the WLWL cause with a larger issue, justice for non-commercial broadcasters nationally. In his words, the Commission "discriminated not only against our station, but against other educational agencies in the allotment of broadcasting facilities."[3]

In March 1934, Harney proposed to the Senate Committee on Interstate Commerce an amendment to a bill being considered by that body, the bill that would soon establish the Federal Communications Commission. The Harney proposal created nothing short of an earthquake in the industry. It called for the new FCC to "reserve and allocate only to educational, religious, agricultural, labor, cooperative, and similar non-profit making associations one-fourth of all the radio broadcasting facilities." The amendment also required the frequencies set aside for non-commercial stations to be "equally desirable as those assigned to profit-making persons, firms, or corporations." Passage of the amendment would have required, of course, a wholesale redistribution of the broadcasting licenses and assignments of the nation. Nevertheless, the plan received considerable support. As Harney was shrewdly aware, educators had for years been criticizing the commercialization of radio and their own inability to maintain more than a small foothold in the medium. In 1930 they formed the National Committee on Education by Radio to lobby for their cause, and that group now threw its weight behind the Harney "25% amendment." The Paulists also rallied to the cause various Catholic organizations and periodicals. The National Catholic Educational Association and, significantly for WWL, the Jesuit Education Association were now supporters of the amendment.4

Harney organized a meeting of Catholic members of the Congress with religious and educational representatives, and successfully forged an alliance. Senators Robert F. Wagner of New York and Henry D. Hatfield of West Virginia served as the congressional leaders in the floor debate that followed. Yet, despite pressure from outside as well as support from within, the Harney plan failed, and the Communications Act of 1934 took effect with only a vague mandate given the new FCC to "study the proposal that Congress by statute allocate fixed percentages of radio broadcasting facilities to particular kinds of non-profit radio programs or to persons identified with particular types or kinds of non-profit activities," and to report its findings. The amendment failed in part because of vigorous opposition from commercial broadcasters, in part because of faulty drafting, and in part because the administrative difficulties envisaged in carrying out the reallocations seemed too gigantic. The "fixed percentage" approach to non-commercial broadcasting was never again seriously considered after 1934.5

The Paulists remained unreconciled to defeat after the failure of the 25% amendment. They now abandoned a "popular front" strategy and reverted to direct measures for securing aid for their embattled station. On January 14, 1935, they filed an application with the FCC calling for a modification of their frequency assignment, but that application affected many more interests than simply those of WLWL. The ramifications of the new proposal were felt across half the continent, and the audacity of its provisions was little short of staggering. It began simply enough--WLWL asked that the FCC assign the station a different dial location, 810 kc. But for that change to be implemented, others would be necessary as well. The 810 frequency was already occupied by WNYC, a New York City licensee, and WCCO, a Minneapolis station. The Paulists asked that

169

both of those broadcasting enterprises be assigned new
frequencies.  WNYC should operate on 1130 kc., joining
two unsuspecting other stations already there, WOV (New
York City) and KSL (Salt Lake City).  WCCO would be
placed on 800 kc.--an assignment that at the moment
belonged to WFAA (Dallas) and WBAP (Fort Worth).  The
application blandly recommended that those two Texas
operations also receive a new assignment, 850 kc., the
clear channel that WWL had fought so intensely to cap-
ture.  Finally, WWL was to be ordered to share the proposed WLWL frequency, 810 kc.  Thus under the scheme
offered by the Paulists, WWL, after five years of legal
struggle, would find itself once more dividing a channel
with another station.  Altogether, the determination of·
WLWL to move to a new frequency could directly affect
the radio activities of seven other stations, and an
even larger number indirectly.[6]

The crucial response to this jerry-built structure
of change would come from WWL.  Father Harney naively
anticipated a favorable response from New Orleans, or
at least no formal opposition.  He misunderstood the
basic nature of the WWL operation, conceiving of it as
primarily concerned with religious and educational broadcasting, as was his own WLWL.  He apparently also believed
that he had secured some pledge of support from the
Loyola Jesuits.  In a July 1935 letter to a fellow
Paulist, he recalled that Wallace Burk had once visited
him, requesting Harney's and WLWL's backing in the campaign to bring public pressure upon the FRC when that
body was considering the WWL-KWKH tangle.  Harney believed that as a consequence of Paulist aid, "the Jesuit
station at New Orleans owes its present position on the
broadcast dial to the friendly and helpful action of
WLWL," and that some recompense would now be forthcoming.
Finally, Harney anticipated bringing ecclesiastical
weight to bear on New Orleans by asking the Papal
Apostolic Delegate in the United States to intervene in
the matter.  Meanwhile, the Paulist Superior and his
colleagues were not overlooking political avenues either;
they availed themselves of the customary Catholic
conduit into federal decision-making, Postmaster General
James A. Farley.  From that official they secured promises of help and boasts of great "time and effort
consumed by me in relation to the matter."[7]

Harney was more than disappointed by the actual
WWL response to the reassignment plan; he was bitterly
angry.  Privately, he warned that the New Orleans
Jesuits would "rue the day," and he cried that "their
determined opposition to our position brands them as

contemptibly ungrateful." Nevertheless, he remained optimistic that the WLWL application might be approved anyway. Realistically, WWL's negative answer should have come as no surprise to any reasonably close observer of the station's record. The WWL management in no way equated themselves with the non-profit broadcasters who had campaigned the previous year for the 25% amendment. Since the WWL decision in 1929 to pursue commercialism, the amount of religious and educational programming on the station was steadily reduced, and with the promise of network affiliation close at hand, such programming would soon be all but completely eliminated. WWL had given no support to the 25% amendment plan, and if anything, sympathized with the National Association of Broadcasters and the proponents of commercial radio who had vehemently and successfully fought it. The primary purpose for which WWL existed in 1935 was to serve as a flourishing source of endowment funds for the University which held its license, and it was at last beginning to perform that function quite well. Thus the fundamental interests of WWL and WLWL were contradictory. The Jesuits at Loyola recognized that basic fact; Harney did not.[8]

WWL wasted no time in voicing complete opposition to the reassignments, with Paul Segal, the Washington attorney who had represented the station in the last round of the clear channel fight, serving in that legal capacity once again. First, Segal attempted to prevent the matter from even reaching the stage of an FCC hearing. He claimed that the Paulist application violated so many Commission rules that hearings would simply impose an unnecessary expense of over $5,000 on WWL. When the FCC refused to accept his argument, he complained that the New Orleans station would appear, but only reluctantly and "under protest." The hearings commenced on June 27, 1935, and were adjourned the following day. They resumed in late October and continued until the beginning of November. Once more, as he had done so often in the past six years, Abell traveled to Washington to testify. The bulk of the argument offered in this case, however, rested on the technical impossibility of the WLWL scheme.[9]

On behalf of the Paulist station, an expert engineering witness claimed that though WWL and WLWL would be operating on the same frequency, no interference problems could physically arise during the daylight hours, and the use of directional antennas would prevent interference after dark. Engineering testimony supplied by WWL, however, warned of adjacent channel interference that would be experienced on 810 kc. due to the presence of WHAS (Louisville) on 820 kc. with 50,000 watts power. It also refused to agree with the WLWL claim that the New Orleans and the New York City transmitters could avoid interference, especially if WWL was granted the requested authority to increase its power to 50,000 watts. Other affected stations joined WWL in opposition for their own special reasons.[10]

It was over a year before the FCC finally announced its decision. During that time attention continued to be focused upon the case by some Catholic opinion-makers. One Catholic periodical, The Sign, in an article on the subject, referred to WLWL as "the oldest and largest Catholic radio station in the country." In doing so, the magazine overlooked the fact that WWL was three years older than the Paulist operation, and was broadcasting with twice the power. Unwittingly though, The Sign was also drawing attention to the plain fact that WWL was now a frankly commercial station, while WLWL's raison d'etre continued to be the propagation of the faith.[11]

In December 1936, the FCC delivered its verdict. The Paulist application was denied. In the words of the Commission: "The ultimate public advantages which would be achieved...are outweighed by the public disadvantages involved therein." There were simply too many "incidental effects" on too many other stations for the proposal to be approved. For WWL, the conclusion of the Paulist dispute meant the failure of the last challenge the New Orleanians would face to a now secure position on their clear channel. For the Paulists, the decision was a severe disappointment hastening their complete abandonment of the WLWL venture. While the station actually earned a small profit in 1936, primarily from a slight excess of donations over operating costs, there seemed no real possibility that circumstance could be long continued. The result was a decision to sell the station to Arde Bulova in March 1937. The Paulist-sponsored magazine, The Catholic World, offered an explanation: "All efforts to make it self-supporting were thwarted by the Federal agencies in Washington that regulate radio. No alternative remained but to sell the facilities." A brief, explosive chapter in broadcasting history had concluded.[12]

* * * * * * * * * *

Paradoxically, while WWL was adopting a fully commercial policy in station operations, University administrators did not feel that policy precluded their radio venture from being tax exempt. The income statements for 1934 and 1935, the first years for which real profits were earned, showed both federal and state income taxes paid. They were not paid, however, without protest; the University raised the issue with the Internal Revenue Service, and in the first of a series of such disputations with IRS officials, argued for an exemption. The claim was made that WWL Development, since its stock was held by a tax-exempt University, and since the bulk of its income was paid to that educational institution, should be considered exempt as well. On April 12, 1935, the IRS denied the petition, stating that WWL Development had been incorporated "with broad powers to engage in business and not for the exclusive purpose of holding title to property for Loyola University...and as your stock carried the right to dividends." The 1935 ruling was accepted as final for the time being, but new Revenue Acts passed by the Congress in 1936 and 1938, and new judicial precedents, were to bring a reopening of the question in the early 1940's. In the meantime, taxes continued to be paid, and as earnings climbed, the governmental share did as well; 1936 saw the income taxes paid exceed $7,000.[13]

The first full year of network affiliation, 1936, showed a startling increase in earnings over a relatively good 1935. Whereas 1935 saw a gross income for WWL Development of $187,783, the following year income reached $307,474 with most of the gain stemming from CBS's payments for the carrying of sponsored network programming. Moreover, the rent or contribution paid to the University by the Development Company soared to $90,253, and even after federal and state taxes, profits of $35,082 were retained in the enterprise. WWL was rapidly turning into a gold mine--a far cry from the anemic operation that had barely maintained an existence just a decade before.[14]

Improving prospects brought changes in their wake for the station, including some that would permanently alter the history of the enterprise. On a minor scale, 1936 saw a revision in the contractual relationship between the University and WWL Development. The income gains made in 1934, 1935, and 1936 encouraged the University administration to rewrite the terms of the agreement, making it even more of a "sweetheart contract" than before. A Supplemental Agreement, signed on December 26, 1936, now required the Development Company to pay to Loyola a minimum of $52,000 annually plus 50% of the remaining profits earned by the station before taxes. Looking ahead to future FCC approval of its application, WWL Development was also authorized "to purchase, install and complete a new standard 50 kw transmitter with all necessary appurtenances" and then to turn over the title for that equipment to the University. The new terms were signed by Father Hynes for Loyola and Andrew Fitzpatrick for WWL Development.[15]

Most significant for the station's future were the management changes of 1937. They marked the first major shift in those positions since the early days of the station's commercial policy. Now the Abell years were about to reach an acrimonious conclusion.

Orie Abell had already re-assumed an old post, Faculty Director. His close friend, Wallace Burk, finally conceded to continuing bad health and resigned that office in 1934. Even while Burk held the position, however, Abell continued to dominate station operations because of his technical expertise and his close personal relations with the lay staff members, especially Pritchard and the aggressive and clever Al Foster. Now in 1937 Abell as Faculty Director faced a new University President, and one not as willing as John Hynes had been to give him the benefit of doubt on policy disagreements. Harold A. Gaudin, S.J., was a Jesuit priest who would preside over the University for only three years, but in that time he reshuffled the entire WWL management team, including Abell himself. Gaudin himself had been educated at Gonzaga University in Spokane, and at the Gregorian University in Rome. He had no previous administrative experience in higher education or connection with WWL. The new President was also facing a difficult personal situation in that he was succeeding Father Hynes, who was almost universally liked and admired.[16]

Trouble between Abell and Gaudin was to come on two fronts: programming policy and the handling of commercial accounts. Regarding the first issue, a problem of image had all along existed, but now with network affiliation and with the station on the verge of 50 kw. service, it became especially acute. Gaudin and the businessmen-directors of WWL Development determined that a station of WWL's emerging prominence should no longer be associated with the hillbilly shows and patent medicine sponsors of the struggling independent days. The "ache and pill station of the nation" phase in WWL's history ought now to be put firmly behind it.

174

Closely related to the programming issue was the question of the handling of commercial accounts. To a substantial extent, this critical sector of WWL operations had been left entirely to Al Foster's personal care, and he had conducted the station's business out of his hip pocket. To a cautious and, according to his close contemporaries, suspicious Jesuit such as Gaudin, as well as to the conservative executives of the Development Company board, this was no longer acceptable now that the stakes of the game were so much higher. The sums of money with which Foster was dealing were too substantial.[17]

Indeed, Al Foster sometimes dispensed with money altogether and operated on the barter system. He would exchange WWL air time for a sponsor's product rather than cash, load up his car with the cases of a headache remedy or a food item, and then proceed to peddle them to any likely grocery or drug stores for whatever they would bring. Certainly, the standard rate cards meant little to him; he would make whatever arrangement with a sponsor necessary to close the sale. Often, the sponsor's check might be made out to him personally, and there were rumors that not all those funds eventually found their way into the WWL account books. Rumors also flew by 1937 that WWL artists who earned talent fees from programs sold by Foster, were expected to return a portion of those fees to the Sales Manager himself.

Certainly, it appeared to Gaudin and his advisors from the business community, that the real center of power at the station lay not in the office of Abell, the Faculty Director, or Pritchard, the nominal Station Manager, but in the wheeling and dealing of Al Foster. Adding to this concern were the incontrovertible figures that showed Foster by far the most handsomely rewarded staff member, earning over $17,000 in commissions in 1936, at a time when announcers and engineers were fortunate to be offered $25 per week. Moreover, there was the constant fear and never proven belief that Al Foster's income actually went far beyond what the auditor's figures read. With those concerns, real or unreal, well in mind, Gaudin determined to professionalize the operations of the station.[18]

The decision was made in April 1937. There would be a change of command at WWL, beginning with the post of Station Manager. Gaudin, operating without the knowledge of Abell or the WWL staff, consulted friends of the University, seeking a recommendation for a new head. From Paul Segal, whose Washington law firm had

175

represented WWL in both the culmination of the clear
channel struggle with Henderson and the Paulist
challenge, came a nomination--Vincent F. Callahan.  The
nominee was what Gaudin had been seeking, a broadcasting
professional.  Callahan was an Irish Catholic from Boston
with considerable radio experience, who was currently
employed by a NBC station in Washington, D.C.  It was
presumed that once a man such as he was brought in, he
could be depended upon to make the other personnel
changes that might be required.[19]

Abell was the first of the WWL team to be informed.
He took the news badly since it could only be interpreted as a judgment on his own recent record at the
station.  Nevertheless, under pressure and reluctantly,
he agreed to travel to Washington, meet with Callahan,
and finalize the details of the latter's coming to New
Orleans.  Abell also agreed to keep the decision secret
for the time being.  Thus when Arthur Pritchard received
a telephone call from Gaudin in mid-May 1937 inviting
him to a meeting at Loyola, he did not anticipate its
purpose.  Pritchard had not yet met Gaudin, though the
latter had been Loyola's President for some months, and
therefore the Station Manager looked upon the conference
as an opportunity to offer some suggestions for improving cooperation between the University and the station.  Instead, he found to his shock that he was being
demoted to Assistant Station Manager and a new man brought
in to direct operations.  Pritchard, ever the good
soldier, agreed to the reduction of his status.[20]

Later, in a hotel room at the Roosevelt, he for
the first time encountered Callahan, who had just arrived
in the city.  Their introduction was Callahan's offering
him a drink--the WWL staff were to find over the next
two years that such invitations would be commonplace
with their new Manager.  Then Pritchard found himself
the target of a barrage of questions, all dealing with
the supposed machinations of Al Foster.  The Englishman
denied vehemently each allegation against the salesman.
It was clear, however, that under Callahan, Foster would
have no future at the station.[21]

The Callahan that Pritchard encountered in May
1937 was of medium height, stocky, with a ruddy complexion and handicapped by a withered arm.  He was
volatile, aggressive, often abusive, and addicted to
horses that never quite ran as fast as he believed they
would.  Memories of his drinking habits were still
vivid for WWL staff members decades after he departed
the scene.  J. D. Bloom would remember that he picked

up Callahan and drove him to the station each morning, and the Manager would inevitably feel the necessity to stop for a brace of breakfast beers on the way. By noon, he had switched to Scotch. Henry Dupre recalls how Callahan might fire a staff member, sometimes Dupre himself, so that someone would be available to serve as a drinking partner in the afternoon. Then the firing would be rescinded the next day. No matter his personal habits, however, he was a good radio man, he knew the business, and he set about successfully putting a substantial measure of professionalism into the operations of the station.[22]

On the second day after assuming control, Callahan wrote a long, confidential memorandum to Gaudin describing his preliminary findings. In it he deplored a multitude of practices that had previously gone on without objection. He revealed an early version of what, in another generation, would be called "payola," pointing out that: "In my observation I have learned that people are getting hats, suits, shoes, through announcements from which the station gets no return." He complained of the staff moonlighting and warned he would demand notification of all employee outside work. A much more careful check of what actually was being broadcast would also be made now: "Effective within a day or two, the engineers in charge of the transmitter will log all local and national programs originating from WWL. This log will be given to me personally; I will look it over, check it, and then turn it over to the auditing department for a further check." He sternly predicted that any employees "who hide any revenue which they receive will be fired without notice."

On the subject of Captain Pritchard, he was quite clear. If there were questionable practices at the station, they were not of the former Manager's doing. He pronounced Pritchard completely honest in his own activities. The problem with his predecessor, in Callahan's view, was that Pritchard simply was without significant knowledge of the broadcasting industry, and as a result, tended to be under the domination of the more experienced Al Foster. Callahan criticized the insufficient number of local accounts, and the poor job of collecting moneys due the station. He promised the use of Dun & Bradstreet reports in evaluating the credit of new accounts, and he stated that cash in advance would be demanded from the questionable ones. The current existence of $3500 in past due receivables would be corrected in a Callahan regime.[23]

Interestingly, Callahan reported that he had already been called upon by Harold Wheelahan, WSMB's chief. In addition to the usual words of welcome, Wheelahan raised the sore issue of WWL continually offering air time at below listed card rates. Callahan left no doubts on this point; the rate card would be followed. As he wrote Gaudin: "Regardless of the activities of any other station, WWL must and will retain its prestige. The prestige of the station can only be maintained by contracts according to the rate card." The focus of much of the unhappiness with WWL operations, Al Foster, was not in evidence when Callahan took over. The new Manager smugly stated: "For some strange reason, Mr. Foster, who appears to have been dominating the station until now, has been on a trip out of town," and he confidently predicted a satisfactory settlement of that personal problem whenever the salesman returned.[24]

In light of his own predilections, Callahan's only reference to programming policy seemed ironically humorous. He noted that in the 4:00-4:30 time period, the station was carrying a show titled "The Cocktail Hour." Piously he reported: "When I found that out, it occurred to me that a radio station operated by the Catholic Church should neither condone nor encourage cocktail hours. I have therefore instructed Mr. Willson to rename the program."[24]

Most important, Callahan looked forward optimistically to the future. He felt relations with Pritchard would be satisfactory, as the Englishman had taken the "reduced post like a soldier," and gave every indication of loyalty. Further, budgets for each department would now be set up with over-spending impossible in the absence of his own permission. He summed up his view of the station: "When the station goes to 50,000 watts, I am confident that there is a marvelous opportunity for WWL to become the outstanding station in this town."[25]

Within two months after Callahan's arrival, a clean sweep of the old WWL management was completed. Foster, seeing the situation clearly, departed the scene immediately; he left to assume the position of Commercial Manager on a St. Louis station, never again returning to Louisiana broadcasting. Pritchard, for whom Callahan had expressed some kind words, received his second rude shock of 1937 when he opened a letter from the Station Manager that bluntly fired him.

Three months salary, $600, was offered in lieu of any notice and in view of his past services to WWL. Pritchard left the station in the summer of 1937 to pursue a career in other fields, permanently forsaking the precarious radio business. The Englishman and the Irishman had not been able to get along after all.

Most wrenching for the station was the departure of Orie Abell. Unable to accept the new order and unwilling to believe the criticisms and allegations leveled at the conduct of WWL affairs during his tenure, he preferred to be replaced in the post of Faculty Director and to terminate an association with the station that extended back for more than a decade. During that time, he took a broadcasting corpse, brought it back to life, put it on a new course, and finally saw his dream for it fulfilled. Abell's WWL, after fighting off a succession of challenges, had become a major financial support for the educational institution he represented. Now that it was reaching the point of even surpassing his dream, of actually wresting the broadcasting leadership from its competitors not just in New Orleans but in the Gulf South as well, he was being shuffled off the scene. He had really built too well. Abell constructed in the end an organization that became too large, too complex and too demanding for a gifted amateur such as himself to direct successfully. The moment had come when he was required to give way to the career executives, to the men for whom broadcasting had become a profession rather than an avocation. Nevertheless, Orie Abell's contribution would never be erased. He would remain, more than anyone else, the founding father of WWL.[26]

Abell's bitterness at the turn of events did not dissipate quickly. Five months after the management change, and even though he was no longer Faculty Director, he took the time to type a long, single-spaced letter to Gaudin tearing into Callahan's methods and accomplishments. From the specifics contained within the letter, it was clear Abell was still keeping in close touch with events at the station. He cited Callahan's supposed inability to develop any significant number of new local accounts, despite the new Station Manager's rosy promises. He further cited the fact that Callahan had taken national time sales away from the now departed Foster, who had earned an 8% commission on those contracts, only to turn that same task of securing national business over to a New York-based station representative firm, the Katz Agency, that was receiving 10% commissions on the same sales. He

179

denounced an increase in the salary budget, a decline
in the quality of announcing, mounting paper work, and
Callahan's inability to recognize the inherent limitations of the New Orleans market, at that time ranked
as only the twenty-seventh largest radio market in the
nation.  Callahan had also raised the station's rates
for local business by 25%, and Abell asked:  "Why is it
that so very, very few contracts are signed up at the
increased rates, if increased rates are meeting with
very little resistance?  The best salesman on the
staff admitted he hadn't signed up a single prospect
the last ten days of October."  In addition, Abell predicted the station would gross more in the five months
of 1937 that his team had directed operations, than in
the seven months of the year under Callahan.  Finally,
he carefully and in detail noted that patent medicine
ads continued to be heard on WWL, even though they were
supposedly one of the reasons why the management change
took place.[27]

     The Abell charges, while true in part, were not
entirely fair to Callahan.  The new Manager had, in fact,
eliminated the most questionable of the medicine accounts,
at the cost of temporarily reduced earnings.  Salaries
were increased, but better personnel were being employed
and the quality of local programming was being upgraded
as a result.  The Katz Agency was earning a higher
commission on paper than Foster had, but in the long
run, a larger volume and a more desirable type of
national business would be attracted to the station by
that firm.  Equally as important, it was certain with
the Katz Agency that 10% was all they were earning.
There had been, on the other hand, too many uncertainties
in Foster's hip pocket system.  Moreover, Callahan was
making the rate card stick and eliminating special deals,
thus winning for WWL some long overdue respect among
its own competitors.  Actually, the overall figures
for the year 1937 were better than satisfactory.  Gross
income had jumped again, this time to $383,237, an
increase of over $75,000 from the previous year, and
WWL Development's annual payment to the University
surpassed the $100,000 mark for the first time,
reaching $110,051.  Much of that business had been con-
tracted by Foster and Pritchard, of course, but prospects
seemed favorable nonetheless.[28]

     In any event, there was no turning the clock back
for Orie Abell.  Gaudin and the WWL Development directors,
if they were to become dissatisfied with Callahan's
performance, would simply seek out another radio professional to replace him.  They would not look back to

the Abell group that had tended the affairs of the station prior to May 1937. A new Faculty Director also sat in Abell's chair, Francis A. Cavey, S.J. He had served at Loyola since 1926 as a professor of philosophy and the Treasurer of the University. He was small in stature, quiet, yet forceful. Cavey would hold the post until his death in 1944. Naturally, he would lack the technical expertise of Abell, and thus his personal relations with the staff would not be close. A new era was beginning for that office. No longer would a Faculty Director be intimately involved in the day to day operations of the station as Abell had been; now they would serve more as a liaison between Loyola and WWL, and particularly as a legal and public symbol of the station's ownership by the University.[29]

As for Orie Abell himself, he remained at the University as a teacher of physics until 1938. In that year he joined the faculty of the new Jesuit High School in New Orleans, then briefly returned to Loyola in 1944 to serve as University treasurer, only to leave again in 1947. He held positions on both the high school and the college level in Dallas and in Mobile during the next three decades before passing away in February 1971. After the trauma of 1937, he never again returned to the field of broadcasting.[30]

## THE CALLAHAN INTERVAL

Vince Callahan's tenure as Station Manager of WWL saw significant steps forward taken, steps that propelled the station to the front rank of broadcasting organizations in the South. He began by tightening the business procedures being employed, introducing office accounting techniques and systems already in use in the nation's larger stations, but up to then not utilized at WWL where trial and error were the rule. The P.I. accounts and most of the more questionable patent medicines that Foster relied upon to increase WWL revenue were gradually eliminated. Foster found these national accounts so lucrative that he, for a time before 1935, opposed the station securing a CBS affiliation. Network programs, in the view of the former Sales Manager, only reduced the quantity of air time available for him to sell. Callahan was not able to throw all the medicine accounts off immediately (indeed some were quite legitimate), for fear of too drastic a decline in WWL income, but he phased them out as quickly as possible.[1]

Foster was replaced as Sales Manager by Paul Beville, but the latter was closely circumscribed in his ability to maneuver. National sales were largely taken from him and placed in the hands of WWL's new station representatives, the Katz Agency. As a result, Beville earned only $9,127 in commissions in 1938 as opposed to the $17,254 Foster collected in 1936 and the $15,416 Foster pocketed for just six months with the station in 1937. Beville's figure was, nonetheless, the most earned by any WWL salesman, and still considerably above the incomes of the on-the-air staff. The popular Henry Dupre's salary for 1938 totaled just $1,559.[2]

The Katz Agency, to whom WWL turned over national time sales, was founded in the 1880's by Emmanuel Katz

to represent California newspapers in New York City.
It grew gradually into a nationwide organization representing some fifty newspapers scattered across the
country.  In the 1930's, the agency took on the responsibility of serving the national sales needs of radio
stations owned by its client newspapers.  A Radio
Department was created, and Eugene Katz, Jr., grandson
of the founder, placed in charge.  Soon the radio business overtook and surpassed the original print sector
upon which the firm had been based.[3]

In May 1937, Eugene Katz was on a necessary business trip.  He had just visited a client in Texas, and
was required to change trains in New Orleans on his way
back to New York City.  Taking advantage of the brief
stop in the Louisiana city, he decided to call upon
what he then regarded as the "top radio station in
town"--WSMB.  Here he met a stone wall; Wheelahan was
not interested, and WSMB already had satisfactory
national representation.  Not quite knowing what to
expect, Katz then chose to visit the WWL offices just
a block away.  He arrived at an opportune moment, just
ten days after Callahan's taking control and immediately
following the release of Al Foster.  Callahan was
determined to change the procedure for handling national
time sales, and to turn that responsibility over to a
firm of professional station representatives.  The Katz
Agency was the first to present itself to him, and
solely because Gene Katz was required to change trains
in New Orleans.[4]

Callahan began at once to regale Katz with "hair-
raising stories" of the confusion the new WWL boss
was encountering in the aftermath of Foster and
Pritchard.  The New Yorker was bewildered both by the
tales and by Callahan himself, who seemed perfectly
capable of proceeding from endearing Irish warmth and
intelligent conversation to verbal abuse, scathing
contempt, and blustering pugnaciousness, all in one
afternoon's chat.  Callahan, Katz later recalled with
masterful understatement, possessed "arcane qualities."
In the months ahead, Callahan's moods were to cause
Katz considerable personal anguish, and that was not
lessened by the broadcaster's propensity for using
meetings with Katz as opportunities for dedicated
drinking at the latter's expense.  Nevertheless, with
WWL soon to be the only 50,000 watt entry in his firm's
stable of stations, Katz chose to grin and bear it.[5]

Negotiations with Callahan were quickly concluded
but formalization of the agreement required the approval

of the Loyola administration. When, at the last moment, the Jesuit educators attempted to change the contract terms, Katz drew himself up and solemnly announced: "Gentlemen, I don't want to seem difficult to do business with but the Katz Agency was founded in 1888, and it has been using this contract form for fifty years. If you don't mind, we would like to stick to it." To which Father Gaudin, Loyola's President, answered the Society of Jesus was a good deal older than that, and it had some considerable experience of its own. Eugene Katz later recalled Gaudin as charming and handsome, but had he "lived to be a hundred, he would not have understood broadcasting."[6]

The national rates that WWL put into effect on September 1, 1937, offered a fifteen minute weekly evening program for $76.50; the same length program in the daytime hours on a weekly basis sold for $38.25. These rates placed WWL slightly above WSMB, the NBC Red affiliate in the city, where the same show sold for $63.75 in the evening and approximately $31 before sunset. Since some 75% of the NBC Red network programs were sponsored, while the same percentage of NBC Blue were sustaining in 1938, the former made WSMB a more formidable competitor than WDSU.

The WWL advantages, however, continued to be power and channel. While WWL broadcast on a clear channel with 10 kw in 1937, and with 50 kw in the offing for 1938, WSMB would see a power increase from just 1 kw to 5 kw in the same years, and WDSU continued with but 1,000 watts. The latter two stations operated on regional channels.

With the advent of WWL's 50,000 watts, its rates, not surprisingly, jumped again. The same weekly quarter hour program in the evening now cost $102, and in the daytime $54. A single evening spot announcement of 100 words inflated in price from $25 to $35. Nevertheless, rates were not high when compared to Northern stations. For example, though CBS was selling an evening hour on its New Orleans affiliate for $275 in 1937, the affiliate in Boston was commanding $425, in St. Louis $500, in Chicago $725, and in New York $1200. The New Orleans and the Southern markets, even with WWL's available power, were not sufficient to command top dollar in station rates.[7]

In keeping with a station about to join the elite corps of 50 kw, clear channel broadcasters, a staff expansion took place, especially in the technical and

the administrative categories. Expenses increased
significantly in 1938, Callahan's initial full year as
Manager, despite the fact that the overall revenue of
the station suffered its first decline in years, from
$383,237 in 1937 down to $351,288. Nevertheless,
operations were still profitable and a rental payment
of over $82,000 was remitted to the University by WWL
Development. It was clear that Callahan believed money
must be spent in order for money to be made, even if,
temporarily, increased operating costs cut into the
year's earnings.[8]

Coming to the forefront now under Callahan was
new departmental leadership. When Abell left his post
of Faculty Director, he also abandoned the title of
Chief Engineer. That position was given to Jefferson
Davis "J.D." Bloom, who had literally grown up with
the station. Born in New Orleans in 1907, he attended
Loyola from 1925-1929, and had been a familiar figure
around WWL in those years. Later he was employed by
two Michigan stations while completing an electrical
engineering degree at the University of Detroit in
1932. Bloom returned to New Orleans the same year and
accepted a job on WWL offered to him by Abell for $25
weekly. It was less money than he had been earning in
Michigan, but since banks were closing all over that
state in 1932, he felt safer in Louisiana. His first
task was to wire the Roosevelt Hotel studios. As Studio
Supervisor from 1932 to 1937, he worked a six day week.
Every fourth day he was required to first open the
studio in the morning, next travel out to the transmitter
site at noon and operate it from 6:00 P.M. until midnight sign-off, and finally sleep over, acting as the
night watchman. In 1937 he succeeded Abell as Chief
Engineer, and in the following year, it was Bloom who
was given the responsibility for the plans and construction of the 50 kw transmitter. He would continue
his new post for the next three decades and more.[9]

Replacing Bloom in charge of studio operations
was Francis Jacob, Jr. Born in 1912, he attended
Jesuit High School in New Orleans, graduating in 1930.
He joined WWL on a full time basis in June 1932, after
a year of part-time transmitter duty at the station.
He, like Bloom, was hired by Orie Abell who seemed
unable to resist a job applicant who could claim a
Jesuit education on either the high school or college
level. Jacob began at $60 monthly, working anywhere
from 60-80 hours each week. He would later play a
major role in bringing about the unionization of the
station's technical staff.[10]

186

By 1939 Callahan's list of employees was a far cry
from Abell's skeleton crew of a decade before. In
addition to Callahan and Cavey, eleven men (no women)
held executive titles. There was now a Director of
Special Events (Henry Dupre), a Director of Merchandising (Louis Read), and a Supervisor of Transmitter
(Edward du Treil). Also employed were thirty-three
other staff members, twenty-two men and eleven women,
most of them musicians, singers, and engineers.
Musicians there were in abundance as Pinky Vidacovich's
orchestra came to play a larger role in programming.
Fifteen years later the American Federation of Musicians
would acknowledge that from the day the Roosevelt studios
opened in 1932 and for the next two decades, WWL "has
not had one day without staff employment in your station
for a group of our members," and during most of that
period, the station averaged eleven or more musicians
on its weekly payroll.[11]

While WWL's application for authorized power of
50,000 watts was first filed by Abell in November 1934,
it was under Vince Callahan that the goal was achieved.
No significant opposition existed to the proposed increase, since KWKH had by 1937 accommodated itself to
the 1100 kc. frequency and was negotiating with the FCC
to make the assignment permanent. Nevertheless, Abell,
a veteran of too many FRC and FCC proceedings, saw no
reason why some extra-curricular political intervention
should not be of assistance. For this purpose, the
station's landlord, Seymour Weiss, and the omnipresent
Jim Farley were employed. Weiss, the old Huey Long
confidante, possessed a new-found influence in Washington since the compacting of the so-called Second
Louisiana Purchase between the heirs of the Kingfish's
power and the Roosevelt administration. In late 1936
the Justice Department announced the dropping of a
bundle of income tax fraud cases being brought against
a number of Longites, including Weiss, and Farley now
magically appeared as the commencement speaker at the
Louisiana State University graduation exercises. For
WWL, the peace settlement offered another avenue for
coaxing the FCC into a favorable decision on the 50 kw
application.[12]

It was largely, however, a war without a battle.
Opposing forces simply did not take the field. The
application was heard by FCC Examiner George H. Hill,
on June 9, 1937, the month after the departure of
Abell and Foster. Paul Segal, George S. Smith and
Charles Denechaud represented the station. Examiner
Hill dutifully noted that the proposed new transmitter

equipment would cost some $120,000, and that a line of credit was established at a New Orleans bank for twice that sum.  He took account of the new population area that would be serviced, and he concluded it "would not be areas such as would be expected to receive primary clear channel daytime service from other stations." Moreover, Hill found WWL's present coverage in rural areas "would be made more reliable by an increase in power."  He recommended the granting of the application. Six months later the Commission itself reiterated the conclusions of the Examiner.  It announced that the University was "fully qualified financially" to operate a 50,000 watts station, that it was already "rendering a meritorious service," and that a need existed for the additional service that would be provided by the new· transmitter power.  On December 30, 1937, it granted the application.[13]

Acting quickly on the favorable decision, WWL employed a consulting radio engineering firm to study the merits of a new lake front site versus the old transmitter location.  The firm's February 1938 report favored the new site near Kenner, Louisiana.  Two weeks later an agreement was reached between RCA and WWL Development by which the manufacturing giant sold the station a "RCA Radio Transmitting Apparatus" for the sum of $112,000, of which $37,333 was paid initially and the remainder financed in 36 monthly installments at a 3% interest rate.  Temporarily, WWL Development retained title to the equipment, and its December 31, 1938, balance sheet reflected the additions.  Capital items now included the following after small amounts deducted for depreciation:

> Transmitting Plant and Equipment....$188,150
> Buildings..........................  25,135
> Land...............................  18,317
> Studio and Office Equipment........   3,897

Correspondingly, approximately $130,000 in notes payable were listed under liabilities.[14]

On early Sunday morning, November 20, 1938, between the hours of 1:00 and 4:00 A.M., the new RCA transmitter was tested.  The announcers on duty invited any distant listeners to wire the station if they were receiving the signal.  In response to the call, WWL received 1,179 telegrams from 47 of the 48 states.  Only Utah failed to reply.[15]

WWL, even before the introduction of 50 kw service, had advanced to a major position in the New Orleans market. In the spring of 1937, a CBS survey interviewed radio owners in Orleans Parish, asking them to name the stations to which they regularly listened. The respondents mentioned an average of three stations per interview. Not surprisingly, the network affiliates scored the highest, but WWL was indicated more often than any other. Of those questioned, 95% answered WWL while 93% included WSMB. In third place, and trailing rather badly behind, was WDSU with a 55% response. It must have come as a distinct shock to the other New Orleans stations to learn that in evening listening, WLW from Cincinnati scored higher than the remaining local broadcasters. Nearly one-third of those surveyed regularly heard the Ohio super power station, while only 11% tuned in WBNO and just 6% WJBW.[16]

The programs which the respondents heard on WWL in 1937 and 1938 were approximately 75% network shows in the evening hours, and some 50% during the daytime. The CBS "personalities" featured on the network in those years included Orson Welles, Cecil B. DeMille, Edward G. Robinson, Jean Hersholt, Phillips Lord, William Powell, Conrad Nagel, Eddie Cantor, Al Jolson, Kate Smith, Benny Goodman, Guy Lombardo, Wayne King, Paul Whiteman, Emily Post, and others. CBS programs on WWL included Myrt and Marge, Ma Perkins, Big Sister, Hilltop House, Little Orphan Annie, Easy Aces, Hollywood Hotel with Dick Powell, Big Town, Major Bowes Amateur Hour, Gang Busters, Hobby Lobby, Lux Radio Theater, among others.[17]

But it was upon local programming that much of the attention at WWL fell in the Callahan period. The Station Manager was determined to upgrade the quality of what was produced in the New Orleans studios, and he could claim justifiable progress. By 1938 the hillbilly groups had been virtually eliminated from the station, thereby appeasing the Loyola administration. Replacing the evicted country music were such programs as Tribute to a Gentleman and Roses to a Lady in which prominent civic and social leaders were fulsomely praised; Deep South featuring a "colored unit of ten negroes in spiritual and jubilee songs, also an old negro deacon as the narrator"; WWL Job Mart on which "ten persons appear each week and tell of their qualifications for positions"; the United Press News, Dupre's Street Broadcast, and heaping quantities of music. Orchestra remotes from the Blue Room of the Roosevelt were heard daily (with the network carrying the programs twice weekly); singers such as Jimmie Willson, Audrey Charles, Dorothy Fields, Louise Hamilton, and the rising Norman Treigle were featured; and Ray McNamara on the studio organ was ever present. Drama was increasingly a feature with efforts such as the WWL Playmakers Lab and the WWL Summer Theatre of the Air. On July 19, 1939, the latter offered an adaption of Oscar Wilde's Lady Windermere's Fan. Three weeks later a production of Ibsen's Hedda Gabler was aired on the same program.[18]

And then there was the Dawnbusters! For two decades it reigned as the single most popular radio program in Louisiana broadcasting, and probably the most remunerative for a station as well. It dominated the morning hours between 7:00-9:00 A.M., especially in the pre-1945 era when the number of radio stations operating was more limited, and the broadcasts were heard by listeners in parts of ten states.

The show had many fathers and gradually evolved into its final form over a period of a few years in the late 1930's. Henry Dupre had begun doing a morning program with phonograph records in the middle years of the decade. Soon a live piano was added, then a string trio, and then through Callahan's suggestion, Pinky Vidacovich's WWL staff orchestra. About a dozen musicians, male and female singers, Dupre as Master of Ceremonies, and a staff announcer were the customary complement. Soon a straight musical format was modified by the addition of comedy, and, in the long run, it would be the humor that would be best remembered.[19]

Certainly, the Dawnbusters was patterned after Don McNeill's successful Breakfast Club program in Chicago. McNeill had taken over that show in 1933, changed its name from The Pepper Pot to The Breakfast Club, and quickly established it on NBC Blue as one of the most popular daytime network shows. Callahan, undoubtedly, had in mind the creation of a regional variation on the McNeill formula when he encouraged the production of a morning musical variety vehicle on WWL. The name of the program was the result of a contest in which listeners were asked to contribute titles with the best receiving a $25 bond. The winner was a Baton Rouge girl, Garnette Schroeder, who coined Dawnbusters (perhaps somewhat suggested by the current CBS hit evening show, Gang Busters). On April 11, 1938, even though the program had already been on for several months listed as simply Henry Dupre or Pinky's Orchestra, the name Dawnbusters appeared for the first time in the newspaper radio schedules. It would not leave those schedules for twenty years.[20]

As early as January 1938, Callahan boasted of the
program to Father Gaudin. He noted that it was then
carried daily except Sunday from 6:30-9:00 A.M., and
that it already had received 30,000 letters and cards.
He termed it "the most outstanding local program in
the City of New Orleans." The Dawnbusters did not
depend upon only local popularity, by any means. For
several months, the show was a weekly feature of the
CBS morning line-up and was carried coast-to-coast.
The official explanation for its discontinuance as a
network "feed," were the "commercial expenditures
necessary" for such a national program. Henry Dupre
recalls it differently. He remembers that Pinky
Vidacovich had written a line for a Cajun-flavored
song: "You got to pick the mirliton, you good for
nothing coushon." Network officials objected to coushon,
claiming it sounded obscene. Pinky knowing a rough
translation would be "fat pig," stubbornly refused.
Coushon stayed, the CBS spot went. Whatever the actual
circumstance, Dawnbusters remained primarily an immensely
successful regional program.[21]

The ingredients were of high quality and blended
effectively. A talented dozen musicians including the
soon to be famous Al Hirt, a clarinetists' clarinetist
in the remarkable Irving Fazola, and Ray McNamara whose
performances on theatre organs were heard in the very
earliest days of radio in New Orleans, formed the solid
core of the program. To that was added a succession of
able singers--Norman Treigle, the great base baritone
whose career on the operatic stage still lay ahead of
him, Bonnie Bell, Gene Paul, Kelly Rand, and most
remembered, the O'Dair Sisters, who began on Dawnbusters
as girls in their mid-teens. Sally, the oldest, was
followed on WWL by her younger sisters Margie and
Dottie. Their last name, chosen for radio purposes,
was the product of another of those inevitable promotion
contests. A female listener won a $25 war bond by
suggesting O'Dair, a name that cleverly combined all
the letters contained in the word "radio."[22]

Most of all, however, there was Pinky and Henry.
Vidacovich called upon his musical talent and his comedy
genius to write a multitude of songs and skits, many
of them reflecting his own Cajun background. It was
Cajun French blended in an idiosyncratic fashion with
English that produced the marvelous dialect that Pinky
Vidacovich captured so well. A prime example was a
novelty piece written and sung by him on a 1945

191

show; it was titled: "When We Kiss This War
Goodbye."

> There'll be a fae' do do when the whistle blow
>     and we kiss this war goodbye.
> Soon as the Japanese surrender, we are going on a
>     bender, when we kiss this war goodbye.
> Now when this thing is over with its sorries
>     and its strife, doggone I'll be so happy,
>     I might even kiss my wife.
> Cause then we'll get some bacon, some
>     sausage, and some meat, and a
>     certain big, fat butcher will get
>     kicked right in his teeth.
> There'll be a fae' do do when the whistle
>     blow and we kiss this war goodbye.
> We'll buy gasoline and tire, set our
>     ration books on fire, when we
>     kiss this war goodbye.
> Till then we've got to sacrifice and
>     econom-acize, and wear that
>     droopy underwear what come in
>     just one size.
> But when this fight is over, there'll
>     be a brand new deal.
> The only ones still fighting will be
>     me and Cleophile.
> There'll be a fae' do do when the whistle
>     blow and we kiss this war goodbye.
> We'll eat butter, jam, and jelly till
>     it almost busts our--stomach;
>     um, something is wrong there!
> Oh, well, it will be alright when we
>     kiss this war goodbye.[23]

Vidacovich portrayed a variety of characters in
the comedy sketches he wrote, and, invariably, Henry
Dupre was written in as the straight man. Pinky's
roles included "the Old Sarge" and his most popular
part, Placide Vidac of Bayou Kop Kop. Placide would
recount to Dupre the antics of some Bayou residents,
among them Wolf Foche, D. D. (the dog doctor of Kop
Kop), Deluge LeBlanc (the rainmaker), Humidity Trosclair
(the sweater, in the absence of rain he could be
employed to sweat over your flowers), Cecile De Mele
(the director of the Kop Kop little theater), Bluebeard
Batiste (the local bigamist), and Chonkee duTeil (the
town crier--for a fee he would agree to cry over a
corpse if the relatives wouldn't). A sample of the
Placide-Dupre repartee that Vidacovich authored was
the following from the 1940's:

Dupre: Placide, I don't find you looking well.
Placide: I guess maybe so. I have to go to the hospital for a crack-up there. You know Cleophile, my wife, she don't like the way I look. But why I got to go to the hospitals? I don't like the way she looks and I don't ask her to go to the hospitals. Furthermore, I don't mind telling you I am afraid of hospitals.
Dupre: Oh, there's nothing to be afraid of, Placide. There'll just take your temperature and--
Placide: Oh, no they won't. I'm too smarts for that. I've put everything in my wife's name.
Dupre: What hospital are you going to, Placide?
Placide: Well, I don't know. Where are the good ones at?
Dupre: Well, you're certainly asking the right man. But don't they have any hospitals in Kop Kop?
Placide: Sure, sure, they've got the Clovise Clinic there.
Dupre: Ah! Why was it named Clovise? Was he killed in the war?
Placide: No, he was killed right there in the clinic. He was the first case that they have at the Clovise Clinic. And right away the doctors then they was have an argument. One say his left kidneys would have to come out, and the other say his right kidneys. So there was, what you call a compromise.
Dupre: They compromised?
Placide: Yeah, they took out his liver.
Dupre: Oh, Placide! But a person can't live without a liver.
Placide: Yeah!--that was their first importants discovery.[24]

Of the sketches that Pinky wrote, but did not take an acting role in, the best remembered were those featuring the Reknits Twins who supposedly owned a Bourbon Street nightclub. Margie O'Dair, in a little girl voice, took the part of Anna Reknits while Billy Newberger and later Al Hirt played her brother. Neither character demonstrated significant intelligence, and the name Reknits spelled backward (a popular 1940's device) was "stinker." Again, Henry Dupre acted as straight man. A sample of their work from the early 1950's follows:

Dupre: Hello, the Reknits Twins. Anna, honey, how are you? How are things at the nightclub?
Anna: Pretty good. We've got a new act, a toe dancer, Tilly Trapanya. She used to be with the ballet.
Dupre: Well, why isn't she with the ballet now?
Anna: She developed what most toe dancers fear

193

most, poor thing.
    Dupre: What is that?
    Anna: An ingrown toe nail.
    Dupre: Oh my! What could be worse than a toe
dancer with an ingrown toe nail?
    Anna: I don't know. Unless, maybe, a fire eater
with ulcers.
    Dupre: Yes, that would be bad.
    Anna: Or a knife thrower with no sense of
direction, or--
    Dupre: Alright! That's enough, that's enough!
Now look, Anna, this ballet dancer, does she still
suffer with her toe nail?
    Anna: Not for the first show. But in the second
show, I felt so sorry for her. There she was doing her
toe tap with the tears just streaming down her cheeks.
You see, it's usually after the first show that she
kicks her husband.
    Dupre: She kicks her husband?
    Anna: Yeah. They always have an argument and she
ends up kicking him. To make matters worse, he's got
a wooden leg.
    Dupre: That makes it worse?
    Anna: Yeah. Sometimes when she kicks him, she aims
a bit too low.
    Dupre: Oh, oh, yes, yes. Well, is her husband in
the act, Anna?
    Anna: No, he won't work. That's what makes Tilly
so mad. Last year when he lost his leg, Tilly almost
divorced him.
    Dupre: Well, where did he lose his leg last year?
In Korea?
    Anna: No, in a barroom.
    Dupre: In a barroom!
    Anna: He's got a bad habit of taking it off when
he's drinking.[25]

    The Dawnbusters was a commercial success from the
beginning, with some sponsors continuing for years.
Griffin Shoe Polish was probably the most constant
supporter with its insistent jingle:

    Keep your shoes shined all the time,
    Cause all the time is the time to shine.

A fifteen minute segment of Dawnbusters was, in fact,
listed in newspaper schedules for a while as "Time to
Shine." Other subscribers included the Dr. Tichenor's
Antiseptic, Bab-O, Dr. LeGrear Livestock and Poultry
Prescriptions, Checkerboard Feeds, and Blackdraught
Cough Syrup. As early as September 1937 the WWL national

rate card signaled out the <u>Dawnbusters</u> for special
charges, separate from those for ordinary daytime programming on the station.[26]

There was no denying, however, that the elaborate
variety showcase was expensive. The staff musicians
received union scale, $27.50, in the 1940's, but comedy
performances meant additional talent fees. Al Hirt
earned an extra $10 for acting in the Reknits sketches.
Of course, the number of people involved in the program
necessarily meant its cost far surpassed that of any
other locally produced show on a New Orleans station.
It was, in Callahan's eyes as well as his successor's,
a trade-off between expense and popularity. The
<u>Dawnbusters</u> attracted enormous attention to WWL, and the
<u>station's</u> schedule all through the day and its revenues
prospered correspondingly--at least until the intrusion
of television created an entirely new set of economics
in the 1950's.[27]

Under Callahan, the WWL public image underwent a
distinct change. From a station that some said had
"more guitars than kilowatts," a middle-of-the-road
program policy now emerged, emphasizing standard popular
music, comedy, and even attempting occasional adventures
into serious drama. It was a personality with many
facets. It incorporated a more vital style of announcing; a "personality cult" between New Orleans radio
announcers and their listeners actually began with
Henry Dupre on WWL. The growing dynamism of Paley's
CBS added sparkle to WWL too, but the station laid
great emphasis on its own home community as well. For
many years, its station identification formula placed
the city first, a then unique arrangement: "This is
New Orleans, WWL...." Certainly, these changes were
more in keeping, not only with the station's front row
position as a 50 kw, clear channel operation, but also
with the desires and inclinations of the Loyola Jesuits
and their advisors on the WWL Development board of
directors.[28]

Not as pleasing though were other aspects of
Callahan's record. The 1938 income figures showed
the first decline in gross broadcasting revenues and
profits since the early 1930's, the result of both
Callahan's commitment to professionalizing and upgrading
the station, the preparations for 50 kw service, and an
economic slump, the Roosevelt Recession, that gripped
the nation in the world's last prewar year. That
slippage only added weight to other unhappiness already
being expressed with the Station Manager. One problem

was basic--Callahan was an abrasive Northerner in a city
that regarded any non-New Orleanians as foreigners,
and especially disliked Yankee carpetbaggers come South
to teach the locals new ways. His social habits probably
were decisive, however. The drinking and the gambling
had, in the eyes of many of the Jesuit Fathers, become
notorious, and they pressed Gaudin for action against
him. Finally, Callahan was less than tactful in his
dealings with the Jesuits, some of whom still were
uneasy with a commercial station with virtually complete
lay direction and control. Since the departure of Abell
in 1937, even the position of Faculty Director seemed
too symbolic. It was to be a recurring concern; a few
Loyola voices would always regard the price in lost
authority being paid for expanding the University's
endowment as higher than acceptable.[29]

By January 1939, the signs of trouble were apparent.
Gaudin wrote Callahan criticizing both the organization
of the sales force and the quality of local programs.
Despite the success of the Dawnbusters, Gaudin still
denied "any marked improvement in talent is discernible."
Within weeks, the decision to change Managers was made,
and a quiet search for a successor was already begun.
Candidates in Pennsylvania, Rhode Island, and Georgia
were contacted and interviewed by the summer of 1939.
One in particular, W. Howard Summerville, was receiving
very serious consideration. On August 5, Gaudin wrote
Summerville in Atlanta, advising him: "Our plans have
not matured and will not do so until the end of this
month. I shall write again as soon as there be something definite." Summerville replied that he was
looking forward to hearing from the President again
"when your plans are definite," and thanked the WWL
Development board "for the time they gave me."[30]

Howard Summerville, often called Slim, was born
in Illinois in 1899, and then moved to Texas with his
family at the age of three. In 1927 he accepted a
position with the Chilton Advertising Agency in Dallas,
the starting point for his long career in radio. Chilton
was serving as the station representative for KRLD
there, and the experience Summerville gained in handling
that client caused him to be offered the post of
Commercial Manager by those broadcasters three years
later. In 1935 he moved to Atlanta as Director and
Commercial Manager of WGST, the CBS affiliate in that
city. Under his management, WGST, the Georgia Tech
station, increased its power from 250 to 5,000 watts

In temperament, he differed drastically from
Callahan. Where Callahan was volatile and overbearing,
Summerville was quiet and methodical with a tendency
toward choosing the safe, cautious course rather than
risk-taking. Where Callahan could often be stubborn,
even bull-headed, Summerville would prefer to be pliable
and mild-mannered in his dealings with station owners.
At WWL he would be especially conscious of the difficulty of his position; he was responsible for the administration of a radio operation and also reporting to a
group of conservative priest-educators whose perceptions
of the requirements and needs of a commercial station
did not always match those of an experienced broadcaster. Some observers came to believe that because
of his diplomatic restraint, WWL's success after 1939
was much more the result of the general prosperity of
the economy and the industry than his management.
Nevertheless, one fact is indisputable. Callahan's
tenure at WWL lasted two years; Summerville's would
last two decades.[31]

As predicted by Gaudin, Callahan was gone by the
end of August 1939. The manner of his firing is not
recorded; it is known that he left for a new position
with a Westinghouse station in Boston, and still later
a non-broadcasting opportunity in Washington, D.C.
Ironically, Harold Gaudin, the Loyola President who
presided over the revolutions in WWL management in 1937
and again in 1939, found himself replaced in his own
office in the same month that Callahan departed. On
August 21, 1939, he was succeeded as the University
head by the Reverend Percy A. Roy, S.J. Father Roy,
another native New Orleanian, was serving as Dean of
the College of Arts and Sciences at the time of the
appointment. No public explanation for the shift in
University leadership was ever announced; the campus
newspaper, The Maroon, simply and without elaboration
reported that Gaudin had been assigned to a new post
in Shreveport. Thus the unsettled conditions at WWL
over the preceeding three years may have claimed one
more casualty.[32]

Moving quickly, Roy traveled to Atlanta and met
with the prospective new Manager. An offer was made
and accepted. On November 28, 1939, with a salary of
$9,100, W. Howard Summerville became WWL's next
Manager, and the last it would have in the station's
radio era. The Callahan interval, a critical two years
in the history of WWL, was concluded.[33]

# 14

## A KEY TO THE MINT

On December 8, 1941, the day after Pearl Harbor,
the Green Hornet's valet, Kato, was suddenly and without comment transformed from a smooth Japanese into a
likable Filipino, complete with an entirely new accent.
Radio was now ready to fight World War II.[1]

December 7 had found WWL offering its usual 1941
Sunday programming.  The station signed on at 8:00 A.M.
with the CBS news show, The World Today.  The morning
hours featured the traditional High Mass from the Holy
Name of Jesus Church on the Loyola campus, and in the
afternoon the New York Philharmonic was scheduled.  At
1:31 P.M., however, a terse United Press bulletin was
received: "WASHINGTON--WHITE HOUSE ANNOUNCES JAPANESE
HAVE ATTACKED PEARL HARBOR."  The WWL program interrupted for the first broadcast of the momentous news was
a local musical half hour featuring the Jacobs Singers.
At 2:00 P.M., the New York Philharmonic concert was
delayed while CBS commentator Elmer Davis gave additional
and fragmentary details of events in Honolulu.  When
conductor Artur Rodzinski finally launched the Philharmonic orchestra into Shostakovitch's Symphony No. 1
in F Major a few minutes later, it was simply background
music for further bulletins tumbling in rapid succession
into the nation's radios.  The evening was to have
included a locally produced quiz program, Jingle Jamboree, and the network's Gene Autry, Crime Doctor, Take
It or Leave It, and Helen Hayes features.  The news
from the Pacific, obviously, radically altered that
Sunday's routine listening, as it would the overall
operations of the country's stations for the next four
years.[2]

* * * * * * * * * *

Some steps had already been taken to prepare radio

199

for war even before Pearl Harbor. Section 606 of the
Communications Act of 1934 authorized the President to
take control of the industry during a period of national
emergency, and, utilizing that power, Franklin Roosevelt
established in September 1940 the Defense Communications
Board, later called the Board of War Communications.
With FCC Chairman James Lawrence Fly at its head, the
Board worked out plans for radio's contribution to the
national defense and its operation in wartime.    In
keeping with those plans, the FCC in early 1942 announced
a policy of granting no applications for the modification
of existing transmitters or for the construction of new
facilities that would involve the use of critical materials.  Only "essential repairs or replacements for the
purpose of maintaining existing services" were permitted.
In effect, the FCC banned the establishment of new stations for the duration of the war, thereby limiting the
industry for the next four years to its 1941 size.
On June 30, 1941, the regulatory authority reported
915 stations licensed or under construction; on the
same date in 1945 the number remained relatively unchanged.[3]

The Commission also ordered reductions in station
power in 1942 "in the interest of conservation of
equipment."  As a result, radiated power was reduced
some 20% by 1943 with a corresponding prolongation of
equipment life (especially that of the high priority
vacuum tubes) and, according to the federal officials,
"without a noticeable change to the broadcast listener."
Previous standing orders were likewise modified.  Stations were no longer required to be on the air for at
least two-thirds of their authorized time.  Instead just
one-third of their broadcast day was now regarded as
sufficient.  In addition, standards for engineers were
relaxed "in recognition of the shortage of radio-
telephone operators because of the additional demands
of military services."  By the final year of the war
the prohibitions on new construction and modifications
were slightly eased.  In January 1945 the FCC allowed
applications from those localities not receiving primary service from any existing stations, while changes
in facilities were permitted if the cost was less than
$500.[4]

One major effect of the ban on new construction
was to substantially increase the worth and the
selling price of already operating properties.  Prospective entrants into the broadcasting field found a
seller's market facing them with stations available

only for prices "far in excess of the value of the physical assets to be transferred." With new competition effectively eliminated by the wartime material shortages and resulting FCC prohibitions, with many foreign markets closed to advertisers, and with the print media unable to absorb additional advertising business because of cutbacks in the available paper stock, radio stations in the war years began to resemble well-stocked gold mines. Advertisers appeared to be virtually throwing money at broadcasters in order that products, many of which were not then available to civilian consumers, might be publicized. Sponsors seemed determined to keep their names before the public in preparation for the days following the war when the items might once again be marketed.[5] The following 1943 Elgin Watch commercial from a WWL-aired CBS program, The Man Behind the Gun, typifies this "institutional" approach:

(Sound of bomber engines in background)
Announcer: Their take-off timed to the split second, these mighty bombers will depend upon exact timing all the way to the target, for seconds may mean the difference between success or failure of their mission. Sure and true before the eyes of many a bomber crew is an Elgin navigation clock. Strapped to many a pilot's wrist is an Elgin service watch. These are among the scores of time-keeping devices and precision instruments being produced in ever increasing quantities by craftsmen of the Elgin Watch Company. Others include split second timers, tank clocks, fine jewels vital to many types of war equipment, time fuses for anti-aircraft projectiles, special timing devices for every branch of our armed services.
Into their production goes a heritage of watchmaking skills that has made Elgin the greatest name in fine American watch-making since 1865. So if your jeweler's supply of beautiful star-timed Lord and Lady Elgin watches is small these days, remember that the work, material, and skill that would be required to produce new Elgins is going instead to help those you love complete their mission successfully on land, on ships, in planes, and submarines. Ask to see the Elgin watches your dealer does have, and keep the desire for these exquisite, supremely accurate watches warm

in your heart.  For once the work of war
is finished, there will be Elgin watches
again for all, and as always, they will
lead in beauty and accuracy.[6]

Not to be overlooked in the expansion of radio
advertising in World War II was the impact of high
excess-profit taxes on the business community.  With
rates ranging up to 90%, those levies created an
enormous temptation for companies to spend on advertising what would otherwise have been paid out to the
federal government in taxes.  For radio, the bene-
ficiary, it was a bonanza.[7]

Total revenues from time sales for all networks
and radio stations between 1938 and 1944 surged from
$117,379,459 in the earlier year to $287,642,747 in
the latter.  Using 1938 as the index year, equivalent
to 100, the progression was:

| | |
|---|---|
| 1938 | 100 |
| 1939 | 111 |
| 1940 | 132 |
| 1941 | 152 |
| 1942 | 161 |
| 1943 | 193 |
| 1944 | 247[8] |

Isolating just stations with annual time sales
of $25,000 or over and excluding the networks, the
picture was equally favorable:

| Year | Broadcast Revenue | Profits before Taxes |
|---|---|---|
| 1938 | $ 73,609,869 | $12,306,054 |
| 1939 | 81,679,851 | 15,650,947 |
| 1940 | 99,063,908 | 21,965,109 |
| 1941 | 117,347,121 | 30,149,416 |
| 1942 | 126,829,928 | 30,646,041 |
| 1943 | 153,388,120 | 46,561,622 |
| 1944 | 199,916,458 | 69,356,960 |

The FCC found that the proportion of the gross
revenue dollar of those stations "devoted to serving
the public,"--in other words, broadcast expenses--
declined from 83¢ in 1938 to just 64¢ in 1944.  The
greatest savings came in the area of program costs.
As a proportion of the revenue dollar, they dropped
from 31¢ to only 23¢.  Part of the explanation for that
saving can be found in the talent lost by stations to
the armed forces during the war.  By January 1944 some

6,000 radio employees were in uniform, about 25% of the industry's total at the beginning of the war. Of the total number of male employees at WWL in 1941, for instance, nearly 60% (28 of 49) entered service by the end of 1943; the majority of those were musicians, artists, or others directly involved in program production. Even when replacements were found, they could not command the salaries their predecessors would have. Additionally, production costs were trimmed as certain types of programs were eliminated in the interests of wartime security. Soon after Pearl Harbor, a Censorship Office was created to deal with the various media. Its radio code of practice suggested to broadcasters the banning of weather information, news of troop or ship movements, war production or casualty data, man-on-the-street programs, and musical request shows. Impromptu interviews, quizzes, game shows, and similar entertainment now tended to disappear from station logs, and with it, the costs of producing those efforts.[10]

Looked at another way, through the ratio of net income before taxes to depreciated tangible broadcast property, America's stations were good investments indeed. Between 1939 and 1944 standard AM licensees tripled the profitability of their operations. Excluding network-owned stations, the ratio of profits to property increased from 56.8% in 1939 to 78.3% in 1942 to 204.1% in 1944. With new investment in equipment and facilities restricted by FCC edict while advertising revenues were climbing sharply, that remarkable record would not be unexpected. Moreover, 50 kw broadcasters such as WWL did even better than the average. Their ratio of earnings to broadcast property by the end of the war reached 340%. Not surprisingly, industry observers regarded the ownership of a 50 kw, clear channel station during World War II as a key to the mint.[11]

* * * * * * * * * *

Some structural changes were also taking place in radio in these same years, though, that did not please broadcasters. For example, they were engaged in a hard-fought renewal of an old struggle. By the late 1930's, ASCAP's total revenue averaged $6 million a year, two-thirds of it derived from radio. All through that decade, broadcasters chafed at what they regarded as ASCAP's exorbitant rates for the use of music on the air, rates that were gradually increased with each contract renewal. Stations paid 3%, then 4%, and in 1935 5% of their gross income for the privilege of using ASCAP music on commercial programs, with a flat

fee charged for sustaining shows. The performing
rights organization refused to issue licenses on anything but a uniform rate basis, and opposed "per-piece"
or "per-program" agreements.[12]

The 1935 contract was scheduled to expire on
December 31, 1940, and both sides began jockeying for
advantageous bargaining positions as early as 1939.
The National Association of Broadcasters, handling
negotiations for the radio forces, pressed the composers for new terms, but found ASCAP employing delaying
tactics. With its authority extending to some 1.2
million pieces of copyrighted music, with other
licensing organizations having a combined total of only
10% as much, and with music involved in an estimated
70% of radio programming, ASCAP was prepared to wait
until the deadline when the broadcasters would have no
alternative but to accept dictated terms.[13]

The NAB chose not to be boxed in, however. Instead,
it called a special meeting of its members in September
1939 and organized Broadcast Music Inc. as an industry-
owned source of music designed to break ASCAP's near
monopoly. Each NAB member station was asked to contribute 2½% of its 1939 gross income to the new corporation. WWL's share was set at approximately $12,000,
considerably less than the $30,000 it was paying to
ASCAP. By June 1940 some 300 commercial radio stations
doing 70% of the dollar volume of the industry's business
were supporters of BMI, which in turn controlled about
140,000 musical selections by the end of the year. Just
as important, by the conclusion of 1940, ASCAP music
was estimated to comprise no more than 36% of the
selections being played on individual stations, and both
NBC and CBS phased it out of their programs entirely.[14]

In March 1940 ASCAP finally announced its own terms
for a new contract. The NAB quickly denounced them as
unreasonable, and it accused its opponents of stifling
the creative talents of American composers and of
actually having forced many musicians out of work
because of excessive fees. To the NAB and the networks,
the new ASCAP proposal was particularly insidious.
Instead of requiring a blanket 5% payment from all
stations as in the past, it now suggested a multi-tiered
structure of fees ranging from 3% for stations with
gross revenues of under $50,000 to 5% for those with
incomes in excess of $150,000 or more, and a new
innovation as well, a separate contract for the networks.
It proposed to charge the chains, which up to now were
exempt from any such payments, an amount equal to 7½%

of their gross incomes.  The ASCAP gambit was clear;
it was divide and, hopefully, conquer.  The music
organization planned to split the smaller stations off
from the BMI counterattack by offering a more attractive arrangement to those local broadcasters than they
had known before.

For the most part the radio ranks held firm, and
as a result, on January 1, 1941, ASCAP music virtually
disappeared from the air.  In its place came seemingly
endless renditions of Jeannie With the Light Brown
Hair (and other songs in the public domain) plus the
newly acquired BMI catalog, as over 650 stations ceased
using all ASCAP music.  One WWL executive later recalled
the tedious task of carefully checking in advance
selections to be played by bands performing on the
station, and closely monitoring the actual programs
themselves to insure there were no last minute changes.
Any variation from the scheduled format required the
show to be cut off the air.  The procedure was good
practice, however, for the same policy was required by
the pressures of wartime security not many months
later.[15]

By the spring of 1941, ASCAP was ready to capitu-
late.  With its dependence on radio's audience now
clear, and with the Justice Department gearing for
antitrust action, compromise was inevitable.  A blanket
license was offered and accepted at the reduced rate of
2.25% of time sales for stations and 2.75% for networks.
Broadcasters were also given, for the first time, an
opportunity to buy the use of ASCAP music on a per-
program basis.  For radio, it was the last major ASCAP
battle; renewals were afterwards negotiated without
crisis, but the scene was never again the same.  BMI had
become a permanent presence and the ASCAP monopoly was
broken.[16]

Also affecting WWL was the hostile eye being cast
by the FCC toward network operations.  Much of this
sudden suspicion stemmed from the convictions of the
FCC's new Chairman, James Lawrence Fly.  Imbued with
the anti-bigness philosophy of the later New Deal
years, he expressed particular concern with the nature
of chain contracts, the extent of common control of
stations, the existence of local broadcasting monopolies,
and the prevalence of newspaper ownership in radio.
Under Fly, the FCC issued a sharply critical Report on
Chain Broadcasting in May 1941, and singled out the
NBC situation, especially.  That network's ownership
of two chains was declared unacceptable, and a divorcement

soon after proposed along with other regulations
governing the general conduct of network-affiliate
relations.

Under the new FCC rules affiliation contracts
could not be so drawn as to prevent a station, if it
desired, from carrying the programs of another network;
affiliates could not prevent another station in their
community from carrying a network program in the event
they rejected it themselves; affiliation contracts
were limited to two years; limitations were placed on
network option time; licensees were forbidden from
contracting away their right to reject unsuitable
or improper network programs; chain organizations
were prohibited from hindering their affiliates'
ability to set or alter rates for non-network time;
and no company was permitted to own more than one network. While the bulk of the regulations affected all
networks and their affiliates, the last applied only
to NBC and its operation of the Red and the Blue
systems. Both NBC and CBS appealed, but to no avail.
On May 10, 1943, the Supreme Court upheld the FCC and
the rules went into effect.[17]

An immediate result of its Supreme Court defeat
was the sale by NBC of its Blue network. On October 12,
1943, the FCC approved the sale to Edward J. Noble, who
soon renamed it the American Broadcasting Company. In
New Orleans, WDSU now became an ABC affiliate, thus
continuing the pattern of four network stations--WWL
(CBS), WSMB (NBC), WNOE (MBS), and WDSU (ABC)--and one
independent, WJBW.[18]

* * * * * * * * * *

An additional dislocation in the World War II
years stemmed from the implementation of the North
American Regional Broadcasting Agreement, a pact which
was signed by the United States, Canada, Cuba, Mexico,
the Dominican Republic, and Haiti. It provided for a
reallocation of radio frequencies among those nations
that was to take effect in March 1941. For the United
States, over 800 stations were required to move to new
frequencies as a result. WWL's shift was from the much-
fought-over 850 kc. channel to the nearby 870 kc.
Percy Roy, the University President, had been informed
of the planned reassignment as early as September 1940
and considered it "a very good reallocation for us."
The new frequency was also a clear channel, and WWL
was granted unlimited time on it, thus ending the
"special, experimental" full time status it had operated

under on 850 kc. since 1934. Each of the other New
Orleans stations found new homes on the radio dial as
well: WDSU at 1280 kc., WJBW at 1230 kc., WNOE at
1450 kc., and WSMB at 1350 kc. For WWL, WDSU, and WSMB
the 1941 assignments would be permanent and continue
into the 1970's.[19]

Other changes on the local level were taking place
too, At WDSU, Joe Uhalt decided to put a period to a
broadcasting career begun twenty years before. Technical violations cited by the FCC, disagreements with
his General Manager, P. K. Ewing, and poor health,
helped propel him toward a determination to retire. In
1943 he sold the station to a partnership of E. A.
Stephens, Fred Weber, and H. G. "Bud" Wall.[20]

Stephens, successful in the automobile business,
was also heavily involved in state politics. He
served as Conservation Commissioner under Governor
Sam H. Jones, an anti-Long reform candidate elected in
1940 after the state had gained an unenviable national
reputation for corruption following newspaper exposure
of political scandals in 1939. The scandals eventuated
in the conviction and imprisonment of a number of Long
machine stalwarts, including WWL's landlord, Seymour
Weiss. On his own, Stephens ran unsuccessfully as a
reform candidate for the United States Senate in 1942
and 1944. During the last campaign, Stephens' successful opponent, John H. Overton, charged that WDSU had
refused him prime time for political broadcasts while
granting "ample and well-placed time" to the station's
owner. A March 1945 hearing on the complaint resulted
in an FCC decision that Stephens "was perhaps more
guilty of a lack of understanding of his obligations
and responsibilities as a licensee than any wilful
intent." Only a verbal reprimand was inflicted.[21]

Wall, another WDSU partner, was described as a
"traditional investor in broadcast properties," and the
holder of a substantial interest in an Indianapolis
station among others. Fred Weber was the only one of
the three new WDSU owners to be active in the daily
management. He was a former Mutual network executive,
who now held the title of Executive Vice President at
WDSU and served as its General Manager.[22]

Before his departure from broadcasting, however,
Uhalt had already left his mark. Under his ownership,
WDSU established a series of firsts in Louisiana
radio--his was the first station to carry a network
program, the first to describe a baseball game and a

207

prize fight, the first to broadcast from an airplane, and the first to move its transmitter from the central city to a suburban location. Moreover, it set a record for "the longest continuous remote pick-up of any station in the South" when it aired in their entirety a month-long congressional committee's hearings investigating a disputed 1933 Senate election. Uhalt struck many of the men who worked for him as gruff and difficult to like, but they did not deny his ability or his record as a broadcasting pioneer.[23]

\* \* \* \* \* \* \* \* \* \*

In 1943, Louisiana State University published the first comprehensive survey of radio listening in the state, and it confirmed the prominent position WWL had come to hold in the industry. Federal census figures for 1940 revealed that radio families in Louisiana now counted over 50% of the total number of families, still well below the national average but higher than most other Southern states. In Orleans Parish, naturally, the figure was considerably higher, 77.2%. But the LSU survey went beyond the census data to examine the listening habits of the average Louisianian. Concentrating on white families, who made up the bulk of radio owners and recognizing that there was no significant programming targeted at black audiences at this time, it found listenership traced a distinct pattern. The audience built slowly with only 4% or less of sets turned on between 5-6 A.M., but by 7 A.M. the percentage had swelled to 23%. At 8 A.M. it reached a temporary peak at 57%, and then began to slide back. About 11 A.M., listeners again increased, reaching a daytime high of 67% at noon. The early afternoon hours saw another slump with a low of somewhat over 40% touched between 3-4 P.M., presumably in the rush of children returning from school and other chores. After 4 P.M. a steady climb began that eventually saw listenership attain its highest point of all, nearly 90% of all sets tuned in between the hours of 8-9 P.M. Then by 11:30 P.M. that vast audience gradually slipped away, as only some 25% remained at the end of the day.[24]

When questioned about their preferences in program content, the largest number of Louisiana radio families preferred comedy with dance music close behind. Only a surprising 2.6% indicated a taste for country music. Thus at least as far as Louisiana was concerned, the format shift made by WWL in 1937 under Callahan was justified. The survey also divided the state into seven distinct regions with the southeastern area

208

including New Orleans designated as Region #7.  Station preferences were than asked of radio families in each region, with 1,704 interviews making up the total sample. The results could not have failed to please the WWL management.[25]

In Region #7, WWL was designated as the station "most frequently listened to" by 26.0% of the respondents.  It was the station most often cited and the other New Orleans broadcasters trailed behind:

| | |
|---|---|
| WWL | 26.0% |
| WSMB | 24.0% |
| WDSU | 22.4% |
| WNOE | 11.8% |
| WJBW | 4.7% |
| Others | 11.2% (including 8.1% for a non-Louisiana station) |

An additional delight was the fact that listeners in four of the other six Louisiana regions also listed WWL as their first preference, a tribute to the station's broad signal coverage.  In Region #2, northeastern Louisiana, WWL ranked third in preference, and only in Region 1, northwest Louisiana where the most popular station was KWKH, was WWL not among the top three. Overall, WWL was mentioned as being regularly heard by 70% of those interviewed.  Far behind was the second choice, WSMB, with support from 40% of the total sample. What had Abell and Callahan wrought![26]

The LSU figures confirmed other ratings available at this time.  In 1944, CBS found that 90% of Orleans parish radio families listened to WWL at least once a week.  In the same year, NBC determined that 36% of Orleans set owners listened most to WWL, even higher than the LSU figure; and again in 1944, the C. E. Hooper Station Index placed the same essential measurement at an even higher 41% in the evening hours, 27% during the day.  Further, CBS calculated that WWL was able to offer primary intense, primary excellent or, at least, secondary good (tertiary) service to counties in seventeen states.[27]

The leadership position that the Loyola station seized by World War II continued to be translated into solid and burgeoning profit figures, as WWL's wide coverage and circulation meant favorable cost per thousand (CPM)--the cost to an advertiser of reaching a thousand listeners--statistics for local and national sponsors both.  It also meant a substantial income for the University. The 1940 financial statement for the school reported total revenues of $571,720 for the year. Tuition accounted for some $195,000 of that amount, but WWL provided even more, $229,680. For a station owned by an educational institution, that was unprecedented. In the early 1940's only thirty colleges still held broadcasting licenses, and of those just nine operated them on a commercial or semi-commercial basis. None of those except WWL occupied a clear channel and offered 50 kw service with a network affiliation. Most educational station incomes came primarily from their supporting academic institutions. For WWL the situation was exactly reversed--it had now become its university's principal support.[28]

Figures for six representative Louisiana stations in 1940 indicate both the extent of WWL's lead in broadcast revenues and the overall profitability of the year:[29]

| | WWL | WDSU | WSMB | WNOE | WJBO | KWKH |
|---|---|---|---|---|---|---|
| Power | 50 kw | 1 kw | 5 kw | 250 w | 1 kw | 50 kw |
| Gross Income From | | | | | | |
| 1) networks | $203,628 | $ 15,487 | $ 77,927 | none | $15,671 | $118,826 |
| 2) national sales | 358,869 | 17,596 | 45,699 | none | 16,649 | 156,678 |
| 3) local sales | 120,745 | 108,479 | 118,040 | 118,040 | 70,848 | 33,962 |
| net profit | 69,509 | 23,286 | 87,746 | 87,746 | 21,742 | 118,410 |

WWL's gross income for 1940 totaled more than twice that of any other Louisiana station. The WWL strength stemmed primarily from its CBS income and from its national time sales. The latter reflected the vast geographic area covered by a 50 kw clear channel station, and therefore, its appeal for major advertisers. In the case of network income, WWL delivered to CBS during 1940 almost 1800 hours of time or an average of approximately five hours per day for network commercial programming. This represented a larger figure than KWKH delivered (1,503) to the same network. Most revealing, however, are the 1940 statistics on the number of hours of sustaining chain shows used by five Louisiana stations (WNOE had not yet acquired its Mutual affiliation)--WWL's total was the smallest of all.[30]

Sustaining hours received, 1940

| | |
|---|---|
| WWL | 1,287 |
| WSMB | 2,273 |
| KWKH | 2,278 |

210

```
WDSU      2,918
WJBO      3,172
```

The conclusion is clear. The Loyola station's own
resources were so considerable that it was more than
able to dispense with the free but unremunerative sustaining hours offered by CBS and instead develop
interesting local programs that could be produced and
sold successfully. The other Louisiana stations lacking
the same degree of capability, were more dependent on
all network offerings as a result. The effect was to
simply widen the lead WWL had already opened. As WWL
sold time the others filled with sustaining programs,
its resources increased even more and perpetuated the
process. The rich were getting richer.

The WWL net profit figure for 1940, a sum less
than that of both WSMB and KWKH was, of course, mis-
leading. While those stations retained virtually all
of their operating incomes after expenses, WWL
Development, under the terms of its agreement with the
University, turned over the bulk of its earnings to
Loyola. If this "rent" had been retained in the radio
organization, as was the case with the others, the WWL
profits would have far surpassed all its rivals. Even
with the rent payment, earnings were three times those
of WDSU and not far behind WSMB in 1940.[31]

Only one fact marred the picture. While WWL
revenues were substantial, they still did not equal
the national average for 50 kw stations in 1940. Broadcast revenues for those elite broadcasting properties
averaged $856,000 in that year, while WWL, reflecting
its smaller, predominantly Southern market was just 75%
of that amount. The conclusion offered by one observer,
that the station's performance in the Summerville years
was good but not record-breaking, seems borne out by
this and later data.[32]

* * * * * * * * * *

The 1940 income statement for WWL reported federal
taxes of $47,000 due on the year's earnings. As
national defense expenditures rose, so did governmental
levies on individuals and businesses. With WWL's
swelling profits offering an ever-growing pot of gold
for the Treasury Department to dip into, the issue of
a tax exemption for the station was raised seriously
once again. The University and its attorneys had never
really accepted the reasoning in the Commissioner of

211

Internal Revenue's 1935 ruling, and now had additional ammunition to use against it.  In May 1938, the United States Court of Appeals for the Second Circuit handed down what appeared to be a highly relevant decision in the case of Roche's Beach, Inc. v. Commissioner of Internal Revenue.33

Roche's Beach, Inc. was a corporation organized by Edward Roche for the purpose of running a bathing beach business in Far Rockaway, Queens County, New York. The company was, however, only a medium through which all profits from the business were funneled into a charitable foundation established by Roche to benefit the destitute, an arrangement not unlike WWL Development's role.  When Internal Revenue denied the Roche's Beach claim for an exemption, the corporation appealed to the Circuit Court and won.  The Court held that the "destination of the income" earned by the corporation is more significant in determining its tax exempt status than the source from which the funds are drawn.  The finding was clear:  "No reason is apparent to us why Congress should wish to deny exemption to a corporation organized and operated exclusively to feed a charitable purpose when it undoubtedly grants it if the corporation itself administers the charity."  No wonder the Loyola attorneys felt emboldened to push again for exempt status!34

Nevertheless, it was recognized that the device of a management company, WWL Development, did pose continuing legal problems, and there was no assurance that the Roche's Beach decision might be the last word on the subject.  Preparations were made, therefore, to simplify the legal structure by eliminating the Development Company entirely.  In September 1940, Father Roy wrote Paul Segal in Washington asking his opinion on the "advisability of us dropping the WWL Development Company," and Roy added:  "We are considering the matter at present."  A week later Segal replied.  He endorsed the idea "from the regulatory or Washington standpoint," and noted the effect would be to "eliminate all confusion in the minds of the Commissioners."  Segal was concerned not just with the tax issue, but with the FCC's suddenly awakened dedication to insuring licensee control of station operations.  The FCC had raised the question as to whether in such arrangements as WWL's, the licensee had not in effect handed over to another corporation the responsibility and control of its franchise.  Pursuing this point, Segal later held a series of private conferences with the Law Department of the Commission and reached a satisfactory meeting of minds.  He reported to New Orleans that the FCC

212

lawyers agreed the use of WWL Development was, at the most, a "mere technical violation of the statute," and that "in fact and in actual operation the station is entirely controlled by the University." He firmly predicted: "We should not need to take into consideration the Federal Communications Commission in connection with this problem of transferring the license to the University." He added meaningfully: "This becomes a tax problem strictly, upon which, I understand, you are working."[35]

A first step toward resolving the problem was taken in December 1940 when the University bought the stock owned in WWL Development by the Marquette Association for Higher Education. By purchasing that stock for $110,500, the University directly, rather than through its Marquette Association arm, became the only significant owner of WWL Development. Good news followed soon after. On April 28, 1941, that Company was declared tax exempt under the provisions of Section 101 of the Internal Revenue Code, the Revenue Acts of 1936 and 1938, and the ruling in the Roche's Beach case. The old adverse IRS decision of six years before was reversed, and some $33,000 in taxes paid between 1936-1940 returned.[36]

The victory proved short-lived. In 1942, the Treasury Department, hard pressed for tax moneys to finance the war effort, reversed itself once again. It announced its intention "not to follow" the rule laid down in Roche's Beach and instead to impose levies on the incomes of companies formerly exempted by the case. On June 1, 1942, WWL Development received the unhappy word from Washington. Basically, the federal authorities retreated to their 1935 position, arguing "the fact that all of your stock is held by an exempt corporation, and that a fixed portion of your income is paid over to Loyola University is not sufficient to make you a corporation organized and operated exclusively for educational purposes within the meaning of section 101(6) of the Internal Revenue Code." No other explanation was offered for the reversal.[37]

The shock galvanized the Loyola administrators into immediate action. Fathers Roy and Cavey set off for Washington to present the WWL argument to whoever would listen and could help. They concentrated particularly on the Congress, and focused upon the Louisiana representatives and senators and upon the Roman Catholic members. Especially helpful in bringing pressure on the Internal Revenue bureaucrats on behalf

213

of the station were Senator Allen J. Ellender and
Congressmen Hale T. Boggs and F. Edward Hebert of
Louisiana, as well as John W. McCormack of Massachusetts.

A brief was also prepared by the University attorneys summarizing the history of Loyola and of WWL
Development, and stressing that the former, not the
latter, determined policy and controlled operations.
Along that line, it noted: "The University has, at
all times, maintained an office in the studios of the
Radio Station for the University's Faculty Director of
WWL, who has always been in active attendance and in
superintendence of the policies and operations." The
brief argued that WWL Development "was organized and
operated exclusively for religious, charitable and
educational purposes and no part of its net income
inures to the benefit of any private shareholder or
individual." Precedents were cited, including Roche's
Beach, and the point made that "in applying income tax
laws, the substance and not the form of the transaction
should control." Copies of the brief were forwarded
to all members of the Senate Finance Committee by
Ellender, and all eight members of the Louisiana House
delegation, as well as others, wrote the Internal
Revenue Commissioner on behalf of WWL. In the meantime,
contingency plans were being laid too. A memorandum
prepared at this time warned that taxes were to be
expected "of anywhere from $137,500 to $350,000," if
the protest was ignored, and recommended that the
Development Company be dissolved and WWL be operated
directly by the University.[38]

The wait was ended in November. On November 10,
Ellender's office wired Percy Roy that the Senator had
just received word from the Acting Commissioner that
for the third time in eighteen months, Internal Revenue
changed its mind. The official news arrived soon after-
ward: "Upon reconsideration and in view of the
additional information submitted, the WWL Development
Company Inc. has been held exempt under section 101(6)
of the Internal Revenue Code and the corresponding
provisions of prior revenue acts." Delighted, Roy
fairly blanketed the Congress with letters of thanks
for the aid rendered. To John McCormack he promised
"each priest at Loyola will say a Mass and each brother
will receive Holy Communion and say the beads that
God may abundantly bless you." Similar tokens of
appreciation were received by a number of key and influential national legislators. Another Washington
battle seemed over and won.[39]

Nevertheless, the Loyola administration and attorneys recognized that WWL Development, despite its temporary acceptance by federal authorities, might still be a potential legal quagmire in the future. Better, therefore, to eliminate the device entirely in order to forestall trouble at a later time. The station, in any event, had outgrown the need for its existence. In December 1942, the Board of Directors of the University, who were at the same time the stockholders of the Development Company, voted to dissolve the latter and to place the management of WWL directly under the former. The Development Company Directors were now reconstituted as the WWL Lay Board of Advisors with the same membership. Formal transfer of assets took place on December 31, 1942, when another chapter in WWL's evolving story, a chapter that began in the office of the Standard Fruit Company thirteen years before, was closed.[40]

* * * * * * * * * *

With the tax issue seemingly settled, the profits resulting from radio's wartime prosperity mounted rapidly. The WWL income figures for the fiscal years ending July 31, 1942, 1943, and 1944 again proved that the "key to the mint" analogy for major station broadcasting in this period was not without solid foundation.

| Fiscal year ended:<br>Gross Income from | July 31, 1942 | July 31, 1943 | July 31, 1944 |
|---|---|---|---|
| 1) CBS | $239,236 | $281,168 | $357,623 |
| 2) National Sales-- | 487,117 | 528,263 | 557,300 |
| 3) Local sales-- | 142,017 | 141,123 | 196,658 |
| 4) Talent fees-- | 16,781 | 35,748 | 49,420 |
| | | | |
| Total Gross Income: | 885,153 | 986,304 | 1,161,001 |
| Net Profit: | 183,275 | 455,789 | 560,989 |

For the first time, fiscal 1944 saw the station's revenues pass the million dollar mark and its net profits surpass a half million. Profits in that year, without any burden of taxes to be paid, constituted a phenomenal 48% of gross broadcasting revenue. In the same year, 1944, FCC calculations revealed that for all commercial AM stations, profits nationally averaged 36% before federal income taxes and a good deal less than that afterwards. Such earnings for the Loyola station made the road for its New Orleans competitors anything but smooth.[41]

215

A portion of the profits from the early war years was put into a studio renovation that began in the spring of 1940. A considerable section of the Roosevelt Hotel's second floor was now turned over to WWL, and two new studios as well as additional office space were created for the flourishing organization. Picture windows were cut into the studio walls "so visitors could watch the artists at work" and new technical equipment introduced. With the completion of the remodeling, the station counted four studios, one of which was set aside for rehearsals. J. D. Bloom, in charge of the construction, claimed the work made WWL "the most modern radio station in the South."[42]

* * * * * * * * * *

Necessarily, the war changed the complexion of both WWL's staff and its programming. The management team, especially, saw fresh faces. While Summerville remained at his post as General Manager throughout the war years, he worked with a new Program Director and a new Commercial Manager. A. Louis Read succeeded Paul Beville in the latter post in 1939. Read was a 1937 Loyola graduate who had done odd jobs at the station, including serving as its mail clerk, during his college days. After leaving Loyola he worked for short periods in the food and in the insurance business before joining WWL full time in 1938. His employment was the implementation of a Gaudin belief that more Loyola alumni should be added to the staff. His first position was decorated with the newly created title of Merchandising Manager. It required him to visit local and regional wholesalers as well as New York distributors, encouraging them to greater use of radio in general and WWL in particular. One year later Read inherited the post of Commercial Manager after the departure of Beville. But with the outbreak of war in 1941, Read entered the Navy and another staff salesman, Larry Baird, assumed the responsibility for the duration and until his predecessor's discharge from service in December 1945.[43]

Henry Dupre, who had become Program Director succeeding Jimmy Willson shortly before the war, left for military duty after Pearl Harbor. His interim replacement was Edward M. Hoerner, a man with considerable radio and stage experience. Ed Hoerner, a singer, first appeared on a 1929 broadcast from Val Jensen's old WJBO then located in the basement of the Orpheum Theatre. He later worked for a brief period at WJBW before joining WWL as a musical artist in 1939. Hoerner also quickly began to move into scriptwriting. He was especially interested in developing more live shows incorporating drama and variety into the afternoon and evening hours, and he soon received Summerville's permission to begin their production. The results of his efforts were under-takings such as Neighborhood Theatre, Jingle Jamboree, Play for Pay, Music from the Southland, and others. Hoerner was designated as the station's Production Manager, and then when Dupre left, as wartime Program Director. It became his responsibility to replace the announcers, singers, and musicians lost to the Armed Forces--not an easy task with the pool of available talent shrunk so drastically by enlistments and the draft.[44]

The sudden death of Father Cavey in 1944 deprived WWL of another member of its management team. His tenure as Faculty Director had been turbulent but also highly successful for the station. Regardless of the amount of credit for the WWL success that could be assigned to him personally in his seven years in the post, his contemporaries agreed that his influence had been a calming one in a period of troubled relations between the downtown broadcasters and the uptown University. Temporarily, Father John Hynes, the well-liked former Loyola President, assumed the office of Faculty Director. He was to hold it only one year before a new approach to the position was introduced in 1945.[45]

Under Summerville, the University's image became somewhat more visible in WWL's programming, though the schedule continued, of course, overwhelmingly commercial. A regular series of fifteen minute to half hour shows titled University Time were developed and broadcast. They featured different academic departments, and usually consisted of short faculty talks or interviews. The law school, for instance, dramatized famous cases and even the signing of the Magna Carta. In 1942 alone, ninety-eight University Time programs were aired on a twice per week basis, mainly in prime Tuesday and Wednesday evening slots.[46]

The most obvious characteristic of programming in the early 1940's was its heavy war orientation. In addition to government announcements carried on spon-sored programs at requested intervals in place of regular commercials, as provided by a National Spot Allocation Plan administered in Washington, whole new vehicles were created to inform citizens and to stimulate civilian morale and support. WWL offered a Camp Polk Program,

centering on activities in that northern Louisiana
Army post and featuring a series of quarter hour play-
lets under the running title, "The Private Life of
Private Price." A similar opportunity was provided the
Air Force in weekly programs featuring men stationed at
Keesler Field in nearby Biloxi, Mississippi. Other
schedule regulars were Eyes on the Sky, a quarter hour
promotion for the Aircraft Warning Service and its
civilian spotters, Calling All Civilians, which dis-
seminated rationing information issued by the Office of
Price Administration, and Skyway to Victory focusing on
the Naval Air Station on Lake Pontchartrain and containing a weekly interview with "A Man Who Has Met the
Enemy." Already established entertainment shows took on
a martial aspect too, as features designed to stimulate
enlistments, war bond sales, and general support for
the war and governmental regulations were included.
The programs, carefully scripted in advance because of
security restrictions in impromptu interviews and talks,
were suffocatingly patriotic. Eternally upbeat in tone,
they contained mawkish rhetoric and oversimplifications
that became uncomfortable listening for their own producers and performers a generation later.[47]

Characteristic of these types of programs and
features was the "People Who Do Things" segment of Music
From the Southland, sponsored by Jax Beer. One evening
in 1944, an Air Force Major, Allen B. Martini, was
honored for his bombing missions in Europe. The script's
prose  probably made the Major, an air combat veteran,
wince:

> (Music swells.)
> Announcer: Yes, Major Martini returned
> eleven times to pour destruction from the
> heaven on the madmen of Naziland. And here
> he is to speak to you. Major Martini,
> for adding new luster to American heroism; for
> making your purpose great and your achievement
> greater; for your crushing attacks on Nazi
> production, the Jackson Brewing Company
> salutes you, Major Allen B. Martini, United
> States Army Air Forces, flyer extraordinary,
> one of those "People Who Do Things."
> (Music swells again.)

The Air Force pilot then delivered a brief talk
encouraging attendance at an up-coming Four Freedoms
War Bond Show in New Orleans that featured "stars of
stage, screen, and radio," and "an exhibition of captured equipment."[48]

The lineup of network shows being carried on the station saw some changes in the war years. Daytime listeners now heard The Goldbergs, Kate Smith, Big Sister, Helen Trent, Our Gal Sunday, Life Can Be Beautiful, Pepper Young, and others. In the evenings the station aired Vox Pop, Sammy Kaye's Orchestra, Al Jolson, The Thin Man, Lux Radio Theatre, Burns and Allen, Major Bowes, Blondie, I Love a Mystery, Dr. Christian, Judy Canova, Frank Sinatra, Dinah Shore, Suspense, Big Town, and It Pays to be Ignorant. And, of course, in the morning, the Dawnbusters continued to reign.[49]

Such was the radio war on the Axis. The world may have been in flames, but for WWL the early 1940's were a triumphant era of patriotic service and rewarding profits.

# 15

## A PERIOD OF ACUTE ADJUSTMENTS

Radio's postwar era began on October 7, 1945, when the FCC announced it was resuming "normal consideration of applications for new stations and changes in existing stations." Two months earlier it had rescinded its wartime order requiring transmitters to be operated with reduced power in order to conserve tubes and parts. What followed the FCC resumption of peacetime business-as-usual was, however, anything but normal.[1]

The phenomenal earnings of broadcasters in recent years--it appeared almost impossible to lose money in radio--and the hiatus in the ordinary expansion of the industry because of the world conflict had combined to build up enormous pressure, a pressure that was to result in a veritable explosion of new licensees and intensified competition over the next few years. In October 1945 there were still only 909 commercial AM stations authorized to broadcast in the United States, but just sixteen months later, that situation was dramatically changed. Some 600 new stations were either already on the air or under construction and more than 700 applications for permits were pending. By June 1948, there were over 2,000 AM broadcasters licensed to operate, plus something new in the air--some 1,000 FM licensees and, menacingly, 109 television stations, the latter representing more and more the darkening cloud of the future.[2]

Translated into community terms, the number of towns and cities with stations grew from 566 on V-J Day to 1,063 in February 1947. The growth was greatest, of course, in the smaller hamlets which lacked radio facilities before the war. The average radio metropolis became one with a population of but 12,500 residents, and the most common situation was now the single station metropolitan area. The latter represented two out of

221

every three radio communities. Nevertheless, broadcasters in all levels of the industry inevitably felt the effect as the audience became more and more fractionated. Clear channel stations, especially, found the new small town transmitters cutting into the listeners they once could claim as their own.[3]

The Federal Communications Commission played a major role in creating this explosive growth by following in its licensing policy an awakened devotion to free competition. No longer would it consider the economic effect of granting new construction permits upon existing stations as it had in the prewar years. Spurring the FCC to its revised stance was a 1940 Supreme Court decision. The case involved an attempt on the part of a Dubuque, Iowa, broadcaster to block the establishment of a competing service in his community on the grounds that there was both an insufficiency of advertising revenue and of talent to support the additional station. The Court rejected the argument, proclaiming instead that "the broadcasting field is open to anyone, provided there be an available frequency over which he can broadcast without interference to others, if he shows his competency, the adequacy of his equipment, and financial ability to make good use of the assigned channel." It added that the purpose of the Communications Act was clearly not "to protect a licensee against competition." Rather, a broadcaster would "survive or succumb according to his ability to make his programs attractive to the public."[4]

Louisiana experienced the same expansive trend in broadcasting as the nation. The state entered World War II with 13 operating stations located in only 7 cities (New Orleans, Shreveport, Monroe, Alexandria, Baton Rouge, Lafayette, and Lake Charles). Two cities, New Orleans and Shreveport, claimed 8 of the 13 stations by themselves; and they were the only communities in the state with more than a single transmitter. But ten years after the Pearl Harbor attack, on December 7, 1951, the radio scene in Louisiana was altogether another story. Instead of the baker's dozen of 1941, there were now 45 standard AM stations on the air, and local service had finally come to much of rural Louisiana. Stations now operated in such towns as Abbeville, Bastrop, Bogalusa, DeRidder, Hammond, Natchitoches, Ruston, and others. Moreover, in the larger metropolitan areas, local competition flourished where it had not existed before, or it became substantially more intense. Alexandria, Baton Rouge, Lafayette, Lake Charles, and Monroe became multiple-station cities, while Shreveport enjoyed five different radio choices. Even a trade organization was formed to facilitate the exchange of needed information on mutual problems and to represent the members in governmental dealings at Baton Rouge. The Louisiana Association of Broadcasters was established in 1947 with James E. Gordon, WNOE's station manager, as its first President.[5]

The stable broadcasting balance in New Orleans was also badly upset by postwar entrants into the field. Where but five AM licensees operated in 1941, ten did a decade later. On February 1, 1951, WBOK, the city's tenth, took the air; and its programming indicated the degree to which specialization had set in. Its fare was directed at only the black population of New Orleans. Thus, as the radio audience became more divided, the community's independent stations found it necessary to tailor their personalities to specific segments of the available market. Only the affluent network outlets could afford to continue the broad, general entertainment programs that had characterized radio's earlier years.[6]

In addition to the chain affiliates--WWL, WSMB, WDSU, and WNOE--and the lone prewar independent WJBW (now controlled by Mrs. Louise Carlson, the divorced wife of the station's founder), four new AM broadcasting organizations began servicing New Orleans prior to WBOK's appearance. They included WJMR, licensed to the Supreme Broadcasting Company in 1946 and quartered in the Jung Hotel; WMRY, operated by Southland Broadcasting and established in 1950; and WWEZ, started in 1947, owned by WWEZ Radio Inc. and located in the Hotel New Orleans on Canal Street. But the station that would loom largest in the future of WWL was WTPS, established in 1947, and the property of the Times-Picayune Publishing Company. The city and the state's most powerful newspaper was back in the radio business once more after an absence of nearly three decades.[7]

The attitude of the stately Times-Picayune towards broadcasting during the 1920's and 1930's was "largely apathetic," if not hostile. By 1939, however, it had finally come to accept the permanence of that rival, and it reluctantly determined to test the waters again, for the first time since its brief alliance with Val Jensen's WAAB in 1922. Leonard K. Nicholson, the newspaper's chief executive officer, chose George M. Healy, Jr., to specifically investigate a new mode of transmission, frequency modulation--FM. Healy, a native of Mississippi who joined the daily in 1926 and rose

rapidly up the administrative ladder, was elected
Treasurer of the publishing corporation in the same
year of 1939.  He favored a return to radio though his
preference was for a standard AM station rather than
experimentation with FM.  Nevertheless, he dutifully
traveled East to meet with Edwin H. Armstrong, the
inventor of the medium.

The FCC had authorized FM broadcasting on an experimental basis just three years before, and the innovation
appeared to offer a number of advantages over AM radio.
The FM signal was static-free, its increased audio frequency range allowed for high fidelity broadcasting, and
stations using it could be placed quite closely to each
other on the dial without interference.  Healy was concerned that the transmission was essentially line-of-
sight, and therefore a station relying upon FM was
limited to local coverage only, but he was sufficiently
impressed by Armstrong and the breakthrough to recommend
to the Times-Picayune officers that such a station be
established.[8]

Full commercial FM broadcasting was authorized by
the FCC in 1940, and thirty-five channels allocated,
but World War II halted its development with only thirty
stations on the air.  By the time the war ended in 1945,
a backlog of four hundred applications had already accumulated, including the Times-Picayune's.  In January 1947,
the station, now designated WTPS, finally began operations.
Its inaugural program featured a brief speech by Leonard
Nicholson ("Never before in our history has an enlightened
and informal public been more essential...") and the
WTPS string ensemble "to demonstrate the clarity and high
fidelity of frequency modulation."  The broadcast
schedule was 2:00-10:00 P.M. daily, and Henry F. Wehrmann,
the newspaper's purchasing agent for twelve years who
had some brief experience with amateur radio during his
days as a Tulane University undergraduate, was named
General Manager.  The format was primarily popular music
and heavy on the playing of recordings.  WWL sent a
"floral offering," congratulating the station on its
entrance into the New Orleans market.[9]

But the Times-Picayune's decision for FM was an
expensive bet on the wrong horse.  In January 1945, the
FCC issued its "Report on Proposed Allocations from
25,000 kc. to 30,000,000 kc."  The document recommended
the shift of all commercial FM stations from the 43-50
mc. range to a much higher location in the radio spectrum,
between 84-102 mc.  The Commission claimed that interference in the lower band was "severe enough to impair

the utility of this service to such an extent that the full development of FM might be retarded." Manufacturers of FM sets and broadcasters already operating FM stations vigorously opposed the switch which would make obsolete over night all existing home equipment, but to no avail as a June 1945 FCC order confirmed a new 92-106 mc. band for commercial FM. Significantly, vocal proponents of the transfer were those interests committed to the early development of television, the service to which the vacated FM frequencies were assigned. The result was to severely delay the progress of FM in the critical years when television was yet in its infancy.

For a time, broadcasters felt obliged to secure FM licenses as an insurance against the possible success of Armstrong's innovation, but by 1948 the shape of the immediate future had become obvious. Television and not FM would dominate, at least for the next decade. The FCC noted a "sudden surge in TV applications and a leveling off of FM interests" in its 1948 Annual Report, and an absolute decline in the number of operating FM stations by 1950. It cited the "economic problems and uncertainties occasioned by the rapid growth of television and the limited number of satisfactory FM receivers" as the explanation. Not until the 1960's, when the rage for high fidelity was coupled with the development of FM stereo, did FM broadcasting come into its own at last.[10]

By 1948 when the trend was clear, WTPS was reverting to Healy's original choice, standard broadcasting. In February a large advertisement in the Times-Picayune announced that the station was beginning AM service. The AM license limited WTPS to daytime hours only, however, so FM was still utilized after sunset. During the daylight hours, simultaneous broadcasting of the same programs on both AM and FM relegated the latter to the role of a superfluous satellite. Probably, the FM activity would have been dispensed with entirely if the FCC had not temporarily denied the newspaper's 1949 application for an evening AM authorization, holding that it would interfere with station CBM in Montreal. Significantly, when WTPS began AM operations, Publisher Leonard Nicholson boasted that the Times-Picayune had always employed "every improved method of communication from carrier pigeon to wirephoto," and he promised "in a not too distant tomorrow we expect to add television to our service." The opposing forces in the New Orleans television battle of the following decade were gathering.[11]

225

When WTPS first took the air in 1947, it joined two other FM ventures already in being. WRCM was the FM affiliate of Supreme Broadcasting's WJMR, both of which were born in 1946. Also coming into existence in the same year was WWLH, an ill-fated FM effort launched by WWL. Its origin dated back to the friendly urging of WWL's Washington firm of legal representatives, Segal, Smith, and Hennessey. As early as November 1943, they had advised Summerville to "prepare FM applications," and Gene Katz in New York echoed the advice. Great things were expected of the new technological development. But four years later, the brilliant future predicted for FM had not materialized, and WWLH was being regarded as "merely a financial burden costing about $1,000 per month." Programming was generally the same as that carried on AM with the one variation coming when WWL preempted a network show in order to air a local news or entertainment feature; WWLH then offered the CBS product. When the passage of a few additional years failed to alter the drab FM picture, Summerville sensed a necessity to conserve his organization's resources in view of the potentially sizeable sums that might soon be invested in a television adventure. WWLH had been established as a hedge against the novelty of frequency modulation experiencing unexpected growth. When it appeared certain that no such growth would occur, the FM operation became simply an expensive liability, and its early death was inevitable. In February 1951, the Loyola administration officially informed the FCC that FM service was being discontinued, and WWLH soon after left the air. That little imagination or effort had been expended in promoting the new service was not admitted.[12]

\* \* \* \* \* \* \* \* \* \* \*

Some of the conservatism evident in the handling of the FM question at WWL probably stemmed from an altered command structure. In August 1945, Father Roy completed the customary six year tenure as the University's President, and handed the office over to Thomas J. Shields, S.J. Roy's successor was forty-five years old and a native of New Orleans, who had first come to Loyola as a Latin instructor in 1932. From 1937-1944 he served as Provincial Superior of the Southern Province of the Society of Jesus. It was Shields' decision not only to accept the administration of the University in 1945, but to also merge the post of WWL Faculty Director with that responsibility. Never before had the two positions been joined; yet now the WWL leadership was being assumed by a Jesuit who, like his predecessors, lacked radio experience, and in this case was without even a science background as well. The basis for Shields' determination to bring together the long separate duties may well have stemmed from a growing belief that the Faculty Director was, since the departure of Abell, exercising little real authority over WWL operations. That situation might be remedied if the Loyola President himself occupied the position. Key decisions were inevitably passed back to the campus anyway for resolution; hence the change seemed only symbolic. Further, the postwar years, from the vantage point of 1945, promised rapid changes in the make-up and the direction of the industry. Critical problems of business strategy would have to be resolved. Better, therefore, that the University President have a working knowledge of station affairs.13

There was some logic in the reasoning. Yet, on the other hand, there was the equally valid issue of whether any University head could afford to devote the amount of time required to really fulfill the responsibilities of a working Faculty Director. Even more, there was the critical question of whether Shields himself was the right choice for the dual role. The evidence indicates that whatever merit existed in the theoretical merger of the positions of President and Faculty Director, Shields was probably not the man to carry the scheme out successfully. Wary and conventional, he could generally be found on the conservative side of every issue. In a time of changed market conditions and a veritable technological revolution in broadcasting, Shields would slow rather than speed WWL's adaption to the new day. In 1952, when Shields was himself succeeded as President, that post and the office of Faculty Director were separated once again.

* * * * * * * * * *

The changed circumstances after V-J Day were to a degree reflected in WWL's revenue figures. Considering the increased competition from both local and regional radio stations going on the air for the first time, together with the emerging threat of television in the New Orleans area and in other markets to which WWL's signal reached, the income of the Loyola broadcasters held up reasonably well.

In 1945 total time sales were $1,172,024, slightly surpassing even the remarkable 1944 figures. But at that point they rested, unknown to Shields and Summerville, on a plateau from which they would not climb farther. Five years later, despite inflation, the gross dollar figures for time sales exceeded 1945 by a bare $1,000, totaling just $1,173,079. The 1950 performance was even less impressive when it was noted that WWL delivered to CBS some 2,800 commercial hours, more than in 1945 and over 1,000 more than in 1940. The station was at best marking time.[14]

Meanwhile, in the industry as a whole, the statistical record was not even that bright. The total of broadcasting revenues for the country's 50 kw. clear channel stations in the years between 1945 and 1949 held briefly, and then commenced a slide that would continue into the following decade. Profits dropped even more rapidly than did revenues.

50 kw. Clear Channel Stations, Averages Per Station[16]

|      | Revenues | Profits Before Taxes |
|------|----------|----------------------|
| 1945 | $1,219,715 | 458,330 |
| 1946 | 1,225,807 | 396,040 |
| 1947 | 1,261,878 | 367,511 |
| 1948 | 1,119,612 | 296,166 |
| 1949 | 1,083,585 | 276,189 |

In Louisiana, the pattern was much the same or even bleaker for stations other than WWL. At WSMB, the NBC affiliate that had represented WWL's closest local competitor, 1945 billings were in excess of $400,000, less than 40% of the Loyola operation. Five years later, WSMB time sales had slipped under $350,000, only a third of WWL's. In the waning moments of Wheelahan's tenure at WSMB, the station's history was marked by a turnover in ownership. E. V. Richards, the theatre impressario who had dominated WSMB since its earliest hours on the air, sold his 50% interest in the operation to United Paramount Theatres, Inc., in 1949. When Paramount merged with the American Broadcasting Company in 1951, the station dropped its NBC affiliation in favor of another with its new parent, ABC. Meanwhile, City Stores, Inc., which now held the stock of Maison Blanche, still controlled the other half interest in WSMB. With Richards gone, Wheelahan left soon after in 1953. The station, once the pride of the city as its first "high power" broadcaster, would not regain its balance until well into the 1960's, as the ownership change brought little favorable immediate effect. By 1955, total broadcast revenues barely exceeded $140,022 and profits had all but disappeared completely.[17]

Faring somewhat more successfully in the late 1940's was James A. Noe's enterprise. Time sales of some $250,000 in 1945 were considerably augmented when the FCC granted WNOE permission in 1949 to increase power to 50 kw. in the daylight hours and 5 kw. after sunset. WNOE's daytime power thus became the equal of WWL's, though on a less desirable frequency. Coupled to its improved signal was an aggressive commercialism. The FCC noted that in 1946, for example, WNOE averaged spot announcements in excess of one thousand per week, with "double spots" during station breaks, a programming device then frowned upon in first class shops, common. As late as 1953, despite continual FCC criticism, the Commission still found WNOE airing twenty or more spots in a thirty minute period. The combination of more power and more commercials boosted Noe's billings to over $325,000 in 1950, though expenses from the installation of the 50,000 watt transmitter resulted in a net loss for the year. By the mid-1950's, however, WNOE too found itself caught in radio's malaise, and revenues plummeted to $176,000 in 1955.[18]

Meanwhile, WDSU, New Orleans' fourth network affiliate, was experiencing ownership changes of its own for the second time in the decade. In 1943 its license had passed from Joe Uhalt to the partnership of Stephens, Weber, and Wall. Then in late 1948, the license was transferred once more; this time to a new partnership consisting of Edgar B. Stern, Sr., and his two sons, Edgar, Jr., and Phillip. Initially, they styled themselves the International City Broadcasting Service, with Edgar, Jr., designated as the managing partner. The Sterns were a wealthy and distinguished New Orleans family. Edgar Stern, Sr., was a native New Orleanian and a Harvard graduate, who had entered a cotton trading firm after leaving college. In 1921 he married Edith Rosenwald, the daughter of Sears, Roebuck and Company's highly successful chief executive officer, Julius Rosenwald. Their son, Edgar, Jr., was born in 1922. He also attended Harvard, earning a degree in Electronic Physics in 1943, and then served as an Army Signal Corps officer until his discharge in October 1946. Phillip, the younger son, worked on the campus radio station at Harvard until his own graduation from that institution in 1947. To a very large extent, their purchase of WDSU was the outcome of a family desire to find Edgar, Jr., an interesting activity in which to engage.[19]

The property that the Sterns purchased had a record of success. Time sales in 1945 totaled $482,842,

surpassing even those of WSMB for the year. Moreover,
WDSU possessed a particularly valuable asset, a television construction permit granted by the FCC in
January 1947, and an authorization to utilize channel 6
for that purpose. It was that asset, the CP, in which
the Sterns were especially interested since it obviated
the necessity of a legal tug-of-war with competing
applicants for the only other remaining unassigned
channel, and thus offered a short-cut to actual TV
operations beginning in New Orleans. Less than two
months after FCC approval of the transfer of control,
WDSU-TV was born. On December 18, 1948, what one New
Orleans newspaper enthusiastically termed "that modern
miracle of electronic science" made its debut in the
Gulf South.[20]

The opening program was televised from Municipal
Auditorium with Don McNeill and his ABC Breakfast Club
cast the featured performers. The station promised it
would provide programs six evenings per week with only
Monday blacked out. Shows from any network would be
offered, utilizing filmed versions which were to be
available "within 24 to 48 hours" after original airing.
By March 1949, WDSU-TV commenced daily at 6 P.M.,
starting with Kukla, Fran, and Ollie, and signing off
at 10:00. Within another year, the sign-on had been
pushed back to 5 P.M. and the sign-off to 11:00.
One Man's Family, Perry Como, Fred Waring, Garroway at
Large, Bing Crosby, the Philco Television Playhouse,
Super Circus, and a considerable number of sports events
had all been shown.

Meanwhile, retail stores energetically advertised
a variety of TV sets at a wide range of prices. A
Philco "Consolette" featuring a ten inch picture tube
"so bright you can view it day or night in a normally
lighted room" was a bargain at $361, while a Major
"Life View Receiver" with a seven inch picture was
"priced for the average pocketbook" at $189.95. Each
name brand carried its own billing: General Electric
was "Daylight Television," RCA was "Eyewitness," Stewart-
Warner "Wonder Window," and Admiral "Magic Mirror."
Most avoided mentioning the very small size of the
picture tube or chose to quote the size in square
inches, thereby citing a figure that sounded more
impressive.[21]

During its first years, WDSU-TV's progress was
largely measured in the reduction of its losses.
In 1950 alone, the station's television operations
lost $116,332 despite time sales of $440,194. Partly,

230

the losses stemmed from the Sterns' penchant for the best of everything, including the latest and often the most expensive equipment. In part, it was the product of the well-provided comfort with which the station personalities were surrounded. "The Country Club," as it was dubbed, was a happy place in which to work thanks to the Stern generosity, and a world apart from the WDSU of the Uhalt days.

Just as important, the losses suffered before profits began to flow in the mid-1950's followed the pattern of the industry generally. Television's share of all the nation's advertising expenditures was only a miniscule 1% in 1949. Income in that sector of broadcasting was still reflecting net losses as late as 1950, and gross revenues did not surpass those earned by radio until 1954. Only then were the years in which radio's profits financed its rival's development finally ended as, in Fred Allen's words, stars and sponsors abandoned radio "like the bones at a barbecue."[22]

\* \* \* \* \* \* \* \* \* \*

The effect of television's emergence on WWL's own fortunes became painfully clear early in 1951 when CBS informed the station that it was reducing the rate at which advertisers could purchase time on its New Orleans affiliate by 10%, from $450 to $405 for an evening hour. The compensation to WWL, based on the system of "converted sponsor hours" then in use, would also be reduced correspondingly. It was to that latter fact that Shields quickly reacted.

In May 1951, he drafted a biting letter to Frank Stanton, the network head. Shields complained that "the implications of this reduction in rate are of such fundamental importance that we believe a formal protest should be made by Loyola University as owner and operator of WWL." He recognized that television competition seemed to underlie the CBS action, but he argued it did not "justify any reduction in WWL rates now nor is it likely to do so for some time." There was, according to the Loyola President, only a single TV station "of modest power" within WWL's principal area of coverage, and only 40,000 television sets in New Orleans and vicinity. He bragged: "With all due allowance for its influence in the immediate vicinity of New Orleans, WDSU-TV cannot purport to compete in area or in influence with WWL." Shields then jabbed at CBS's own sprawling enterprises. While acknowledging

231

a certain "family pride in the advance made by CBS in other fields which are related to broadcasting only remotely," he nevertheless conjectured those very "extraneous activities" had somehow encroached on the network's basic strength and was now threatening "the income to which WWL is reasonably and logically entitled." He cited the CBS ventures in phonograph recordings, color television, and electronics manufacturing specifically, questioning whether they had not drained off the organization's resources. If reductions were to be made, they should take effect only in those communities adversely affected by television, and not be "imposed upon stations where these adverse conditions do not prevail."[23]

Stanton's response was prompt and well presented. Stanton clarified the central issue: "Why should a radio station which has thus far suffered relatively little loss to television be asked to reduce its rate equally with all other stations on the network-- including those stations that currently face a good deal of television competition?" The CBS President readily admitted that it was a question the network had itself seriously pondered, and the answer CBS formulated was, in his words, "the only one under which nation-wide network radio, as we know it today, can continue." He admitted that the conclusion had been reached that CBS "could hope to maintain most of our present advertisers only if we reduced network rates." The problem became one of deciding whether to reduce rates "city by city, in direct proportion to the audiences the stations had lost to television," or to seek "a uniform rate reduction all across the country, in all areas, regardless of the amount of television competition." It rejected the first course, even though it seemed on the surface to be the most equitable, after a careful study of the consequences. Stanton predicted the first alternative would require a drastic cut in the rates of stations "in the most important markets of the country," and at those lessened earnings levels, the affected broadcasters would be compelled to "either go out of business or at least be forced to withdraw from an unproductive network contract." When national advertisers then found that CBS could not give them access to the needed markets, they in turn would withhold financial support and "their invaluable network programming." Finally, with the most popular shows disappearing from the CBS line-up, "even the stations relatively little affected by television would no longer have the big day-long audiences that attract local and national spot business."[24]

In short, Stanton maintained, to cut rates un-
evenly would be to destroy "the entire, complex fabric
of national network radio," and to lead to a serious
deterioration in the health of even local business.
He saw television competition as "a countrywide network
problem, common to all stations, regardless of the
amount of audience they have presently lost to television." But Stanton's rebuttal was not yet finished.
He added "as a completely secondary point," some
comments correcting Shields' impression of the WWL
audience. A January 1951 Association of National
Advertisers report was cited by the network executive,
indicating that WDSU-TV had reduced the WWL listenership to such an extent that a 5% drop in the station's
time charges was warranted. The 5% figure, Stanton
remarked, was "not too far off from the reduction CBS
has asked for the entire network." He also updated
Shields' estimate of the number of TV sets in the New
Orleans area; the correct number was now supposedly
56,400 as of May 1, 1951. Lastly, Stanton singled
out the fact that WWL, like other clear channel stations,
had lost a significant portion of its audience to the
postwar multiplication of AM licensees. A 1949 Broadcast Measurement Bureau study was recalled by him, a
study that reflected a decline in WWL's evening
audience from 926,460 families in 1946 to 659,040
three years later. Dryly, Stanton observed: "This
change, too, cannot help but have a bearing on the
advertiser's view of station and network values."[25]

Shields had lost the debate; he was probably never
destined to win it. Stanton accurately referred to the
time as "a period of acute adjustments," and for WWL
there were even more to come. Shields estimated that
the 1951 rate reduction would alone cost his station
some $38,000 in lost income for the year. That amount
would seem small indeed, however, compared to the rate
slash executed by CBS in 1955. From the 1951 figure of
$405 per evening hour, the network drastically pared
its station rate for WWL to just $215, and, under a
new system, quoted that single rate for the entire day.
Network evening programs of the sort carried for the
past two and a half decades had all but vanished, as
the big stars and shows moved over to television. The
daytime hours, which still retained the women's serials
spawned in radio's golden age, were now equally if not
more valuable than the former prime evening hours.[26]

For a time, while evening network radio lived out
its final days, WWL launched an aggressive publicity
campaign to retain its listeners. Using the slogans,

233

"A Sky-Full of Stars" and "Wonderful, Wonderful, Listening," it advertised regularly and splashily in the city's newspapers. The ads featured pictures of the various CBS personalities who were still appearing on radio--Horace Heidt, Arthur Godfrey, Amos & Andy, Bing Crosby, Red Skelton, Jack Benny, and Edgar Bergen-- and the print commercials were duplicated in type by the other network affiliates in New Orleans. Gradually, as those stars shifted to the newer medium, the ads were no longer run, and the day of the disc jockey dawned.

Part record introducer, part sage, and ever the salesman, the DJ had never really been absent from radio, even in its most glorious era. With the advent of the many, small postwar stations, though, he became essential. The DJ promised low overhead and high commercialism, a combination that was difficult for any struggling broadcaster to resist. If large network-connected operations, such as WWL's, eschewed the DJ while radio times remained flush, even they were pushed to employ him by the radically altered economics of AM broadcasting in the mid-1950's. For a time, WWL continued the live shows such as the Dawnbusters and kept its staff orchestra on the payroll, but more and more the schedule slots vacated by the departed CBS entertainment offerings were filled by record programs. Such titles as Hits for Missus began to appear and in late 1954 even Pinky Vidacovich was pressed into that service. Under the title Pinky's Alley, he played records and performed his skits five nights per week from 8-9 P.M. The show's life was only two years, but the disc jockey phenomenon was to be permanent. Gradually, radio would find a solution to the television riddle; it would become mobile, following its listeners everywhere, and personal, tailoring its programs to loyal if limited sectors of the mass audience. In the end it would stage a remarkable comeback, but from the vantage point of the 1950's, the prospects were none too bright as yet. By 1956 an estimated 90% of the population were "within range" of at least one television station, and 75% could tune in two or more.[27]

* * * * * * * * * *

The WWL management faced two more unexpected challenges to the station's equilibrium at this same time--the internal test of unionism and an external threat from the Treasury Department once again re-opening the long debated tax question. In the first case, WWL was somewhat belatedly feeling the effects of the labor movement in broadcasting. Strikes in the industry, for example, had taken place as early as 1926 when the International Brotherhood of Electrical Workers (IBEW) sought to gain recognition as the bargaining agent for employees at KMOX in St. Louis.

As unions appeared in radio, they took various forms. Some were organized only within the industry; others such as the American Federation of Musicians, as well as the IBEW, were already in existence and moved into the medium because it was either providing work for their members or because they were invited to organize certain stations. The National Association of Broadcast Employees and Technicians was the first union formed solely to represent broadcast employees, and in 1934 it negotiated a contract for the technical personnel of NBC. But the major movement towards unionization in radio did not begin until the passage of the National Labor Relations Act in 1935.[28]

Announcers and actors were a group who often felt themselves particularly exploited by station owners. Subjected to long hours and low wages, commonly as little as $10 per performance for actors with kickbacks all too customary, they saw the 1935 law as a means of rectifying inequities. The result was the chartering of the American Federation of Radio Artists in 1937 with initial locals in New York City, Hollywood, and Chicago. Its first slate of officers included Eddie Cantor as AFRA President and Jascha Heifetz and Lawrence Tibbett as Vice Presidents. Later, in 1952, it would merge with another group, the Television Authority, to become the American Federation of Television and Radio Artists.[29]

At WWL, members of the American Federation of Musicians had been employed since 1932, but none of the other staff were represented by unions prior to World War II, and the same was true of other New Orleans stations. The pattern was first broken by the WWL engineers in 1941. Unhappy with the irregularity of their on-duty shifts, they carried their complaint to J. D. Bloom. But when the Chief Engineer, in sympathy with the cause, presented the demand from his section to Summerville, he found a resistance to any change. Convinced then that a union was the only means of securing better schedules from an otherwise unbending manager, they turned to the IBEW for assistance. Facing a solid front of technical employees and the imperatives of the Law, Summerville and the Loyola authorities acquiesced. A dozen years later, the

Business Manager of Local 1139 of the IBEW would testify "the best contracts maintained with this Local" were with WWL, and those agreements were secured "without threat of a strike or breakdown in any instance during collective bargaining."[30]

The experience of WWL's announcers followed somewhat the same pattern, though feelings were even more strained in the process. The announcers of the wartime years, principally John Kent, Fred Hammond, Don Lewis, and Bill Brangel, chafed under a weekly base salary of $37.50, that had not seen increases corresponding to the substantial rise in the station's earnings during the early 1940's. They received a sympathetic hearing from Program Director Ed Hoerner, but he was powerless to remedy Summerville's parsimony. By 1946 the situation had become almost explosive. The announcers were able to supplement their salaries with talent fees earned through associating themselves by name with various continuing programs (e.g. Don Lewis served for years as the Esso Reporter), but in the months after the war's end, many of those stipends began to taper off. Hoerner, who was still filling Henry Dupre's shoes as Program Director while the latter awaited discharge from military service, cautioned his men continuously against choosing the alternative of union organization. Once more he promised to carry their cause to the General Manager. The result was not only another refusal to modify the salary structure, but also a rumored warning passed on to the announcers that Summerville was taking steps to fire them all for their recalcitrance.[31]

True or not, the rumor was sufficient to move them to immediate action. A few took the lead in calling upon the New Orleans IBEW representative to organize the announcing staff. While the IBEW was primarily a union for technical personnel, it indicated a willingness to take in the new WWL applicants in the absence of an AFRA local. In 1946, AFRA maintained locals in only two Southern cities, Atlanta and Charlotte. Summerville and Shields stubbornly demanded an NLRB election to verify the staff sentiment, and found themselves, as a result, on the minority side of a unanimous vote in favor of unionization.[32]

Negotiations began on the first union contract with management represented by neither Summerville or Shields, but instead by Charles H. Logan, a New Orleans attorney who headed a firm of labor relations specialists. Usually assisting Logan was a Loyola graduate and lawyer, J. Michael Early, who had been employed for a

236

time as a Field Examiner for the National Labor Relations Board. During the late 1940's, he began handling the WWL "account" for Logan, and on the basis of that performance over the years, he would be offered and accept the post of General Manager at the station in August 1961. Speaking for the employees at this first contract session and at similar meetings in later years were the union's national representative and the shop steward at WWL, generally John Kent until he left to join WDSU-TV in the 1950's. As shop steward, Kent felt himself in an especially insecure position, and he believed he was more than once close to being fired by the unforgiving Summerville. Kent and some of his colleagues grumbled at the decision of the Manager and the Faculty Director not to deal directly with their employees, using instead the Logan firm of bargaining experts.[33]

Under the contract finally negotiated, the announcers received a substantial and immediate salary increase, improved working hours, the introduction of overtime and of double time on holidays, and the regularization of talent fees. The WWL management's initial reluctance to satisfy staff grievances thus resulted in even higher eventual costs with the intervention of union organization. In 1945 the salaries of program department personnel, exclusive of musicians, were only $30,901. Five years later, with the union now in place and without any significant increase in revenues or staff, salaries had more than doubled, totaling $61,442. The adage "penny wise and pound foolish" might well have applied in this case. The organizational relationship between management and labor at the station was clarified more logically in 1947 when the announcing staff transferred from the IBEW to a newly created AFRA local in New Orleans.[34]

If the ownership of WWL suffered a setback in dealing with its own employees, it continued an almost unbroken series of victories in its periodic matches with the Washington bureaucracy. The reopening of the tax issue was only the latest round in that series of contests. If it seemed the 1942 Treasury Department decision granting WWL an exempt status had closed the matter, the Revenue Act of 1950 came as a distinct shock to the Loyola administration. The Congress had become concerned about the frequency with which tax-exempt organizations were becoming involved in competitive commercial enterprises. Private foundations, universities, churches, trade associations, fraternal societies, and certain classes of cooperatives might thereby "wage competition with a major and often decisive advantage over other businesses." Consequently, the legislators included in the 1950 Act an "unrelated business income tax" designed to eliminate the unfair competition, and they excluded from that impost only churches and the profits of business "substantially related" to the exempt functions of the organizations conducting them. As the New Orleanians soon found to their consternation, the Internal Revenue Service had every intention of applying the new tax to the earnings of WWL. Once more the Jesuits and their legal advisers prepared for a Washington struggle, as Father Shields promised to use "every means possible to avoid the tax."[35]

Shields presented his case in an October 1950 hearing. He began by denying that WWL posed unfair competition for its rival stations, and by disclaiming any "abuse of a tax-free status." While admitting there may well have been abuses by other educational institutions in the operation of private enterprises, such was not the case here. According to Shields: "From the moment the radio station made a profit, we can show that every penny was spent on what is really a public service (at a saving to the federal and state government) in the form of education." The Loyola President's views on the competitive situation were not shared, however, by many of WWL's rival broadcasters who, despite Shields' disclaimers, were convinced the non-taxed privilege granted WWL a strong advantage in negotiating advertising rates. A WDSU executive later commented: "In principle we know it's wrong if one horse carries 140 pounds and the other 110 pounds." Their perceptions of the market situation were not easily changed.[36]

Shields then directed his attention to the issue of the "unrelated" nature of the broadcasting business, arguing strongly that the station was in fact substantially related to the tasks of the University. He contended that the function of a college was "the imparting of knowledge, formulation of character, broadening of culture, etc., by means of instruction, lectures, exhortations, and demonstrations," all of which were also the functions of a radio station. Because of that similarity, he saw an educational institution holding a broadcasting license as in a "totally different class from those which derive revenue from altogether unrelated businesses." To further support his point, Shields cited the fact that students in English, Speech, Dramatics, and Music had found WWL

238

"an unparalleled outlet for demonstrating, improving
and utilizing their talents," and he deemed their
experience "a laboratory course." The Physics Department likewise benefited, supposedly, from the aid of
WWL engineers "in constructing or repairing electronic
equipment." Finally, he called the federal officials'
attention to the fact that in all station advertising
"even in national and trade magazines, under the letter
WWL appears the description 'a department of Loyola
University.'"[37]

In effect, Shields portrayed WWL in a fashion that
was not notably consistent with its current nature.
The rhetoric of the Jesuit President was considerably
more appropriate to the station of the 1920's than the
one actually existing in 1950. A 50 kw., highly successful, professional operation such as WWL's was far
removed from the educationally-oriented adjunct to the
curriculum that Shields seemed to be describing, and
the Internal Revenue men were not unaware of the difference. Shields' argument did not win the day on that
point.

The petitions, appeals, briefs, and legal maneuvers
dragged on for months. Gradually, the Loyola spokesmen
came to rest their case on the contention that the
University should be considered "a church" under the
meaning of the 1950 Law. They argued, "the Catholic
Church is an organic unity (like a body) and you cannot
exempt the whole without exempting its parts," and that
Loyola was "the Church teaching and fulfilling its
mission of teaching." Very effectively, one Loyola
argument turned the church-state issue to the benefit
of the University:

> The point may here be made that Loyola
> University receives no direct aid from the
> state government or from the United States
> Government for its support. In fact, if the
> question of direct aid was broached (as even
> the question of Catholic school children
> riding on some state buses) in such an in-
> stance the cry would be immediately raised
> by those opposed to the Catholic Church that
> such aid is a violation of the so-called
> American principle of "Separation of Church
> and State." And the point might be made
> that it is just a little discouraging to
> have this "principle" scored against an
> institution positively and negatively, so
> that you are damned if you are and damned

239

if you are not.  Looks like we lose on it
either way.[38]

It was a well-conceived thrust.  If Loyola was not
eligible for state or federal aid because it was associated with the Catholic Church, then it must also be
considered as such on the tax question.  Hence the
"church" exemption under the 1950 Act was in order.

Nevertheless, Internal Revenue held fast.  In
August 1954, four years after the passage of the ominous
tax law and the re-opening of the WWL status debate,
the Tax Rulings Division informed Shields that "the
exemption is applicable only to an organization which ·is
itself a church or association or convention of churches."
The Division's Director added: "Religious organizations,
including religious orders, if not themselves churches,
and all other organizations which are organized and
operated under church auspices, are subject to the...
tax, whether or not they carry out a religious, educational, or charitable function approved by the
church."[39]

The latest decision from Internal Revenue ended a
battle not the war.  Once more the University sought a
reconsideration and once more arguments were presented.
It is not unlikely that the Louisiana congressional
delegation did yeoman service again.  In the past,
effective use had been made of the Capitol Hill group
as intermediaries, and such was the case now.  Perhaps
as a result, a shift in Loyola's favor seemed to occur
in January 1956 when proposed tax regulations were
issued by Internal Revenue.  No longer was a religious
order required to prove itself a church in the strictest
sense.  It became sufficient to prove it was an integral
part of an overall religious body and was engaged in
the "ministration of sacerdotal functions."  Such a
qualified religious order would be exempt from the
unrelated business tax in "all its activities, including
those which it conducts through a separate corporation
or other separate entity which it wholly owns and which
is not operated for the primary purpose of carrying on a
trade or business for profit."  The regulation seemed
to deserve the title:  "The WWL Corollary."[40]

Closely observing the entire process were network
executives at CBS's New York Headquarters.  A long,
internal memorandum to CBS Radio head, Arthur Hayes,
and to William A. Schudt, Jr., Vice President in charge
of Station Relations, recounted the whole tax story in
detail with predictions as to its future course.  The

purpose was clear. The network was considering a possible offer to purchase the station in the event the outcome of the tax dispute was unfavorable for Loyola. To the CBS officials, there seemed at least the possibility that the University administration might be open to a bid in that case, particularly since, under the terms of the 1950 law, the institution would apparently not be taxed on the sale of business assets such as WWL. For the network, such a purchase offered an opportunity for shaving a lead which NBC had built in chain-owned stations. The proposed regulations, however, lessened the chances for the transaction ever taking place, and the memorandum recognized the fact. Loyola's position was said to be "improved" but the exemption was "not as yet a fait accompli."[41]

It became one, finally, in July 1958. The Tax Rulings Division informed the University that "upon reconsideration" the earlier holdings "that station WWL constitutes an unrelated trade or business are hereby revoked." For the third time in less than twenty years, the Internal Revenue Service had seen fit to reverse itself on the issue of WWL taxes. It was a remarkable record of inconsistency on the part of the government and an equally remarkable record of legal and political success on the part of the New Orleans station.[42]

The years following World War II were, as Frank Stanton wrote to Shields, "a period of acute adjustments." The challenges of increasing competition, of new technologies, of internal tensions, and of governmental threats posed sudden and startling problems for WWL, creating the most critical moments in the station's history since the precarious days of the early 1930's. Management decisions were required that severely taxed the capabilities of its cautious and conventional leadership; its responses may not always have been the wisest choices. Nevertheless, considering the unprecedented nature of postwar developments, the WWL managers probably emerged from the period with at least passing grades on the majority of tests faced. But the most bitter and far-reaching test of all, however, was WWL's struggle to win a place of its own in the high stakes game of television.

# 16

## FORGING A STRATEGY FOR SURVIVAL

"No one created the American television system,"
it has been said. "It evolved in a series of patchwork
progressions, affected variously by governmental regulations, corporate aims, technological advances, advertising and marketing requirements, and to some degree,
by public reaction." It was into those troubled, foreign
waters that WWL ventured in the 1940's, at first half-
heartedly, then later with a sense of almost frantic
desparation as a television hurricane seemed likely to
engulf radio broadcasters.[1]

Television, as a potential communications medium,
had existed for at least as long as its sister service
of radio. It too had been made possible by the electronic
discoveries of the late 19th and early 20th centuries.
An experimental program, in which Secretary of Commerce
Herbert Hoover participated, was transmitted by wire
between New York and Washington in 1927, and in 1928 a
Schenectady station televised the first dramatic program.
Real development did not begin, however, until a
Russian-born engineer, Vladimir Zworykin, and his
associates perfected an electronic screening device and
picture tube in 1931. By 1938, David Sarnoff pronounced
home television "technically feasible," and the following
year his NBC organization began telecasting from the New
York World's Fair. Two years later, after some false
starts and not a little bureaucratic indecision, the FCC
at last authorized full commercial operation on eighteen
channels located in the "very high frequencies" between
50-294 mc., though that number of VHF channels was later
reduced to thirteen in 1946 and just twelve in 1947.
Before manufacturers could begin large-scale production,
progress was interrupted by the war and the diversion
of electronic parts and equipment to military needs.
Nevertheless, six commercial stations were on the air

by 1945, and some ten thousand television receivers were in use.[2]

Immediate postwar shortages of materials made it impossible to construct new stations or to produce home receivers for some months after the end of the global conflict, and the new industry's emergence was even more complicated by a controversy over color.  Two camps had now arisen--one, led by RCA, sought a rapid development of television, utilizing the crowded VHF range in the spectrum and monochrome or black-and-white standards. CBS headed the opposition.  It pushed its own color television system, and asked the FCC to assign TV to an even higher section of the spectrum, the "ultra-high frequencies" from 300 to 3,000 megacycles.  Here, the CBS executives claimed, there was room for thousands of stations that would not interfere with one another, as well as the potential for better quality reception in color.  The CBS faction accused RCA of attempting to clamp pre-war standards on the new medium, to which RCA retorted its opponents were seeking to stall TV development indefinitely in the interest of preserving vested radio interests and gaining time to make up lost ground in the newer service.

As the battle raged, both potential manufacturers and station owners waited on the sidelines for a resolution, unwilling to risk supporting the wrong team. Since the RCA and the CBS systems were incompatible with each other, a choice was required of the FCC.  In March 1947, the Washington regulators rendered their verdict; the CBS color system was declared not ready for commercial use, and the utilization of VHF channels and RCA's black-and-white process was reaffirmed.  That decision was cast into a questionable light six months later when FCC Chairman Charles R. Denny resigned his Washington duties to become a NBC Vice President.  Nevertheless, the 1947 ruling seemed to end television's pioneer stage, and a stampede into the field began.  By 1948, 108 stations were authorized to operate, and retail set sales were five times greater than in 1947.[3]

For WWL, the first halting steps towards television were taken during World War II.  In November 1943, George S. Smith, a partner in Paul Segal's Washington firm of communications attorneys, advised Summerville that the moment was appropriate for television to be seriously considered.  Smith argued it "now offers the speculative possibilities that audio broadcasting did in 1922 but on a more expensive scale."  Acting upon that advice, an application for a construction permit

244

was filed by the University early in 1944, but with the wartime ban on TV development no immediate action was taken by the FCC on the petition. Channel 6 was requested, but that request was to have a short life. Despite Smith's original recommendation, which prompted the WWL application, Paul Segal intervened with quite a different interpretation of the near-term prospects for television. The unsettled issue of color versus monochrome systems and of the placement of TV in the radio spectrum caused him to recommend to the University administrators a withdrawal of the institution's bid for a CP until the direction of the emerging medium was clarified. Accordingly, in March 1946, Segal transmitted to the FCC a Loyola resignation, thus ending WWL's first flirtation with television.[4]

But with the settlement of the color controversy in favor of RCA in 1947 and the rush for channels that followed, WWL's voluntary restraint was inevitably tested. In December 1947, the ever-cautious, ever-conservative Father Shields drafted an in-house memorandum summarizing the TV question as he perceived it at that moment. It was obvious he was feeling some pressure to act positively on the matter. Shields began by taking pride in the fact that "Loyola has hitherto kept pace with the development of radio" and owned "one of the more powerful and leading stations in the country." But now the issue of television had arisen, "another step in the progress of radio," and therefore, "it would seem that WWL in accord with its policy as a leading station of the country should install television." Moreover, Shields noted, since the number of channels assigned to New Orleans was limited, "it would appear that immediate application for a license is indicated."[5]

For Shields, however, negative factors far outweighed any impetus to test the waters. He pointed out that TV was "not yet widespread in the country," nor was it possible "to transmit television scenes from place to place over long distances such as is done with ordinary radio (chain) programs." He further took notice of the smallness of home screens, their expense, and their less than satisfactory performance in terms of picture quality. He contended that TV was still "in the experimental stage," and that the improvements which would eventually be made would mean "the television installations of the present will become obsolete." The wisest course, he wrote, should be one of "extreme caution and prudence," and on that point he quoted the lines of Alexander Pope:

245

Be not the first by whom the new is tried
Nor yet the last to lay the old aside.6

For Shields, WWL represented a very different enterprise from those of other broadcasting licensees. It
rendered a "public service in the form of education by
the profits accruing from operation of the station since
every cent of said profits is dedicated to and used for
the education of youth." Since WWL was the "essential
and largest part" of the University's endowment, "every
possible safeguard must be taken that the earning power
of the radio station be preserved." Television would
impair that earning power. Installation costs were
estimated at $250,000 while maintenance and operating
expenses would average another $200,000 yearly. Moreover,
those figures did not seem likely to be offset by significant new revenues.

Shields predicted that TV's use would be confined
to the evening hours only "for no one has time to look
at pictures during the day when men are at work, children
at school, and women busy with their household duties."
He expected WWL radio to operate in the mornings and
afternoons with no competition from television. WDSU-TV,
which would be on the air some twelve months later, was
indeed operating on such a schedule during the first few
years of its existence. Shields then centered his attention on those evening hours between 6 P.M. and 10 P.M.
He admitted a rival station might begin telecasts in
that prime time, and without competition from WWL,
"could take the ascendency...here in the city of New
Orleans." The ascendency would be limited to the city's
immediate area, however, because of the short range of
the TV signal, and the Jesuit did not envision the
prospect hurting his institution financially, "since
without greater power we are selling not only coverage
of the city, but also the country districts."

As Shields perceived the situation, WWL had little
to gain from sailing into the uncharted waters of television. The large required investment "would not benefit
us one bit in the coverage of what is sold as WWL
territory except in the city of New Orleans," and in
addition, the income from the home community could not
compensate for the outlays involved. Even if the station
should lose as much as $100,000 per year because of its
failure to meet television competition, WWL would still
have found itself ahead since expenses, if a TV license
was secured, would likely be twice the amount of the
lost profits. Shields saw no threat in an expansion of
television to the countryside, the smaller towns and

246

cities that WWL's clear channel coverage reached so
effectively; he termed such a possible expansion "a
wholly gratuitous supposition." For any such development to take place, he concluded accurately, a substantial number of new channels would have to be made
available by the FCC, and in that case, Loyola would
have sufficient time to itself apply for one of those.

A quite different aspect of the television issue
was then raised by Shields. A "very great difficulty"
for him was his belief that much of the programming
"involves women who are scantily clothed." Compounding
the problem was the fact that even the advertising on
the medium was often sex-appeal based. As a result,
he warned: "Loyola will be confronted with the em-
barrassment of deleting pictures which an amoral (for
so many do not even acknowledge a moral standard in
these matters) clientele may desire." Along the same
line, Shields saw television's heavy use of sports
such as horse racing and wrestling as not in "good
taste if exhibited by an educational institution."[7]

Shields' position was clear. After his analysis
of both the present and the likely future, he determined
that a television venture would not be in the best
interests of the University at that moment. Acting upon
his memorandum, the WWL Advisory Board confirmed the
decision on December 19. Yet, Shields had failed to
convince his own General Manager; Summerville was
"uneasy" with the Board's action and "feared that we
might be making a mistake." The President himself
was still troubled by enough doubt to seek more advice,
and, therefore, composed letters to Gene Katz in New
York City and to Paul Segal in Washington. He enclosed
his memorandum on television and asked them to comment
on it, "pointing out any errors." Segal's reply was
brief, recommending that, notwithstanding the Board's
decision, the "first draft of a television application"
be prepared. Segal assured the Jesuit that such a pre-
cautionary step "will not commit anyone, but I think
it is essential that it be available as against a quick
decision, which you may well make soon."[8]

It was Gene Katz, already a confirmed advocate of
television, who carried the weight of the counterattack
against Shields' negativism. He believed that TV was
"the coming advertising medium," and he urged WWL to
"protect its position by going ahead promptly" with an
application: "We know it will cost a lot to get going
in TV, but we believe it will cost less than to be out
of TV." Katz predicted that by 1950 it would be possible

247

to receive transmissions from both the East and West
Coasts, while it was already "possible to televise in
New Orleans this evening events which happened in New
York or Washington this morning by air-expressed
film." As to the quality of reception, Katz stated:

> Pictures now received on ordinary
> low-priced sets are, in our observation,
> very acceptable. In my home I have the
> cheapest RCA receiver, $325.00. On the
> night of our record-breaking snowstorm,
> I sat in my living room from 8:30 to 12:30
> watching championship tennis matches
> at Madison Square Garden. I was amazed
> at my ability to watch a fast-moving game
> for a 4-hour stretch over TV without eye-
> strain. Images are satisfactory.[9]

Prices were coming down too, Katz promised, with
$150 sets to be on the market by 1949. Some 150,000
sets were currently in use and "only a small minority
are in bars." It was, therefore, a respectable association for a church-related institution.

Most important, Katz saw it as "a question of now
or never." He cautioned: "There are only so many
channels available for New Orleans. If you don't get
one and if there is no re-deal, WWL will be out forever
or will be forced to pay a fancy price for a channel
someone else has been granted." He turned then to the
question of the earning power of the WWL broadcasting
operation. To safeguard the University, a satisfactory
level of income must be preserved. In order to do that,
Katz reasoned, "WWL must be able to supply the up-to-
date product which advertisers want. When TV comes to
New Orleans, advertisers will want it. If WWL can't
supply it, its revenues will decrease." The wisest
course would be to insure the University "against the
technological obsolescence of its present plant by
building a new one to supply the product which will be
in demand."

He disputed Shields' suggestion of $200,000 a year
maintenance costs: "It might be that high for the
first year, but as receivers increase in number and
rates are increased, operating expenses will decrease.
He pointed to a Philadelphia station, on the air only
since September 15, that was already meeting its costs
out of time sales of $2500-3000 weekly. There was,
the New Yorker enthused, "a terrific advertiser appeal

in TV which makes local merchants want to be first on
the air with a TV program." It was inevitable that TV
would "replace" radio during the peak and most profitable
hours in metropolitan areas--"it's as irresistible a
progression as the supplanting of silent movies by
talkies." Even in the daytime, WWL's primacy was in
danger. Katz recalled that TV's greatest audiences yet
had been amassed for the 1947 World Series, a daytime
event, and he observed that Saturday and Sunday afternoons were already important time periods for the small
screen.

Realistically, the rise of a New Orleans television
industry without a WWL share of the business could
wreak havoc on the station's future. With TV stations
in operation, "only the poorer homes" would be left for
radio, a less attractive audience from a sponsor standpoint. Moreover, WWL's "outside market" in the rural
areas of Louisiana, Alabama, and Mississippi, as well
as other states, were, according to Katz, "not very
exciting to national advertisers. Who is going to buy
WWL to reach them alone? Without the New Orleans
market WWL would get very little business." He admitted
WWL's TV audience might never be as large as its present
AM listeners, but little would be left of that body of
listeners after television stations in New Orleans and
in other Southern cities began to siphon them off.

Finally, Katz turned to the issue of sexual standards raised by Shields. He acknowledged "some cheesecake in TV and some cases where program material offends
religious standards of decency and modesty." Yet, he
argued, "cheesecake is being broadcast by WWL now, but
not in visual form. If you were to analyze the hundreds of soap operas and network comedy shows now being
broadcast by WWL from the point of view of what constitutes cheesecake to the ear, you would find many
offenses. However, custom and habituation to the verbal
form of such material has dulled our criticism."
Optimistically, he foresaw TV's potential for good:
"For every case which borders on the offensive, it will
bring ten exciting, stimulating and educational eye
messages to the people of New Orleans, helping to make
them better able to understand a complicated world."
He suggested that, instead of Shields' quotation from
Pope, one from Robert Browning might be more appropriate:
"Progress is the law of life."[10]

The two men represented differing temperaments and
conflicting attitudes towards change. Shields, the
cleric and the educator, evidenced both an unenterprising

prudence and even a meloncholy pessimism. Rather than pursuing a determined effort to maximize profits, which economists traditionally have stated are the objective of the firm, he unconsciously adopted the so-called "minimax" principle--not an attempt to maximize profits in the classic manner but rather a strategy of obtaining the greatest security within the confines of a strategy which minimized losses. He urged a policy calculated to "guarantee" WWL the smallest loss rather than the most profits; in effect, Shields was "satisficing" rather than "maximizing" by agreeing to settle for a return that was "good enough" although not optimal. He was inherently prepared for the worst rather than the best, seeking to hedge against the poorest return "by looking primarily at the most satisfactory of the generally unsatisfactory states of nature which may materialize." One social scientist has designated such inclinations as those of "administrative man" rather than "economic man."

For Katz, on the other hand, the future was both considerably brighter and inevitable. His thrust was in accord with the dictum of management critic, Peter Drucker: "An established company which in an age demanding innovation is not capable of innovation is doomed to decline and extinction." A business strategy based on such a thesis presumes that existing products or services as well as existing technologies will sooner or later decline rather than prosper, and that neither time nor resources should be spent "defending yesterday." Focusing upon the future, of course, entailed risks. Katz, perhaps in part because it was not his resources directly at stake, was more prepared to accept the uncertainty of the future than Shields. Nevertheless, WWL's national sales representative seemed more conscious that "through risk-taking...any businessman earns his daily bread," and that profits are "the premium for the risk of uncertainty."11

If Katz's argument was to prove faulty at any point, it was in his seeming low regard for the future of radio. Rather than "replace" radio, as the automobile replaced the carriage, television would find the earlier medium a very healthy competitor by the 1960's. The two technologies would adjust to each other's strengths and weaknesses and find considerable market space for peaceful co-existence. As early as 1954, a few minds were already being changed about the inevitable demise of radio, and it was being termed "that lively corpse."12

250

Shields' response to the Katz advice and to the urgings of Segal and Summerville was to compose a "Memorandum No. 2 re Television" for submission to the WWL Advisory Board. In it he noted that "pressure has been brought to bear for further consideration of the advisability" of filing for a television channel, and that "those of the radio industry interested in television are very enthusiastic about its future." But the Jesuit President remained unconvinced, and despite the pressure and the enthusiasm, he continued to hold that such a venture "will cost Loyola huge sums of money to operate a television station," and that "it will be some time" before any profits could be realized. For Shields the issue reduced itself to a single question: "Is Loyola justified in spending hundreds of thousands or even a million and a quarter dollars in the hope television will some day prove profitable?" He scorned such spending as "speculation," and cited an "acid-test" to prove his point: "Have the enthusiasts for television invested heavily of their own private savings in stock of television companies?" It was a rhetorical question for Shields knew his opponents were not "selling standard securities in order to invest totally in television."[13]

Even granting television might be profitable, Shields admitted, would it be profitable enough: "With the high cost of production of television programs, the station margin of profit can hardly be as great as on audio radio." With that small return on investment, he warned, "it would take many years for Loyola to recover expenditures, and after a lapse of those fifteen or twenty years we would be in no better position than we are today." Furthermore, with other TV stations in the city, each restricted by the nature of the signal itself to the New Orleans area, "the Loyola video station would be, not predominant like WWL (which because of power and coverage of great areas of the country is now predominant) but simply one of the group, and perhaps the poorest since other stations could take programs we could not take because of our religious and educational status." On the last point, Shields was returning to the voluntary censorship issue which he had raised in his initial memorandum. It was an issue which he perceived as peculiarly tied to the new service of television, and not one that had been a major problem or concern in AM broadcasting.

Finally, the University head delved into the subject of macroeconomics. He predicted the onset of an "inevitable and devastating depression" in the United

251

States, and foresaw the emergence of television "just when the depression arrives." A wiser course, Shields counseled, would be to wait and perhaps at a later time purchase "a station and channel already developed, for in time of depression, video stations not solidly financed and dependent upon profits from advertising could be obtained cheaply."[14]

As strenuously as Shields campaigned against a plunge into TV, he was unable to prevent the step being taken. In the end, the WWL decision-makers were virtually stampeded into acting. In early 1948, the Sterns, not yet in control of WDSU, filed an application for a construction permit. In so doing, the Sterns were requesting Channel 10, the last remaining unclaimed commercial VH frequency allocated to New Orleans. Previously, channel 6 had been assigned to the Stephens-Wall-Weber partnership at WDSU, channel 4 to Maison Blanche and WSMB, and channel 7 to the Times-Picayune and WTPS. At that moment, it appeared highly likely that the Stern move might well close the VHF television scene to WWL for years to come. For a firm engaged in broadcasting, the "minimal condition is existence," and that is synonymous with an FCC authorization. There was, therefore, a sense of what Gene Katz had called "now or never" in the offices at Loyola and WWL that February.[15]

An urgent telegram was wired by Paul Segal in Washington to Shields: "Filing of Sterns Application for Channel Ten Renders It Imperative That Loyola File Similar Application Within Ten Days." Segal and his associates foresaw the real likelihood of irreparable damage to WWL's fortunes if immediate action was not taken. The WWL Board acted at once. Despite the President's earlier, strong opposition, it voted on February 23 to file a competing application for Channel 10, and Denechaud telegrammed the vote to Segal the same day. Shields was overruled, but loyally he supported the decision and dutifully enlisted in the campaign for the FCC grant. On March 3, the WWL application was transmitted to the Secretary of the Commission. It had been signed by Shields the previous day.[16]

The FCC's Form 301 ("Application to Construct a New Broadcasting Station") was the appropriate document for putting the WWL case before the Washington bureaucrats. A significant portion of the information filed consisted of an estimation of probable expenses. The Loyola planners gauged the cost of a TV transmitter at $90,000, the antenna system at another $20,000, and the necessary studio equipment at $70,000--a total including other miscellaneous items of some $204,000. They estimated operating expenses during the first year of telecasting at $150,000, and they anticipated revenues of but $75,000. A healthy loss was thus projected.[17]

The loss would not have been untypical. In 1948, the FCC reported that the television industry as a whole showed an overall loss of $15 million. One business periodical in 1949 commented wryly that "never before in history have so many men lost so much money so fast--and so willingly."[18]

The WWL estimate of its probable first deficit was, if anything, conservative. Its projected outlays were below those being incurred by the bulk of the broadcasters who launched television ventures in these years. Fortune concluded in 1949 that the minimum possible investment in TV in a metropolitan area for the potential broadcaster would be about $400,000 "before he warms up his first camera," and the minimum operating charges for the first year another $400,000. But WWL anticipated spending a good deal less. According to Fortune:

> Television operation is from the very first at least twice as costly as radio operation, because there must be two of everything. In all operations there are both video and audio; there must be present the same number of audio technicians, announcers, etc., as were necessary in radio, plus the proliferation of video needs. But in addition to this, TV requires another doubling of almost everything for reserves: cameras break down or black out. And then you need a third doubling of camera equipment for the sake of point of view: the viewer's eye is quickly bored by a stationery camera giving a simply front-view picture.[19]

Indeed, the National Association of Broadcasters adhered to a "two by four" formula, which set TV expenses at from two to four times those of radio, while a media columnist chose five as his measure--"five times as difficult, five times as expensive, and five times as effective as radio." It took some degree of business courage and vision, therefore, for radio men to accept "the grim insecurity of plowing in hundreds of thousands of dollars without an immediate, countable clear return certain at hand."[20]

With multiple applicants for the same channel, the Sterns, Loyola, and a fresh entrant into broadcasting, the New Orleans Television Company, the FCC, as a matter of routine, informed the contenders that a hearing would be required. Before the hearing could be held, however, television suffered a rude jolt. On September 30, 1948, the Commission issued a "freeze order." No new or pending applications for TV construction permits would be acted upon by the FCC until the order was lifted at some indefinite date in the future. The nation's would-be television entrepreneurs, including WWL, found themselves in a regulatory limbo that was to last almost four full years.[21]

By the fall of 1948, the FCC had become only too aware of the fact that with just twelve channels available for TV in the VHF range, it would be impossible to meet the public's demand for more stations without creating unacceptable picture interference. To avoid any interference in transmission, FCC rules prohibited stations closer than 190 miles apart being placed on the same channel. With but twelve channels with which to work, licensing enough stations to satisfy both applicants and the public was out of the question. The freeze permitted the Commission time to investigate the alternative of opening up new channels in the UHF range for the first time, and even to explore again the subject of color television. The latter issue had re-entered the picture when CBS in the spring of 1949 successfully televised in color surgical operations from an Atlantic City Hospital to a medical convention.[22]

While the FCC studied these subjects during the freeze, a sparring for positions of competitive advantage marked the New Orleans broadcasting scene. In October 1948, the Sterns dropped out of the triangular contest for Channel 10 because of their acquisition of WDSU and its previously issued construction permit. Then in a significant development, a request by Maison Blanche to extend the time limit on its CP for Channel 4 was denied by the Commission with the result that the department store was forced to surrender its unused permit in January 1950. Channel 4 thereby became available and seemingly offered another path into the new medium.

The WWL decision-makers acted quickly. On February 16, Shields signed a new Form 301 modifying his station's application for a CP from Channel 10 to 4. The Commission, of course, placed the modification in its "pending file" and reminded Shields of the freeze in effect "until a final determination on allocations has been reached." The New Orleanians were naturally expecting that reaction, but saw a virtue in filing anyway. As Segal advised, it was necessary to make "a clear and open declaration of our intention to use Channel 4, so that should there be some other applicant for this frequency, we shall be in a position to ask him to change to something else on the basis that we have had a request pending for a long time for Channel 4." Meanwhile, the Times-Picayune was taking the opposite course. In August 1949, its construction permit for a station on Channel 7 had expired. In explanation, an executive of the newspaper stated: "In the light of present and probable national economic trends and the serious and fundamental uncertainties confronting the television broadcasting art,...it would be impractical to construct a television station in New Orleans at this time." Despite that judgment, the publishers, nevertheless, reversed themselves one year later, and in May 1950 filed a new application seeking WWL's then vacated Channel 10.[23]

The circumstances were again altered in March 1951 when the FCC once more intervened. It issued its "Third Notice of Further Proposed Rule-Making" containing a revised table of channel assignments. The channels it now assigned to the city of New Orleans were 2, 4, 6, and 7 in the VHF band and three in the UHF, 20, 26, and 32. Channel 2, however, was reserved for educational, non-commercial use. Channel 10, which had formerly belonged to the city and for which the Times-Picayune had a pending application was assigned to Baton Rouge by the Commissioners. Temporarily, at least, the New Orleans newspaper was in the position of having filed for a non-existent channel. Paul Segal in Washington quickly perceived the effect of the FCC move. He wrote Denachaud: "There are only two unused commercial television channels proposed to be assigned to New Orleans. There are now three applications pending. This means inevitably that there would be a hearing upon the applications with attendant inconvenience, delay, trouble, and expense." He advised a possible solution, petitioning the FCC to remove the non-commercial restriction on Channel 2.[24]

Shields was reluctant to take that action; it was a question of image in the academic world. He pleaded such a petition would put him in a "very embarrassing position," since Loyola was a member school in the American Council on Education, an organization that was clamoring for more educational channels to be set aside by the FCC. Not for the first time were the interests

of the University as a commercial broadcaster and its
identity as an institution of higher learing in apparent
conflict, and again, as often in the past, the commercial
necessity prevailed.  Now Loyola counter-proposed to
the FCC that Channel 2 become a commercial assignment,
and even that an additional commercial channel--Meridian,
Mississippi's, Channel 11--be given to New Orleans.  The
University claimed the "VHF assignments proposed by the
Commission for New Orleans were inadequate to serve the
needs of that area since a considerable period of time
would elapse before converters or new receivers capable
of utilizing ultra high frequency signals could be
distributed."  Loyola argued that to rely on UHF for
service would simply be to perpetuate the existing TV
monopoly of WDSU.  On the issue of Channel 2, the WWL
attorneys argued the regulatory agency was "without
legal power to reserve channels" for non-commercial
use.[25]

While the counter-proposals were pending in Washington, Shields traveled to New York for a meeting with
Katz and with the officials of CBS.  Upon his return, he
admitted that he had learned much about TV, including
the fact that "if we want to retain our affiliation with
the national chain, we will have to have television."
He pointed out that CBS had already threatened one of its
affiliates with loss of service if it did not begin telecasting immediately after the lifting of the freeze, and
Shields warned that WWL's separation from the network
would be disastrous.  Moreover, the Jesuit had considerably altered his views on the future prospects of
television.  He believed that WWL "could not only break
even but make a certain amount of profit on television,
now that the pioneering days are over when television
stations operated for months and years at tremendous
loss."  He also had become convinced that, while radio
would not "fail entirely," it would experience diminishing
incomes in the years ahead.  Shields placed the initial
investment for a TV station at $350,000, not including
land and buildings.  Since the Roosevelt Hotel location
seemed unsuitable for television, he estimated an
additional $50,000-200,000 for real estate.  He granted
the costs were high, but believed that WWL "can profit
by the mistakes made by pioneer stations."  The negative
Shields of 1948 had become the convert of 1951 as the
industry's red ink gradually turned to black.  In 1950,
non-network-owned stations earned $800,000, the first
time they had returned an aggregate profit.[25]

On April 11, 1952, the FCC issued its long-awaited
"master plan" for television, hundreds of pages of fine

print unimaginatively titled the Sixth Report and Order on Television Allocations. In lifting the freeze, the FCC established a set of priorities of which the first was: "To provide at least one television service to all parts of the United States." The twelve VHF channels could accommodate some 500 stations, given the necessary miles of separation for licensees on the same channel, and those were spread among the country's larger cities with at least one in each state. When the VHF channels were exhausted, 70 UHF channels capable of accommodating 1500 stations were assigned. New York City, for instance, received seven VHF's and two UHF's, and altogether over 1250 towns and cities were provided with TV service. About 10% of the assignments made were reserved for non-commercial, educational use.[26]

As welcome as the ending of the freeze was for WWL, the FCC's assignment decisions for the Gulf South community represented a discouraging setback. The counter-proposals for adding Channel 11 and opening up Channel 2 to commercial operation were both denied. As if that were not enough, the FCC went even farther and deleted another VHF assignment from the city, Channel 7, substituting a UHF replacement, Channel 61. New Orleans as a result could claim only three VHF possibilities, 2, 4, and 6, with the first of those still designated educational. Four UHF opportunities now existed, 20, 26, 32, and 61, but local broadcasters were highly skeptical of their profit potential at a time when existing sets were not equipped to receive UHF.

An expensive $50-75 converter was required to adapt a home TV for UHF, an amount that only a small minority of set owners might be prepared to spend. As late as mid-1953, only 15% of all sets manufactured in the nation were UHF-equipped, and the FCC found that the only UHF stations earning profits were those without VHF competition. The mixing of VHF and UHF stations in the same city was an invitation to disaster for the latter. Not only were UHF operations more expensive to build, requiring taller antennas and more powerful transmitters, but they also faced the economic fact that the networks showed an obvious preference for the wider VHF audience, thereby depriving the higher frequency stations of the most popular programming available. The necessary revenues from time sales required to cover back-breaking start-up costs thus proved extremely difficult to amass. In the months immediately following the freeze, over one hundred UHF stations were established and subsequently soon failed, many as early as 1953 and 1954. A decade later, only 7% of the commercial UHF assignments were actually on the air, and not until 1962 were all new television sets required to be equipped to receive both services.[27]

For WWL and for other New Orleans television interests, the April 1952 FCC announcement created a special problem--it reduced to just one, Channel 4, the number of unoccupied commercial channels. In September 1952 when the Commission replaced Channel 2 with Channel 8, formerly in Mobile, the tightness of the situation was not eased for 8, like its predecessor, carried an educational reservation. On April 26, the WWL Advisory Board met to develop a course of action. Agreement was reached that the essential task was to "avoid the expense and time which may be consumed by a hearing before the FCC," and to "expedite" the WWL application as quickly as possible. The Jesuit administrators and their lay advisers, many from the WWL Development days, together with Paul Segal from Washington and Summerville, Bloom, and Hoerner representing the station, deemed it imperative that theirs be the only application for Channel 4. To insure that eventuality one member of the Board was assigned the responsibility of contacting the Times-Picayune management in order to dissuade the newspaper from creating a contest, while Denechaud was asked to seek out Seymour Weiss and to request the hotel owner to prevail upon ex-Governor Noe not to intrude WNOE into the picture, a possibility that had been recently rumored. Applications from non-local groups were regarded as not of serious concern in view of the FCC's avowed partiality towards community ownership.[28]

Segal also advised an immediate acquisition of the necessary land for the transmitter, the transmitter itself, the antenna, cameras and equipment, as well as the drafting of a program outline. The possession of these, Segal promised, would "put us in a much more favorable position to have our application granted." It was a calculated risk since it was entirely possible the FCC might still reject the WWL bid, and the properties could then represent a wasted investment. Nevertheless, the Board, in an act of faith, chose to assume the risk. The danger of financial loss seemed mitigated, however, by the probability that the properties could always be sold to the eventual winner in the competition for Channel 4, if Loyola did not gather in the prize.[29]

In June, a new Form 301 was filed with the FCC to comply with the technical requirements of the Commission's Sixth Report and Order. The transmitter placement was

258

now listed as Gretna, Louisiana, across the Mississippi River from New Orleans, while the studio site was still shown as the Roosevelt, even though plans were already formulated for a change of location. Cost figures had changed considerably since the 1948 proposal. The transmitter, listed at $90,000 four years before, now had increased to nearly $160,000. Studio equipment jumped from $70,000 to $118,000, and most startling of all, the antenna system from $20,000 to $105,000. With the addition of over $100,000 for land and buildings, the application for a CP placed the necessary station investment at $545,000. Operating expense for the first year was estimated at another $617,000, but surprisingly, a profit was anticipated with revenues of $635,000 projected.

In September 1953, an amendment to the Form 301 of the previous year was submitted, principally showing a change in studio location from the Roosevelt to newly acquired property at 829 Camp Street in New Orleans. Land and buildings, reflecting the purchase, were now valued at $250,000, and the total station investment at $702,000. Profit figures were even more hopeful, however with operating costs of $862,000 expected, significantly less than an anticipated income of $919,000. There was no denying, nonetheless, that a television venture was an enormously expensive proposition, with needed starting capital soaring far beyond what even the pessimists of five years before had predicted.[30]

Meanwhile, the quiet campaign to forestall competing local applications for Channel 4 was failing badly. By the summer of 1952, Jimmy Noe had filed his own Form 301, though WWL efforts "to persuade Governor Noe to request an ultra-high-frequency channel" were continuing. The campaign ended in 1953 when the other shoe dropped, the Times-Picayune also filed for the sought-after channel. On September 30, the FCC officially informed the University that the three applications were "mutually exclusive" and that a consolidated hearing would be required. The direct fears of WWL's management had materialized; a lengthy, costly, and unpredictable struggle would have to be fought in the halls of the Federal Communications Commission. At times, it would rival in bitterness and intensity the clear channel war with Henderson in the 1930's. Once more the future of the station would be determined more by actions in Washington, D.C., a thousand miles away, than in its own studios. Once again WWL's fortunes would lie more in the outcome of a political-legal clash than in the skills of its station personnel.[31]

# 17

## POINTS OF PREFERENCE

A former FCC Chairman called it: "The Whorehouse Era...when matters were _arranged_, not adjudicated." According to another Washington veteran: "It was like a race track up here. Guys running up and down the hall, barging into offices trying to find another arm to twist." Rumors of political favoritism were rampant, and one academic critic accused the FCC of "dealing a heavy blow to good government." In this climate of influence peddling and favor seeking, the three claimants for New Orleans' single remaining VHF channel sought justice from the Federal Communications Commission. If they restrained themselves from _ex parte_ communications with the Commissioners or from employing the good offices of their favorite Washington elected representatives, they might have seemed almost the only competitors for a FCC grant who did show such forebearance.[1]

For the _Times-Picayune_, Noe, and WWL the adjudication process began with the exchange of "supplementary material" in December 1953. Loyola's consisted of two thick volumes containing biographies of University and station executives, estimated budgets, descriptions of studio facilities, proposed work schedules, policy statements, programming information, complimentary letters, and a mass of other data. The volumes began with a short and laudatory history of both Loyola and WWL before proceeding to capsule biographies of which the first was the University's new President.[2]

In the spring of 1952, Father Shields, having completed more than the customary six years in the office, passed the presidency to W. Patrick Donnelly, S.J., a man of considerable experience in educational administration. Donnelly had last served as head of Spring Hill College in Mobile, another Jesuit institution. In order to prepare himself for the broadcast decisions to be

261

made, he undertook visits to television stations in
eleven different cities, including Chicago, New York,
Washington, Dallas, and Atlanta, and held conferences
with their managements.

Significantly, the new President quickly chose to
separate his office from that of the everyday WWL
management. Rejecting Shields' merger of the two posts,
Donnelly appointed a separate Jesuit Faculty Director,
W. D. O'Leary. A native of Georgia, as was the President, O'Leary, who possessed both an M.D. degree and
a M.A. in Psychology, preceeded Donnelly as Spring Hill's
chief administrator, and had assumed control of Loyola's
School of Dentistry in 1948. Given the FCC's distaste
for absentee ownership of stations, the presence of a
full-time Faculty Director on the premises, rather than
the Shields system of splitting time, showed greater
promise of adding strength to Loyola's bid for Channel
4. As for Shields himself, in September 1953, he was
appointed principal of a Jesuit high school in Dallas,
Texas.3

The volumes of supporting material testified to
WWL's past record as a commercial radio station. It
revealed that for a composite week in 1953, some 78%
of the total programming was classified as entertainment, about 11% as news, just 2% as religious, and but
1% as educational. In that composite week, 438 commercial and 151 non-commercial spot announcements were
carried. The projected figures for television operations were not significantly different than those for
radio. An expected 108 hours per week were to be
telecast as opposed to the usual 157 radio hours. About
69% of the TV programming was to be commercial; 64% of
the present AM time was sponsored. Some 41% of the
television schedule would be taken from CBS, a bit less
than CBS's 44% of the WWL schedule on radio. The WWL
planners placed the estimated number of commercial
spot announcements at 302 weekly, a third less than
radio in 1953, but a figure likely to grow as television
prosperity gathered momentum. Entertainment would
dominate the TV program log, and the educational-
religious categories were expected to be less than 4%
of on-the-air-time.4

The Loyola station proposed to use a large number
of filmed programs including the Buster Crabbe Show,
Cowboy G-Men, Two-Gun Playhouse, Lillie Palmer Show,
Wrestling from Hollywood, and Washington Spotlight.
The costs of these ranged from a low of $30 (Last
Edition) to a high of $250 (Gene Autry Show) per program,

and they would be spotted throughout the seven day schedule. Equally important were the live productions that would be mounted in WWL's own studios. These included religious programs, e.g. In Which We Live (Protestant, Sunday mornings at 10:00) and We Believe (Catholic, Sunday mornings at 10:30), as well as educational, e.g. Art Museum and Great Books, both also Sunday offerings. Entertainment proposals consisted of shows such as Dixieland America, Music with Mac (Ray McNamara), Jill's Hollywood (Jill Jackson), Jive Five (Al Hirt), and Southern Hospitality.

Costs of the live productions were estimated at figures as low as $18.83, not including talent paid at a staff salary, for ten minutes of Ray McNamara on the organ each weekday morning to $510 for Show Business Show Case, to be broadcast on Friday evenings. The latter would require Henry Dupre as Master of Ceremonies, a five-piece studio orchestra, and professional variety acts. It would "spot light" WWL radio and TV talent heard during the day "and brought back for a repeat performance at a time when a general audience is available." The $500 cost did not include the salaries of the staff announcer and orchestra utilized. The local programs projected and the sample scripts supplied left no doubt that the WWL planners in 1953 saw TV as little more than visual radio. The shows revealed an unmistakeable aural broadcasting quality, and few if any imaginative uses of the new medium were suggested. Fortunately, most of the proposals never saw an actual airing when WWL-TV was eventually born.[5]

A full statement of the station's expected program policies was also provided the FCC. According to that statement, the policies were founded on "the fundamental premise that the television broadcaster has a definable and constant responsibility toward the community as a whole and toward its major integral component--the family home." It promised adherence to the Television Code of the National Association of Radio and Television Broad-casters so that "decency, propriety, and good taste shall always prevail." In regard to religious programs, WWL recognized a "specific responsibility" to make "adequate program space available" for all faiths, something that had not been a part of the station's policy until relatively recently. No comments were made regarding the carrying of paid political advertisements that had not been heard on WWL radio since the days of Huey Long, but the implication was present that the old AM policy would not be binding on the television opera-tion.[6]

The estimated revenues from the first year of telecasting were to be derived as follows:

Sale of Station Time

| | |
|---|---:|
| To network | $262,080 |
| To national advertisers | 630,000 |
| To local advertisers | 187,500 |
| | $1,079,580 |

After deductions for agency and representatives'
commissions, and following an addition for talent fees
charged, total broadcast revenues of $919,155 were an-
ticipated. After expenses, an "indicated net income"
of $77,521 was predicted. Salaries formed much the
largest portion of first year costs, over $500,000,
with film rentals, the next most important item, far
behind at $64,000. Individual staff salaries were to
begin at $60 per week for secretaries, move up to $80
for camera men, and $126 for studio supervisors. De-
partment heads such as the Engineering Director (J.D.
Bloom) and the Program Director (Ed Hoerner) would
receive $12,000 yearly, and Summerville as General
Manager $25,000. The staff orchestra members would each
earn $75.66 weekly, announcers $95, and singers
$74.50.[7]

The sales policy published confined commercial
announcements to no more than six minutes in a half
hour program. A suggested rate card offered three
classes of time and purchase options ranging from ten
seconds to one hour. A one-minute announcement in prime
evening time could vary from $90 to $120, depending on
its frequency. The rates included transmitter charges,
use of film facilities, the services of an off-camera
staff announcer, recorded music as background, the
necessary technical staff, and normal rehearsal time.
They did not include such items as talent, set construction, and remote lines.[8]

On January 4, 1954, a "hearing conference" with
FCC Examiner Elizabeth C. Smith and the three contestants
was held. The parties discussed the fact that in the
previous month the Commission had authorized "compatible"
color television broadcasting based on the standards
developed by a National Television System Committee
supported by RCA, the major set manufacturers, and
eventually even CBS. The Channel 4 competitors agreed
to supplement their already filed applications with
proposals on the use of color. But the adoption of the
new standards and the submission of color data did not

necessarily precipitate any rapid development of the new process. By 1956, for instance, WDSU-TV had sunk some $500,000 in color and did not expect to earn back the investment for some time yet. That station first began to carry network programs in color in July 1954 and would not acquire a color camera of its own until the following year.[9]

Loyola's color proposal was modest. It promised available network color shows as well as films, and the production of live programs "on a trial basis from time to time, to an extent indicated by popular interest, the availability of receiving sets, and similar relative considerations." It made no commitment as to the number of such programs that would be aired. The Times-Picayune, on the other hand, took more concrete steps. George Healy headed a group from the newspaper who traveled to RCA installations in New York City and in New Jersey to study color operations first hand. A proposal was then filed calling for daily live color programs totaling almost 17 hours per week in addition to film. Noe's submission was, like WWL's, much less detailed. His simply stated an intention to use network color shows "when they become available" and to purchase equipment for the use of color film and slides. No live programs were contemplated by him. On the issue of color, at least, the Times-Picayune seemed to have taken an early lead in the competition with its fulsome and probably unrealistic plans.[10]

* * * * * * * * * *

The procedure followed in determining which of the three contenders would receive the eventual authorization to telecast on Channel 4 had not changed markedly since the days of W. K. Henderson when the issue was a clear AM channel. The applicants first submitted a statement of points upon which they intended to rely in the comparative hearing. Cross-examination of witnesses was then based on material filed in the original applications and supplements and in the points of reliance. After the record was closed, an initial decision would be rendered by the hearing examiner, Elizabeth C. Smith in this case. Exceptions to the decision were inevitably filed by the losers, and oral arguments presented to the Commissioners themselves sitting en banc. The Commission, after further deliberation, would finally announce its ruling, and the next appeal for the vanquished, if they continued to persist in their claim, must be to the federal courts, possibly ending in the chamber of the United States Supreme Court.

In a hearing, the competing parties had a wide margin of choice as to the evidence they presented, selecting, of course, that which might reflect most favorably on themselves and adversely on their opponents. The lengthy process has been described as "ritualistic, formalistic, wasteful, and inefficient." Faced with the necessity of deciding among mutually exclusive applications for the same grant, the FCC was forced over the years to develop some general criteria upon which to base its choice. It was understood, of course, that the applicants were to be "decent and law-abiding, with sufficient intelligence and integrity to fulfill the public responsibility" placed upon the broadcaster. More was needed, however, if the Commissioners were really expected to make any sort of rational decision.[11]

The criteria upon which the FCC came to rely, though not always consistently, featured a preference by the regulatory body for local ownership, participation by the prospective licensees in civic activities, integration of ownership and management, diversification of background, broadcast experience, a commendable record of past broadcasting performance, suitable and realistic proposed programming and operating plans, and diversification of ownership of the mass media of communications. In the New Orleans television case, the applicants would be examined on all those grounds, with some becoming more significant than others in the eventual decision.[12]

In pursuing localism, it has been said, the FCC "appears to conceive of the station owner as a kind of latter-day Mark Twain who understands the needs and concerns of his community in an imaginative and sensitive way." Such an owner would, hopefully, be more amenable to providing "civic, social and business groups appropriate access to the facility." In much the same way, the integration of ownership and management meant that in a contest between applicants, preference would be shown to an owner-manager who supposedly should be more concerned with community needs than a station head reporting to an absentee proprietor.[13]

Diversification of background was a criteria resting upon the theory that a bid for a license from a firm whose investors came from varied business and professional fields might be more civic-minded than one from a single-interest group. Yet, one of the FCC's own hearing examiners admitted there was "no empirical data to support this belief and...very little logic to recommend it."

The desirability of previous broadcast experience and
an impressive performance record, especially in the
creation of local live programs, formed obvious criteria
upon which the FCC relied, along with an evaluation of
proposed plans and policies for future station operation.
For WWL, the final criteria of diversification in the
ownership of communications mass media would be an important weapon to use against the Times-Picayune. The
most striking aspect of this criterion was the forcing
of newspaper applicants into an unfavorable contesting
position against their rivals since the FCC had come to
believe local concentration of media ownership did
"represent a potential hazard, not only to market competition for advertising but, more important, to the
free flow of ideas."[14]

A major highlight of the years following World War
II was the widespread entry of newspaper publishers into
FM broadcasting and television. The reasons were simple
enough, both were promising public services expected
eventually to be profitable, and they served as a protection for the newspaper properties against that same
competition. As for the FCC, it had long been worried
about the problem, and warned of "the spectre of the
octopus reaching out ever-further to control mass
media" as early as 1941. In that same year, prompted
by President Roosevelt, the FCC launched an investigation
that was not closed until 1944 when the Commission
finally announced a specific rule on cross-media concentration was impossible. It chose instead to adopt a
case-by-case approach, but even that policy tended to
be marked by rampant inconsistency as the years went by.
As Judge Henry J. Friendly later noted: "On some
occasions the Commission has preferred a non-newspaper-
owner, on grounds of diversification, over a newspaper
applicant at least as well or better qualified. On
other occasions, it has awarded licenses to newspaper-
owning or affiliated applicants despite the availability
of other well-qualified contenders without newspaper
affiliation." Friendly called the wobbling "intolerable"
and urged the Commission to "develop enough courage to
penetrate the fog it has helped create."

Eventually, the FCC came to regard newspaper ownership as a "discrediting factor, not a disqualifying
factor" for an applicant. In 1954 when the New Orleans
Channel 4 hearing began, newspapers controlled over
18% of all AM stations, 33% of FM, and 37% of TV. Those
who feared that cross-media concentration might mean
the constriction of one medium to protect the interests

of another, combined advertising schemes that would con-
stitute unfair competition for media rivals, and re-
straints on the free flow of ideas were not consoled by
those figures.[15]

The FCC referred to its own hearing criteria as
"guideposts." The word emphasized their imprecise
nature; they were "capable of infinite manipulation."
According to one scholar, they actually became "spurious
criteria, used to justify results otherwise arrived at."
In an era in which the FCC possessed an "almost invisible
prestige" under a barrage of allegations of political
favoritism and questionable ethics, the criteria were,
nevertheless, the only ostensible rules of the game.[16]

On February 11, 1954, the WWL owners submitted
their "Statements of Matters Relied Upon by Loyola
University." They claimed a "superior local live and
film programming service" as well as a "superior ability
to carry out its proposal." Heavy emphasis was placed
on "better background and experience than the other
applicants," the "length and character of local residence"
of the owners, their participation in community affairs,
and their broadcasting record. Not overlooked either
was the desirability of diversification in New Orleans
media ownership. Overall, the points especially stressed
were "the comparative history of the applicants" and the
need for diversification in media control, both of which
under the FCC's usual criteria should have been strong
suits in the WWL hand.[17]

The Times-Picayune chose its own ground on which to
fight. It cited its "116 years of operation in New
Orleans," which gave it a great familiarity with community
needs, and the fact that all of its nine officers were
residents of the city. The newspaper was quick to note
Loyola's top two officials "have not resided in New
Orleans longer than six years" and none of the University's officers were life-long residents, while six of
the Times-Picayune's were. A "more stable corporate
management than Loyola" was also claimed, especially
with the educational institution's presidency rotated
at least once each decade and the latest occupant in
the office only since the preceeding year. The publishing firm sought to use Loyola's own instructional
mission against it, warning that deficit operations in
television could be absorbed by the newspaper, while
for WWL they would result in either a curtailment of
broadcast service or the diversion of capital "which
would otherwise be used for educational purposes."

Moreover, WTPS-TV operations would be under the direct supervision of George Healy, a senior Vice-President and stockholder in the publishing company, thus providing an integration of ownership and management. On the other hand, in the case of WWL-TV, the Faculty Director was not an officer of the University and had no owner-ship interest in it in the ordinary sense.[18]

The Times-Picayune argued it was promising more scheduled hours than Loyola, and a considerably more elaborate plan for color telecasts. It also warned that WWL intended to simply carry over its radio talent and programs to TV, while the WTPS proposal provided "opportunities for more different entertainment per-sonnel on a greater variety of shows." A detailed description of the supposedly superior technical facilities and production capabilities of the Times-Picayune was offered as additional proof of the news-paper's case. The journalists took a much more aggressive tack in their presentation than had the educators. While Loyola praised its own record, it criticized its opponents only indirectly. The Times-Picayune, however, followed an offensive-minded strategy, attacking head-on what it considered to be some of its competitor's weak points. But even the newspaper did not carry its offensive as far and press it as hard as the veteran of Louisiana political wars, ex-Governor James A. Noe.[19]

His application for a CP had been filed by a part-nership formed in October 1953 and styled James A. Noe and Company. The partners were Noe himself, his son, Harry Allsman (a Louisiana oilman and public official), and Raymond F. Hufft (a one-time general manager of WNOE, a businessman, and a state official). There was little doubt that Noe Sr. would be the managing partner. His broadcasting interests in 1954 included the owner-ship of KNOE and KNOE-TV in Monroe, Louisiana, and WNOE in New Orleans, and a 50% share of KOTN in Pine Bluff, Arkansas. Noe promised he would be "in direct charge of station policies and planning and supervision of day-to-day operations" of the proposed WNOE-TV.[20]

Among its "points of reliance," James A. Noe and Company cited the fact that Loyola University was actually controlled by "a church group having its head-quarters outside of the State of Louisiana"--more specifically in Rome, Italy--and that there was "no assurance of continuity of top management interest and direction" at the college since the Jesuit administrators were subject "to transfer to other assignments at any time." Furthermore, in view of the fact that Loyola was

269

the property of "an absentee Church Order," it could not present a "well-balanced" point of view in its television programming. The Noe statement warned of Loyola's "fixed principles of thought dissemination representative of a minority group of the population," and urged that the educational institution be confined to its teaching occupation or "to applying for a non-commercial television outlet presently available in New Orleans." Against both the Times-Picayune and Loyola, Noe argued his previous television experience in the operation of KNOE-TV in Monroe.[21]

Noe's concentration on the religious affiliation of WWL continued to be the principal focus of his attack. In June 1954 he demanded specific information relating to the Society of Jesus and its world-wide activities. Noe's attorneys likened the Jesuits to a holding company in business, controlling and influencing the policy of broadcasting media in many locations. Loyola vigorously opposed the demand, claiming that it was an attempt to obtain evidence on a matter not relevant to the proceedings. The applicant in this case, it argued, was the University, not the Society of Jesus, and it was "controlled and operated solely by its officers and board of directors." The religious beliefs of those individuals were immaterial. Noe, nevertheless, won a partial victory. In late July Examiner Smith ordered the University to furnish Noe's counsel a statement by Father Donnelly clarifying the "extent of control, if any, which has been, is now or would be exercised by the Society of Jesus or by the Roman Catholic Archdiocese of New Orleans over Loyola University...insofar as such control relates in any manner whatsoever to the construction and operation of the proposed television station." The issue of outside control was to become almost the whole of Noe's case in the oral testimony that followed in the fall of 1954.[22]

In preparation for the cross-examination to come, Paul Segal briefed each of the Loyola and WWL officials who would be taking the stand. He also asked them to observe other FCC hearings in progress in order that they might familiarize themselves with the procedures followed and the nature of the questions which might be asked. In a rather distinct departure from the prevailing mores of the period, Segal sternly warned his clients against extra-mural contacts with federal officials on behalf of the WWL application.[23]

On Monday morning, October 4, the cross-examination phase of the hearing began in a small room in the

Interstate Commerce Commission building in Washington
with Donnelly as the first witness.  The Jesuit
President was questioned for more than two hours by
Warren Woods, Noe's counsel, primarily on the "outside
control" issue.  Donnelly vigorously denied the station
was controlled "from abroad" or by the New Orleans
archdiocese.  He admitted the Society of Jesus operated
29 universities and colleges and some 30 high schools in
the United States, but he held that the policies of
those institutions were not dictated by the Order's
Superior General in Rome.  Under Wood's probing, Donnelly
acknowledged that the Loyola administration could not
"assume heavy financial obligations without approval by
higher authority"--specifically, the same Superior
General--but that procedure was adhered to simply to
"keep religion from getting a bad name."

Then  Woods turned to an especially sensitive
matter--the airing of non-Catholic religious programs on
WWL, and Donnelly found himself temporarily on the
defensive.  The Jesuit acknowledged a complaint had been
filed with the FCC in August 1953 by Rev. Walter D.
Langtry, chairman of the radio and television committee
of the New Orleans Council of Churches, protesting the
absence of any locally originated Protestant religious
programs on WWL.  Donnelly explained, however, there
had been no recent requests for such offerings up to the
time of Langtry's complaint "and that is why the station
did not carry them."[24]

* * * * * * * * * *

The issue was one of long-standing.  During its
first twenty years of existence, the station had in fact
followed a policy of refusing to carry any non-Catholic
religious programs.  The policy was maintained, in the
words of Father Shields, "in spite of great pressure
and some financial loss."  But by the end of World War II,
the implications of that stance became more serious than
ever.  In 1945 some Protestant organizations filed suit
against a Philadelphia station to compel it to allow them
time for their denominational programs.  Soon afterwards,
WWL itself received an ominous letter from the Protestant
War Veterans of the United States asking for the names
of any Protestant broadcasts carried on the Loyola
station.  Paul Segal was quick to warn Shields and
Summerville of the potential for trouble in WWL's policy,
reminding them of the FCC regulation that at least im-
plicitly gave to other denominations the right to
occasionally schedule their own programs over a station
which regularly broadcasted the offerings of another

271

religious body.  The Washington attorney cautioned the
University "not to give non-Catholic religious groups
any particular specific reason to present a case" against
it before the FCC.[25]

For Shields, the problem posed a dilemma.  At that
moment, the Southern Baptist Conference was asking to
have its annual convention broadcast by WWL.  It was
willing to purchase the time, and it claimed that WWL's
clear channel signal enabled that station alone among
all New Orleans and Deep South broadcasters to reach
the rural areas where most Southern Baptists resided.
Shields feared if he refused to air the convention, a
complaint would be filed with the FCC, charging his
station with religious discrimination.  The consequence,
he bemoaned, might be "the only large radio station under
Catholic direction in the western hemisphere and, other
than the Vatican Station, the only large Catholic radio
in the world, will go off the air."  That outcome would
likewise mean "financial ruin" for Loyola, the sole
Catholic university in the South.  He also foresaw if
Loyola was forced to sell WWL, the probable buyers would
be "Protestants or Jews" with the result that "one of the
most powerful stations in the country would be wide open
for the broadcasting of all types of heresy."[26]

On the other hand, if WWL agreed to carry the
material, Shields feared the University would find
itself in the position of, in one Jesuit's words,
"propagating a false religion."  At the least, it
would be "implicit formal cooperation" with a corresponding "spiritual harm to souls" by "acquainting them
with a false doctrine."  Caught by the dilemma, Shields
and his predecessor, Father Percy Roy, presented their
difficulty to Archbishop Joseph F. Rummel of New Orleans
in a two hour meeting with the prelate on the evening of
May 4, 1945.  According to Shields, the Archbishop
"manifested the utmost sympathy, interest, and understanding," and asked the two Jesuits to secure the
opinions of leading Catholic moralists and theologians
to aid Rummel in making a final determination.  Dutifully,
Loyola's President prepared statements of the case and
sent them off to Catholic scholars in various parts of
the country--Massachusetts, New York, Illinois, Kansas,
California, and New Orleans.[27]

The responses were virtually unanimous in their
support for the inauguration of a new WWL policy offering
time to all bona fide religious organizations.  The
Rector of Notre Dame Seminary in New Orleans, for
example, replied that just as a local transit company,

272

which happened to be owned by Catholics, would "be allowed to transport people to heretical churches," so also could the station give Protestant groups access to its facilities. A Jesuit theologian in Indiana found nothing "intrinsically wrong" with the broadcasting of Baptist services. He pointed out there was no participation in the services themselves by the WWL personnel, "merely a communication" of religious activity to those who did desire to participate. The necessity of saving the station seemed to be the most important consideration since, he wrote: "In these days the Church can ill afford to withdraw into silence, or to lose such opportunities for keeping its vivifying influence before the people as are offered by the control of a big radio station." A California Jesuit agreed. Joseph D. O'Brien, S.J., admitted the selling of time for non-Catholic programs constituted "material cooperation," but held "the good to be accomplished by keeping your license far outweighs the evil which will result." O'Brien did advise that the Baptists be made to pay for any time they received, and none be offered to them free of charge.[28]

On June 16, Shields forwarded the collected theological responses to Archbishop Rummel, pointing out what he termed "the unanimity of opinion of so many noted men." Two weeks later, Rummel added his own conclusion. Satisfied with the learned support for the step, he advised Shields to proceed with the granting of time to qualified non-Catholic religious organizations. The station began to carry non-Catholic programs originating at the network, commencing with the CBS feature, Columbia Church of the Air. The soul-searching of Shields and Roy may seem rather quaint to a later generation, but as Catholic broadcasters in the 1940's, they were breaking new ground. The issue for them was novel and perplexing indeed, yet they finally reached an accommodation with it that satisfied the regulatory requirements. In so doing, the Loyola officials sacrificed the doctrinal monopoly they had formerly enjoyed on WWL, but they exchanged it for continued existence, the necessary first condition for any commercial operation. They placed what they believed to be paramount--the financial viability of the University--first and foremost, and they insured that viability through the medium of radio rather than in spite of it, as was the case with other educational institutions that chose to dabble in the business of broadcasting.[29]

273

The issue arose once more, however, in the summer
of 1953 when Reverend Langtry, on behalf of the New
Orleans Council of Churches, filed his complaint with
the FCC. Langtry related that he had contacted WWL,
offering the assistance of his Radio and Television
Committee in developing local religious programs. Ed
Hoerner had conferred with the minister, thanked him
for the offer of aid, but explained that all of the time
available on Sunday mornings for religious programming
was already allocated. Langtry was not convinced.
While the Program Director's position appeared to be a
reasonable one on the surface, the actual effect of the
policy, it seemed to Langtry, was "to bar local Protestant
voices, and to make the station the voice of Roman
Catholicism." He discounted WWL's broadcasting of
Columbia Church of the Air, which did feature Protestant
and Jewish segments, since it was a network offering
and in the New Orleans minister's view "had little or
no local appeal." Langtry brought the matter to FCC
attention when WWL filed for a television channel,
since his organization viewed "with disquiet such an
extension of the influence of a definitely partisan
station, which has for so many years refused to allow
any of the local spokesmen for the Protestant Churches
to appear, either through the purchase of time or on a
sustaining basis."[30]

Langtry could not have raised the issue at a more
inopportune moment. It was just the type of damaging
evidence that could wreck any dreams of winning the
Channel 4 fight. The WWL management reacted immediately.
A letter was drafted, signed by Ed Hoerner, and quickly
forwarded to Langtry. In it Hoerner began by expressing
surprise that the minister should have felt compelled to
submit to the FCC what obviously was simply a misunder-
standing. The Program Director was quite sure that
Langtry's goal could be accommodated, and a meeting of
the two men was suggested. Later, when Paul Segal
was questioned about the episode by the FCC, he termed
it a "mistake of somebody on the staff of WWL." Segal
added that when the matter "reached the proper level"
at the station, it was corrected. By the time of the
hearing in October 1954, the New Orleans Protestant
churches had a regularly scheduled thirty minute program of their own each Sunday afternoon on WWL. In
view of the 1945 decision to accept such programming,
it was undoubtedly an error to wait until the raising
of an FCC complaint in 1953 before such an offering
was scheduled. Only quick, remedial action prevented
the issue from impairing Loyola's standing in the quest
for the television grant.[31]

\* \* \* \* \* \* \* \* \* \*

Other WWL witnesses followed Donnelly to the stand,
but without significant fireworks. Those erupted on the
second day of the hearing when George Healy took the
stand and faced Paul Segal's cross-examination. The
WWL attorney worked hard at showing Healy's lack of
knowledge of the broadcasting operations at WTPS despite
his title as the executive in overall charge of television and radio. Since Healy was also serving as the
newspaper's editor, a real question arose as to the
possibility of absentee ownership at the station. Under
questioning, Healy found himself very hard put to comment
on the character of WTPS programs and even on the advertising rates and policies in effect at the station. In
his memoirs, the newspaper editor later acknowledged
that he "rejoiced" when he was eventually relieved of
the responsibilities of broadcasting; he had found the
assignment difficult, and he discovered the "print and
electronic media are far apart."[32]

More sparks flew when the next Times-Picayune witness, John F. Tims, took the stand. Angry words were
hurled between Warren Woods and the newspaper's attorney,
William J. Dempsey, when the former attempted to introduce through Tims, the President of the publishing
corporation, the subject of attempted monopoly. In 1950
the Times-Picayune had instituted a unit plan for the
sale of all classified advertising space. Under it
advertisers were required to run the same ad copy in
the less popular States if they wished space in the more
influential Times-Picayune. A limited variation of this
"forced combination" policy had been in effect since the
1930's. The broadened action caused consternation at
the rival afternoon Item where an antitrust suit was
planned. The Item management refrained, however, when
the Justice Department filed its own suit in June 1950.
The Times-Picayune was accused of attempting to establish a monopoly and of seeking to injure or destroy its
competitor. The combination rate itself was challenged
as an unreasonable restraint of interstate trade.[33]

In May 1951 a federal district court in New Orleans
held the newspaper defendant guilty on almost all counts,
and ordered it to abandon the unit advertising rate.
Naturally, an appeal was carried to the Supreme Court
in Washington and argued there in March 1953. Two months
later, a decision was announced and the Times-Picayune
officials were jubiliant. By a five to four majority,
the Court found the government had not substantiated its
case against the newspaper, and the unit plan had not

275

unduly handicapped the Item. David Stern, the Item's owner, called the decision "the last blow to competitive journalism," and he growled, "competitive journalism is healthy in a democracy." The verdict signaled the approaching end of Stern's paper as an independent entity.[34]

Woods' attempt to resurrect the monopoly case was not successful. The hearing examiner announced sharply that she did not intend to retry the Supreme Court decision of the previous year. Noe's attorney was required to move on to other topics. The most surprising admission he was then able to elicit from Tims was the baring of WTPS's financial performance. The station had lost over $600,000 since its founding in 1946. As a consequence, WTPS eliminated its staff orchestra, broadcast no dramatic programs, and confined its schedule to sports, news, and recorded music. Compared to WWL, it was an extremely limited operation and a distinctly unsuccessful one.[35]

On October 7, Jimmy Noe took his place on the witness stand, to be questioned by both Segal and Dempsey. Time and again he was asked technical questions to test the depth of his broadcasting knowledge, and Noe was forced to concede there were many facets of station activities with which he was unfamiliar. At one point Segal switched to queries on programming, and noted that the Noe TV proposal contained the promise of a ceramics show. Bluntly, he asked the ex-Governor if he even knew what ceramics was. The witness replied caustically that he did not, but added: "When you were studying law, I was picking cotton and working in the oil fields."

Questions centered particularly on the partnership's ability to finance a television station. The evidence was shaky, and an FCC lawyer reported a serious doubt in the agency that Noe had the necessary financial qualifications. The costs of construction were to be met in large part by a $600,000 loan from an unnamed bank, and no evidence was introduced to verify the availability of the money. Noe agreed that the partnership would "have to borrow money to put the thing over," but no elaboration was given by him. Further, while his own personal contribution to the starting capital was to be some $300,000, the balance sheet which he submitted revealed current assets of some $134,000 and current liabilities of nearly $900,000, the latter consisting principally of bank loans. The figures appeared to indicate that his share of the investment would also be based on borrowed money. The financial data was the most telling

276

evidence against the Noe application.[36]

A few more witnesses were heard, but the testimony they supplied was conventional. On November 3, Examiner Smith "closed the record" of the comparative hearing, and instructed the parties to submit their proposed findings to her. No new evidence could now be introduced.[37]

On July 7, 1955, Elizabeth Smith released her decision. It occupied 110 pages of close-packed print, and its final conclusions were not pleasant reading for Segal or his clients. Smith began by reiterating that the preliminary investigation of the applicants by the FCC's Broadcast Bureau had found both Loyola and the Times-Picayune "legally, technically, and financially qualified" to construct and operate a television station. Noe also had met the test on the first two grounds, but failed the third. It became necessary for him to answer the "threshold question" of financial ability before his proposal could be scrutinized in conjunction with the others. But the Noe partners did not provide the necessary proof during the hearing, and therefore, they were disqualified from further consideration. The Examiner thenceforth focused her attention only on the competing applications of the newspaper and the university.[38]

She found little to choose between the two conflicting bids for Channel 4, as she methodically measured each against the usual FCC criteria. In the area of program proposals, she saw no decisional significance to the number of hours each promised to telecast or the balance between live, film, and network shows that each desired to maintain. She did find a significant difference in special programming for areas outside of New Orleans. Loyola proposed no offerings of this sort, while the Times-Picayune planned four weekly segments in its schedule "designed to bring about regular participation of persons and groups" from neighboring communities. Contacts were already claimed with eighteen such communities looking to the eventual production of programs. On this relatively subsidiary test, the Examiner held the newspaper merited a preference.

A more important gain was made by the journalists when Smith evaluated the color proposals of both parties. Here she found the WWL plans vague and minimal. On the other hand, the Times-Picayune had detailed its plans for producing live studio programs in color, the equipment to be used, the sets and scenery to be built, and the time to be allocated. The WWL staff made a severe tactical error in not taking their color proposal more seriously. Realizing the march that had been stolen on them, Segal and his associates scorned the good faith of the newspaper's plans, claiming they had been formulated "solely to overwhelm and influence the Commission in this proceeding." But no substantial proof could be mustered by Loyola's attorneys to prove their contention that the WTPS color programs would never materialize. Smith concluded, therefore, that the Times-Picayune deserved "a material preference as against Loyola on this point."[39]

Turning to other criteria, she found that both applicants projected an adequate staff, suitable studio facilities and equipment, and both offered reasonable assurance of meeting their commitments. On the matter of past performance, Loyola claimed a superiority based on the record of WWL in its three decades of existence, and Smith agreed that the University earned a preference on this point. She quickly offset it, however, by concluding that WTPS operations had been in the public interest too, and that the newspaper had a long record of service to the community. In what the WWL supporters regarded as one of the strongest facets of their case, they did not win a clear victory. The factor of local ownership was likewise regarded as a near draw, despite the controversy over outside control of WWL from Rome that developed during the hearing. The publishing organization did win "a slight preference" on the criteria of participation in civic and community life. Smith found the Times-Picayune officers and directors "proportionately more active in a greater number and variety" of civic projects, and over a longer span of time.[40]

Next, no decisional preference was found on the bases of integration of ownership and management, diversification of business interests, and, startlingly, ownership of mass communication media. On the surface, the concentration of control represented by one corporation owning two newspapers, an AM and FM station, and a television outlet should have proved damaging to the Times-Picayune case. Yet, despite the best WWL expectations of success on this point, it resulted instead in a standoff. Smith neatly equated the potential power of the publishers with the holding of broadcast licenses by other Jesuit educational institutions in California, Pennsylvania, Missouri, and New York. She contended that Loyola had not "substantiated its claim of superiority" on this criterion.[41]

The FCC official now reached her ultimate conclusion. She had found neither proposal to be deficient in any important aspect, and believed each promised "well-balanced and meritorious programming." The deciding factor, she argued, was the preference earned by the Times-Picayune "on two important facets of proposed programming"--color and the provision of time for outlying communities. Especially important, she felt, were the WTPS color efforts since the end-product would be to "encourage and foster a new and challenging phase of visual broadcasting in the New Orleans area without delay." For Smith, the record of the proceedings thus meant that "the public interest, convenience, and necessity would be better served by a grant of the application of Times-Picayune Publishing Company."[42]

The news of the Examiner's decision came as a severe shock to the members of WWL staff. They generally assumed a ruling in favor of their station was inevitable. They had feared the issue of religious control; instead they had been undone by the unexpected matter of color. On the day after the release of Smith's ruling, Segal wrote Donnelly an apologetic letter. Regrettably, he warned, there would be "a very substantial expense... before us in connection with the preparation of exceptions, briefs, oral argument and the other procedural steps which now will be Herculean." There would also, he predicted, be a lengthy delay, and probably, it would be well into 1956 before a final verdict was rendered. As to the Examiner's decision, Segal expressed himself satisfied with "the factual portion," but was convinced Smith had "fallen deeply in error when she came to her conclusion." He, nevertheless, took an optimistic view. Her findings were merely advisory; the Commission itself would make the real determination.[43]

Addressing himself to the specific points raised in the decision, Segal characterized the "outlying communities" issue as of "relatively small importance." He was vehement, however, on the matter of color. On this, Smith was "clearly wrong." Color had been "injected into this case by the Times-Picayune as a makeweight, as a substitute for a real issue of principle." He hoped he would be able to convince the Commissioners of that. Moreover, Segal intended to emphasize the real decisional factors in the case, the restrictive advertising practices of the newspaper, the past performances of WTPS and WWL, the independence of Loyola's station from those operated by other Jesuit-affiliated institutions, and the diversification of the media of mass communication, among others. He ended with words of encouragement for the Jesuit President: "Meanwhile, be of good cheer; we have not sevened out yet."[44]

Segal was correct; the next steps in the FCC's deliberative process were time-consuming. Not until May 1956 did the attorneys finally present their oral arguments to the Commission. Segal was the first to plead his case, followed by Dempsey, and then Woods. The WWL attorney vigorously challenged the Examiner's choice of WTPS. On the color issue, he maintained Loyola's plans were "practical and feasible," while the WTPS scheme was not. He also raised the issue of the Times-Picayune's real purpose in seeking a license, contending that broadcasting was being used as a means of advancing the interests of the newspaper rather than out of any concern for the medium. He then ridiculed any attempt to compare the past performances of WWL and WTPS. With a little humor, he termed the operations of the latter "picayune," and he contended the clearly superior record of WWL as one of the most powerful and successful stations in the country plainly entitled it to the preference in the Channel 4 struggle.

On behalf of the Noe partnership, Warren Woods was his usual aggressive self. He referred to the ex-Governor as the "poor boy" among the applicants, but determinedly maintained, nevertheless, that his client did have sufficient funds available to furnish an adequate starting capital. Even though it had been the Times-Picayune which had won the favor of the Examiner, Woods stubbornly persisted in pressing the "outside control" issue against Loyola. He warned a grant to the University would subject the television station to foreign manipulation, and discussed once more both the Langtry episode and the now defunct all-Catholic religious programming policy. When the attorneys concluded their arguments, the FCC took the case under advisement.[45]

Its decision was released on Friday, July 13, 1956, just six weeks after oral arguments had been presented-- the Times-Picayune called it "an unprecedented swift action." The FCC trod well-traveled ground in reaching its ruling, examining the same facts as Elizabeth Smith had the previous year and reaching the same general conclusions except on a very few crucial points. The decision of the Commissioners was a unanimous 6-0 verdict in favor of the Loyola application, reversing the recommendation of their own hearing examiner.

The FCC found no substantial points of preference between Loyola and the Times-Picayune on most criteria. It agreed with Smith that the civil record of the

publishing corporation principals warranted a preference
over Loyola and so did their broader range of business
interests, though on the latter, the advantage was of
only "secondary significance." Those gains for the
newspaper were more than offset by a major breakthrough
for Segal--the Commissioners agreed with him that the
past broadcasting record of WWL entitled it to a "substantial preference" over both the Times-Picayune and
Noe. Indeed, the findings on this point strongly indicated that the performances of both WTPS and the Noe
stations had not fulfilled their promise or potential.
The Commission next reached the factors that the Examiner
had found decisive--programming for outlying communities
and plans for the introduction of color telecasting.
On the first, it agreed with the Examiner, but stated
"in view of the overall parity otherwise found in the
respective program proposals of the applicants, such
preference is necessarily minor in nature." The color
question prompted the regulatory body to recall a precedent established in an earlier case; the promise of
local live color programs by one applicant when another
planned only to carry network color shows at first was
not to be regarded as a determining factor in the award
of a channel. As the Commission stated in its conclusion
on this point:

> We see no matters present in this proceeding
> which would warrant a different conclusion
> here. Accordingly, we do not award a preference.
> All applicants propose use of color. The
> difference lies chiefly in their judgments
> as to when it will be possible to undertake
> color programs on a somewhat extensive scale.
> The correctness of such varying judgments
> cannot be tested on the record before us.[46]

The Times-Picayune suffered another reverse on the
test of integration of ownership and management.
Segal's close questioning of George Healy during the
hearing had revealed the editor's limited acquaintance
with broadcasting and even the operation of his own
radio station. The FCC found, therefore, that his
function with the television station, in view of his
newspaper responsibilities, would necessarily be
"representative rather than a matter of individual
concern." The University earned a preference on this
point since WWL's Faculty Director served on Loyola's
Board of Directors and also was "in daily contact" with
the station.

Finally, the Commissioners came to the area of diversification of mass communication media ownership, a criterion upon which Segal had expected Loyola to gain advantage. He had been disappointed by the Examiner; he was not disappointed by the Commission. The FCC agreed that the ownership of two of three newspapers of the community and one of the two VHF licenses did represent "a trend toward concentration...of significant comparative consideration, emphasized somewhat by the forced combination rate policy which has been practiced in the newspaper operation." It found the same tendency toward concentration involved if a second television grant was given to Noe, who already operated KNOE-TV in Monroe. Noe was also eliminated from serious consideration by his inability to demonstrate an adequate financial capability.[47]

The result was clear. The FCC had found two major points of preference in favor of Loyola--the past performance of WWL and the diversification of communications interests--as well as minor ones. It, therefore, denied the applications of the Times-Picayune and the Noe partnership and awarded the construction permit for a new commercial television station in New Orleans to Loyola University. It was, at that moment, over ten years since the University had first applied for permission to begin service in the new medium. Robert A. Marmet, an attorney in Segal's firm, summed up the elation the WWL forces felt in a telegram to Donnelly: "WHO SAID FRIDAY THE 13TH WAS UNLUCKY."[48]

* * * * * * * * * *

Yet, it was not a complete triumph. Two clouds still marred the television horizon. One was the obvious intention of the losers to appeal. As early as mid-August, the Times-Picayune petitioned the FCC for a rehearing of the case, asking the federal agency to correct the "many errors in its findings." Healy was not hopeful himself that much could be done. He believed the decision to have been a political one, a gesture on the part of the Eisenhower administration working through the FCC to win the support of the Catholic community in the United States in a presidential election year. No evidence has survived, however, to support that conclusion, and Paul Segal had been most explicit in his instructions to the Loyola Jesuits that they strictly avoid politicians of any stature while the case was under consideration. His refrain was always the same: "We will win this case on the record of our radio station." When the FCC in

282

July 1957 denied the request for a rehearing, both the
Times-Picayune and Noe carried their efforts to United
States Court of Appeals in the District of Columbia.
The Times-Picayune questioned whether the FCC had given
the decision of the Examiner "the consideration and
weight required by law," and it branded the 1956 ruling
of the Commission "arbitrary and capricious." Noe's
brief centered on the "outside control" issue; he was
nothing if not persistent. Noe contended that Loyola,
by reason of its connection with the Society of Jesus,
was a corporation whose stock was voted by representatives
of aliens. Thus under the Communications Act of 1934, it
ought to be ineligible to hold a television license.[49]

The appeals of the Times-Picayune and of the Noe
partnership were consolidated, but while the case was
still under advisement, the newspaper chose to withdraw.
Its interests had changed dramatically. On July 14,
1958, David Stern III, board chairman of the New Orleans
Item, announced its sale to the Times-Picayune. Since
memories of the anti-trust suit of the early 1950's had
not yet faded, the Justice Department was approached for
approval of the transaction. Part of the price of that
approval proved to be the sale of WTPS and the abandonment of the fight for a television license. In the end,
WWL's strongest rival voluntarily left the field, but
not before its campaign for the Channel 4 grant had substantially delayed the eventual settlement and run up
the cost of gaining the construction permit. On
September 15, 1958, the first issue of the merged
States-Item was published in New Orleans; and in
Washington, Jimmy Noe now found himself alone in pressing
an appeal of the FCC ruling.[50]

Some support for Noe's position did come from an
amicus curiae brief filed by the Protestants and Other
Americans United for Separation of Church and State.
The POAU, which had intervened in many suits involving
Catholic issues, claimed WWL was following a "conscious
anti-Protestant policy," and the awarding of a TV
license to it would, therefore, violate the First
Amendment. The Court of Appeals did not agree. On
October 16, it unanimously announced its refusal to
overturn the decision of the FCC. It was satisfied
the Commission's conclusion granting the license to
Loyola "was based on a careful and reasoned weighing
of the various points of preference awarded between
Noe and Loyola, in accordance with governing law."
It found no validity in Noe's claim of alien control
or the POAU's vision of a deliberate anti-Protestant

strategy.  Undaunted, the Noe group took the final step, asking the Supreme Court to review the case.  Not surprisingly, Noe met with another rebuff.  The teletype machine at WWL clattered the news on March 2, 1959--the Supreme Court in a brief order rejected Noe's arguments and let stand the earlier FCC and Court of Appeals rulings.  Nearly three years after the FCC announced its decision in favor of Loyola, the University's last opponent finally succumbed.[51]

The second cloud on WWL's television horizon had been manufactured by the FCC even before the Commission decided in favor of Loyola in July 1956.  Ironically, the University, which found itself in partnership with the FCC in their defense against the Times-Picayune and Noe appeals, was simultaneously attacking a policy supported by the federal regulators.  The 1956 grant of Channel 4 to the Jesuit educators had only been conditional, pending the outcome of a rulemaking proceeding begun earlier, and until such time as a resolution was achieved, the actual construction of Loyola's television station was stayed.  The victory seemed a hollow triumph to the WWL principals unless work could begin soon.

* * * * * * * * * *

Deintermixture, the FCC called it.  It was a plan born in the frustration of creating a viable UHF service.  By the mid-1950's, it was apparent that UHF stations were not faring well.  Some had already gone off the air, many others had cancelled their construction permits without even an attempt to act upon them.  As late as 1958, over 80% of the commercial outlets on the air operated on VHF channels even though less than 30% of all channels were allocated to that band.  A variety of factors accounted for UHF becoming a disaster area, including viewer inertia, the unwillingness of set manufacturers to promote all-channel receivers and converters, the high retail cost of this equipment, superior VHF signal strength and quality, and VHF's entrenched position stemming from its earlier start and the four year FCC freeze.  The VHF channels had the coverage and the circulation that advertisers craved, and the networks chose them for affiliates as a result, further solidifying their supremacy.[52]

The FCC, of course, was well aware of the plight of the UHF band and was anxious to take corrective action.  It considered a wide range of proposals before issuing its report on June 25, 1956.  The Commission concluded the best long range solution was the shift of all television

to the ultra high frequency area, but it also recognized
that prior to such a shift, there would have to be a
research program directed towards the improvement of UHF
reception. In the meantime, the Commission would follow
an interim policy of "selective deintermixture." The
process would involve reallocating channel assignments
in a number of communities to make them all or predominantly VHF or UHF. Supposedly, it would force
viewers in UHF cities to purchase all-channel receivers
or converters, and thus give the stations in the higher
frequencies a fighting chance for life. The FCC
announced its intention to deintermix thirteen markets in
its June 1956 report, and one of those was New Orleans.[53]

    In the Crescent City, the FCC planned to delete the
Channel 4 assignment and to substitute instead another
UHF Channel, 42. Channel 4 would be moved to Mobile,
and New Orleans would be left with just two VHF assignments, 6 and 8, with the latter remaining tied to an
educational reservation. Under the proposal the city
would become predominantly UHF with five channels in
that range--20, 26, 32, 61 and the now tentatively
shifted 42. Since the Commission had come to believe
that a chief cause for the sad plight of UHF stations
was the past policy of intermixing UHF and VHF assignments, quite logically their rehabilitation should
begin with a reversal of the process--deintermixture.
Further, the best candidates for the successful implementation of the new policy were said to be markets
with but one or no commercial VHF stations operating.
If, as a congressional committee later commented,
"economic injury results to those who have applied for,
or received, grants of VHF channels which are deleted in
the process of deintermixing particular markets, that,
too, is an unavoidable concomitant of the strengthening
and preserving of UHF broadcasting for the benefit of
the public generally."[54]

    The WWL managers were not as cavalier in accepting
their possible loss of the Channel 4 prize. After
struggling to win it at the cost of thousands of dollars
in legal fees and months of tedious delay, it was not
to be expected that they would acquiesce in the proposed
changes. The FCC invited interested parties who opposed
the plan to file written statements stating their case.
It was an invitation Loyola readily accepted. On
December 3, 1956, a brief was submitted, hitting hard
the FCC's reasoning in making the policy recommendations.
The document denounced the "inequity" of a situation in
which the city would be left with a single commercial
VHF assignment and a large number "of unused and

unwanted UHF channels." It reported the University
between 1951 and 1956 had expended almost $100,000
for travel, printing, telephone and telegraph services
seeking the Channel 4 CP, and that figure did not include
legal fees. In addition, Loyola had diverted the
attention and time of the WWL radio staff to prepare
the television case, an undetermined but substantial
cost. Those expenses were not incurred in order for
the University to be given a UHF station as a consolation
prize. It wanted no part of Channel 42.[55]

The brief cited a number of specific points of
opposition, many of them based on technical grounds. It
particularly argued the low percentage of sets in the
New Orleans area equipped for UHF reception, a figure
estimated at about 40%, was insufficient for viable
deintermixture, and the carrying out of the FCC intentions
would simply create a near monopoly situation for WDSU.
The real solution, the brief contended, was not to remove
Channel 4 but just the reverse, to give the city more
VHF alternatives, specifically Channels 2 (from Baton
Rouge), 11 (from Meridian, Mississippi), and 13 (from
Biloxi). To nail down its case, Loyola employed students
in its College of Business Administration to conduct a
door-to-door survey of New Orleans television viewing
habits. Of the more than 3,000 persons interviewed,
only 4% indicated the choice of a UHF station in the
prime evening hours. The brief concluded "the audience
is dominated 31-to-1 daytime and 19-to-1 nighttime by
the very-high-frequency station"--Channel 6--and as a
result, New Orleans was "uniquely the wrong place in
which to eliminate a VHF assignment for replacement
with a UHF assignment."[56]

This time the WWL licensees had considerable
governmental support for their position, and Paul Segal
did not warn the New Orleanians against employing
political help. The case became one of Louisiana against
the FCC as key members of the state's congressional
delegation openly joined the Loyola camp. Especially
prominent were F. Edward Hebert and Hale Boggs, both
holders of considerable power in the House of Representatives and both elected from New Orleans area districts.
The Boggs and Hebert interventions included the filing
of written reports from a Washington engineering firm
attempting to prove the technical unsuitability of the
community for UHF reception, and a plea for more VHF
channels to be assigned instead. The solution of the
congressmen was to make the city all-VHF rather than
predominantly UHF. It was a form of deintermixture,

286

but the exact reverse of the FCC's conception. According to the two politicians, "the preservation and further development of adequate television service to the residents of the city of New Orleans and the surrounding area may be achieved" only with VHF outlets. They branded UHF as a second rate service that would cost the citizens of their community an extra $12,000,000 in receiving set expenses.[57]

The only local support for the FCC's proposal came from the sole operating UHF station in New Orleans. On November 1, 1953, WJMR-TV, owned by Supreme Broadcasting Company, had gone on the air using Channel 61. Later it shifted to Channel 20, where it was transmitting at the time of the deintermixture controversy. Along with WDSU-TV, it was the city's only other viewing choice, carrying CBS and ABC programs while Channel 6 featured NBC. It took issue with the Loyola brief on a number of key points. It disputed, for example, the WWL contention that only 40% of the sets in the community could receive a UHF signal; it put the number at 75% and claimed all new sets presently being sold in the city were equipped for all channels. It also poked fun at the private survey done by Loyola's College of Business, remarking wryly that it "no doubt spells the end of the professional radio and TV audience researchers." Contrary to the Loyola figures, Supreme claimed 25% of the average nighttime audience. Facing the Boggs-Hebert intervention, the WJMR-TV owners reacted with mock dramatics: "Only a man who has been stabbed by his best friend, or who has discovered sudden infidelity on the part of his ever loving wife, could understand Supreme's feelings on the matter of these comments." Not so humorous, however, was a reference to sizeable campaign contributions from WDSU and WWL being the price of the congressmen's support. Item by item, Supreme contradicted each contention of the elected officials, and criticized "their exertion of political pressure on a matter which is clearly a question of engineering logistics." It was "such unwarranted attacks" on the FCC, in the opinion of Supreme Broadcasting, that had "held back the UHF broadcasters that might otherwise be on the air today." Television must look to UHF for its future development, and for New Orleans itself, it would be far better to delete even Channel 6 and switch it to UHF than "to sacrifice the presently available UHF channels to the fires of political expediency."[58]

It was a strong response, replete with both statistical and rhetorical rebuttals, but it was to no avail. The WWL record of winning Washington battles extended back for almost thirty years in a virtually unbroken string. The victories achieved there more than made up for any shortcomings in the internal operations. The deintermixture clash with the FCC, like so many others before the regulatory authorities, ended in a decision favorable to the WWL interests. On March 8, 1957, Father Donnelly received telegrams from Senators Russell Long and Allen Ellender and Congressman Hale Boggs jubilantly informing the Jesuit that the stay of construction on Loyola's CP for Channel 4 had just been lifted by the FCC. Long along with Boggs and Hebert had been involved in lobbying the Commission on behalf of WWL. The FCC had reached the conclusion that it "would be more in the public interest to add an additional VHF channel, thus making New Orleans a predominantly VHF community, than it would to make New Orleans a UHF city by deleting one or both of the present VHF assignments." It based that finding on the size of the metropolitan area and VHF's supposedly better ability to cover larger areas, the relatively small number of viewers who had converted their sets for UHF reception (despite Supreme Broadcasting's comments to the contrary), and Mobile's less than pressing need for the channel in question. Along with retaining Channel 4 in New Orleans, another VHF alternative, Channel 12, was shifted from Beaumont, Texas, to New Orleans. The Boggs-Hebert plan that also was endorsed by Loyola had been adopted almost in its entirety.[59]

Selective deintermixture proved considerably less than a fruitful policy for the FCC. Of the thirteen markets in which the Commission proposed to implement the strategy, only five saw it finally carried out. Under intense political pressure from local opponents of the scheme, the Commissioners did not, in most instances, adhere to the principles they enunciated in June 1956. One observer noted, however, that the policy would have failed even with zealous advocacy on the part of the FCC. "It offered too little, too late" for the failing UHF licensees, many of whom had already ceased to broadcast. For the FCC, the decade of the 1950's was hardly its finest hour. Once more it proved the truth of an observation by a contemporary critic, that in the United States, "regulation by commission has not been able to match the ingenuity, imagination, and inventiveness of American business." For Loyola, on the other hand, the latest vacillation of the FCC cleared the last cloud and removed the final obstacle. After more than a decade of internal debate, planning, and legal struggle, WWL-TV was poised on the edge of reality.[60]

# 18

## RETROSPECT

Progress was swift now. Immediately following the
FCC announcement that the construction stay had been
lifted, Summerville predicted that the new station would
be on the air in four months. He was only a little too
optimistic; the delay was just six months.1

The principal task to be accomplished was the renovation of the studio on North Rampart Street. Originally,
the TV station was to be installed in a Camp Street
building in the central business district. By the fall
of 1953, however, the staff had taken a second look at
that property and found it wanting. They also discovered
at the same time a much more favorable site on Rampart
Street at the edge of the French Quarter. Here they saw
a combination of structures, that formerly housed the
Zetz 7-Up Bottling Company, offering them 37,000 square
feet of working area. The bottling plant was purchased
in November 1953 for some $300,000 with most of that sum
provided by a loan from a bank headed by one of WWL's
advisory board members. Two months later, the never-used
Camp Street building was sold for its original purchase
price.2

With the March 1957 FCC clearance, remodeling of
the Rampart Street property began in earnest. Only the
outer walls of the structure were retained, as a complete transformation of the interior now took place.
The result was rather breathlessly described as "a
rhapsody in ultramodern design" with dark marble panels
stretching upwards from the sidewalk to cover the
exterior, to the first floor level, and the second level
faced with "massive aluminum louvres which screen the
interior from the direct rays of the western sun." A
principal feature of the station was a 60 x 180 foot
studio that could be separated into two by the insertion
of a soundproof divider. The whole complex was a world

apart from the cramped, makeshift spaces with which Orie Abell had coped in the precarious days of the 1920's. Meanwhile, the transmitter was placed in a two-story concrete building on the west bank of the Mississippi in the Jefferson Parish suburb of Gretna. That structure, together with the antenna system, was completed in July 1957.[3]

On the programming side, preparations for actual operations had been underway for months. Closed circuit productions of proposed shows were regularly utilized as training devices for both talent and technical personnel, special events were simulated, and coordination with the CBS network well practiced. Earlier a baker's dozen of key staff members attended a two-week professional orientation course in television offered at a Houston station. By the fall of 1957, preparations were complete.[4]

The formal opening of WWL-TV was set for the evening of September 7, exactly six months to the day after the FCC had finally issued a construction permit. In advance of the opening the Loyola administration scheduled cocktail parties and nightly tours through the new facilities for faculty and station families, business associates, and local and national dignitaries. The New Orleans newspapers carried multi-page descriptions of the city's newest television outlet, featuring elaborate biographies of the principals, both at the University and at the studio, and the usual congratulatory statements and advertisements. One of the latter pictured tall television towers shaking hands with the legend: "WDSU-TV Welcomes WWL-TV to the Wonderful World of TV." The Loyola station itself ran a large ad promoting its offerings with the pointed statement: "Now all your favorite CBS television programs are on every TV set." Pictured were the most popular CBS stars--Ed Sullivan, Phil Silvers, Gale Storm, James Arness, Jimmy Durante, Garry Moore, and Edward R. Murrow. Most of these had previously been carried on the UHF station in the city.[5]

The first evening of telecasting began with a thirty-minute dedication program, entitled The Newest Look on TV. The master of ceremonies was Ed Hoerner, and present for short speeches were Senator Russell Long, Congressman F. Edward Hebert, and the Lieutenant Governor of the state. The station signed on at 6:30 P.M. with the dedicatory show. The schedule for the remainder of the evening consisted of:

| 7:00 | Gale Storm Show |
| 7:30 | S.R.O. Playhouse |
| 8:00 | Jimmy Durante Show |
| 8:30 | Two for the Money |
| 9:00 | Gunsmoke |
| 9:30 | Miss America Pageant |
| 11:00 | Movie: Now Voyager |

As the station settled into a regular routine in the weeks that followed, it began the day at 7:00 A.M. with Captain Kangaroo and continued until after midnight with late movies. Serial dramas dotted its daytime schedule during these first months of operation--Love of Life, Search for Tomorrow, The Guiding Light, and others-- and the soothing personalities of Arthur Godfrey and Garry Moore were regularly featured. For the children, Henry Dupre, about to end the Dawnbusters era, could be found performing as "Uncle Henry" on an afternoon cartoon show, Popeye and Pals. In the prime evening hours, Alfred Hitchcock, United States Steel Hour, Studio One, and the not-yet-discredited quiz shows, led by the $64,000 Question, were available for viewing. The WWL-TV ads proclaimed it: "Wow! What a Lineup!" And the station promised there was: "More on Channel 4."[6]

* * * * * * * * * *

For television in general, it was "boom land." The 108 stations of the 1948 freeze period had grown to 500, and 40 million homes--80% of the nation's total were tuning them in. Channels in the VHF range were described as "gold-mining claims," much as AM licenses had been during the Second World War. For WWL-TV, it was the right time to be born.[7]

The station, despite enormous start-up costs, was profitable from almost the very first. By the end of July 1958, after some eleven months on the air, the gross income from television broadcasting exceeded $1.6 million with the largest shares almost equally divided among network, national spot, and local time sales. Net profits of nearly $300,000 were earned on that total, a good return even though those figures did not take into account an unsecured bank loan of some $430,000, used to finance the start of operations and upon which no payments had yet been made. Nevertheless, the gross income figure for less than one year's telecasting significantly exceeded the highest amounts recorded by

WWL radio in its most successful years in the 1940's. On the other hand, the net profit figures for television, although not insubstantial, were less than radio had earned on a smaller volume in the preceeding decade.[8]

Meanwhile, WWL-AM was faring a good deal less well. For the fiscal year ended July 31, 1958, its gross income had declined to $766,015. Noticeably meager were the network time sales of only $98,000, a far cry from the halcyon days of the past. Profits, at least, were still being earned as radio was demonstrating a surprising capacity for survival. As Broadcasting magazine phrased it: "It is as though silent films persisted side by side with talkies." Nevertheless, for WWL the focus on television and the need to curtail the amounts spent on an apparently declining AM service seemed to necessitate the release of the station's long-time pride, its staff orchestra, and an accompanying painful decision to terminate the beloved Dawnbusters show. Radio staff orchestras were now all but unknown in the United States, except in New Orleans, and the luxury was simply too great an expense. Moreover, "union troubles" with the musicians were becoming an increasing headache. To Father Aloysius B. Goodspeed, S.J., who had succeeded to the post of Faculty Director upon the death of O'Leary in 1955, fell the responsibility of executing the fatal decision in 1959. There were, he recalled, "a few hard feelings" on the part of some staff, but there was no turning back. For twenty years and more the Dawnbusters had entertained WWL audiences, and it still remains well-remembered, the single most popular program ever broadcast in the Deep South. It simply out-lived its own time.[9]

In January 1960, Howard Summerville, after two decades as General Manager, departed the station as well, the victim to a large extent of the emergence of an entirely new era in broadcasting. Some months of tension and uncertainty ensued until J. Michael Early, whose first close acquaintance with WWL had been as a labor relations attorney, was given the post in August 1961. By 1966, a decade after WWL-TV first took the air, its "average daily circulation," the mean number of viewers who were tuned to its programs at any time, exceeded its two competitors. By the 1970's, the University's annual income or profit from the combined TV, AM, and FM (reinstituted in 1970) operations considerably exceeded $1,000,000 and approached twice that figure.[10]

Certainly, Father Edward Cummings, Loyola's
President in 1922, could never in his wildest flight
of fancy have envisioned the enterprise he was launching
that March day when he sought only to raise funds for a
few new campus buildings.  He and his associates looked
upon radio as a token publicity device, a tool to be
employed and then probably discarded or left to the
attention of a few technically-minded amateurs.  Instead,
fifty years later it had become the financial mainstay
of the University which spawned it almost off-handedly
five decades before.  The transformation was the handiwork of a passing parade of dedicated radio professionals
stretching from Joe du Treil to Al Foster to Vince
Callahan to Henry Dupre and Pinky Vidacovich and others.
It also was a result of the application of the considerable legal skills of a Charles Dolle and a Paul Segal,
and the perceptive sense of the future of a Gene Katz.

Most of all, the WWL success could be attributed
to two factors that were paramount.  The first was the
Loyola Jesuits' mastery in waging the political battles
common to the industry.  Broadcasting is a regulated
and highly competitive field, and the bodies of the
losers are strewn across the pages of its history in
numbers too many to count.  The station owners who survive the combat must have able and influential governmental allies and adroit legal representation.  Loyola
chose wisely in both areas, and supported them with
careful and usually well-considered policy decisions.
It did not ask its forces to fight a campaign that could
not be won, and it generally timed its forward moves
expertly.  It accepted the rules, written and unwritten,
of the regulatory game in broadcasting, unreasonable
as they sometimes seemed, and worked its will within
the system.  The victories it won in Washington were,
in the long run, more important to the profitability of
the enterprise than the ordinary business strategies
employed at home.  The history of WWL is, therefore, a
classic case study in survival and success in a regulated sector of the modern American economy.

The second paramount factor in WWL's ascendancy
was the single-minded determination of Orie Abell to see
his station grow.  No other individual looms so large
in the WWL story as the Jesuit physicist who controlled
its fortunes from 1924 to 1937.  Abell typified the
classic American entrepreneur, absolutely convinced
that growth was a good to be pursued almost without
thinking.  The fact that he was a priest and that the
institution he represented was a university, in no way
modified his tactics or his plans.  He utilized

commercial practices and approaches and espoused a
traditional business philosophy in order to insure the
financial viability of his institution.

Under Abell, WWL set itself entirely apart from the
conventional educational stations of the time, and he
openly admitted their interests and those of his own
organization were at variance. He recognized a simple
entrepreneurial dictum--the first duty of a business is
to survive. WWL did survive under Abell's leadership,
and he put it on the path of profitability. The bulk
of the nation's educational broadcasters, who chose a
different and what they regarded as a "higher" road,
eschewing commercialism, failed that survival test. In
insuring the growth of his station, Abell also solidified
the strength of the University. The two for him were
twin sides of the same coin. Suffice to say, without
Abell, there would have been no WWL, and Loyola itself
would have become a very different and probably less
valuable institution.

And what of the listeners that WWL's enterprise in
radio served during these years? It offered them entertainment and information of varying quality--sometimes
outstanding, sometimes trivial--and in so doing, it
opened for those millions a window to the world that
might otherwise have remained closed. A former NAB
President, Governor LeRoy Collins, once commented that
the media he represented had a responsibility to contribute constructively to the molding of a character
and stature of the American people. But as Collins saw
it, this was not a cross to bear; it was instead broadcasting's glory.[11]

Preface

[1]Ralph W. Hidy, "Business History," International Encyclopedia of the Social Sciences (New York:  Macmillan Company, 1968), VI, 474.

[2]Les Brown, Television:  The Business Behind the Box (New York:  Harcourt, Brace, Jovanovich, Inc., 1971), p. 179.


CHAPTER 1:  The Coming of Radio Telephony

[1]New Orleans, The Times-Picayune, 31 March 1922.

[2]Elliott N. Sivowitch, "A Technological Survey of Broadcasting's 'Pre-History,' 1876-1920," Journal of Broadcasting 15 (Winter 1970-1971): 1-2.

[3]Erik Barnouw, A History of Broadcasting in the United States, vol. 1:  A Tower in Babel (New York:  Oxford University Press, 1966), pp. 9-19.

[4]Sivowitch, pp. 8-9; Helen M. Fessenden, Fessenden:  Builder of Tomorrows (New York:  Coward-McCann, Inc., 1940), p. 81; Gleason L. Archer, History of Radio to 1926 (New York:  American Historical Society, 1938), p. 86.

[5]Fessenden, p. 153.

[6]Archer, p. 87.

[7]Sivowitch, pp. 11-13; Barnouw, pp. 21-27.

[8]Sivowitch, pp. 16-17.

[9]"The Wireless Ship Act of 1910," Frank J. Kahn, ed., Documents of American Broadcasting, 2d ed., (New York:  Appleton-Century-Crofts, 1973), pp. 5-6; Frederic P. Lee, "Federal Radio Legislation," The Annals of the American Academy of Political and Social Science 141-142 (1929): 36.

[10]E.E. Bucher, "A Resume of Early Radio Development," The Radio Industry (Chicago:  A.W. Shaw Company, 1928), pp. 50-51.

[11]"The Radio Act of 1912," Kahn, pp. 7-17; Murray Edelman, The Licensing of Radio Services in the United States, 1927 to 1947 (Urbana: The University of Illinois Press, 1950), pp. 1-2.

¹²Hiram Percy Maxim, "The Amateur in Radio," The Annals of the American Academy of Political and Social Science 141-142 (1929): 32.

¹³Kahn, p. 8.

¹⁴William Peck Banning, Commercial Broadcasting Pioneer: The WEAF Experiment, 1922-1926 (Cambridge, Mass.: Harvard University Press, 1946), p. 19; Barnouw, p. 55.

¹⁵Ibid., pp. 37-51; Sydney W. Head, Broadcasting in America, 2d ed., (Boston: Houghton Mifflin Company, 1972), p. 130.

¹⁶Banning, p. 19.

¹⁷Barnouw, pp. 61-61; Gordon B. Greb, "The Golden Anniversary of Broadcasting," Journal of Broadcasting 3 (Winter 1958-1959): 3-4; R. Franklin Smith, "Oldest Station in the Nation," Journal of Broadcasting 4 (Winter 1959-1960): 42.

¹⁸Archer, pp. 199-202; Barnouw, pp. 66-68.

¹⁹Ibid, p. 69.

²⁰Archer, p. 204.

²¹Barnouw, p. 91; Radio Broadcast, April 1923, p. 524; W. Elliot Brownlee, Dynamics of Ascent: A History of the American Economy (New York: Alfred A. Knopf, 1974), p. 261; Charles Hull Wolfe, Modern Radio Advertising (New York: Funk & Wagnalls Company, 1949), p. 94.

²²U.S., Department of Commerce, Bureau of Navigation, Radio Service, Radio Stations of the United States, July 1, 1913 (Washington, D.C.: Government Printing Office, 1913), pp. 123-124; Ibid., July 1, 1916, pp. 122-123; Ibid., June 30, 1921, pp. 105-112.

²³The Times-Picayune, January 18, 1921.

²⁴U.S., Federal Communications Commission, License Division Records, Washington, D.C. [Hereafter cited as FCC-LDR]; Ray Poindexter, Arkansas Airwaves (North Little Rock, Ark.: by the author, 1974), p. 3

²⁵WGV and WWL Files, FCC-LDR.


CHAPTER 2: The State, the School, the Station

¹Donald B. Dodd and Wynelle S. Dodd, eds., Historical

296

Statistics of the South, 1790-1970 (University, Alabama: University of Alabama Press, 1973), section 1, passim.

[2]Ibid., pp. 74-76.

[3]Perry H. Howard, Political Tendencies in Louisiana, rev. and exp. ed. (Baton Rouge: Louisiana State University Press, 1971), pp. 607, 10.

[4]Ibid., p. 16; Dodd and Dodd, pp. 17, 29, 57, 61; U.S. Department of Commerce, Bureau of the Census, Historical Statistics of the United States: Colonial Times to 1957 (Washington, D.C., 1960), p. 279.

[5]Howard, pp. 11-17; Dodd and Dodd, p. 29; George M. Reynolds, Machine Politics in New Orleans, 1897-1926 (New York: Columbia University Press, 1936), p. 42.

[6]Allan P. Sindler, Huey Long's Louisiana: State Politics, 1920-1952 (Baltimore: Johns Hopkins Press, 1956), pp. 27-28; U.S. Department of Commerce, Statistical Abstract of the U.S., 1922 (Washington, D.C., 1923), p. 573; Edwin Adams Davis, The Story of Louisiana, (New Orleans: J.F. Hyer Publishing Co., 1960), I, 360.

[7]Reynolds, p. 13; Edward F. Haas, DeLesseps S. Morrison and the Image of Reform (Baton Rouge: Louisiana State University Press, 1974), pp. 7-9.

[8]Reynolds, p. 44; Glenn Martin Runyan, "Economic Trends in New Orleans, 1928-1940" (Master's Thesis, Tulane University, 1967), pp. 2-3.

[9]Ibid.

[10]Ibid., pp. 35-36.

[11]Joy J. Jackson, New Orleans in the Gilded Age: Politics and Urban Progress, 1880-1896 (Baton Rouge: Louisiana State University Press, 1969), pp. 202, 204-206; I.A. Timmreck, "History of Loyola University," unpublished MSS, Documents Center, Loyola University, New Orleans, LA.

[12]Orie L. Abell, S. J., "Brief History of Radio Station WWL," unpublished MSS, WWL Records, Documents Center, Loyola University, pp. 1-2 [hereafter cited as WWL Records, LU]; Interview with L.J.N. du Treil, New Orleans, 3 October 1974.

[13]Orie L. Abell, S.J., "Radio Broadcasting Station WWL," The Radio Graphic, August 1931, p. 71; "WWL--A Radio Pioneer" The Southern Jesuit, February 1936, p. 2; du Treil interview.

[14]Barnouw, p. 37; Abell, "Radio Broadcasting Station WWL," p. 71; du Treil interview.

[15]Thomas T. Eoyang, An Economic Study of the Radio Industry in the United States (New York: Columbia University, 1936), p. 155; Walter C. Johnson and Arthur T. Robb, The South and its Newspaper, 1903-1953 (Westport, Conn.: Greenwood Press, Publishers, 1974), p. 109; George E. Lott, Jr., "The Press-Radio War of the 1930's" Journal of Broadcasting 14 (Summer 1970) 275.

[16]Carroll Atkinson, American Universities and Colleges That Have Held Broadcast Licenses (Boston: Meador Publishing Co., 1941), pp. 12-17; Carl J. Friedrich, "Radiobroadcasting and Higher Education" Studies in the Control of Radio 4 (May 1942) 17-19; Barnouw, p. 99; Hiram L. Jome, Economics of the Radio Industry (Chicago: A.W. Shaw Company, 1925), p. 167.

[17]Soards' New Orleans City Directory, 1923 (New Orleans: Soards Directory Co., Ltd., 1923), pp. 822, 1774; Thomas Ewing Dabney, One Hundred Great Years: The Story of the Times-Picayune (Baton Rouge: Louisiana State University Press, 1944), p. 444.

[18]Interview with Ted R. Liuzza, New Orleans, 11 September 1975; Clarke Salmon to Theodore G. Deiler, 7 April 1922, Radio Division Files, Department of Commerce Records, National Archives, Washington, D.C. [hereafter cited as NA]; Sammy R. Danna, "The Rise of Radio News," in American Broadcasting: A Source Book on the History of Radio and Television, eds., Lawrence W. Lichty and Malachi C. Topping (New York: Hasting House Publishers, 1975), p. 338; Radio Broadcast April 1923, p. 524.

[19]The New Orleans Item, 7 April 1922; WWL File, FCC-LDR.

[20]Times-Picayune, 2 April 1922, 10 May 1922.

[21]"WWL Fetes 24th Anniversary," WWL Spotlight, March 1946, p. 6; du Treil interview.

[22]Abell, "Brief History...," p. 1; du Treil interview; Karl Maring, S.J., "Loyola's 'Physics Experiment' of 1922," The Louisiana Physics Teacher, Spring 1972, pp. 18-19.

[23]U.S. Department of Commerce, Radio Service Bulletin No. 60, 1 April 1922, p. 23; WWL Files, LDR-FCC.

[24]Arthur Enderlin to General Manager, WWL, 16 April 1974, Station Files, WWL [Enderlin was Chief Radio Officer of the San Jose at the time of its grounding.]

[25]Abell, "Brief History...," p. 1.

298

[26]Times-Picayune, 2 April 1922.

[27]Ibid.; Margaret E. Carey, "Radio Station WWL," unpublished article, WWL records, LU, p. 5.

[28]Columbia Broadcasting System, CBS Listeners and Dealers, 1937, vol. 1, pp. 136-137 and vol. 2, pp. 140-141.

[29]In Re Loyola University (WWL), 5 F.C.C. 43 (1937); CBS File, WWL Records, LU; Interview with Jefferson Davis Bloom, New Orleans, 3 September 1974; Interview with Joseph H. Uhalt, Jr., New Orleans, 11 May 1976.

[30]Interview with Howard Miller, CBS Radio Research, New York City, 25 June 1976.

[31]Barnouw, II, 58; FCC, Report on Chain Broadcasting, pp. 38-39, 66.

[32]Ibid., p. 39; Supplemental Agreement between WWL Development Co. and Loyola University, 19 January 1933, WWL Development Co. File, WWL Records, LU.

[33]New Orleans Item, 2 November 1935.

[34]Ibid., 17 February 1935, 3 November 1935; Times-Picayune, 17 February 1935, 15 December 1935, 16 December 1935.

CHAPTER 3:    Static in the 360 Jungle

[1]Dabney, p. 442; Soards' New Orleans City Directory, 1922, p. 843; WAAB File, LDR-FCC.

[2]New Orleans States, 14 September 1924; Jess Baker Covington, "A History of the Shreveport Times" (Ph.D. dissertation, University of Missouri, 1964), pp. 95-96, 115; Soards' 1922, p. 1251; Luizza interview.

[3]Ewing to Cong. James B. Aswell, 4 April 1922, Radio Division Files, NA.

[4]John B. Draper to Ewing, 17 April 1922, Radio Division Files, NA.

[5]New Orleans Item, 6 April 1922.

[6]Ibid., 7 April 1922; Hermann Deutsch, "Birth of New Orleans Radio Remembered," New Orleans States-Item, 14 July 1967.

[7]Ibid.

[8]Times-Picayune, 7 April 1922.

[9]New Orleans Item, 7 April 1922.

[10]Ibid., and 12 April 1922.

[11]Times-Picayune, 9 April 1922; New Orleans Item, 9 April 1922.

[12]Times-Picayune, 2 May 1922, 5 May 1922, 11 May 1922; New Orleans Item, 8 April 1922, 10 April 1922.

[13]WAAC, WBAM, and WCAG Files, LDR-FCC; Times-Picayune, 30 April 1922.

[14]WAAG and WGAQ Files, LDR-FCC; Shreveport Times, 28 June 1935; Radio Service Bulletin No. 63, 1 July 1922, p. 3; Lillian Jones Hall, "A Historical Study of Programming Techniques and Practices of Radio Station KWKH, Shreveport, Louisiana, 1922-1950" (Ph.D. dissertation, Louisiana State University, 1959), pp. 18-21.

[15]Barnouw, pp. 91-93.

[16]Sullivan to Deiler, 8 April 1922, Radio Division Files, NA; Deiler to Commissioner of Navigation, 8 April 1922, Radio Division Files, NA.

[17]Ibid., A.J. Tyrer to Deiler, 3 May 1922, Radio Division Files, NA.

[18]New Orleans Item, 21 May 1922.

[19]Times-Picayune, 14 May 1922.

[20]Ibid.; Banning, pp. 134, 136; N.R. Danielian, A.T.&T.: The Story of Industrial Conquest (New York: The Vanguard Press, 1939), pp. 110-113.

[21]Times-Picayune, 14 May 1922; Radio Broadcast, May 1922, p. 3.

[22]Wolfe, p. 622; Orrin E. Dunlap, Jr., Dunlap's Radio and Television Almanac (New York: Harper and Brothers, 1951), p. 70; Banning, p. 90-93; Barnouw, p. 96; Eoyang, p. 154.

[23]New Orleans Item, 21 May 1922.

[24]C.M. Jansky, Jr., "The Contribution of Herbert Hoover to Broadcasting" Journal of Broadcasting 1 (Fall 1957) 241-243; Edward F. Sarno, Jr. "The National Radio Conferences" Journal of Broadcasting, 13 (Spring 1969) 190-192; Laurence F. Schmeckebier, The Federal Radio Commission (Washington: The Brookings Institution,

1932), pp. 4-5; Archer, p. 250.

[25]Schmeckebier, p. 5; Barnouw, p. 100.

[26]Sarno, pp. 195-198; Radio Service Bulletin No. 72, 2 April 1923, p. 10; Radio Service Bulletin No. 76, 1 August 1923, p. 11.

[27]WWL File, LDR-FCC.

[28]New Orleans States, 9 July 1922.

[29]New Orleans Item, 7 May 1922.

[30]New Orleans States, 9 July 1922.

[31]Radio Service Bulletin, No. 75, 2 July 1923, p. 10; New Orleans States, 15 October 1922, 1 July 1923; New Orleans Item, 18 March 1923; Radio Service Bulletin, No. 87, 1 July 1924, p. 9.

[32]Radio Service Bulletin, No. 67, 1 November 1922, p. 7; WBAM File, LDR-FCC; WAAC File, LDR-FCC; New Orleans States, 18 November 1923.


CHAPTER 4:   Troubled Growth, 1924-1925

[1]Bloom interview; du Treil interview.

[2]Abell, "Brief History...," p. 2A; Maring, p. 19.

[3]Abell, "Brief History...," p. 2; du Treil interview; Loyola University, The Maroon, 16 October 1924, Documents Center, Loyola University.

[4]New Orleans States, 16 November 1924; Abell, "Brief History...," p. 2; WWL File, LDR-FCC; Bloom interview.

[5]Abell, "Brief History...," p. 3; du Treil interview.

[6]Leslie J. Page, Jr., "The Nature of the Broadcast Receiver and its Market in the United States from 1922 to 1927" Journal of Broadcasting 4 (Spring 1960) 176; Radio Broadcast, June 1923, July 1923, December 1923, April 1924; New Orleans States, 2 March 1924; Soards' New Orleans City Directory, 1923, p. 1774, and 1925, pp. 1845-1846.

[7]Eoyang, p. 158.

[8]Ibid, p. 159.

301

[9]Herman S. Hettinger and Walter J. Neff, Practical Radio Advertising (New York: Prentice-Hall, 1938), p. 55.

[10]New Orleans States, 5 October 1924.

[11]David R. Mackey, "The Development of the National Association of Broadcasters" Journal of Broadcasting 1 (Fall 1957) 307; Sarno, pp. 193-194; Stanley Adams, "The ASCAP Story," The New York Times, 16 February 1964.

[12]Archer, p. 308; Barnouw, p. 119; Radio Broadcast, July 1923, p. 181.

[13]Barnouw, p. 120; Mackey, p. 308; Katharine Pringle and Henry F. Pringle, "ASCAP Makes the Piper Pay," Nation's Business, April 1950, p. 88; Bruce Robertson, "A New Harmony for an Old Discord," Broadcasting-Telecasting, 25 October 1954, p. 84.

[14]Jome, p. 174; Paul Schubert, The Electric Word: The Rise of Radio (New York: The Macmillan Company, 1928), p. 228.

[15]Banning, pp. 136-137; Danielian, pp. 121-122; Archer, pp. 320-321.

[16]Banning, pp. 137, 139, 205; Danielian, pp. 123-124; Archer, p. 321; The New York Times, 14 March 1924.

[17]Radio Broadcast, August 1924, p. 300; Barnouw, pp. 118-119; New Orleans States, 29 June 1924.

[18]WTAF File, LDR-FCC; Radio Service Bulletin No. 76, 1 August 1923, p. 8; New Orleans States, 23 March 1924.

[19]WABZ File, LDR-FCC; Radio Service Bulletin No. 82, 1 February 1924, p. 3; New Orleans States, 21 September 1924, 26 October 1924, 30 November 1924.

[20]WBBS File, LDR-FCC; Radio Service Bulletin No. 83, 1 March 1924, p. 3.

[21]WCBE File, LDR-FCC; Radio Service Bulletin No. 83, 1 March 1924, pp. 4, 17; Soards' New Orleans City Directory, 1923, p. 1502; New Orleans States, 30 November 1924; Times-Picayune, 4 June 1975; Radio Stations of the United States, 1 July 1916, p. 123; Uhalt interview.

[22]WEBP File, LDR-FCC; Radio Service Bulletin No. 88, 1 August 1924, p. 6; New Orleans States, 25 May 1924, 15 June 1924, 27 July 1924.

[23]New Orleans States, 13 April 1924.

[24] Ibid., 3 August 1924.

[25] Ibid., 16 March 1924, 27 April 1924.

[26] Ibid., 15 June 1924, 6 July 1924, 13 July 1924.

[27] Ibid., 20 July 1924, 27 July 1924.

[28] Ibid., 16 September 1924, 18 September 1924, 21 September 1924, 25 September 1924.

[29] Ibid., 5 October 1924.

[30] Ibid., 9 November 1924.

[31] Laure Fletcher Lemoine, "A History of Radio Station WSMB, New Orleans, Louisiana, 1925-1967" (Master's thesis, Louisiana State University, 1969), p. 11; Laura de Vincent, "Julian Saenger's Dream Palace," New Orleans States-Item, 7 February 1976; New Orleans States, 7 February 1932; Interview with Harold Wheelahan, Jr., New Orleans, 12 May 1976.

[32] New Orleans States, 9 November 1924, 8 February 1925; WCAG File, LDR-FCC; Radio Service Bulletin, No. 100, 1 August 1925, p. 7.

[33] WSMB File, LDR-FCC; Radio Service Bulletin, No. 97, 1 May 1925, p. 4; New Orleans Item-Tribune, 19 April 1925; Dabney, p. 444 n.; Frank Luther Mott, American Journalism:  A History, 1690-1960 (New York:  The Macmillan Company, 1962), p. 664; New Orleans States, 19 April 1925.

[34] New Orleans Item-Tribune, 25 January 1925, 19 April 1925; Liuzza interview.

[35] Lemoine, p. 17; Albert F. McLean, Jr., American Vaudeville as Ritual (Lexington:  University of Kentucky Press, 1965), pp. 23-24; John E. DiMeglio, Vaudeville U.S.A. (Bowling Green, Ohio: Bowling Green University Press, 1973), pp. 11-12.

[36] Lemoine, p. 14, 27; New Orleans States, 31 May 1925; New Orleans Item-Tribune, 19 April 1925.

[37] Radio Service Bulletin, No. 98, 1 June 1925, pp. 13-16.

[38] WAAC, WCAG, WJBO, WOWL Files, LDR-FCC; New Orleans States, 19 October 1924 and 21 September 1925.

[39] Radio Service Bulletin, No. 98, 1 June 1925, pp. 13-16.

CHAPTER 5:   New Law, New Power, New Quarters

[1]Marvin R. Bensman, "The Zenith-WJAZ Case and the Chaos of 1926-1927," Journal of Broadcasting 14 (Fall 1970) 423-430.

[2]"United States v. Zenith Radio Corporation et al.," Kahn, p. 25; Bensman, p. 431; Schmeckebier, pp. 12-13.

[3]Bensman, p. 431; New York Times, 2 May 1926; Edelman, pp. 3-4.

[4]O.H. Caldwell, "The Administration of Federal Radio Legislation," The Annals of the American Academy of Political and Social Science  141-142 (1929) 45; Bensman, 432-435; Edelman, p. 4.

[5]Fred L. Israel, ed., The State of the Union Message of the Presidents (New York:  Chelsea House, 1966), III, 2699; Donald G. Godfrey, "The 1927 Radio Act:  People and Politics," paper presented at the meeting of the Broadcast Education Association, Chicago, Illinois, March 1976.

[6]"The Radio Act of 1927," Kahn, pp. 37-41; Schmeckebier, pp. 2, 20, 60; Edelman, p. 6.

[7]Lawrence W. Lichty, "A Study of the Careers and Qualifications of Members of the Federal Radio Commission and the Federal Communications Commission" (Master's thesis, Ohio State University, 1961), pp. 89, 144, 150-151.

[8]Annual Report of the Federal Radio Commission to the Congress of the United States for the Fiscal Year Ended June 20, 1927 (United States:  Government Printing Office, 1927), pp. 9-10 [hereafter cited as FRC Annual Report with respective year]; Schmeckebier, p. 24.

[9]Abell, "Brief History...," pp. 3-4.

[10]New Orleans States, 19 January 1925; Abell, "Brief History...," pp. 4-5; WWL File, LDR-FCC; FRC Annual Report, 1928, pp. 95-96.

[11]Abell, "Brief History...," pp. 4-5.

[12]Ibid., pp. 5-6; New Orleans States, 6 May 1928.

[13]Abell, "Brief History...," pp. 6-7; New Orleans States, 6 May 1928.

[14]Abell, "Brief History...," pp. 7, 19-20; Maring, p. 19; Theodore Deiler to Chief, 16 April 1931, Radio Division, WWL Folder, Radio Division Files, NA [hereafter cited as RDF-NA]; Bloom interview; Interview with Francis Jacob, New Orleans, 6 September 1974.

[15]New Orleans States, 3 July 1928; New Orleans Item, 3 July 1928; Abell, "Brief History...," p. 7; The Maroon, 9 November 1928.

[16]Abell, "Brief History...," p. 7; The Maroon, 5 October 1928, 7 December 1928.

[17]G.J. Murphy to Deiler, 22 September 1928, Deiler to Radio Division, 24 September 1928, Deiler to Radio Division, 8 October 1928, WWL Folder, RDF-NA.

[18]Deiler to Radio Division, 26 November 1928, Chief, Radio Division to Deiler, 6 December 1928, WWL Folder, RDF-NA.

[19]Abell to Chief, Radio Division, 14 December 1928, Chief, Radio Division to Abell, 29 December 1928, Deiler to Chief, Radio Division, 2 January 1929, WWL Folder, RDF-NA.

[20]Leer Marshan, "Tracing the Growth of WJBW" Radio Graphic, August 1931, p. 67; WJBW File, LDR-FCC.

[21]Uhalt interview; New Orleans States, 26 June 1927, 24 October 1927; WDSU File, LDR-FCC; Uhalt to Deiler, 4 May 1928, WDSU Folder, RDF-NA.

[22]New Orleans States, 13 May 1928, 6 July 1928.

[23]Deiler to Chief, Radio Division, 8 August 1928, RDF-NA.

[24]Federal Communications Commission, Report on Chain Broadcasting, May 1941, pp. 3-8; Ned Midgley, The Advertising and and Business Side of Radio (New York: Prentice-Hall, Inc., 1948), pp. 67-68, 89; John W. Spalding, "1928: Radio Becomes a Mass Advertising Medium," Journal of Broadcasting 8 (Winter 1963-1964); Robert Metz, CBS: Reflections in a Bloodshot Eye (Chicago: Playboy Press, 1975), p. 20.

[25]FCC, Chain Broadcasting, p. 4; Spalding, pp. 31-32.

[26]Earl Smith, "WDSU" Radio Graphic, August 1931, p. 61; Lemoine, p. 43; New Orleans Item-Tribune, 24 March 1929; New Orleans States, 3 February 1929.

[27]Smith, "WDSU," p. 61; Uhalt to Federal Radio Commission, 27 May 1927, WDSU Folder, RDF-NA.

[28]New Orleans States, 6 July 1928; FRC Annual Report, 1928, pp. 170, 178.

[29]WWL File, LDR-FCC; New Orleans States, 6 July 1928.

CHAPTER 6: The Clear Channel War - Round One

[1]Glenn Frank, "Radio as an Educational Force," The Annals of the American Academy of Political and Social Science, 177 (January 1935) 120; Maurice E. Shelby, Jr., "John R. Brinkley: His Contribution to Broadcasting," in Lichty and Topping, pp. 560-561; see transcripts of Henderson broadcasts, KWKH Folder, RDF-NA.

[2]U.S., Congress, House, 72nd Cong., 1st sess., 13 July 1932, Congressional Record 75: 15263.

[3]John Tebbel, The Media in America (New York: Thomas Y. Crowell Company, 1974), p. 356.

[4]Maude Hearn O'Pry, Chronicle of Shreveport, (Shreveport: Journal Printing Company, 1938), p. 355. Margery Land May, Hello World Henderson (Shreveport: by the author, 1931), pp. 35-40.

[5]Hall, pp. 23-24; WGAQ Files, LDR-FCC.

[6]Radio Service Bulletin, No. 72, 2 April 1923, p. 10, and #83, 1 March 1924, p. 8; William G. Patterson to Commissioner of Navigation, 4 May 1925, KWKH Folder, RDF-NA.

[7]Henderson to Deiler, 25 March 1926, KWKH Folder, RDF-NA.

[8]Louis L. McCabe to Deiler, 6 April 1926, KWKH Folder, RDF-NA; New York Herald-Tribune, 11 April 1926.

[9]KWKH and KSBA File, LDR-FCC; Hall, p. 36-39; The Shreveport Times, 21 September 1975.

[10]KWKH File, LDR-FCC; The New York Times, 19 and 25 August 1927 and 14 October 1927.

[11]Edward N. Brady to Calvin Coolidge, 14 September 1927, KWKH Folder, RDF-NA.

[12]Schmeckebier, p. 27; U.S., Congress, Senate, 70th Cong., 1st Sess., March 1, 1928, Congressional Record 69: 3834-3835; Transcript of Henderson broadcast of 14 February 1928, KWKH Folder, RDF-NA.

[13]Lloyd Hanson to Sam Pickard, 1 December 1927, Henderson broadcast transcripts, and Sykes to W.D. Terrell, 27 January 1928, KWKH Folder, RDF-NA.

[14]The New York Times, 25 August 1927; FRC Annual Report, 1928, p. 82; U.S., Congress, House, 70th Cong., 1st sess., March 12, 1928, Congressional Record 69: 4571.

[15]Schmeckebier, pp. 28, 31-32; FRC Annual Report, 1928, pp. 17-18, 48-49; May, pp. 20-21.

[16]Abell, "Brief History...," p. 12; Abell background in James D. Carroll, S.J., to the author, 6 August 1976.

[17]Abell, "Brief History...," p. 12; The Maroon, 9 November 1928.

[18]Caldwell, p. 49.

[19]FRC Annual Report, 1928, p. 117.

[20]Times-Picayune, 21 February 1929; Shreveport Times, 21 February 1929.

[21]FRC Annual Report, 1928, p. 47; Schmeckebier, p. 54.

[22]Bloom interview; The Maroon, 25 January 1929; Times-Picayune, 10 February 1929.

[23]Abell, "Brief History...," pp. 12-13.

[24]The Maroon, 9 February 1929; Times-Picayune, 8 and 22 February 1929; Shreveport Times, 9 and 17 February 1929; New Orleans States, 20 February 1929.

[25]T. Harry Williams, Huey P. Long (New York: Alfred A. Knopf, Inc., 1969), p. 205; See Henderson-Long correspondence in Folders 419, 420, 922, and 1375, Box 13, Huey P. Long, Jr., Papers, Department of Archives and Manuscripts, Louisiana State University Library, Baton Rouge, Louisiana; Ernest G. Bormann, "This is Huey P. Long Talking," Journal of Broadcasting, 2 (Spring 1958) 113-114.

[26]Times-Picayune, 22 February 1929; Shreveport Times, 3, 21, and 22 February 1929.

[27]Times-Picayune, 9 February 1929; Shreveport Times, 31 January, 2 and 9 February 1929; May, p. 23.

[28]Shreveport Times, 19 February 1929; May, pp. 23-24; The Maroon, 22 February 1929.

[29]Times-Picayune, 21 February 1929; Shreveport Times, 20 February 1929.

[30]Times-Picayune, 22 February 1929; Shreveport Times, 22 February 1929.

[31]May, p. 24; Shreveport Times, 22 February 1929; Times-Picayune, 22 February 1929; Abell, "Brief History...," p. 9; New York

Times, 3 November 1929.

   32Shreveport Times, 22 February 1929; New Orleans Item, 22
February 1929; Abell, "Brief History...," p. 10.

   33Shreveport Times, 22 February 1929; Times-Picayune, 23
February 1929.

   34Ibid., 22 June 1929; New York Times, 10 July and 6 August
1929; Abell, "Brief History...," p. 11; FRC Annual Report, 1929,
pp. 47, 76.

   35Abell, "Brief History...," p. 10.

   36FRC Annual Report, 1929, p. 55; Schmeckebier, p. 54; U.S.
Congress, Senate, Committee on Interstate Commerce, Commission on
Communications, 71st Cong., 1st sess., 1930, p. 100.

CHAPTER 7:   Commercial Expectations and Realities, 1929-1931

   1Abell, "A Brief History...," pp. 14-15; The Maroon, 22
March 1929.

   2Abell, "A Brief History...," p. 15.

   3Standard Rate and Data Service, Radio Advertising, March 1929,
p. 26 [hereafter SR & DS].

   4Wolfe, pp. 94-95; Frederick H. Lumley, Measurement in Radio
(Columbus:  The Ohio State University, 1934), p. 196; Herman S.
Hettinger, A Decade of Radio Advertising (Chicago:  The University
of Chicago Press, 1933), pp. 44-45; The Maroon, 12 April 1929.

   5Hettinger, pp. 138-139.

   6Ibid., pp. 140, 160-161.

   7Ibid., pp. 140, 147, 151; FRC Annual Report, 1930, p. 12;
"A Brief Historical Note on the Mechanical Reproduction Announcement
Requirement," Journal of Broadcasting 4 (Spring 1960) 119-122.

   8U.S., Congress, Senate Report of the Federal Radio Commission
on Commercial Radio Advertising, S. Doc. 137, 72nd Cong., 1st sess.,
1932, pp. 22-23, 26 [hereafter cited as FRC Commercial Radio
Advertising]; Interview with Eugene Katz, Katz Agency, New York
City, 24 June 1976.

   9Hettinger, p. 262; Banning, p. 147.

[10]FRC, Commercial Radio Advertising, p. 179.

[11]Hettinger, pp. 140-141.

[12]John A. Abbo and Jerome D. Hannon The Sacred Canons
(St. Louis: B. Herder Book Co., 1952), pp. 203-205; Letter of
Rev. Charles E. O'Neill, S.J. to author, 7 September 1976.

[13]Thomas J. Shields, S.J., to Lorenzo Malone, S.J., 17 April
1946, WWL Development Co. File, WWL Records, LU.

[14]Davis, II, 281-284; Leo Brownson, "B.S. D'Antoni: Banker-
Sportsman," The New Orleanian, 15 February 1931, p. 23; Jeff Radford,
"Can an Old Hotel Change its Sheets?" New Orleans Magazine,
September 1975, pp. 39-40; New Orleans States, 8 February 1925.

[15]Davis, II, 284; Brownson, p. 23; Agreement between WWL
Development Company, Inc., and Loyola University, 29 October 1929,
WWL Development Co. File, WWL Records, LU.

[16]Ibid.; Abell, "A Brief History...," p. 17; Interview with
Arthur C. Pritchard, New Orleans, 4 September 1974.

[17]Abell, "A Brief History...," p. 16; Statements of Harold A.
Gaudin, S.J., and Francis A. Cavey, S.J., 21 March 1939, WWL
Development Co. File, WWL Records, LU; Statement of Wallace A.
Burk, S.J., 23 September 1930, Federal Radio Commission, Docket
889 File, Washington National Records Center, Washington, D.C.
[hereafter cited as WNRC].

[18]Barnwell R. Turnipseed III, "The Development of Broadcasting
in Georgia, 1922-1959" (Master's thesis, University of Georgia,
1960), pp. 31-35; Atkinson, p. 56.

[19]Abell, "A Brief History...," p. 15.

[20]SR & DS, October 1929, p. 32.

[21]Ibid.

[22]Abell, "A Brief History...," p. 18.

[23]Ibid., p. 19; The Maroon, 22 November 1929, 10 January 1930;
Barnouw, p. 229.

[24]Abell, "A Brief History...," pp. 23, 27.

[25]Ibid., pp. 25-26; Jacob interview; Bloom interview.

[26]Abell, "A Brief History...," pp. 27, 34, 36; Times-Picayune,
9 September 1930.

[27]Abell, "A Brief History...," p. 26.

[28]New Orleans Item, 21 September 1930; Times-Picayune, 21 September 1930; Sammy R. Dana, "A History of Radio Station KMLB, Monroe, Louisiana, with Emphasis on Programming Policies and Practices, 1930-1958" (Master's thesis, Louisiana State University, 1960),pp. 1, 6-7.

[29]Abell, "A Brief History...," pp. 24, 27; New Orleans States, 20 April 1924, 4 May 1924.

[30]Abell, "A Brief History...," p. 35; Pritchard interview.

[31]Abell, "A Brief History...," pp. 28, 33.

[32]Ibid., 34, 36.

[33]Ibid., P. 39; Hettinger, pp. 162-163.

[34]Testimony of Wallace A. Burk, S.J., 14 February 1933, Federal Radio Commission Docket 1757 File, WNRC; Abell, "A Brief History...," p. 35.

[35]Ibid., pp. 43-44; Times-Picayune, 21 September 1930; Lemoine, p. 50.

[36]Wheelahan interview; New Orleans Item, 19 October 1930; New Orleans States, 19 October 1930; Lemoine, p. 50.

[37]Pritchard interview; Abell, "A Brief History...," p. 43.

CHAPTER 8: Daylight Burglars and Clear Channels

[1]Theodore N. Beckman and Herman C. Nolen, The Chain Store Problem: A Critical Analysis (New York: McGraw-Hill Book Company, Inc., 1938), pp. 14-18; Godfrey M. Lebhar, Chain Stores in America, 1859-1950 (New York: Chain Store Publishing Corporation, 1952), p. 25.

[2]Beckman and Nolen, p. 3, 37; Lebhar, p. 59; Carl G. Ryant, "The South and the Movement Against Chain Stores," The Journal of Southern History 39 (May 1973) 221.

[3]Lebhar, pp. 113-115.

[4]Beckman and Nolen, pp. 234-235.

[5]Ibid., p. 231; Lebhar, pp. 116-122, 156.

[6]May, pp. 69-71; Statement of William Kennon Henderson, 28 April 1931, Federal Radio Commission, Docket 1145 File, WNRC.

[7]May, p. 72; New York Times, 27 April 1930.

[8]Transcripts of Henderson broadcasts of 11 January 1930 and 1 June 1931, KWKH Folder, RDF-NA; May, p. 57.

[9]Henderson transcript, 7 January 1930, KWKH Folder, RDF-NA; May, p. 48.

[10]U.S., Congress, Senate, 71st Cong., 2nd sess., 6 January 1930, Congressional Record 72: 1108.

[11]Section 29, "Radio Act of 1927," Kahn, p. 49; New York Times, 11 January 1930.

[12]Photograph of Radio Digest Award in FRC, Docket 889 File, WNRC; Nation's Business, April 1930, p. 30; Congressional Record, 9 January 1930, 72:1288.

[13]New York Times, 17 and 25 January 1930, 22 February 1930; Congressional Record, 17 January 1930, 72:1788; James W. Wesolowski, "Obscene, Indecent, or Profane Broadcast Language as Construed by the Federal Courts," Journal of Broadcasting 13 (Spring 1969) 203-215.

[14]Henderson testimony, 23 September 1930, FRC, Docket 889 File, WNRC; New York Times, 27 April 1930, KWKH File, LDR-FCC.

[15]Hall, p. 69; Elisabeth Salassi, "Hello World," Shreveport Magazine, April 1950, p. 17; Henderson statement, 28 April 1931, FRC, Docket 1145 File, WNRC; Henderson testimony, 17 February 1933, FRC, Docket 1757 File, WNRC.

[16]Shreveport Journal, 4, 21, 22, and 23 October 1930.

[17]Henderson transcript, 1 June 1931, KWKH Folder, RDF-NA; Henderson testimony, 17 February 1933, FRC, Docket 1757 File, WNRC.

[18]Hello World Doggone Coffee Label in FRC, Docket 1145 File, WNRC; Henderson testimony, 23 September 1930, FRC Docket 889, WNRC; Viola Carruth, Caddo: 1,000 (Shreveport: Shreveport Magazine, 1970), p. 140.

[19]FRC, Examiner's Report No. 470, In Re Loyola University (WWL) et al, 8 April 1933, p. 13; FRC, Henderson statement, Docket 1145 File, WNRC.

[20]Henderson transcript, 1 June 1931, KWKH Folder, RDF-NA.

[21] Ibid.; May, p. 78.

[22] Burk testimony, 23 September 1930, FRC, Docket 889 File, WNRC; Abell, "A Brief History...," p. 21.

[23] Ibid., pp. 21-23; Henderson and Burk testimony, FRC, Docket 889 File, WNRC.

[24] FRC, Examiner's Report No. 59, In Re Hello World Broadcasting Corporation, 20 January 1931, p. 1; Deiler to Chief, Radio Division, 10 June 1930, WWL Folder, RDF-NA.

[25] FRC to Chief, Radio Division, 1 July 1930, Chief, Radio Division to Radio Supervisor, Atlanta, 2 July 1930, Abell to Chief, Radio Division, 8 October 1930, WWL Folder, RDF-NA.

[26] Abell, "A Brief History...," p. 24.

[27] Van Nostrand to Chief, Radio Division, 17 July 1930, Abell to Chief, Radio Division, 8 October 1930, WWL Folder, RDF-NA; Abell, "A Brief History...," $\frac{1}{2}$. 25.

[28] Van Nostrand to Chief, Radio Division, 17 and 18 July 1930, WWL Folder, RDF-NA.

[29] Sullivan to Deiler, 12 September 1930, Deiler to Chief, Radio Division, 13 September 1930, WWL Folder, RDF-NA.

[30] Shreveport Times, 23 September 1930; Times-Picayune, 24 September 1930; The Maroon, 10 October 1930; Henderson testimony, FRC, Docket 889 File, WNRC; KWEA File, LDR-FCC; FRC, Examiner's Report No. 447, In Re Hello World Broadcasting Corp. (KWEA), 20 January 1933, p. 1, 5.

[31] Times-Picayune, 24 September 1930; New Orleans States, 23 September 1930; Henderson testimony, FRC, Docket 889 File, WNRC.

[32] Times-Picayune, 22 and 24 September 1930; Burk testimony, FRC, Docket 889 File, WNRC.

[33] Abell testimony, Ibid.; New Orleans States, 24 September 1930; Times-Picayune, 24 September 1930.

[34] Batcheller to Chief, Radio Division, 19 November 1930 and 13 December 1930, WWL Folder, RDF-NA.

[35] FRC, Examiner's Report No. 59, pp. 2-4.

[36] Schemeckebier, p. 54; U.S., Congress, Senate, 71st Cong., 3rd sess., 30 January 1931, Congressional Record, 74:3565-3566.

[37]Ibid.

[38]Henderson transcript, 26 January 1931, FRC, Docket 1145 File, WNRC; Deiler to Chief, Radio Division, 22 January 1931, KWKH Folder, RDF-NA.

[39]Deiler to Chief, Radio Division, 3 February 1931, McCabe to Deiler, 14 February 1931, KWKH Folder, RDF-NA; FRC, Examiner's Report No. 249, In Re Application of Hello World Broadcasting Corporation et al, 12 September 1931, pp. 1-2.

[40]Ibid.; Abell, "A Brief History...," p. 40.

[41]Ibid.; Burk testimony, 11 June 1931, FRC, Docket 1145, WNRC.

[42]Henderson Statement, 28 April 1931, FRC, Docket 1145 File, WNRC.

[43]FRC, Examiner's Report No. 249, pp. 2-4.

[44]Abell, "A Brief History...," p. 47; Henderson testimony, FRC, Docket 889 File, WNRC.

[45]Copy of time-sharing agreement, 14 September 1931, FRC, Docket 1757 File, WNRC.

[46]FRC, Order of the Commission, In Re Application of Hello World Broadcasting Corporation et al, 4 December 1931, pp. 1-6.

[47]Erwin G. Krasnow and Lawrence D. Longley, The Politics of Broadcast Regulation (New York: St. Martin's Press, 1973), p. 7; Tebbel, p. 367.

[48]Don R. LeDuc and Thomas A. McCain, "The Federal Radio Commission in Federal Court," Journal of Broadcasting 14 (Fall 1970) 393-394, 404.

CHAPTER 9:  The Ache and Pill Station of the Nation

[1]Broadus Mitchell, Depression Decade (New York: Harper & Row, 1947), pp. 32-33; William E. Leuchtenburg, Franklin D. Roosevelt and the New Deal (New York: Harper & Row, 1963), pp. 18-19.

[2]Robin Von Breton Derbes, "The WPA Saved New Orleans," New Orleans Magazine, July 1976, p. 137; Statistical Abstract of Louisiana, 1974 (New Orleans: University of New Orleans, 1974), p. 165; John Robert Moore, "The New Deal in Louisiana," in The New Deal: The State and Local Levels, eds. John Braeman, Robert H.

313

Bremner, and David Brody (Columbus: Ohio State University Press, 1975), p. 137.

[3]Roman Heleniak, "Local Reaction to the Great Depression in New Orleans, 1929-1933," Louisiana History 10 (Fall 1969): 291-296.

[4]Runyan, pp. 27, 42, 45, 62; Heleniak, pp. 297-300.

[5]Wolfe, pp. 94-95; Federal Communications Commission, Second Annual Report, 1936, p. 57; Cooperative Analysis of Broadcasting: Fourth Year Report (Princeton, NJ: Crossley Incorporated National Research Organization, 1934), p. 6; Harvey J. Levin, The Invisible Resource: Use and Regulation of the Radio Spectrum (Baltimore: Johns Hopkins Press, 1971), p. 363.

[6]Eoyang, pp. 179-181; FRC, Commercial Radio Advertising, pp. 41, 46; Levin, 362.

[7]Ibid., pp. 361-363.

[8]"Statement of Income and Expenses, 1931-1957," WWL Records, LU; Abell, "A Brief History...," p. 43.

[9]Price, Waterhouse & Co., The Third Study of Radio Network Popularity (New York: Columbia Broadcasting System, 1932), p. 11.

[10]Abell, "A Brief History...," pp. 55-56.

[11]SR & DS, Radio Advertising, March 1932, p. 60.

[12]Ibid

[13]Bloom interview; Pritchard interview.

[14]Head, p. 278; Hettinger, p. 168; Carl J. Friedrich and Jeanette Sayre, "The Development of the Control of Advertising on the Air," Studies in the Control of Radio 1 (November 1940): 8-9; Wolfe, p. 646.

[15]Hettinger, pp. 168-170; Mark Ethridge, "The Government and Radio," The Annals of the American Academy of Political and Social Science 213 (January 1941): 111.

[16]Bloom interview; Pritchard interview; Interview with Henry Dupre, New Orleans, 27 September 1974.

[17]Transcripts of WWL commercial copy, File, WWL Records, LU.

[18]Ibid.

314

[19]Radio Time (New Orleans), 12 June 1933, 18 June 1933, 25 March 1934, 20 May 1934, 28 October 1934; Abell, "A Brief History...," p. 38.

[20]Harvey J. Levin, Broadcast Regulation and Joint Ownership of Media (New York University, 1960), p. 44; Karl A. Bickel, New Empires: The Newspaper and the Radio (Philadelphia: J.B. Lippincott Company, 1930), pp. 65, 67; Lott, p. 276.

[21]Alfred M. Lee, The Daily Newspaper in America (New York: The Macmillan Company, 1937), pp. 559-561; Barnouw, p. 202; Levin, p. 47.

[22]Ibid., pp. 108-109, 121-123.

[23]Lott, p. 277; Robert A. Rutland, The Newsmongers: Journalism in the Life of the Nation, 1690-1972 (New York: The Dial Press, 1973), p. 331; Sidney Kobre, Development of American Journalism (Dubuque, Iowa: Wm. C. Brown Company, Publishers, 1969), p. 710.

[24]Lott, pp. 277-281; Lee, pp. 564-565; E.H. Harris, "Radio and the Press," Annals of the American Academy of Political and Social Science 177 (January 1935): 166-168.

[25]"News on the Air," Business Week, 24 March 1934, p. 12; Lott, pp. 282-284; Clarence C. Dill, "Radio and the Press: A Contrary View," Annals of the American Academy of Political and Social Science 177 (January 1935): 170.

[26]Johnson and Robb, pp. 154, 162; Abell, "A Brief History...," p. 37.

[27]See New Orleans newspapers for June 1932 and thereafter for this policy change; Minutes of Board of Directors, Loyola University, 14 October 1953, WWL-TV File, WWL Records, LU.

[28]Pritchard interview; Bloom interview; Dabney, pp. 463-464; Covington, p. 114.

[29]For examples of WSMB ads, see Times-Picayune, 19 September 1932 and 23 February 1933, also New Orleans Item, 2 October 1932; for WDSU examples see same dates; for WWL examples, see Item, 17 September 1933 and Times-Picayune, 23 May 1934.

[30]New Orleans States, 2 October 1932; Pritchard interview; Times-Picayune, 24 May 1934; Item, 1934-1935 passim.

[31]Abell, "A Brief History...," p. 49.

[32]WWL Development Co. File, WWL Records, LU; Katz interview; Interview with Charles I. Denechaud, Jr., New Orleans, 5 November 1974.

[33]Abell, "A Brief History...," p. 48; Pritchard interview; Supplemental Agreement between WWL Development Co. and Loyola University, 19 January 1933, WWL Development Co. File, WWL Records, LU.

[34]Marquette Association for Higher Education File, University Records, LU.

[35]1933 Supplemental Agreement, WWL Development Co. File, WWL Records, LU.

[36]Profit and Loss Statement, 30 November 1933, Ibid.

[37]Abell, "A Brief History...," p. 50.

[38]Ibid., pp. 53-54, 58, 64-66; "WWL--A Radio Pioneer," The Southern Jesuit, February 1936, pp. 2-4; The Maroon, 29 April 1932.

[39]Abell, "A Brief History...," pp. 50-51; "WWL Expands," The New Orleanian, February 1932, p. 11.

[40]Williams, pp. 374-375; Jeff Radford, "Can an Old Hotel Change Its Sheets?" New Orleans Magazine, September 1975, pp. 39-40.

[41]Williams, pp. 374-375; F. Edward Hebert, "Earl Long, Robert Maestri, Jimmy Noe, Chep Morrison, Bathtub Joe and Me," New Orleans Magazine, August 1976, p. 308.

[42]Abell, "A Brief History...," p. 51; Burk testimony, 14 February 1933, FRC, Docket 1757 File, WNRC; Bloom interview.

[43]Abell, "A Brief History...," p. 51; Burk testimony, 14 February 1933, FRC, Docket 1757 File, WNRC.

[44]Abell, "A Brief History...," p. 67; FRC, Commercial Radio Advertising, pp. 148-150.

CHAPTER 10:  The Clear Channel War - The Final Round

[1]Harnett T. Kane, Louisiana Hayride (New York:  William Morrow & Company, 1941), p. 151; Deiler to Chief, Radio Division, 27 November 1931, KWKH Folder, RDF-NA; New Orleans States, 28 December 1930.

[2]New Orleans Item, 2 February 1931.

[3]Huey P. Long, Every Man a King (New Orleans: National Book Co., Inc., 1933), p. 273; Williams, pp. 490-491.

[4]For correspondence originating from Long's Pere Marquette Building offices, see Folder 528, Box 15, Huey P. Long, Jr., Papers, LSU.

[5]Pritchard interview.

[6]Ibid., Hynes to Long, 5 February 1932, Long File, WWL Records, LU.

[7]Transcripts of Henderson broadcasts of 28 November 1932, 19 December 1932, 22 December 1932, FRC, Docket 1757 File, WNRC.

[8]Henderson testimony, 17 February 1933, FRC, Docket 1757 File, WNRC, Examiner's Report No. 470, pp. 10-11.

[9]Ibid., p. 67; FRC, Examiner's Report No. 470, pp. 10-11.

[10]Henderson transcript, 4 December 1932, FRC, Docket 1757 File, WNRC.

[11]Henderson transcripts, 19 December 1932, 16 January 1933 and Henderson testimony, 17 February 1933, Ibid.

[12]Henderson testimony and Henderson bankruptcy petition, Ibid.; FRC, Examiner's Report No. 470, p. 11.

[13]Hello World Broadcasting Corporation financial statement, 30 December 1932, and Henderson testimony, 17 February 1933, FRC, Docket 1757 File, WNRC; FRC, Examiner's Report No. 470, p. 11.

[14]Ibid., pp. 4-8.

[15]Ibid., pp. 9-10.

[16]Ibid., pp. 11-23.

[17]Pritchard interview; FRC, Order of the Commission, In Re Applications of Loyola University (WWL) et al, 15 September 1933, p. 7; Hall, pp. 89-90.

[18]Chicago Tribune, 6 May 1934; Abell, "A Brief History...," p. 30.

[19]Arthur M. Schlesinger, Jr., The Age of Roosevelt, vol. 3: The Politics of Upheaval (Boston: Houghton Mifflin Company, 1960), p. 55.

[20]Chicago Tribune, 6 May 1934; Frank Freidel, Franklin D. Roosevelt: Launching the New Deal (Boston: Little, Brown and Company, 1973), p. 65; Alfred B. Rollins, Jr., Roosevelt and Howe (New York: Alfred A. Knopf, 1962), p. 416.

[21]Chicago Tribune, 6 May 1934; Abell, "A Brief History...," p. 30; Broadcasting, 15 June 1934; p. 39; Congressional Record, 5 June 1934, 78:10503; Barnouw, A History of Broadcasting in the United States, vol. 2: The Golden Web (New York: Oxford University Press, 1968), p. 28.

[22]Lawrence W. Lichty, "The Impact of FRC and FCC Commissioners' Backgrounds on the Regulation of Broadcasting" Journal of Broadcasting, 6 (Winter 1961-1962): 99-100; Interview with Thomas O. Hanley, Atlanta, Georgia, 29 December 1975 [Hanley is the son of the former FRC member]; Abell, "A Brief History...," p. 30.

[23]FRC Order, 15 September 1933, pp. 2-8.

[24]Shreveport Times, 16 September 1933; Abell, "A Brief History...," p. 57; Congressional Record, 5-6 June 1934; 78:10503, Broadcasting, 15 June 1934.

[25]Abell, "A Brief History...," p. 30; Chicago Tribune, 6 May 1934; George Q. Flynn, American Catholics and the Roosevelt Presidency, 1932-1936 (Lexington: University of Kentucky Press, 1968), pp. 17, 37, 175.

[26]Pritchard interview; Bloom interview; Bormann, pp. 115-116, 119; U.S. Congress, Senate, Committee on Interstate Commerce, Federal Communications Commission, 73rd Cong., 2nd sess., 1934, p. 189.

[27]Abell, "A Brief History...," p. 30; Chicago Tribune, 6 May 1934.

[28]WWL and KWKH File, LDR-FCC; Broadcasting, 15 June 1934; Shreveport Times, 9 June 1934.

[29]Thomas K. McGraw, "Regulation in America: A Review Article," Business History Review 49 (Summer 1975): 162-163; Kasnow and Longley, p. 7.

[30]The Shreveport Times, 28 June 1935 and 21 September 1975; Hall, p. 101; Richard McCaughan, Socks on a Rooster: Louisiana's Earl K. Long (Baton Route: Claitor's Book Store, 1967), p. 84.

[31]The Shreveport Times, 28 June 1935 and 21 September 1975; Times-Picayune, 30 May 1945.

³²The Shreveport Times, 29 May 1945.

³³Beckman and Nolen, p. 231; Richard Hofstadter, The Paranoid Style in American Politics and Other Essays (New York: Alfred A. Knopf, 1965), pp. 4, 30.

³⁴David H. Bennett, Demagogues in the Depression (New Brunswick, N.J.: Rutgers University Press, 1969), p. 4.


CHAPTER 11:  A Profit-Making Enterprise - At Last

¹Barnouw, II, 6.

²Lester V. Chandler, America's Greatest Depression, 1929-1941 (New York: Harper & Row, Publishers, 1970), p. 129; Federal Communications Commission, Report on Social and Economic Data Pursuant to the Informal Hearing on Broadcasting, Docket 4063, Beginning October 5, 1936, July 1, 1937, p. 5. [hereafter cited as FCC, Report on Social and Economic Data].

³Ibid., pp. 5, 23; Dick Perry, Not Just a Sound: The Story of WLW (Englewood Cliffs, N.J.: Prentice-Hall, Inc., 1971), p. 45.

⁴FCC, Report on Social and Economic Data, p. 24; FCC, Report on Chain Broadcasting, pp. 3-4, 30.

⁵Hettinger and Neff, p. 310; Barnouw, I, 239.

⁶Ibid., I, 273; Kenneth G. Bartlett, "Trends in Radio Programs," Annals of the American Academy of Political and Social Science 213 (January 1941): 16-17, 20; Hettinger and Neff, p. 108.

⁷Head, p. 171; Gilbert Seldes, The Great Audience (New York: Viking Press, 1950), p. 113; Raymond W. Stedman, The Serials (Norman: University of Oklahoma Press, 1971), pp. 251, 257, 269, 293, 307; Harrison B. Summers, ed., A Thirty Year History of Programs Carried on National Radio Networks in the United States, 1926-1956 (Columbus: Ohio State University, 1958), p. 42.

⁸Ibid., pp. 152, 185, 331; George A. Willey, "The Soap Operas and the War," Journal of Broadcasting 7 (Fall 1963): 339.

⁹Bartlett, p. 19.

¹⁰U.S., Department of Commerce, Bureau of the Census, Census of Business, 1935: Radio Broadcasting, pp. 1, 19. 44.

¹¹Ibid., pp. 38, 67; Barnouw, I, 236; Interview with Don Lewis, New Orleans, 7 February 1975.

319

[12]Broadcasting Year Book, 1935, p. 98; Variety Radio Directory, 1937-1938, p. 479.

[13]Baton Rouge State-Times, 19 June 1941; Nellie Graham Colbert, "A History of Radio Station WJBO, Baton Rouge, Louisiana with Emphasis on Programming Policies and Practices, 1934-1952" (Master's thesis, Louisiana State University, 1960), pp. 10-11, 34; Variety Radio Directory, 1937-1938, p. 480; In Re T.B. Lanford et al., I F.C.C. 212 (1935); In Re Evangeline Broadcasting Company, i F.C.C. 253 (1935).

[14]Samuel D. Reeks, "A Station for the Majority," The Radio Graphic, August 1931, pp. 69-70; Radio Time 20 May 1934 and 30 September 1934; WNOE File, LDR-FCC; Sindler, p. 118; New Orleans States-Item, 19 October 1976.

[15]New Orleans Item, 3 October 1934; The Maroon, 5 October 1934.

[16]Bill C. Malone, Country Music U.S.A. (Austin: University of Texas Press, 1968), pp. 35-37; John H. DeWitt, Jr., "Early Radio Broadcasting in Middle Tennessee," Tennessee Historical Quarterly, 31 (Spring 1972): 90; Richard A. Peterson, "Single Industry Firm to Conglomerate Synergistics: Alternative Strategies for Selling Insurance and Country Music," in Growing Metropolis: Aspects of Development in Nashville, eds. James Blumstein and Benjamin Walter (Nashville: Vanderbilt University Press, 1975), pp. 346-347.

[17]Elizabeth Mae Roberts, "French Radio Broadcasting in Louisiana, 1935-1958" (Master's thesis, Louisiana State University, 1959), p. 36; Radio Time, 12 November 1933 and 30 December 1934.

[18]Abell, "A Brief History...," p. 38; Radio Time, 14 January 1934, 20 May 1934, 3 March 1935.

[19]Ibid., 18 February 1934, 24 June 1934, 2 September 1934.

[20]Dupre biography, Memorandum of Material Filed by Loyola University, 16 December 1953, in Support of Television Application to the Federal Communications Commission, vol. 1, p. 396 [hereafter cited as 1953 TV Application]; Dupre interview; Radio Time, 17 June 1934 and 16 September 1934.

[21]Vidacovich biography, 1953 TV Application, I, 398; Radio Time, 6 August 1933, 15 October 1933; Eunice Ruby, "The Dawnbusters," New Orleans Magazine, July 1976, p. 80.

[22]William J. Dempsey and William C. Koplovitz, "Radio Economics and the Public Interest," Annals of the American Academy of Political and Social Science 213 (January 1941): 97; Program log, 10 September 1935, Programs File, WWL Records, LU.

[23]Interview with George Wagner, New Orleans, 21 April 1975; Programs File, WWL Records, LU.

[24]1934 and 1935 Auditor's Reports for WWL, in J.K. Byrne & Co. CPA Files, New Orleans [hereafter cited as Auditor's Report].

[25]Ibid.

[26]Ibid.

[27]Columbia Broadcasting System, Listening Areas of the Columbia Broadcasting System, Inc., 1933.

[28]Columbia Broadcasting System, CBS Listeners and Dealers, 1937, vol. 1, pp. 136-137 and vol. 2, pp. 140-141.

[29]In Re Loyola University (WWL), 5 F.C.C. 43(1937); CBS File, WWL Records, LU; Bloom interview; Uhalt interview; Lemoine, p. 45.

[30]Miller interview.

[31]Barnouw, II, 58; FCC, Report on Chain Broadcasting, pp. 38-39, 66.

[32]Ibid., p. 39; Supplemental Agreement between WWL Development Co. and Loyola University, 19 January 1933, WWL Development Co. File, WWL Records, LU.

[33]New Orleans Item, 2 November 1935.

[34]Ibid., 17 February 1935, 3 November 1935; Times-Picayune, 17 February 1935, 15 December 1935, 16 December 1935.

CHAPTER 12:   The Twilight of the Abell Years

[1]America, 31 March 1934, p. 615; Rev. Joseph I. Malloy, C.S.P. to Rev. James M. Gillis, 9 January 1933, Box 4, WLWL Papers, Paulist Archives [hereafter cited as PA], New York City; Radio talk delivered by Rev. John B. Harney, C.S.P., on WLWL, 21 March 1934, WLWL Papers, PA; John B. Harney, C.S.P., "Education and Religion vs. Commercial Radio" (pamphlet published by the Paulists, 1934), p. 3.

[2]WLWL File, LDR-FCC; Harney, "Education and Religion...," p. 5; In Re Missionary Society of St. Paul the Apostle (WLWL) et al., 3 F.C.C. 527 [hereafter cited as In Re WLWL].

[3]America, 31 March 1934, p. 615; Harney, 21 March 1934, radio talk, WLWL Papers, PA.

[4]The Commonweal, 30 March 1934, pp. 592-593 and 20 April 1934, p. 673; Friedrich, pp. 51-52; Harney "Education and Religion...," pp. 1-2; Harney testimony, 15 March 1934, U.S., Congress, Senate, Committee on Interstate Commerce, Federal Communications Commission Hearings, 73rd Cong., 2nd sess., 1934, p. 135 [hereafter cited as FCC Hearings].

[5]Friedrich, pp. 51-53; Barnouw, II, 24-27; Section 307c, Communications Act of 1934, Kahn, pp. 69-70; Carl J. Friedrich and Evelyn Sternbert, "Congress and the Control of Radio-Broadcasting," Studies in the Control of Radio, October 1943, p. 21; S.E. Frost, Jr., Education's Own Stations (Chicago: University of Chicago Press, 1937), pp. V-VII. R. Franklin Smith "A Look at the Wagner-Hatfield Amendment," in Problems and Controversies in Television and Radio, eds. Harry J. Skornia and Jack William Kitson (Palo Alto, Calif.: Pacific Books, 1968), pp. 173-176.

[6]In Re WLWL, 3 F.C.C. 519.

[7]Harney testimony, 15 March 1934, FCC Hearings, pp. 189-192; Harney to Rev. John H. Sullivan, C.S.P., 5 July 1935, Harney Papers, PA; Harney to Rev. Thomas F. Burke, C.S.P., 20 February 1935, Harney Papers, PA; James A. Farley to Berlyt Stephens, 27 September 1936, Box 4, WLWL Papers, PA.

[8]Harney to Sullivan, 5 July 1935; Pritchard interview.

[9]Petition to FCC prepared by Paul M. Segal, 21 May 1935, Box 5, WLWL Papers, PA; WWL Brief prepared by Paul M. Segal, 8 June 1935, Box 5, WLWL Papers, PA; In Re WLWL, 3 F.C.C. 526.

[10]Ibid., pp. 530-531, 537.

[11]The Sign, October 1936, p. 132; The Commonweal, 8 February 1935, p. 428.

[12]In Re WLWL, 3 R.C.C., 536-537; WLWL Income Statement for 1936, Box 3, WLWL Papers, PA; The Catholic World, June 1937, p. 364.

[13]Brief in behalf of WWL Development Co. Inc. in Support of Claim for Exemption from Income, Excess Profits, Capital Stock, and Social Security Taxes, 1942, Taxes Folder, WWL Records, LU [hereafter cited as 1942 Tax Brief]; 1936 Auditor's Report.

[14]Ibid.

[15]Supplemental Agreement, 26 December 1936, WWL Development Co. Folder, WWL Records, LU.

[16]Bloom interview; du Treil interview, Interview with Rev. Francis L. Janssen, S.J., New Orleans, 5 January 1977; I.A. Timmreck and Francis L. Janssen, S.J., "Loyola University: A Compendium of Historical Information" (unpublished manuscript, Loyola University Documents Center), pp. 161-162.

[17]Denechaud interview; Bloom interview; Dupre interview.

[18]Bloom interview; Dupre interview; Pritchard interview; 1936 Auditor's Report.

[19]Katz interview; Pritchard interview; Bloom interview.

[20]Ibid., Abell, "A Brief History...," pp. 34-35.

[21]Pritchard interview.

[22]Timmreck interview; Bloom interview; Dupre interview; Jacob interview.

[23]Callahan to Gaudin, 18 May 1937, Callahan File, WWL Records, LU.

[24]Ibid.

[25]Ibid.

[26]Pritchard interview; Dupre interview; Abell, "A Brief History...," p. 44.

[27]Abell to Gaudin, 2 November 1937, Callahan File, WWL Records, LU; Jacob interview.

[28]Bloom interview; Dupre interview; Jacob interview; Katz interview; 1937 Auditor's Report.

[29]Interview with J. Michael Early, 8 November 1974, New Orleans; Cavey biography, Faculty Directors File, WWL Records, LU; Interview with Leon Soniat, 19 May 1976, New Orleans.

[30]Abell biography, Jesuit Archives, St. Charles College, Gran Coteau, Louisiana.

CHAPTER 13:  The Callahan Interval

[1]Interview with A. Louis Read, New Orleans, 12 January 1976; Bloom interview; Timmreck interview.

[2]1936, 1937, and 1938 Auditor's Reports.

[3]Katz interview.

[4]Ibid.

[5]Ibid.

[6]Ibid.

[7]Standard Rate & Data Service, June 1938, p. 89, and December 1938, p. 95; Thomas Porter Robinson, Radio Networks and the Federal Government (New York:  Columbia University Press, 1943), p. 112; Hettinger and Neff, pp. 319-323; WSMB and WDSU Files, LDR-FCC.

[8]1938 Auditor's Report.

[9]Bloom interview; Bloom biography, 1953 TV Application, I, 358.

[10]Jacob interview; Jacob biography, 1953 TV Application, I, 368-369.

[11]Summer Theatre of the Air Brochure, Programs File, WWL Records, LU; John Scheuermann, Jr., Secretary-Treasurer of Local 174, American Federation of Musicians to General Manager, WWL, 9 December 1953, in 1953 TV Application, II, Part c.

[12]Abell to Gaudin, 4 May 1937, Power File, WWL Records, LU; Sindler, pp. 126-127.

[13]FCC, Examiner's Report No. I-491, 26 August 1937, pp. 1-5; In Re Loyola University (WWL), 5 F.C.C. 43-47.

[14]Glenn D. Gillett to Gaudin, 10 February 1938, Transmitter File, WWL Records, LU; Agreement between RCA and WWL Development Company, 26 February 1938, Transmitter File, WWL Records, LU; Bloom interview; 1938 Auditor's Report.

[15]Unsigned, undated memo, Power File, WWL Records, LU.

[16]CBS, Station Audience Study-Station Ratings, Spring 1937, CBS Radio Research Files, New York City.

[17]Jacob interview; For CBS personalities and programs, see typical schedules in New Orleans newspapers, 1937 and 1938, passim.

[18]Lewis interview; Jacob interview; Callahan to Gaudin, 28 January 1938, Callahan File, WWL Records, LU; Summer Theatre of the Air brochure and WWL Playmakers Lab brochure, Programs File, WWL Records, LU.

[19]Interview with Wallace Dunlap, Westinghouse Broadcasting, Washington, D.C., 14 November 1975; Interview with John L. Vath, New Orleans, 13 May 1976; Interview with Marshall Pearce, New Orleans, 13 May 1976; Dupre interview; 1953 TV Application, p. 396.

[20]Frank Buxton and Bill Owen, Radio's Golden Age: The Programs and the Personalities (n.p.: Easton Valley Press, 1966), p. 51; Ruby, p. 80; Times-Picayune, 11 April 1938; New Orleans Item, 11 April 1938.

[21]Callahan to Gaudin, 28 January 1938, Callahan File, WWL Records, LU; 1953 TV Application, p. 396; Ruby, p. 81.

[22]Ruby, p. 80-82; Dupre interview; Interview with Dottie O'Dair and Al Hirt, WWL, Eric Tracy Show, 31 March 1975; Interview with Ray McNamara, WSMB, Fiftieth Anniversary Program, 21 April 1975.

[23]Roy Reed, "The Cajuns Resist the Melting Pot," The New York Times Magazine, 29 February 1976, pp. 10, 42, 44; Dawnbusters, undated 1945 show, recording in WWL Station Files, New Orleans.

[24]Various undated Dawnbusters recordings, WWL Station Files.

[25]Ibid.

[26]Dupre interview; Ruby, p. 80; Undated Dawnbusters recordings, WWL Station Files; New Orleans Item, 1 February 1940 and 5 December 1941.

[27]Dupre interview; Ruby, p. 80; Jacob interview; Lewis interview.

[28]Jacob interview; Dunlap interview; Read interview.

[29]1938 Auditor's Report; Jacob interview; Dupre interview; Read interview; Bloom interview; Katz interview.

[30]Gaudin to Callahan, 27 January 1939, Callahan File, WWL Records, LU; Gaudin to Dale Robertson, WBAX, Wilkes-Barre, Pa., 5 August 1939; Gaudin to Stephen P. Willis, East Providence, Rhode Island, 5 August 1939, Gaudin to W. Howard Summerville, WGST, Atlanta, 5 August 1939, Summerville to Gaudin, 7 August 1939, Summerville File, WWL Records, LU.

[31]Summerville biography, 1953 TV Application, p. 353; Dupre interview, Katz interview; Jacob interview; Lewis interview; Soniat interview; Vath interview; Read interview.

[32]Read interview; Timmreck and Janssen, p. 165; The Maroon, 22 and 29 September 1939.

[33]Summerville to Cavey, 14 November 1939 and Roy to Summerville, 18 November 1939, Summerville File, WWL Records, LU.

CHAPTER 14:  A Key to the Mint

[1]Lichty and Topping, p. 305.

[2]New Orleans Item, 6 December 1941.  Ned Midgley, The Advertising and Business Side of Radio (New York:  Prentice-Hall, Inc., 1948), p. 2.

[3]Friedrich and Sternberg, p. 25; Carl J. Friedrich, "Controlling Broadcasting in Wartime," Studies in the Control of Radio, November 1940, p. 12; FCC, Seventh Annual Report, 1941, p. 21; FCC, Eighth Annual Report, 1942, p. 30; FCC, Eleventh Annual Report, 1945, p. 11.

[4]FCC, Ninth Annual Report, 1943, pp. 46-47; FCC, Eleventh Annual Report, 1945, p. 11.

[5]Ibid., p. 12; Barnouw, II, 165.

[6]Undated The Man Behind the Gun recording, broadcast by WWL in 1943, WWL Station Files.

[7]Barnouw, II, 165-167.

[8]FCC, Public Service Responsibility of Broadcast Licensees, 7 March 1946, pp. 49-50.

[9]Ibid., p. 52.

[10]Ibid., p. 49; Poindexter, p. 296; Staff File, WWL Records, LU; Barnouw, II, 156.

[11]FCC, An Economic Study of Standard Broadcasting, 31 October 1947, pp. 12, 14-15.

[12]Robertson, pp. 84-85; Eldridge Peterson, "Radio Quarrel with Composers," Printers' Ink, 28 June 1940, pp. 26, 30; National Association of Broadcasters, Let's Stick to the Record (Washington: by the authors, 1940), p. 4; New York Times, 22 March 1940.

[13]Peterson, "Radio Quarrel...," p. 4; New York Times, 3 November 1940 and 17 December 1940.

[14]Robertson, p. 85; ASCAP File, WWL Records, LU; New York Times, 3 November 1940.

[15]NAB, Let's Stick to the Record, pp. 12-13; Robertson, p. 85; Interview with Edward M. Hoerner, New Orleans, 21 May 1976; Pringle and Pringle, p. 89.

[16]Robertson, p. 85; Pringle and Pringle, p. 89.

[17]James Lawrence Fly, "Regulation of Radio Broadcasting in the Public Interest," Annals of the American Academy of Political and Social Science 213 (January 1941) 102-108; FCC, Report on Chain Broadcasting; FCC, Ninth Annual Report, 1943, p. 4.

[18]Ibid., p. 50; Radio Daily, 1944 Radio Annual, pp. 444-445.

[19]FCC, Sixth Annual Report, 1940, pp. 45, 47; FCC, Seventh Annual Report, 1941, pp. 21-22; Roy to Paul Segal, 17 September 1940, License File, WWL Records, LU.

[20]WDSU File, LDR-FCC; In Re WDSU, Inc., 10 F.C.C. 126; Interview with Marian (Mrs. Joseph H.) Uhalt, New Orleans, 14 May 1976.

[21]Read interview; Sindler, pp. 139, 165, 175, 197; Howard, pp. 264-265; George E. Simmons, "Crusading Newspapers in Louisiana," Journalism Quarterly 16 (December 1939) 328.

[22]Read interview; Radio Daily, 1944 Radio Annual, p. 444.

[23]Smith, "WDSU," p. 61; Program Notes, Broadcast Pioneers Twelfth Annual Mike Award Banquet, 29 February 1972, WDSU Files, New Orleans; Lewis interview; Soniat interview; Uhalt, Jr., interview.

[24]Edgar A. Schuler, Survey of Radio Listeners in Louisiana (Baton Rouge: Louisiana State University Press, 1943), pp. 15, 17, 61-63.

[25]Ibid., p. 41.

[26]Ibid., pp. 54-56.

[27]CBS, Listening Areas: 7th Series, 1944 (New York: Columbia Broadcasting System Research Department, 1945); J. Leonard Reinsch, Radio Station Management (New York: Harper & Brothers, 1948), p. 10.

[28]Loyola University, Annual Financial Report to the FCC, 1940, WNRC [beginning in 1938, the FCC required from each licensee an annual financial report containing a balance sheet, an income statement, and other miscellaneous information; this report is now submitted on FCC Form 324]; Atkinson, pp. 11, 56-57.

[29]WWL, WDSU, WSMB, WNOE, WJBO, KWKH Annual Financial Reports to FCC, 1940, WNRC.

[30]Ibid.

[31]Ibid.

[32]FCC, An Economic Study of Standard Broadcasting, p. 11.

[33]WWL Annual Financial Report to 1940; Roche's Beach, Inc., v. Commissioner of Internal Revenue, 96 F. 2d. 776.

[34]Ibid., p. 778.

[35]Roy to Segal, 17 September 1940, License File, WWL Records, LU; Segal to Roy, 24 September 1940, and Segal to Denechaud, 18 November 1940, WWL Development Co. File, WWL Records, LU.

[36]Roy to Denechaud, 18 December 1940, Ibid.; Commissioner of Internal Revenue to WWL Development Co., 28 April 1941, Taxes File, WWL Records, LU.

[37]Guy T. Helvering, Commissioner of Internal Revenue, to WWL Development Company, Inc., 1 June 1942, Ibid.

[38]Roy to Ellender, 11 August 1942, and Ellender to Roy, 21 October 1942, Ibid.; "Brief in behalf of WWL Development Company, Inc.," undated 1942, Ibid., undated memorandum "Re: WWL Development--Tax Exemption," Ibid.

[39]Frank Wurzlow, Jr., Secretary to Senator Ellender, to Roy, 10 November 1942 and Roy to McCormack, 17 November 1942, as well as other letters written same date, Ibid.

[40]WWL Development Co. File, WWL Records, LU.

[41]1942, 1943, and 1944 Auditor's Reports; FCC, An Economic Study of Standard Broadcasting, p. 17.

[42]Maroon, 10 May 1940.

[43]Read interview; Radio Daily, 1944 Radio Annual, p. 445.

[44]Hoerner interview.

[45]Faculty Directors File, WWL Records, LU; Katz interview; Bloom interview; Dupre interview.

[46]Programs File, WWL Records, LU.

[47]Ibid.; Charles A. Siepman, "American Radio in Wartime," in

<u>Radio Research, 1942-1943</u>, edited by Paul F. Lazarsfeld and Frank
N. Stanton (New York: Essential Books, 1944), p. 125; Soniat
interview; Hoerner interview.

[48]Undated 1944 <u>Music From the Southland</u> recording, WWL
Station File.

[49]WWL schedules in <u>Times-Picayune</u> and <u>New Orleans Item</u> for
various dates, 1942, 1943, 1944.


CHAPTER 15:   A Period of Acute Adjustments

[1]FCC, <u>Twelfth Annual Report</u>, 1946, pp. 10-11.

[2]FCC, <u>Economic Study of Standard Broadcasting</u>, p. 1; FCC;
<u>Fourteenth Annual Report, 1948</u>, p. 26.

[3]FCC, <u>Economic Study of Standard Broadcasting</u>, pp. 26-27, 96.

[4]<u>Ibid</u>., p. 1; <u>Federal Communications Commission v. Sanders
Brothers Radio Station</u>, 309 U.S. 470 (1940); Richard A. Givens,
"Refusal of Radio and Television Licenses on Economic Grounds,"
<u>Virginia Law Review</u> 46 (November 1960) 1392.

[5]<u>Broadcasting Yearbook, 1952</u>, pp. 150-154; Interview with
John Pennybacker, Baton Rouge, May 1976; Articles of Incorporation,
Louisiana Association of Broadcasters, 12 August 1947, LAB Records,
Baton Rouge.

[6]<u>New Orleans Item</u>, 1 February 1951.

[7]<u>Broadcasting Yearbook, 1952</u>, pp. 152-153; <u>In Re Charles C.
Carlson (WJBW)</u>, 12 F.C.C. 902 (1948).

[8]Interview with George W. Healy, Jr., New Orleans, 12 May
1976; Don V. Erickson, <u>Armstrong's Fight for FM Broadcasting</u>
(University, Alabama: The University of Alabama Press, 1973),
p. 4; Lawrence D. Longley, "The FM Shift in 1945," <u>Journal of
Broadcasting</u> 12 (Fall 1968) 253.

[9]<u>Ibid</u>., p. 354; Head, p. 180; <u>Times-Picayune</u>, 3-4 January
1947.

[10]Longley, pp. 355-360; <u>Broadcasting</u>, 16 January 1945; FCC,
<u>Thirty-First Annual Report, 1965</u>, p. 117.

[11]<u>Times-Picayune</u>, 13, 16, 17 February 1948; <u>In Re Times-
Picayune Publishing Co. (WTPS)</u>, 13 F.C.C. 509 (1949).

[12]George S. Smith to Summerville, 29 November 1943, WWL-TV File, LU; Thomas J. Shields, S.J., "Memorandum No. 1 re Television," 17 December 1947, WWL-TV File, LU; Times-Picayune, 3 January 1947, 16 May 1947; Shields to FCC, 1 February 1951, WWL-TV File, LU; Katz interview.

[13]Shields biography, 1953 TV Application, I, 34-36.

[14]WWL Annual Financial Reports to FCC, 1945 and 1950, WNRC.

[15]Barnouw, II, 285-286.

[16]FCC, Twelfth Annual Report, 1946, p. 13; FCC, Fourteenth Annual Report, 1948, p. 35; FCC, Sixteenth Annual Report, 1950, p. 116.

[17]WSMB Annual Financial Reports to FCC, 1945, 1950, 1955, WNRC; Lemoine, pp. 76-77; In Re Paramount Television Productions, Inc. et al., 17 F.C.C. 264 (1953).

[18]WNOE Annual Financial Report to FCC, 1945, 1950, 1955, WNRC; In Re James A. Noe (WNOE), 13 F.C.C. 448; FCC, Examiner's Report, In Re Loyola University et al., 6 July 1955, p. 78; New Orleans States, 7 October 1954.

[19]Times-Picayune, 17 December 1948; FCC, Application of Edgar B. Stern, Sr., et al, 9 February 1948, Docket 8935 File, WNRC; Davis, II, 17 and III, 566; Read interview.

[20]WDSU Annual Financial Report to FCC, 1945, WNRC; Read interview; Times-Picayune, 17 December 1948; New Orleans Item, 17 December 1948.

[21]Times-Picayune, 17, 18, 20, 21, 24, 26 December 1948; New Orleans Item, 17, 20 December 1948, 4 March 1949, 1 April 1950.

[22]WDSU Annual Financial Report to FCC, 1950, WNRC; Hoerner interview; Read interview; James A. Perry, "A Soul-Baring Session with Terry Flettrich," New Orleans States Item, 22 March 1975; Head, p. 321; Barnouw, II, 244, 290; Broadcasting Yearbook, 1975, p. A-5, A-7; Roger G. Noll et al., Economic Aspects of Television Regulation (Washington, D.C.: The Brookings Institution, 1973), p. 15.

[23]Shields to Stanton, 22 May 1951, CBS File, WWL Records, LU: Interview with Eric H. Saline, Director, Affiliate Relations, CBS Radio Network, New York City, 24 June 1976.

[24]Stanton to Shields, 4 June 1951, Ibid.

[25]Ibid.

[26]Ibid.; Shields "Memorandum Concerning Radio Station WWL," 5 August 1951, WWL-TV File, WWL Records, LU; Saline interview; Miller interview; Agreement between CBS Radio and Loyola University, 1 July 1955, WWL File, CBS Radio Records, CBS, New York City.

[27]Times-Picayune, 7 October 1951, 3 November 1952, 7 July 1955; New Orleans Item, 16 October 1953, 20 December 1954; Head, pp. 219-220; Barnouw, II, 216-219; WWL Advertising Brochure, "The South's Greatest Salesman," Summer 1956, Katz Agency File, WWL Records, LU; FCC, Twenty-Second Annual Report, 1956, p. 93.

[28]Martin J. Maloney, "The Collision of Radio, Unions, and Free Enterprise," in Broadcasting and Bargaining: Labor Relations in Radio and Television, ed. Allen E. Koenig (Madison: University of Wisconsin Press, 1970), p. 13; Robert L. Coe with Darrel W. Holt, "The Effect of Unionism on Broadcasting," in Koenig, p. 22; Gregory Schubert and James E. Lynch, "Broadcasting Unions: Structure and Impact," in Koenig, pp. 41, 56.

[29]Stedman, p. 310; Allen E. Koenig, "American Federation of Television and Radio Artists Negotiations and Contracts," (Master's thesis, Stanford University, 1962), pp. 4-6, 8.

[30]Bloom interview; M.A. Downey, "IBEW Men at Work," Louisiana State Federation of Labor 1953 Review, pp. 82, 103; Robert L. Grevemberg to Summerville, 27 October 1953, 1953 TV Application, II, Part B.

[31]Soniat interview; Lewis interview; Hoerner interview.

[32]Soniat interview; Lewis interview; Hoerner interview; Ernest La Prade, Broadcasting Music (New York: Rinehart & Company, Inc., 1956), p. 94.

[33]Soniat interview; Early interview; Hoerner interview.

[34]Soniat interview; Hoerner interview; WWL Annual Financial Reports to FCC, 1945, 1950.

[35]Testimony Mortimer M. Caplin, 10 September 1969, U.S., Congress, Senate, Committee on Finance, Tax Reform Act of 1969, 91st Cong., 1st sess., 1969, pp. 1-15; Shields Memorandum, 7 March 1950, Tax File, WWL Records, LU.

[36]Shields Statement to Internal Revenue Service, 10 October 1950, Taxes File, WWL Records, LU; David Chandler, "Four-Six-Eight...Who Do We Appreciate?" New Orleans Magazine, June 1971, p. 31; Uhalt, Jr., interview; Read interview; Wall Street Journal, 18 August 1959.

[37]Shields Statement.

[38]Unsigned brief, "An Endeavor to Prove that Loyola University is an Integral Part of the Roman Catholic Church," Taxes File, WWL Records, LU.

[39]H.T. Swartz, Director, Tax Rulings Division to Loyola University, 13 August 1954, Ibid.

[40]Federal Tax Regulations, 1959 (St. Paul: West Publishing Co., 1959), pp. 566-567; Shields, "Memorandum" 5 August 1951.

[41]K.W. Hoehn to Arthur Hayes, William A. Schudt, Jr., and R. Dunne, 24 February 1956, WWL File, CBS Radio Records, NYC; "C.B.S. Steals the Show," Fortune, July 1953, p. 82.

[42]H.T. Swartz to Loyola University, 16 July 1958, Taxes File, WWL Records, LU.


CHAPTER 16:  Forging a Strategy for Survival

[1]Les Brown, Television:  The Business Behind the Box (New York:  Harcourt, Jovanovich, Inc., 1971), p. 61.

[2]Leo Bogart, The Age of Television (New York:  Frederick Ungar Publishing Co., 1972), pp. 8-9; Broadcasting Yearbook, 1975, p. A-5; Head, pp. 188-193.

[3]Ibid.; Lawrence P. Lessing, "The Television Freeze" Fortune, November 1949, pp. 126, 157; "CBS Steals the Show," p. 82; Robert Pepper, "The Pre-Freeze Television Stations" in Lichty and Topping, p. 140.

[4]Smith to Summerville, 20 November 1943, FCC to Smith, 27 March 1944, Segal to FCC, 26 March 1946, TV Files, WWL Records, LU; Hoerner interview; Katz interview.

[5]Shields memorandum, 17 December 1947, TV Files, WWL Records, LU.

[6]Ibid.

[7]Ibid.

[8]Shields to Katz, 5 and 23 January 1948, Shields to Segal, 5 January 1948, TV Files, WWL Records, LU.

[9]Katz to Shields, 7 January 1948, TV Files, WWL Records, LU.

[10] Ibid.

[11] Joseph W. McGuire, Theories of Business Behavior (Englewood Cliffs, N.J.: Prentice-Hall, Inc., 1964), pp. 22, 47, 126, 182; Herbert A. Simon, Administrative Behavior (New York: The Macmillan Company, 1961), pp. xxv-xxvi; Peter F. Drucker, Management: Tasks, Responsibilities, Practices (New York: Harper & Row, 1974), pp. 72, 786, 791.

[12] Richard Austin Smith, "TV: The Coming Showdown" Fortune September 1954, p. 140.

[13] Shields, "Memorandum No. 2 re Television," TV Files, WWL Records, LU.

[14] Ibid.

[15] Kenneth Harwood, "Broadcasting and the Theory of the Firm" Law and Contemporary Problems 34 (Summer 1969) 494; FCC, Docket Files 8935 and 8936, WNRC.

[16] Segal, Smith and Hennessey to Shields, 23 February 1948, Denechaud to Segal, 23 February 1948, TV Files, WWL Records, LU; David E. Tolman to T.J. Slowie, 3 March 1948, FCC, Docket File 8936, WNRC.

[17] FCC Form 301, 2 March 1948, Docket File 8936, WNRC.

[18] Earl B. Abrams, "Losing Money in Television Isn't New," Broadcasting-Telecasting, 3 May 1954, p. 70; "TV: The Money Rolls Out" Fortune, July 1949, p. 73.

[19] Ibid., pp. 74, 77.

[20] Ibid, pp. 74, 144.

[21] FCC Order, In Re Applications of Edgar B. Stern et al., 29 April 1948, Docket Files 8935-8937, WNRC; Lessing, p. 123.

[22] Bogart, p. 9; Lessing, pp. 164, 167.

[23] Docket 8935 File, WNRC; FCC Form 301, 16 February 1950, Docket 8936 File, WNRC; Segal to Summerville, 31 March 1950, TV Files, WWL Records, LU; Examiner's Report, In Re Loyola University et al., 7 July 1955, p. 61a; Slowie to Frederick H. Walton, Jr., 3 May 1950, Volume 12, Docket 8936 File, WNRC.

[24] FCC, Sixth Report and Order, 11 April 1952, 41 F.C.C. 150, 489; Segal to Denechaud, 25 April 1951, TV Files, WWL Records, LU.

[25] Shields Memorandum, 5 August 1951, TV Files, WWL Records, LU; Abrams, p. 70.

[26]FCC, Sixth Report and Order; Louis M. Kohlmeier, Jr., The Regulators: Watchdog Agencies and the Public Interest (New York: Harper & Row, 1969), pp. 204-206.

[27]FCC, Sixth Report and Order, pp. 492-493; "'63 Pre-Freeze Areas Critical for VHF" Broadcasting-Telecasting, 4 January 1954, p. 33; "UHF Fares On Par with VHF in One Station Areas" Ibid., p. 31; Kohlmeier, pp. 207-208; Krasnow and Longley, pp. 100-101.

[28]In Re Amendment of Section 3.606 of the Commission's Rules and Regulations, 43 F.C.C. 916 (1952); WWL Advisory Board Meeting Minutes, 26 April 1952, TV Files, WWL Records, LU.

[29]Ibid.

[30]Segal to Summerville, 7 August 1952, and FCC to Shields, 30 September 1953, Ibid.

CHAPTER 17:  Points of Preference

[1]Sterling Quinlan, The Hundred Million Dollar Lunch (Chicago: J. Philip O'Hara, Inc., 1974), p. 5; Louis L. Jaffe, "The Scandal in TV Licensing" Harper's Magazine, September 1957, p. 77.

[2]1953 TV Application.

[3]Ibid., I, 23-26, 34.

[4]Ibid., I, 48-68.

[5]Ibid., I, 71-239.

[6]Ibid., I, 251-254.

[7]Ibid., I, 459-464.

[8]Ibid., I, 467-468.

[9]Examiner's Report, 7 July 1955, p. 1; Broadcasting-Telecasting 21 December 1953, p. 27, and "The Plunge Into Color, As Made by WDSU-TV," 16 January 1956, pp. 70, 74.

[10]Examiner's Report, 7 July 1955, pp.

[11]R.H. Coase, "The Economics of Broadcasting and Government Policy," American Economic Review 56 (May 1966) 445; Jaffe, p. 78.

[12]Henry J. Friendly, The Federal Administrative Agencies (Cambridge, Mass.: Harvard University Press, 1962), pp. 57-58.

[13]Noll et al., p. 104; Paul W. Cherington, Leon V. Hirsch, and Robert Brandwein, Television Station Ownership: A Case Study of Federal Agency Regulation (New York: Hastings House, Publishers, 1971), p. 17.

[14]H. Gifford Irion, "FCC Criteria for Evaluating Competing Applicants," Minnesota Law Review 43 (January 1959), pp. 485-488; Noll et al., pp. 106-107.

[15]Christopher H. Sterling, "Newspaper Ownership of Broadcast Stations, 1920-1968" Journalism Quarterly (Summer 1969) 231-234; Friendly, pp. 66-67.

[16]Irion, p. 488; Jaffe, p. 79; Anthony Lewis, "FCC Prestige at Record Low" New York Times, 16 November 1958.

[17]"Statement of Matters Relied Upon by Loyola University," TV Files, WWL Records, LU.

[18]"Matters Relied Upon by The Times-Picayune Publishing Company as a Basis for Preference Over Loyola University," TV Files, WWL Records, LU.

[19]Ibid.

[20]Examiner's Report, 7 July 1955, pp. 62-65.

[21]"Points of Reliance of James A. Noe and Company," TV Files, WWL Records, LU.

[22]Memorandum Opinion and Order, In Re Applications of Loyola University et al., 22 July 1954, 43 F.C.C. 2673.

[23]Hoerner interview; New Orleans Item, 5 October 1954.

[24]Times-Picayune, 5 October 1954; New Orleans States, 5 October 1954.

[25]Thomas J. Shields, S.J., "Justification of Non-Catholic Religious Programs on WWL" Religious Difficulties File, WWL Records, LU.

[26]Ibid.

[27]Ibid.; Gerald Kelly, S.J., to Percy A. Roy, S.J., 14 May 1945, Religious Difficulties File, WWL Records, LU.

[28]D.C. O'Meara, S.M., to Shields, undated, Ibid.; T.L. Bouscaren, S.J., to Roy, 12 May 1945, Ibid.; Joseph D. O'Brien, S.J., to Roy, 21 May 1945, Ibid.

[29]Shields to Rummel, 16 June 1945, Ibid.; Shields memo, 1 July 1945, Ibid.; Examiner's Report, 7 July 1955, pp. 13-14.

[30]Langtry to FCC, 25 August 1953, Religious Difficulties File, WWL Records, LU.

[31]Hoerner to Langtry, undated, Ibid.; Segal, Oral Argument before FCC, 25 May 1956, Docket File 8936, WNRC.

[32]New Orleans Item, 6 October 1954; Times-Picayune, 6 October 1954; Examiner's Report, 7 July 1955, pp. 39-40; George W. Healy, Jr., A Lifetime on Deadline (Gretna, La.: Pelican Publishing Company, 1976), p. 195.

[33]New Orleans States, 6 October 1954; Times-Picayune, 7 October 1954; Richard J. Barber, "Newspaper Monopoly in New Orleans: New Lessons for Antitrust Policy" Louisiana Law Review 24 (April 1964) 509; John Wilds, Afternoon Story: A Century of the New Orleans States-Item (Baton Rouge: Louisiana State University, 1976), pp. 250-252.

[34]Times-Picayune Publishing Co. et al. v. United States 345 U.S. 594 (1953); Wilds, pp. 253-257.

[35]Times-Picayune, 7 October 1954; New Orleans Item, 7 October 1954; Examiner's Report, 7 July 1955, pp. 39-41.

[36]New Orleans Item, 7 October 1954; Times-Picayune, 7 October 1954; New Orleans States, 11 October 1954; Examiner's Report 7 July 1955, pp. 63, 65-71.

[37]Times-Picayune, 4 November 1954.

[38]Examiner's Report, 7 July 1955, p. 91.

[39]Ibid., pp. 97-100.

[40]Ibid., pp. 100-104.

[41]Ibid., pp. 104-108.

[42]Ibid., p. 109.

[43]Hoerner interview; Segal to Donnelly, 8 July 1955, TV Files, WWL Records, LU.

[44]Ibid.

[45]Times-Picayune, 26 May 1956; Oral Arguments, 25 May 1956, Docket File 8936, WNRC.

[46]Times-Picayune, 14 July 1956; In Re Loyola University et al. 44 F.C.C. 874 (1956), pp. 951-966.

[47]Ibid., pp. 968-974.

[48]Ibid., pp. 975-976; Marmet to Donnelly, 13 July 1956, File, WWL Record, LU.

[49]New Orleans States, 15 August 1956; Healy interview; Letter Aloysius B. Goodspeed, S.J., to the author, 23 April 1976; Brief or Appelant, The Times-Picayune Publishing Company v. FCC, U.S. Court of Appeals for the District of Columbia Circuit, 13 January 1958; Noe v. FCC, 260 F. 2d 739 (1958).

[50]Ibid., Wilds, pp. 266-269; Editor & Publisher, 19 July 1958, pp. 1, 52; Healy, pp. 194-195.

[51]Noe v. FCC, pp. 742-743; Teletype copy, 2 March 1959, TV File, WWL Records, LU.

[52]Harvey J. Levin, "Economic Structure and the Regulation of Television" Quarterly Journal of Economics 72 (August 1958) 431-433.

[53]Business Week, 30 June 1956, p. 34; "Notes, The Darkened Channels: UHF Television and the FCC" Harvard Law Review 75 (June 1962) 1583-1586; "Television Service and the FCC" Texas Law Review 46 (November 1968) 1119-1122; Douglas W. Webbink, "The Impact of UHF Promotion" Law and Contemporary Problems 34 (Summer 1969) 543.

[54]FCC, In Re Amendment of Section 3.606, Table of Assignments, Television Broadcast Stations (New Orleans, Mobile), Docket 11752; U.S., Congress, Senate, Committee on Interstate and Foreign Commerce, The Television Inquiry: Allocations Phase. 84th Cong., 2d sess., 1956, pp. 8-9.

[55]Comments of Loyola University, 3 December 1956, TV Files, WWL Records, LU, pp. 3-4.

[56]Ibid., pp. 18-38.

[57]WJMR-TV, Reply Comments, 21 December 1956, TV File, WWL Records, LU, pp. 13-29.

[58]New Orleans Item, 1 November 1953; WHMR-TV, Reply Comments, pp. 7-31.

[59]Joseph A. Todd to Donnelly, 3 December 1956, Russell Long to Donnelly, 8 March 1957, Hale Boggs to Donnelly, 8 March 1957,

TV Files, WWL Records, LU; FCC, In Re Amendment of Section 3,606, 7 March 1957, 22 F.C.C. 396-405.

[60]"Notes, The Darkened Channels," pp. 1589-1590; Lawrence D. Longley, "The FCC and the All-Channel Receiver Bill of 1962" Journal of Broadcasting 13 (Summer 1969) 294; Marver H. Bernstein, Regulating Business by Independent Commission (Princeton, N.J.:  Princeton University Press, 1955), p. 296; Webbink, p. 543.


CHAPTER 18:  Retrospect

[1]Times-Picayune, 9 March 1957.

[2]Board of Directors Minutes, Loyola University, 20 October 1953, 1 November 1953, 17 November 1953, 5 January 1954, FCC, Docket File 8936, WNRC; Theodore A. Roy, S.J., to Donnelly, 30 October 1953, TV File, WWL Records, LU.

[3]New Orleans Item, 6 and 8 September 1957.

[4]In Re Loyola University et al., 44 F.C.C. 901.

[5]Donnelly to Marmet, 3 September 1957, TV Files, WWL Records, LU; Times-Picayune, 7 September 1957.

[6]Ibid., 7, 8, 9 September 1957; New Orleans Item, 4 June 1958.

[7]Erik Barnouw, Tube of Plenty:  The Evolution of American Television (New York:  Oxford University Press, 1975), pp. 198-199; FCC, Twenty-third Annual Report, 1957, p. 105.

[8]Financial Statement, 31 July 1958, TV File, WWL Records, LU.

[9]Ibid.; "Broadcast Evolution:  From Radio to Radio" Broadcasting-Telecasting, 23 January 1956, p. 78; Goodspeed to author, 23 April 1976.

[10]Ibid.; Broadcasting-Telecasting, 18 January 1960; Early interview; Cherington et al., p. 196; Loyola University of the South Institutional Report, April 1974, Chapter 5, Loyola records, LU.

[11]John E. Coons, ed., Freedom and Responsibility in Broadcasting (Evanston, Ill.:  Northwestern University Press, 1961), p. 3.

# BIBLIOGRAPHY

## I. Archival Materials

Essential to the completion of this study were the records
of both WWL itself and of Loyola University now housed in the
Documents Center on the Loyola campus. The material is arranged
topically for the most part with individual folders on key station
personnel. The specific files in which items utilized here can
be located are indicated in the appropriate chapter documentation
of this book. Also housed in the Documents Center are unpublished
manuscript histories of the University by I.A. Timmreck, Francis L.
Janssen, S.J., and others, and the uncompleted and immensely
helpful chronicle of WWL written by Orie L. Abell, S.J., in 1937
and titled "Brief History of Radio Station WWL."

Also valuable were materials located in the offices of WWL
at 1024 North Rampart Street in New Orleans. Most particularly,
these included recordings of programs aired by the station during
the past thirty-five years as well as some miscellaneous correspondence. Financial statements and revenue data for WWL were
examined in the offices of the University's accountants, J.K.
Byrne and Company of New Orleans.

Elsewhere in Louisiana, the Huey P. Long, Jr., Papers in
the Department of Archives and Manuscripts at the Louisiana
State University Library, Baton Rouge, were helpful in illuminating
the role of the Kingfish in the Clear Channel War of the 1930's.
Also in Baton Rouge, material in the office of the Louisiana
Association of Broadcasters was consulted. At Gran Coteau,
Louisiana, Jesuit Archives are maintained at St. Charles College.
Those archives proved helpful in providing biographical data on
Jesuits associated with Loyola and with WWL over the years.

In New York City, the records and correspondence of CBS
Radio concerning its New Orleans affiliate provided significant
insights. These were made available to the author at the CBS
headquarters at 51 West 52nd Street in New York City. The Paulist
Archives at 415 West 59th Street in that city contain not only
the files of the ill-fated WLWL but also data on WWL not available
even in New Orleans.

Indispensable to any history of broadcasting are the materials
collected at various sites in the Washington, D.C., area. These
include, most notably, the records of the Commerce Department and
its Radio Service Section and later Radio Division in the National
Archives; the records of the License Division of the Federal
Communications Commission, housed at the agency's headquarters
at 1919 M Street, N.W.; and the annual financial statements filed
by broadcasting stations since the late 1930's as well as docket

339

files of cases decided by the Federal Radio Commission and the Federal Communications Commission, all stored at the Washington National Record Center in Suitland, Maryland. The Broadcast Pioneers Library, a privately funded repository for broadcast history material located in the headquarters of the National Association of Broadcasters, 1771 N Street, N.W., provided valuable data as always.

## II.  Interviews and Communications

The author was fortunate enough to interview or to communicate with a significant number of persons associated with either Louisiana broadcasting, Loyola University, or the radio and television industry in general. More often than not, they answered my questions with candor and patience. The following people provided the greatest assistance:  Jefferson Davis "J.D." Bloom, Charles I. Denechaud, Jr., Charles P. Dufour, Wallace Dunlap, Henry Dupre, L.J.N. "Joe" du Treil, J. Michael Early, Aloysius B. Goodspeed, S.J., Thomas O. Hanley, S.J., George W. Healy, Jr., Edward M. Hoerner, Francis Jacob, Francis L. Janssen, S.J., Eugene Katz, Jr., Don Lewis (William Lastrapes), Ted R. Liuzza, Howard Miller, Charles E. O'Neill, S.J., Marshall Pearce, John H. Pennybacker, Arthur C. "Captain" Pritchard, A. Louis Read, Eric H. Saline, John Kent (Leon Soniat), I.A. Timmreck, Joseph H. Uhalt, Jr., Marian (Mrs. Joseph H) Uhalt, Sr., George Wagner, Harold M. Wheelahan, Jr., John L. Vath. Tapes of the majority of the interviews are in the possession of the author.

## III.  Public Documents

The most important government documents pertaining to broadcast history, other than those already described under the heading of Archival Materials, are the Annual Reports of both the Federal Radio Commission (1927-1934) and the Federal Communications Commission (1934-  ), the decisions of those two agencies (with the latter's contained in the series F.C.C. Reports), and the various special studies published by them. Especially informative among the special studies were the 1932 FRC Report on Commercial Radio Advertising, the 1936 FCC Report on Social and Economic Data..., the 1941 FCC Report on Chain Broadcasting, the FCC's 1946 Public Service Responsibility of Broadcast Licensees, and the FCC's 1947 An Economic Study of Standard Broadcasting.

Department of Commerce publications which were consulted consisted of the annual Radio Stations of the United States, especially for the years 1912-1922, and the monthly Radio Service Bulletin, especially for the early and mid-1920's. The Census of Business, 1935, published by the Bureau of the Census within the

Commerce Department, contains a special section on radio broadcasting
and provided information on the industry not otherwise available.
The Bureau's Historical Statistics of the United States: Colonial
Times to 1957 and the Department's annual Statistical Abstract of
the United States volumes provided background data that was useful.

Legislative branch material included the Congressional Record,
particularly for the period from 1926-1935, as well as various
Senate or House investigations of broadcasting and radio regulation. The activities of the Senate Committee on Interstate
and Foreign Commerce often touched upon those subjects. Testimony
in its 1930 hearings on a Commission on Communications, its 1934
Federal Communications Commission hearings, and its 1956 Television
Inquiry: Allocations Phase was examined with profit.

## IV. Newspapers

The New Orleans press is a basic source for the radio era
in the Crescent City. The three local dailies, the Times-Picayune,
the New Orleans Item (published as the Item-Tribune for a period
on Sundays), and the New Orleans States covered the subject fulsomely in the 1920's, almost not at all in the following decade,
and only tepidly thereafter. In 1958 the States and the Item
were merged to form the New Orleans States-Item.

The Maroon, the student newspaper of Loyola University, gave
occasional space to WWL news, especially during the period prior
to October 1932 when the station was still located on the Loyola
campus. Back issues of the Maroon are housed in the University's
Documents Center. During the early 1930's, a short-lived weekly
titled Radio Time was published to counteract the boycott of broadcasting stories imposed by the city's major newspapers. Copies
of Radio Time have been preserved in the Special Collections
Department of Tulane University's Howard-Tilton Library.

The Shreveport Times and the Shreveport Journal were consulted
for radio history in that Louisiana city; in Baton Rouge, the
State-Times served the same purpose. Outside Louisiana, selected
issues of the New York Times, the Wall Street Journal, the New
York Herald-Tribune, and the Chicago Tribune were of assistance.

## V. Periodical Literature and Published Articles

For the industry in general, Broadcasting and the annual
Broadcasting Yearbook have been essential sources for any re-
searcher since their inception in the 1930's. From 1945 to 1957,
the weekly publication styled itself Broadcasting-Telecasting.
For the preceding decade of the 1920's, Radio Broadcast is the
most useful periodical source. Invaluable also for any economic

341

study of this subject are the editions of the Standard Rate and Data Service monthly compendium of time charges for the nation's broadcasting stations. Back issues of these, at times called Radio Advertising, are retained by the Library of Congress.

The following articles published in newspapers, magazines, journals, and secondary works were of value in the preparation of this study:

Abel, John D.; Clift, Charles III; and Weiss, Frederic A. "Station License Revocations and Denial of Renewal, 1934-1969." Journal of Broadcasting 14 (Fall 1970): 411-421.

Abell, Orie L., S.J. "Radio Broadcasting Station WWL." The Radio Graphic, August 1931, pp. 71-72.

Abrams, Earl B. "Losing Money in Television Isn't New." Broad-casting-Telecasting, 3 May 1954, p. 70.

Adams, Stanley. "The ASCAP Story." New York Times, 16 February 1964.

Barber, Richard J. "Newspaper Monopoly in New Orleans: New Lessons for Antitrust Policy." Louisiana Law Review 24 (April 1964): 503-554.

Bartlett, Kenneth G. "Trends in Radio Programs." The Annals of the American Academy of Political and Social Science 213 (January 1941): 15-25.

Bensman, Marvin R. "The Zenith-WJAZ Case and the Chaos of 1926-1927." Journal of Broadcasting 14 (Fall 1970): 423-440.

Bormann, Ernest G. "This is Huey P. Long Talking." Journal of Broadcasting 2 (Spring 1958): 111-122.

"A Brief Historical Note on the Mechanical Reproduction Announce-ment Requirement." Journal of Broadcasting 4 (Spring 1960): 119-122.

Brownson, Leo. "B.S. D'Antoni: Banker-Sportsman." The New Orleanian, 15 February 1931, pp. 23, 28.

Bucher, E.E. "A Resume of Early Radio Development." The Radio Industry. Chicago: A.W. Shaw Company, 1928.

Caldwell, Orestes H. "The Administration of Federal Radio Legis-lation." The Annals of the American Academy of Political and Social Science 141-142 (1929): 46-55.

"CBS Steals the Show." Fortune, July 1953, pp. 79-82, 164-166.

Chandler, David. "Four-Six-Eight...Who Do We Appreciate?"
New Orleans Magazine, June 1971, pp. 28-31, 62-63.

Coase, R.H. "The Economics of Broadcasting and Government Policy."
American Economic Review 56 (May 1966): 440-447.

Coe, Robert L. and Holt, Carrel W. "The Effects of Unionism on
Broadcasting." In Broadcasting and Bargaining: Labor
Relations in Radio and Television. Edited by Allen E.
Koenig. Madison: University of Wisconsin Press, 1970.

"Commercial Radio Stations and Their Time on the Air." Broadcast
Advertising, March 1930, p. 25.

Danna, Sammy R. "The Rise of Radio News." In American Broadcasting: A Source Book on the History of Radio and
Television, pp. 338-344. Edited by Lawrence W. Lichty and
Malachi C. Topping. New York: Hastings House, Publishers,
1975.

daVincent, Laura. "Changing the Picture at Loew's." New Orleans
States-Item, 12 January 1976.

_____. "Julian Saenger's Dream Palace." New Orleans States-
Item, 7 February 1976.

Dempsey, William J. and Koplovitz, William C. "Radio Economics
and the Public Interest." The Annals of the American
Academy of Political and Social Science 213 (January 1941):
97-101.

Derbes, Robin Von Breton. "The WPA Saved New Orleans." New
Orleans Magazine, July 1976, pp. 74-78.

Deutsch, Hermann. "Birth of New Orleans Radio Remembered."
New Orleans States-Item, 14 July 1967.

DeWitt, John H., Jr. "Early Radio Broadcasting in Middle
Tennessee." Tennessee Historical Quarterly (Spring 1971):
80-94.

Dill, Clarence C. "Radio and the Press: A Contrary View." The
Annals of the American Academy of Political and Social Science
177 (January 1935): 170-175.

Dodds, Wendell H. and Harwood, Kenneth. "Governmental Issues in
U.S. Broadcasting, 1946-1955." Journal of Broadcasting 1
(Spring 1957): 161-167.

Dodson, Orland. "The Friendly Giant is Fifty." Shreveport Times, 21 July 1975.

Downey, M. A. "IBEW Men at Work." Louisiana State Federation of Labor 1953 Review, pp. 82-103.

Ethridge, Mark. "The Government and Radio." The Annals of the American Academy of Political and Social Science 213 (January 1941): 109-115.

"FCC Dose for TV Ills is Mild." Business Week, 30 June 1956, p. 34.

Fly, James Lawrence. "Regulation of Radio Broadcasting in the Public Interest." The Annals of the American Academy of Political and Social Science 213 (January 1941): 102-108.

Frank, Glenn. "Radio as an Educational Force." The Annals of the American Academy of Political and Social Science 177 (January 1935): 119-122.

Friedrich, Carl J. "Controlling Broadcasting in Wartime." Studies in the Control of Radio, November 1940, No. 2.

_____. "Radiobroadcasting and Higher Education." Studies in the Control of Radio, May 1942, No. 4.

_____. and Sayre, Jeanette. "The Development of the Control of Advertising on the Air." Studies in the Control of Radio, November 1940, No. 1.

_____. and Sternberg, Evelyn. "Congress and the Control of Radio Broadcasting." Studies in the Control of Radio, October 1943, No. 5.

Givens, Richard A. "Refusal of Radio and Television Licenses on Economic Grounds." Virginia Law Review 46 (November 1960): 1391-1406.

"Gov't Approves Plan to End Competition in New Orleans." Editor & Publisher, 19 July 1958, pp. 9, 52.

Greb, Gordon. "The Golden Anniversary of Broadcasting." Journal of Broadcasting 3 (Winter 1958-1959): 3-13.

Harris, E. H. "Radio and the Press." The Annals of the American Academy of Political and Social Science 177 (January 1935): 163-169.

Harwood, Kenneth. "Broadcasting and the Theory of the Firm." Law and Contemporary Problems 34 (Summer 1969): 485-504.

Hays, Charlotte. "Norman Newhouse, The Invisible Man, and Other Tales of the T-P's Ruling Family." Figaro, 4 February 1976, pp. 10-12.

Hebert, F. Edward. "Earl Long, Robert Maestri, Jimmy Noe, Chep Morrison, Bathtub Joe and Me." New Orleans Magazine, August 1976, pp. 58-73.

Heleniak, Roman. "Local Reaction to the Great Depression in New Orleans, 1929-1933." Louisiana History 10 (Fall 1969): 289-306.

Hettinger, Herman S. "Broadcasting in the United States." The Annals of the American Academy of Political and Social Science 177 (January 1935): 1-14.

Irion, H. Clifford. "FCC Criteria for Evaluating Competing Applicants." Minnesota Law Review 43 (January 1959): 479-498.

Jaffe, Louis L. "The Scandal in TV Licensing." Harper's Magazine, September 1957, pp. 77-84.

Jansky, C. M., Jr., The Contribution of Herbert Hoover to Broadcasting." Journal of Broadcasting 1 (Summer 1957): 241-249.

LeDuc, Don R. and McCain, Thomas A. "The Federal Radio Commission in Federal Court." Journal of Broadcasting 14 (Fall 1970): 393-410.

Lee, Frederic P. "Federal Radio Legislation." The Annals of the American Academy of Political and Social Science 141-142 (1929): 36-44.

Lessing, Lawrence P. "The Television Freeze." Fortune, November 1949, pp. 123-127, 157-168.

Levin, Harvey J. "Economic Structure and the Regulation of Television." Quarterly Journal of Economics 72 (August 1958): 424-450.

Lewis, Anthony. "F.C.C. Prestige at Record Low." New York Times, 16 November 1958.

Lichty, Lawrence W. "The Impact of FRC and FCC Commissioners' Backgrounds on the Regulation of Broadcasting." Journal of Broadcasting 6 (Spring 1962): 97-110.

Liuzza, Ted R. "WSMB, New Orleans." The Radio Graphic, August 1931, pp. 63-64.

Longley, Lawrence D. "The FCC and the All-Channel Receiver Bill of 1962." Journal of Broadcasting 13 (Summer 1969): 293-303.

_____. "The FM Shift in 1945." Journal of Broadcasting 12 (Fall 1968): 353-364.

Lott, George E., Jr. "The Press-Radio War of the 1930's." Journal of Broadcasting 14 (Summer 1970): 275-286.

Mackey, David R. "The Development of the National Association of Broadcasters." Journal of Broadcasting 1 (Fall 1957): 305-325.

McGraw, Thomas K. "Regulation in America: A Review Article." Business History Review 49 (Summer 1975): 159-183.

Maloney, Martin J. "The Collision of Radio, Unions, and Free Enterprise." In Broadcasting and Bargaining: Labor Relations in Radio and Television. Edited by Allen E. Koenig. Madison: University of Wisconsin Press, 1970.

Maring, Karl, S.J., "Loyola's 'Physics Experiment' of 1922." The Louisiana Physics Teacher, Spring 1972, pp. 18-19.

Marshan, Leer. "The Friendly Broadcasting Station: Tracing the Growth of WJBW." The Radio Graphic, August 1931, pp. 67-68.

Maxim, Hiram P. "The Amateur in Radio." The Annals of the American Academy of Political and Social Science 141-142 (1929): 32-34.

Moore, John R. "The New Deal in Louisiana." In The New Deal: The State and Local Levels, pp. 137-165. Edited by John Braeman, Robert H. Bremner, and David Brody. Columbus: The Ohio State University Press, 1975.

"Notes: The Darkened Channels, UHF Television and the FCC." Texas Law Review 46 (November 1968): 1102-1217.

Page, Leslie J., Jr. "The Nature of the Broadcast Receiver and its Market in the United States from 1922 to 1927." Journal of Broadcasting 4 (Spring 1960): 174-182.

Pepper, Robert. "The Pre-Freeze Television Stations." In American Broadcasting: A Source Book on the History of Radio and Television, pp. 139-147. Edited by Lawrence W. Lichty and Malachi C. Topping. New York: Hastings House, Publishers, 1975.

Perry, James A. "A Soul-Baring Session with Terry Flettrich."
    New Orleans States-Item, 22 March 1975.

Peterson, Eldridge.  "Radio Quarrel with Composers, Now Approaching
    Climax, Is Acute Advertising Problem."  Printers' Ink,
    28 June 1940, pp. 36-40.

Peterson, Richard A.  "Single-Industry Firm to Conglomerate
    Synergistics:  Alternative Strategies for Selling Insurance
    and Country Music."  In Growing Metropolis: Aspects of
    Development in Nashville, pp. 341-357.  Edited by James
    Blumstein and Benjamin Walter.  Nashville:  Vanderbilt
    University Press, 1975.

"The Plunge into Color as Made by WDSU-TV."  Broadcasting-
    Telecasting, 16 January 1956, pp. 70-78.

Pringle, Katharine and Henry F.  "ASCAP Makes the Piper Pay."
    Nation's Business, April 1950, pp. 35-37, 88-90.

Radford, Jeff.  "Can an Old Hotel Change its Sheets?"  New Orleans
    Magazine, September 1975, pp. 37-48.

Reeks, Samuel D.  "A Station for the Majority:  WABZ, The Life of
    New Orleans."  The Radio Graphic, August 1931, pp. 69-70.

Robertson, Bruce.  "A New Harmony for an Old Discord."  Broadcasting-
    Telecasting, 25 October 1954, pp. 84-87, 103.

Ruby, Eunice.  "The Dawnbusters."  New Orleans Magazine, July 1976,
    pp. 80-88.

Ryant, Carl G.  "The South and the Movement Against Chain Stores."
    Journal of Southern History 39 (May 1973):  207-222.

Salassi, Elisabeth.  "Hello, World."  Shreveport Magazine, April
    1950, pp. 16-17, 46.

Sarno, Edward F., Jr.  "The National Radio Conferences."  Journal
    of Broadcasting 13 (Spring 1969):  189-202.

Schubert, Gregory and Lynch, James E.  "Broadcasting Unions:
    Structure and Impact."  In Broadcasting and Bargaining:
    Labor Relations in Radio and Television.  Edited by
    Allen E. Koenig.  Madison:  University of Wisconsin
    Press, 1970.

Seipman, Charles A.  "American Radio in Wartime."  In Radio
    Research, 1942-1943.  Edited by Paul F. Lazarsfeld and
    Frank N. Stanton.  New York:  Essential Books, 1944.

Shelby, Maurice E. "John R. Brinkley: His Contribution to
    Broadcasting" In American Broadcasting: A Source Book
    on the History of Radio and Television, pp. 560-568.
    Edited by Lawrence W. Lichty and Malachi C. Topping.
    New York: Hastings House, Publishers, 1975.

Simmons, George E. "Crusading Newspapers in Louisiana." Journalism
    Quarterly 16 (December 1939): 325-333.

Sivowitch, Elliot N. "A Technological Survey of Broadcasting's
    'Pre-History,' 1876-1920." Journal of Broadcasting 15
    (Winter 1970-1971): 1-20.

Smith, Earl. "WDSU." The Radio Graphic, August 1931, pp. 60-62.

Smith, R. Franklin. "A Look at the Wagner-Hatfield Amendment."
    In Problems and Controversies in Television and Radio,
    pp. 171-178. Edited by Harry J. Skornia and Jack William
    Kitson. Palo Alto: Pacific Books, 1968.

_____. "Oldest Station in the Nation." Journal of Broad-
    casting 4 (Winter 1959-1960): 40-55.

Smith, Richard Austin. "TV: The Coming Showdown." Fortune,
    September 1954, pp. 138-140, 164.

Spalding, John W. "1928: Radio Becomes a Mass Advertising Medium."
    Journal of Broadcasting 8 (Winter 1963-1964): 31-44.

Sterling, Christopher H. "Newspaper Ownership of Broadcast Stations,
    1920-1968." Journalism Quarterly 46 (Summer 1969): 227-236.

_____. "Second Service: Some Keys to the Development of FM
    Broadcasting." Journal of Broadcasting 15 (Spring 1971):
    181-194.

"Television Service and the FCC." Texas Law Review 46 (November
    1968): 1102-1217.

"TV: The Money Rolls Out." Fortune, July 1949, pp. 73-77, 142-148.

Webbink, Douglas W. "The Impact of UHF Promotion: The All-Channel
    Television Receiver Law." Law and Contemporary Problems 34
    (Summer 1969): 535-561.

Wesolowski, James W. "Obscene, Indecent, or Profane Broadcast
    Language as Construed by the Federal Courts." Journal of
    Broadcasting 13 (Spring 1969): 203-215.

Willey, George A. "The Soap Operas and the War." Journal of
    Broadcasting 7 (Fall 1963): 339-352.

"WWL - A Radio Pioneer." The Southern Jesuit, February 1936, pp. 1-3.

In addition to the above, selected issues of the following Catholic periodicals were reviewed for pertinent items: America, The Catholic World, Commonweal, and Sign.


VI. Books

In the research for this history, the following published works were utilized:

Abbo, John A. and Hannon, Jerome D. The Sacred Canons. St. Louis: B. Herder Co., 1952.

Archer, Gleason L. Big Business and Radio. New York: American Historical Society, 1939.

_____. History of Radio to 1926. New York: American Historical Society, 1938.

Atkinson, Carroll. American Universities and Colleges That Have Held Broadcast Licenses. Boston: Meador Publishing Co., 1941.

Banning, William Peck. Commercial Broadcasting Pioneer: The WEAF Experiment, 1922-1926. Cambridge: Harvard University Press, 1946.

Barnouw, Erik. A History of Broadcasting in the United States, 3 vols. New York: Oxford University Press, 1966-1970.

_____. Tube of Plenty: The Evolution of American Television. New York: Oxford University Press, 1975.

Beckman, Theodore N. and Nolen, Herman C. The Chain Store Problem: A Critical Analysis. New York: McGraw-Hill Book Company, Inc., 1938.

Bennett, David H. Demagogues in the Depression. New Brunswick, N.J.: Rutgers University Press, 1969.

Bernstein, Marver H. Regulating Business by Independent Commission. Princeton: Princeton University Press, 1955.

Bickel, Karl A. New Empires: The Newspapers and the Radio. Philadelphia: J.B. Lippincott Company, 1930.

Bogart, Leo. The Age of Television. New York: Frederick Ungar Publishing Co., 1972.

Brown, Les. Television: The Business Behind the Box. New York: Harcourt, Brace, Jovanovich, Inc., 1971.

Brownlee, W. Elliott. Dynamics of Ascent: A History of the American Economy. New York: Alfred A. Knopf, 1974.

Buxton, Frank and Owen, Bill. Radio's Golden Age: The Programs and the Personalities. n.p.: Easton Valley Press, 1966.

Carruth, Viola. Caddo: 1,000. Shreveport: Shreveport Magazine, 1970.

Columbia Broadcasting System. Listening Areas of the Columbia Broadcasting System, Inc., 1933. By the authors.

_____. Listening Areas: 7th Series, 1944. New York: Columbia Broadcasting System Research Department, 1945.

_____. CBS Listeners and Dealers, 1937, 2 vols. By the authors.

Chandler, Lester V. America's Greatest Depression, 1929-1941. New York: Harper & Row, Publishers, 1970.

Chase, Francis, Jr. Sound and Fury: An Informal History of Broadcasting. New York: Harper & Brothers Publishers, 1942.

Cherington, Paul W.; Hirsch, Leon V.; and Brandwein, Robert, eds. Television Station Ownership: A Case Study of Federal Agency Regulation. New York: Hastings House, Publishers, 1971.

Coons, John E., ed. Freedom and Responsibility in Broadcasting. Evanston, Ill.: Northwestern University Press, 1961.

Cooperative Analysis of Broadcasting: Fourth Year Report, 1936. Princeton: Crossley Incorporated National Research Organization, 1934.

Dabney, Thomas Ewing. One Hundred Great Years: The Story of the Times-Picayune. Baton Rouge: Louisiana State University Press, 1944.

Danielian, N.R. A.T. & T.: The Story of Industrial Conquest. New York: The Vanguard Press, 1939.

Davis, Edwin A. The Story of Louisiana, 4 vols. New Orleans: J.F. Hyer Publishing Co., 1960.

DiMeglio, John E. Vaudeville U.S.A.. Bowling Green, Ohio: Bowling Green University Popular Press, 1973.

Dodd, Donald B. and Wynelle S., eds. Historical Statistics of the
South. University, Ala.: The University of Alabama Press,
1973.

Drucker, Peter F. Management: Tasks, Responsibilities, Practices.
New York: Harper & Row, Publishers, 1974.

Dunlap, Orrin E., Jr. Dunlap's Radio and Television Almanac. New
York: Harper & Brothers, 1951.

Edelman, Murray. The Licensing of Radio Services in the United
States, 1927-1947. Urbana: University of Illinois Press,
1950.

Emery, Walter B. Broadcasting and Government. East Lansing:
Michigan State University Press, 1971.

Eoyang, Thomas T. An Economic Study of the Radio Industry in the
United States. New York: Columbia University, 1936.

Erickson, Don V. Armstrong's Fight for FM Broadcasting. University,
Ala.: University of Alabama Press, 1973.

Federal Tax Regulations, 1959. St. Paul: West Publishing Co., 1959.

Fessenden, Helen M. Fessenden: Builders of Tomorrows. New York:
Coward-McCann, Inc., 1940.

Flynn, George Q. American Catholics and the Roosevelt Presidency,
1932-1936. Lexington: University of Kentucky Press, 1968.

Freidel, Frank. Franklin D. Roosevelt: Launching the New Deal.
Boston: Little, Brown and Company, 1973.

Friendly, Henry J. The Federal Administrative Agencies. Cambridge:
Harvard University Press, 1962.

Frost, S.E., Jr. Education's Own Stations. Chicago: University
of Chicago Press, 1937.

Haas, Edward F. DeLesseps S. Morrison and the Image of Reform:
New Orleans Politics, 1946-1961. Baton Rouge: Louisiana
State University Press, 1974.

Head, Sydney W. Broadcasting in America, 2nd ed. Boston: Houghton
Mifflin Company, 1972.

Healy, George W., Jr. A Lifetime on Deadline: Self-Portrait of
a Southern Journalist. Gretna, La.: Pelican Publishing
Company, 1976.

Hettinger, Herman S.  A Decade of Radio Advertising.  Chicago:
     University of Chicago Press, 1933.

_____.  and Neff, Walter J.  Practical Radio Advertising.
     New York:  Prentice-Hall, 1938.

Hofstadter, Richard.  The Paranoid Style in American Politics and
     Other Essays.  New York:  Alfred A. Knopf, 1965.

Howard, Perry H.  Political Tendencies in Louisiana.  Baton Rouge:
     Louisiana State University Press, 1971.

Israel, Fred L., ed.  The State of the Union Messages of the
     Presidents, 3 vols.  New York:  Chelsea House, 1966.

Jackson, Joy J.  New Orleans in the Gilded Age.  Baton Rouge:
     Louisiana State University Press, 1969.

Johnson, Walter C. and Robb, Arthur T.  The South and its Newspapers,
     1903-1953.  Westport, Conn.:  Greenwood Press, 1974.

Jome, Hiram L.  Economics of the Radio Industry.  Chicago:  A.W.
     Shaw Company, 1925.

Kahn, Frank J., ed.  Documents of American Broadcasting, 2nd ed.
     New York:  Appleton-Century-Crofts, 1973.

Kane, Harnett T.  Louisiana Hayride:  The American Rehearsal for
     Dictatorship, 1928-1940.  New York:  William Morrow & Company,
     1941.

Kobre, Sidney.  Development of American Journalism.  Dubuque, Iowa:
     Wm. C. Brown Company, Publishers, 1969.

Kohlmeier, Louis M., Jr.  The Regulators:  Watchdog Agencies and
     the Public Interest.  New York:  Harper & Row, 1969.

Krasnow, Erwin G. and Longley, Lawrence D.  The Politics of
     Broadcast Regulation.  New York:  St. Martin's Press, 1973.

LaPrade, Ernest.  Broadcasting Music.  New York:  Rinehart &
     Company, Inc., 1956.

Lazarsfeld, Paul F. and Kendall, Patricia L.  Radio Listening
     in America.  New York:  Prentice-Hall, Inc., 1948.

Lebhar, Godfrey M.  Chain Stores in America, 1859-1950.  New York:
     Chain Store Publishing Corp., 1952.

Lee, Alfred M.  The Daily Newspaper in America.  New York:  The
     Macmillan Company, 1962.

Leuchtenburg, William E. Franklin D. Roosevelt and the New Deal. New York: Harper & Row, 1963.

Levin, Harvey J. Broadcast Regulation and Joint Ownership of the Media. New York: New York University, 1960.

_____. The Invisible Resource: Use and Regulation of the Radio Spectrum. Baltimore: Johns Hopkins Press, 1971.

Long, Huey P., Jr. Every Man a King: The Autobiography of Huey P. Long. New Orleans: National Book Co., 1933.

Lumley, Frederick H. Measurement in Radio. Columbus: The Ohio State University Press, 1934.

McCaughan, Richard. Socks on a Rooster: Louisiana's Earl K. Long. Baton Rouge: Claitor's Book Store, 1967.

McGuire, Joseph W. Theories of Business Behavior. Englewood Cliffs, N.J.: Prentice-Hall, Inc., 1964.

Maclaurin, W. Rupert. Invention and Innovation in the Radio Industry. New York: Macmillan Company, 1949.

McLean, Albert F., Jr. American Vaudeville as Ritual. Lexington: University of Kentucky Press, 1965.

Malone, Bill C. Country Music, U.S.A. Austin: University of Texas Press, 1968.

May, Margery Land. Hello World Henderson: The Man Behind the Mask. Shreveport: by the author, 1930.

Metz, Robert. CBS: Reflections in a Bloodshot Eye. Chicago: Playboy Press, 1975.

Midgley, Ned. The Advertising and Business Side of Radio. New York: Prentice-Hall, Inc., 1948.

Mitchell, Broadus. Depression Decade. New York: Harper & Row, 1947.

Mott, Frank Luther. American Journalism: A History, 1690-1969. 3rd Ed. New York: Macmillan Co., 1962.

National Association of Broadcasters. Let's Stick to the Record. New York: by the authors, 1940.

Noll, Roger G. et al. Economic Aspects of Television Regulation. Washington: The Brookings Institution, 1973.

O'Pry, Maude H. Chronicles of Shreveport. Shreveport: Journal Printing Company, 1928.

Owen, Bruce M.; Beebe, Jack H.; and Manning, Willard G., Jr. Television Economics. Lexington, Mass.: Lexington Books, 1974.

Perry, Dick. Not Just a Sound: The Story of WLW. New York: Prentice-Hall, Inc., 1971.

Poindexter, Ray. Arkansas Airwaves. North Little Rock: by the author, 1974.

Price, Waterhouse & Co. The Third Study of Radio Network Popularity Based on a Nation-Wide Audit Conducted by Price, Waterhouse & Co., Public Accountants. New York: Columbia Broadcasting System, 1932.

Quinlan, Sterling. The Hundred Million Dollar Lunch. Chicago: J. Philip O'Hara, Inc., 1974.

Radio Daily, The 1944 Radio Annual. New York: Radio Daily, 1944.

Reinsch, J. Leonard. Radio Station Management. New York: Harper & Brothers, 1948.

Reynolds, George M. Machine Politics in New Orleans, 1897-1926. New York: Columbia University Press, 1936.

Robinson, Thomas P. Radio Networks and the Federal Government. New York: Columbia University Press, 1943.

Rollins, Alfred B., Jr. Roosevelt and Howe. New York: Alfred A. Knopf, 1962.

Rutland, Robert A. The Newsmongers: Journalism in the Life of the Nation. New York: The Dial Press, 1973.

Schlesinger, Arthur M., Jr. The Age of Roosevelt, Vol. 3: The Politics of Upheaval. Boston: Houghton Mifflin Company, 1960.

Schmeckebier, Laurence F. The Federal Radio Commission. Washington: The Brookings Institution, 1932.

Schubert, Paul. The Electric Word. The Rise of Radio. New York: Macmillan Company, 1928.

Schuler, Edgar A. Survey of Radio Listeners in Louisiana. Baton Rouge: Louisiana State University Press, 1943.

354

Seldes, Gilbert. _The Great Audience_. New York: Viking Press, 1950.

Simon, Herbert. _Administrative Behavior_. New York: Macmillan Company, 1961.

Sindler, Allan P. _Huey Long's Louisiana: State Politics, 1920-1952_. Baltimore: Johns Hopkins Press, 1956.

_Soards' New Orleans City Directory_, 1922-1932. New Orleans: Soards Directory Co., Ltd.

Soule, George. _Prosperity Decade_. New York: Holt, Rinehart & Winston, 1947.

_Statistical Abstract of Louisiana, 1974_. New Orleans: University of New Orleans, 1974.

Stedman, Raymond W. _The Serials_. Norman: University of Oklahoma Press, 1971.

Summers, Harrison B., ed. _A Thirty Year History of Programs Carried on National Radio Networks in the United States, 1926-1956_. Columbus: The Ohio State University, 1958.

Tebbel, John. _The Media in America_. New York: Thomas Y. Crowell Company, 1974.

_Variety Radio Directory, 1937-1938_. New York: _Variety_, 1937.

_Variety Radio Directory, 1940-1941_. New York: _Variety_, 1940.

Wilds, John. _Afternoon Story: A Century of the New Orleans States-Item_. Baton Rouge: Louisiana State University Press, 1976.

Williams, T. Harry. _Huey Long_. New York: Alfred A. Knopf, Inc., 1969.

Wolfe, Charles H. _Modern Radio Advertising_. New York: Funk & Wagnalls Company, 1949.

VII. Other Unpublished Material

Aarnes, Hale. "The Organization and Administration of Radio Stations Owned and Operated by Educational Institutions." Ph.D. dissertation, University of Missouri, 1949.

Billeaud, Frances P. "A History of KLFY-TV, Lafayette, Louisiana, 1955-1961." Master's Thesis, Louisiana State University, 1963.

355

Colbert, Nellie G. "A History of Radio Station WJBO, Baton Rouge, 1934-1952." Master's Thesis, Louisiana State University, 1960.

Covington, Jess B. "A History of the Shreveport Times." Ph.D. dissertation, University of Missouri, 1964.

Danna, Sammy R. "A History of Radio Station KMLB, Monroe, Louisiana, 1930-1958." Master's Thesis, Louisiana State University, 1960.

Godfrey, Donald G. "The 1929 Radio Act: People and Politics." Paper presented at the Broadcast Education Association meeting, Chicago, 20 March 1976.

Hall, Lillian J. "A Historical Study of Programming Techniques and Practices of Radio Station KWKH, Shreveport, 1920-1950." Ph.D. dissertation, Louisiana State University, 1959.

Koenig, Allen E. "American Federation of Television and Radio Artists' Negotiations and Contracts." Master's Thesis, Stanford University, 1962.

Lemoine, Laura F. "A History of Radio Station WSMB, New Orleans, 1925-1967." Master's Thesis, Louisiana State University, 1969.

Lichty, Lawrence W. "A Study of the Careers and Qualifications of Members of the Federal Radio Commission and the Federal Communications Commission." Master's Thesis, The Ohio State University, 1961.

Roberts, Elizabeth M. "French Radio Broadcasting in Louisiana, 1935-1958." Master's Thesis, Louisiana State University Press, 1959.

Runyan, Glenn M. "Economic Trends in New Orleans, 1928-1940." Master's Thesis, Tulane University, 1967.

Ryant, Carl G. "The Unbroken Chain: Opposition to Chain Stores During the Great Depression." Master's Thesis, University of Wisconsin, 1965.

Smeyak, G. Paul. "Presidential Radio Use: 1920-1928." Paper presented at the Broadcast Education Association meeting, Chicago, 20 March 1976.

Turnipseed, Barnwell R., III. "The Development of Broadcasting in Georgia, 1922-1959." Master's Thesis, University of Georgia, 1960.

Wallace, Wesley H. "The Development of Broadcasting in North Carolina, 1922-1948." Ph.D. dissertation, Duke University, 1962.

WSMB, Fiftieth Anniversary Program, Interview with Ray McNamara, 21 April 1975.

361